GLOBAL RESTRUCTURING
AND PERIPHERAL STATES

GLOBAL RESTRUCTURING AND PERIPHERAL STATES

The Carrot and the Stick in Mauritania

Mohameden Ould-Mey

LITTLEFIELD ADAMS BOOKS

LITTLEFIELD ADAMS BOOKS

Published in the United States of America
by Rowman & Littlefield Publishers, Inc.
4720 Boston Way, Lanham, Maryland 20706

3 Henrietta Street
London WC2E 8LU, England

British Cataloging in Publication Information Available

Library of Congress Cataloging-in-Publication Data

Ould-Mey, Mohameden.
Global restructuring and peripheral states : the carrot and
the stick in Mauritania / Mohameden Ould-Mey.
p.   cm.
Includes bibliographical references and index.
1. Structural adjustment (Economic policy)—Mauritania.
2. World Bank—Mauritania. 3. International Monetary
Fund—Mauritania. 4. Non-governmental organizations—
Mauritania. 5. Competition, International. I. Title.
HC1050.O95   1996   338.9661—dc20   95–39780

ISBN 0–8226–3050–8 (cloth : alk. paper)
ISBN 0–8226–3051–6 (pbk. : alk. paper)

Printed in the United States of America

♾™ The paper used in this publication meets the minimum requirements of
American National Standard for Information Sciences—Permanence of
Paper for Printed Library Materials, ANSI Z39.48–1984.

To my parents and to Nabgha and Humam

Ignorance will come to an end when everything
is presented as it actually is.
Muammar Al Qaddafi, *The Green Book*

Contents

Figures and Tables

FIGURES

TABLES

Abbreviations and Acronyms

AAFED	Abu Dhabi Arab Fund for Economic Development
ADB	African Development Bank
ADF	African Development Fund
AFESD	Arab Fund for Economic and Social Development
AFR70	Africa 70 (Italy)
AFVP	Association Française des Volontaires du Progrès
AGFUND	Arab Gulf Fund for United Nations Development
AGSECAL	Agricultural Sector Adjustment Loan
AIPAC	American Israeli Political Action Committee
BALM	Banque Arabe Libyenne Mauritanienne
BAMIS	Banque Arabe Mauritanienne Islamique
BCM	Banque Centrale de Mauritanie
BIMA	Banque Internationale de Mauritanie
BMAA	Banque Mauritanienne Arabe Africaine
BMCI	Banque Mauritanienne pour le Commerce International
BMDC	Banque Mauritanienne pour le Développement et le Commerce
BNM	Banque Nationale de Mauritanie
BRPM	Bureau de Recherches et de Participations Minières (Morocco)
CAID	Canadian Agency for International Development
CARITAS	Organisation Caritative Internationale
CCCE	Caisse Centrale de Coopération Economique
CCI	Centre du Commerce International (CNUCED/GATT)
CDSS	Country Development Strategy Statement
CFA	Communauté Financière Africaine
CGTM	Confédération Générale des Travailleurs de Mauritanie
CHATC	Chinese Agency for Technical Cooperation
CHNCEE	Chinese National Company for Export of Equipment
CIA	Central Intelligence Agency
CMSN	Comité Militaire de Salut National
CNN	Cable News Network

CNUCED	Conférence des Nations Unies pour le Commerce et le Développement
CSA	Commissariat à la Securité Alimentaire
CSLM	Confédération des Syndicats Libres de Mauritanie
DGCS	Direzzione Generale Di Cooperatzione Allo Sviluppo (MOFA)
DGIC	Directorate General for International Cooperation (MOFA)
DOULOS	Communauté DOULOS
EATC	Egyptian Agency for Technical Cooperation
EC	European Community
EDF	European Development Fund
EEC	European Economic Community
EIB	European Investment Bank
EMN	Etablissement Maritime de Nouakchott
ESAF	Enhanced Structural Adjustment Facility
EU	European Union
FAC	Fonds d'Aide et de Coopération (France)
FAD	Fonds Africain de Développement
FAO	Food and Agriculture Organization
FBIS	Foreign Broadcast Information Service
FENU	Fonds d'Equipement des Nations Unies
FIRVA	Fonds d'Insertion et de Reinsertion dans la Vie Active
FIS	Front Islamique de Salut
FLAM	Forces de Liberation des Africains de Mauritanie
FLN	Front de Liberation Nationale
FND	Fonds National pour le Développement
GATT	General Agreement on Trade and Tariffs
GCC	Gulf Cooperation Council
GDP	Gross Domestic Product
GNP	Gross National Product
GPO	Government Printing Office
GTFDI	Guidelines on the Treatment of Foreign Direct Investment
GTZ	German Agency for Technical Cooperation
Hamas	Harakit Al-Muqawama Al-Islamiya (Islamic Resistance Movement)
IBRD	International Bank for Reconstruction and Development
ICVA	International Council of Voluntary Agencies
IDA	International Development Association
IDB	Islamic Development Bank
IDRC	International Development Research Centre
IFAD	International Fund for Agricultural Development
IFIs	International Financial Institutions
ILO	International Labor Organization
IMF	International Monetary Fund
IQDF	Iraqi Development Fund
ITALPIANTI	Italiapianti (NGO)
JICA	Japan International Cooperation Agency
KFAED	Kuwait Fund for Arab Economic Development
KFTCIC	Kuwait Foreign Trade Contracting and Investment Company
KFW	Development Bank (Federal Republic of Germany)

LWF	Lutheran World Federation
MATC	Moroccan Agency for Technical Cooperation
MDR	Ministère du Développement Rural
MEF	Ministère de l'Economie et des Finances
MIFERMA	Mine de Fer de Mauritanie
MIGA	Multilateral Investment Guarantee Agency
MND	Movement National Démocratique
NAFTA	North American Free Trade Agreement
NATO	North Atlantic Treaty Organization
NICs	Newly Industrialized Countries
NIEO	New International Economic Order
NGO	Non-Governmental Organization
OAU	Organization of African Unity
OECD	Organization of Economic Cooperation and Development
OMVS	Organisation de la Mise en Valeur du Fleuve Senegal
OPEC	Organization of Petroleum Exporting Countries
OPT	Office des Postes et Télécommunications
Oxfam	Oxfam, United Kingdom
PACs	Political Action Committees
PANPA	Port Autonome de Nouakchott dit Port de l'Amitié
Para	Paragraph
PASA	Programme d'Ajustement du Secteur Agricole
PASEP	Programme d'Ajustement du Secteur des Entreprises Publiques
PCMSN	Présidence du Comité Militaire de Salut National
PCR	Programme de Consolidation et de Relance
PDIAR	Projet de Développement Institutionel Administratif et de la Réforme
PFP	Policy Framework Paper
PG	Présidence du Gouvernement
PIC	Public Information Center
PLO	Palestine Liberation Organization
PPM	Parti du Peuple Mauritanien
PRDS	Parti Républicain Démocratique et Social
PREF	Programme de Redressement Economique et Financier
RAMS	Rural Assessment and Manpower Surveys
RIM	République Islamique de Mauritanie
SAF	Structural Adjustment Facility
SAL	Structural Adjustment Loan
SAP	Structural Adjustment Program
SDA	Social Dimension of Adjustment
SDF	Saudi Development Fund
SDI	Strategic Defense Initiative
SDR	Special Drawing Right
SECAL	Sectoral Adjustment Loan
SMAR	Société Mauritanienne d'Assurance et de Réassurance
SMB	Société Mauritanienne de Banque
SMCP	Société Mauritanienne de Commercialisation de la Pêche
SMCPP	Société Mauritanienne de Commercialisation des Produits Pétroliers

SNA	System of National Accounts
SNIM	Société Nationale Industrielle et Minière
SOATIC	Soviet Agency for Technical Coopération
SOMAGAZ	Société Mauritanienne de Gaz
SONADER	Société Nationale pour le Développement Rural
SONELEC	Société Nationale d'Eau et d'Electricité
SONIMEX	Société Nationale d'Import et d'Export
SOS	Save Our Soul (International Code Signal for Extreme Distress)
TATC	Tunisian Agency for Technical Cooperation
TDH	Terre des Hommes (France)
TECPLAN	Techniplan
UAE	United Arab Emirates
UBD	Union des Banques de Développement
UDP	Union pour la Démocratie et le Progrès
UFD	Union des Forces Démocratiques
UM	Ouguiya
UN	United Nations
UNDP	United Nations Development Program
UNEF	United Nations Equipment Fund
UNHCR	United Nations High Commission for Refugees
UNICEF	United Nations Children Fund
UNIDO	United Nations Industrial Development Organization
UNPF	United Nations Population Fund
UNSO	United Nations Soudano-Sahelian Office
USAID	United States Agency for International Development
USSR	Union of Soviet Socialist Republics
UTM	Union des Travailleurs de Mauritanie
VOA	Voice of America
WFP	World Food Programme
WHO	World Health Organization
WV	World Vision
ZOA	ZOA Care (Netherlands)

Preface

Structural adjustment programs (SAPs) represent the most pervasive development policy and theory in progress in developing countries since the early 1980s. This book examines the genesis, process, impact, and implication of SAPs at the global, national, and local levels. It analyzes how structural adjustment programs were conceived by the Group of Seven (G-7) and executed by international financial institutions such as the International Monetary Fund (IMF) and the World Bank in close collaboration with fiscally bankrupt Third World states. It specifically demonstrates the ways in which these programs succeeded in reversing nationalistic policies through a carrot-and-stick strategy of providing loans in exchange for fundamental changes in the political economy of borrowing countries. The unfolding of these programs within the Mauritanian state, economy, and society is presented as a case study that is based on intensive field work involving the collection and analysis of primary documents such as the texts of World Bank loan agreements, IMF/World Bank policy framework papers (PFPs), IMF standby arrangements, Paris Club accords, and various minutes of proceedings of meetings between negotiation teams from the Mauritanian government and the multilateral institutions.

Although the book draws upon several analytical approaches in geography, political science, and international relations, its main theoretical framework attempts to synthesize and advance the schools of uneven development and regulation theory by collapsing them into a *geopolitical economy* approach emphasizing the global shift in the balance of power between states and blocs of states and the resulting reconfiguration of international relations. I argue that the processes of economic liberalization and management decentralization pursued everywhere today actually represent further centralization of the world economy, indeed the emergence of a *global command economy* where the conception, formulation, design, and funding of development policy is increasingly controlled by a few international institutions, mechanisms, and forums such as the G-7, the IMF, the World Bank, the Paris Club, the Consultative Group, and international nongovernmental organizations (NGOs). The unfolding of these processes within peripheral states brings to light three fundamental implications. First, SAPs are unleashing a profound process of denationalization of the state where it is restructured from a national to a multilateral state, virtually deprived of its sovereignty over development policies. Second, the national economy is being controlled by a complex multitude of international economic investors and is experiencing a systematic process of devaluation, a phenomenon that is contributing to the bizarre acceleration of net resource transfer from the South to the North. Third, the process of democratization brought about by SAPs is paving the road for a profound sociopolitical fragmentation that is actually diffusing and containing the explosive social impacts of economic reforms. I conclude that the process of democratization (the most praised dimension of structural adjustment) brought about by SAPs at the national/local levels will remain superficial amid undemocratic relations at the global/international levels where SAPs are conceived and designed.

The bulk of this work was originally presented as a doctoral dissertation in geography at the University of Kentucky, and several persons and institutions have contributed to it through varying degrees of intellectual, moral, and material support. My gratitude goes first to John Pickles for his mentorship and friendship. I am equally grateful to Robert Olson for his intellectual and moral support. Many thanks also go to Paul Karan, Peter Little, Susan Roberts, and Richard Ulack for their comments and suggestions; to Gyula Pauer and Richard Gilbreath for their assistance in the making of a map of Mauritania; and to E. K. Esawi for providing help and offering his generous computer skills.

Many anonymous Mauritanian state officials and employees deserve my deep gratitude for their assistance and support in my year-long enterprise of collecting adjustment-related documents in Nouakchott. I am grateful too to Miguel Saponara from the World Bank for sending me copies of three nonconfidential World Bank documents (International Development Association President Reports no. P–293–MAU and P–4550–MAU, and Mauritania's fourth PFP). My gratitude goes also to Mohamed Ali Ould-Mey, whose meticulous reading of Mauritanian Arabic newspapers and prompt correspondence kept me informed on the continuous unfolding of adjustment-related events in Mauritania while I was in the United States.

The preliminary stages of this work received generous financial support from the Islamic Educational Scientific and Cultural Organization (ISESCO) and strong moral support from the faculty of the Department of Geography at the University of Nouakchott. Later, the Department of Geography at the University of Kentucky provided a teaching assistantship, without which the work would not have been completed. To all I wish to express my deep gratitude. I offer special thanks to everybody at the University of Kentucky Interlibrary Loan Service, particularly Barbara Hale and Janet Layman, for their superb job of ordering for me so many books and other library materials. I also wish to thank Jonathan Baltzell and Wanda Lane from the Stanton Academic Computer Center at Francis Marion University for assisting me in printing the manuscript. My thanks go also to both publishers of *Third World Quarterly* and *Journal of Third World Studies* for granting me permission to reprint significant parts of two articles I recently published in their journals. Last but not least, I express my gratitude to Littlefield Adams Books' anonymous reviewer for his/her great review and succinct suggestions and to acquisitions and production editors for their efficient coordination and production of this volume.

1

Concrete and Theoretical Contexts

Introduction

During the past fifteen years, development policy and research were dominated by the concepts and the processes of restructuring in the industrialized countries (North America, Western Europe, and Japan) and adjustment to that restructuring in the rest of the world (developing countries, Eastern Europe, and the former Soviet Union). Like the processes of recovery following the Great Depression of the 1930s and reconstruction following World War II, the process of restructuring and adjustment following the economic crisis of the 1970s refers to a new strategy of capital accumulation that involves a restructuring of power relations between capital and labor, a redefinition of the balance of power between nations, and a reconfiguration of state policies with a significant shift away from the welfare state. Among the many geographic implications (shifting balance between regions, spatially uneven development, urban-rural and international migrations, social conflicts, and so on) of restructuring and adjustment, there are three main levels of manifestation that highlight the salient features of the process. First, at the national level the process is illustrated by worldwide national austerity programs and budget cuts, the rise of unemployment and growing job insecurity (shift from permanent employment to part-time, homework, and temporary employment), downsizing of companies through massive layoffs, and increased mobility of capital across international borders. Second, at the geopolitical and international level the process is manifested in the increasing tension between internationally organized finance and domestically organized politics, between the global nature of the economy and the national character of politics. Though there is no global state, the role of global-like institutions and mechanisms in the process of socioeconomic regulation is illustrated by the increasing role of multilateral financial institutions, the expanding United Nations responsibilities (particularly the post–Cold War expansion of UN peacekeeping operations and recent propositions by Canada to establish a permanent UN army), and the expanding U.S. global military and media apparatuses. Third, at the conceptual level the process raises discrepancies between the hegemonic discourse of free market, liberal democracy, state deregulation, and management decentralization, on the one hand, and the emerging global command economy (IMF/World Bank centralization of money and credit), the still undemocratic nature of international relations (veto power in the UN system), and the greater centralization of military power, knowledge, and technology, on the other hand. This discrepancy between reality and discourse and the question of defining what constitutes market and democracy continue to fuel a variety of debates between universalism and particularism, between liberalism and Marxism, and between structuralism and poststructuralism.

These manifestations raise three research questions: (1) How did the process of restructuring and adjustment originate and what are the real forces behind it? (2) What are the implications of this process for peripheral states in their relations with core states? and (3) How did the process of adjustment unfold within particular peripheral states, economies, and societies? To answer these questions, I based my research methodology on two forms of investigation. The first form of investigation consisted of a general survey of adjustment literature with an attempt to unpack and unravel the genesis and genealogy of SAPs, particularly at the international level. My evidence was based on (1) the analysis of documents and declarations coming out of the G–7 economic summits held between 1975 and 1995 and (2) the analysis of how development policies adopted by G–7 economic summits constitute the essentials of the policies of SAPs implemented by international financial institutions in their dealings with borrowing peripheral states. The second form of investigation focused on the articulation of the above global policies at the national level. For this purpose I focused on Mauritania as a borrowing peripheral state within which the unfolding of SAPs was exemplary in terms of its speed, scope, and depth. Mauritania may be considered a typical developing country when judged by the following criteria: (1) its previous colonial status, its recent independence in 1960, and the fragility of its institutions, particularly the state apparatus; (2) the artificial nature of its international borders, which cut across the same tribes or clans on its Western Saharan, Algerian, Malian, and Senegalese borders; (3) its geographic and geopolitical position on the margins of the Arab world and sub-Saharan Africa, in the middle of an ecological and cultural transition zone; (4) its socioeconomic development indicators of some $500 gross national product (GNP) per capita and a life expectancy of less than fifty years; and (5) the uncertainty of its environment, where over the past twenty-five years successive waves of drought and rural-urban migrations had devastated the socioeconomic fabric of the traditional society and the geographic distribution of the population, creating what was often referred to as a society of environmental refugees. Today, Mauritania's capital city, Nouakchott, is one of the fastest growing cities in the world with over 25 percent of the country's total population.

This work is organized into nine chapters: chapter 1 presents an introduction to the concrete and theoretical contexts of the research, defines the research questions, and describes the methods of investigation. The concrete context of the research consists of (1) identifying the salient features of three IMF/World Bank adjustment programs implemented by the Mauritanian government between 1984 and 1995; (2) noting the significance of these programs as the most important socioeconomic and political changes in the country since 1984; and (3) emphasizing the necessity of adopting an epistemology capable of grasping the complexity and totality of SAPs in their origins, processes, and outcomes. The theoretical context situates the research within the larger intellectual and policy debate centered around economic restructuring in the industrialized countries and its corollary process of economic and political adjustment in the developing countries. This section underlines geography's critical and theoretical contribution to the restructuring and adjustment debate, particularly within the theoretical framework of uneven development and regulation theory. It also suggests the relevance of collapsing these two approaches into one, a geopolitical economy approach whose central argument is that *interstate competition and struggle for control of power and wealth are neither theoretically nor empirically less significant in the actual making of history than internal social and class struggle within states.* Moreover, the chapter outlines briefly the significance of SAPs during the past decade and the various approaches to their study, the importance of resource transfer from South to North despite the discourse of aid, and the overall economic failure of SAPs, particularly in sub-Saharan Africa, where the Mauritanian economy belongs.

Chapter 2 outlines and examines the main elements of global restructuring and adjustment and their implications for peripheral states. First, it addresses how the economic crisis of the 1970s developed out of a fundamental contradiction between nationalist, protectionist policies seeking to achieve accumulation at the national level, on the one hand, and global policies working toward the destruction of all borders, barriers, and policies that interfere with the free movement of capital worldwide, on the other hand. Second, adjustment is presented as a comprehensive Western strategy (with military, political, economic, and cultural components) whose agents are the industrialized countries, particularly the Group of Seven and its leader, the United States, which has engineered, funded, and supported SAPs since 1980. Third, the other elements of the global strategy of adjustment outlined in this chapter include (1) the role of World Bank studies in discrediting the nationalist model of development, (2) the role of military intervention and media propaganda in suppressing other alternatives to adjustment, (3) the way in which post–Cold War changes tend to consolidate the North/South divide, and (4) the identification of Islamic militancy as one main threat to adjustment. Finally, the last section of this chapter assesses the role of the instruments of adjustment, particularly the role of the borrowing state and how it is crucial to the implementation of SAPs.

Chapter 3 provides a background to the Mauritanian context within which SAPs were implemented. It begins by introducing the historical geography of Mauritania as a necessary background to the circumstances that surrounded the creation of Mauritania and the birth of the colonial state, as well as the development of the postcolonial independent state. It then describes briefly the main tenets of nationalist development planning adopted by the state throughout the 1960s and 1970s. The last section of this chapter introduces subsequent chapters by outlining a brief summary of the sequence of SAPs in Mauritania and their impacts on the state and the economy.

Chapter 4 describes the process of denationalization of the Mauritanian state, i.e., its transition from a national to a multilateral state. It begins with a brief conceptualization and contextualization of denationalization as a state form congruent with the current strategy of capital accumulation at the global (rather than the national) level. Then it demonstrates how and to what extent the Mauritanian state is being denationalized. The influence of international forces in shaping state policy is shown through a thorough analysis of the interplay between the government and international financial institutions such as the IMF, the World Bank, the Paris Club, and the Consultative Group. This is done through a detailed analysis of the geneses and processes of (1) formulation of public policy, (2) articulation of development strategies, (3) engineering of fiscal policy, (4) management of foreign debts, and (5) design of public investment programs. In all these various aspects of public policy, it is argued that the role and agency of the state remain important yet secondary to the role of multilateral institutions.

Chapter 5 continues the analysis of the denationalization of the state by pointing out the increasing penetration of lender missions and NGOs within state apparatuses. It analyzes how missionaries from the international community of lenders (World Bank missions) and donors (NGOs) are scrambling for the conception and implementation of national and local development projects and therefore competing with the state in its own backyard. Specific examples from the preparation and implementation of one structural adjustment program and one sectoral adjustment program are provided to illustrate the emerging division of labor between the government and the community of lenders and donors in terms of the overall organization and control of the national economy.

Chapter 6 discusses the scope and extent of the economic restructuring and the internationalization and devaluation of the Mauritanian economy following the denationalization of the state. After a detailed survey of major economic and sectoral adjustment programs in Mauritania, the chapter addresses the rationale and impact of successive devaluations of the national currency and their negative impact on the purchasing power of the nation as a whole vis-à-vis the world market. The chapter also shows how the reins of the national economy are increasingly controlled by a complex multitude of international investors entwined by the World Bank and how their control over policy design and project financing turned the state into an executor of World Bank/IMF development policies and a guarantor of international loans.

Chapter 7 assesses the social dimension and impact of SAPs, particularly social policy and social differentiation under adjustment. First, it argues that social policy of adjustment is primarily aimed at containing the sociopolitical ramifications of economic and financial reforms while gathering vital data at the household and informal sector levels for a *global planning system*. It therefore constitutes a by-product of SAPs, not an original and genuine social policy. Second, it describes social differentiation under adjustment, particularly the growing social disparity as reflected in the rise of a comprador international class, the decline of salaried and wage earners in the middle class, and the homogenization of a class of urban and rural poor engaged in various strategies of survival in the so-called informal sector.

Chapter 8 examines the political implications of SAPs, particularly the processes of democratization and sociopolitical fragmentation. It underlines the significance of democratization as the buzzword of the post–Cold War era and stresses the organic linkages between economic liberalization and multiparty politics. It demonstrates that the role of popular protest in bringing multipartyism to Africa was significant yet secondary to the role played by Western pressure to liberalize African politics following a decade of sustained efforts to liberalize African economies through SAPs. Western pressures for democratization in Mauritania are presented to illustrate the above argument. It also argues that the process of denationalization of the state following the adoption of SAPs weakened the public sector and created a sense of social insecurity among people who felt that the state was no longer able and/or willing to protect them. This lies behind the three trends of sociopolitical fragmentation that are developing along the paths of ethnicity, multipartyism, and Islamism.

Chapter 9 begins by summarizing the main findings of the research. At the international level, the global strategy of restructuring and adjustment of the 1980s and 1990s has reconstituted and reinvigorated the political, economic, and military power of the West and accelerated the recompradorization of the peripheral states of the world economy by reversing their nationalist policies. At the national level, the Mauritanian state has been denationalized, the economy internationalized and devalued, and the society democratized and fragmented. The chapter concludes with a critique of SAPs' democratization and points to the necessity of its demystification, since even genuine democratic relations at the national and local levels will always remain superficial amid undemocratic relations at the international and global levels, where SAPs are conceived and designed. It also presents a general critique of representative democracy and suggests the necessity of materializing direct democracy.

Concrete Context of SAPs

In the mid-1980s the Mauritanian government embarked on a full-scale structural adjustment program with the sponsorship and assistance of the International Monetary Fund, the World Bank, the Paris Club, the Consultative Group for Mauritania, and a growing number of international nongovernmental organizations. The program was articulated around a government strategy of trading control over economic policy for loans and other forms of capital inflow from the world market via international financial institutions. So far, two three-year programs have been fully implemented and a third one is under way. The Economic and Financial Recovery Program (1985–88) initiated the adjustment process and focused on three types of reforms: (1) a macroeconomic reform focusing on a devaluation of the national currency (by 40 percent between January 1984 and February 1985) and the adoption and continuation of a flexible exchange rate policy, a ceiling of credit and its reorientation from the public sector to the private sector, a freezing of public expenditure, and a liberalization of the prices of most goods and many services; (2) a sectoral reform aiming at the privatization of ownership and/or management of public enterprises, the restructuring of the banking system, and the definition of new strategies for the productive sectors of mining, fishing, and agriculture; and (3) an institutional reform with new regulations promoting private investment and reforming the administrative system. The Economic Consolidation and Growth Program (1989–91), as its name indicates, expanded and consolidated the above reforms with an attempt to contain their negative social impacts. The policy framework paper of the third program (1992–95) was presented to the executive boards of the IMF and the World Bank in September 1992, after two years of shuttle missions between Washington and Nouakchott. The first policy measure implemented in the framework of this program was another devaluation of the national currency by 42 percent.

Reforms such as the above have been in progress almost everywhere in developing countries throughout the 1980s and 1990s. In Mauritania, they represent the major socioeconomic and political changes for the past decade. The central focus of this work analyzes the international context of these reforms and their unfolding within the Mauritanian state, economy, and society. It locates and traces their origins and motives and shows how they brought about a rearticulation of space/power relations between the global, the national, and the local. Because such an approach of inquiry involves a multitude of institutional, economic, and sociopolitical issues of international and national development, it needs (1) the scope and scale of the discipline of geography (in 1994, the

Association of American Geographers had forty-three specialty groups); (2) the depth of political economy, particularly what Pickles and Watts have called the new postparadigmatic[1] geography of regional political economy; and (3) the insight of what I call *geopolitical economy*, where competition between nation-states (or blocs of nation-states) is *not less* important in the dynamic of the making of history than internal social struggles within those nation-states. Therefore, the work deals with adjustment as a complex whole whose totality is a crucial element that must be grasped in any attempt at understanding the unfolding of structural and institutional reforms within and without the state apparatus. These reforms are comprehensive and deal simultaneously with structural, sectoral, and institutional policies. Focusing on one aspect of adjustment can easily lead to the loss of the overall process. Because adjustment policies are in progress worldwide today, they must be analyzed as a development strategy or a philosophy of development, which must be understood as a whole and beyond the simple analysis of the statistics of gross domestic product (GDP), inflation, debt, unemployment, and so on. While such statistics are based on the analysis of national data, at some point one must go beyond the state categorical analysis to better understand many state policies, particularly those related to SAPs, whose consistency and uniformity in almost all developing countries during the past fifteen years indicate that they must have been the result of careful planning. Yet adjustment is often equated with liberalism and laissez-faire economic policies where market forces are believed to be working at their optimum. However, the analysis of the concrete unfolding of adjustment demonstrates clearly that it actually represents a sophisticated form of global planning (indeed a global command economy) advocated and presented within the context of a hegemonic discourse of liberalism, "the context of the newly emerging neo-liberal discourses and reemerging ideologies of individual freedom, private property, and market-based planning."[2]

This work is primarily concerned with the difficult search for "truth" through the ticklish enterprise of unraveling the genesis and tracing the genealogy of state policies, particularly within their international context. It is less interested in either predictions or prescriptions for the future, since the overall academic performance on these two levels has been quite poor in the past decades. Derek Bok, president of Harvard University, warns against the detachment of academia when he writes, "Armed with the security of tenure and the time to study the world with care, professors would appear to have a unique opportunity to act as society's scouts to signal impending problems long before they are visible to others. Yet rarely have members of the academy succeeded in discovering the emerging issues and bringing them vividly to the attention of the public."[3] Though the primary reason behind this academic failure needs further study, it could be attributed to the systematic separation of work and politics as part of the overall professional specialization desired and often required for efficiency and productivity at the workplace. One of the main concerns of dominant academic and intellectual circles is to keep social peace at the workplace through *the politics of the exclusion of politics* or at least its separation from work. Such separation is embodied in the often futile efforts to try to find technical explanations and solutions for what are actually political issues and problems. This academic compartmentalization of politics and science continues to produce not only poor but also misleading knowledge.

During my numerous interviews and correspondences with state officials and adjustment experts, particularly in the course of my search for adjustment-related documents in Mauritania and the United States, this categorization of politics and science became obvious. Indeed, the secrecy of documents and information is positively correlated to their importance and relevance for unraveling the real significance of policies. For example, a (public) document such as the *standby arrangement* that the IMF signs conjointly with borrowing governments is considered *confidential* and therefore kept away from the public because its propagation would touch the fabric of power relations and their intellectual representations. Its propagation would particularly discredit the widely believed *apolitical nature* of the IMF and expose its political leverage and influence over the process of policy-making in countries dealing with it. It would also reveal that the peripheral state is not as powerful and sovereign as people generally believe and would even reveal that governments are not as much interested in the well-being of their peoples as they always claim. Instead of releasing such an important document, which exposes the real balance of power between the borrowing state and the IMF, governments would keep it confidential, while the IMF would issue a press release that would state briefly the amount of money involved in the standby, structural adjustment facility (SAF), or enhanced structural adjustment facility (ESAF) arrangement without specifics concerning the conditions agreed upon because these are considered politically *sensitive*. This is how politics becomes an *epistemological problem* that cannot be overcome by simply ignoring it, as classic academic research unfortunately does avowedly. Moreover, the partisan reading and interpretation of policies stemming from such a document would be presented to general readers and policymakers in a variety of IMF periodical publications including *International Financial Statistics*, *Finance and Development*, and *IMF Survey*. It is clear that the IMF and borrowing governments do not want publicity for their deals. Such secrecy continues to raise serious suspicion in the minds of the general public since both the IMF and borrowing governments are considered public institutions that should be accountable to the public.

This problem of "public information" was partly behind the August 1993 World Bank decision to establish a Public Information Center (PIC). Although the World Bank is generally more open to research than the IMF, it nevertheless has its own categories of documents and information, whose secrecy varies in accordance with their significance for the study of adjustment. First, there are published documents such as *World Development Report* that are distributed worldwide not only to inform general readers and policymakers but also to influence their opinions and perceptions and therefore the process of decision making. Because such documents provide carefully prepared answers to macroeconomic development questions of the day, they influence the tenets of development theory and the findings of development research on a global scale. Second, formal reports such as *Economic and Sectoral Memorandum*, *Staff Appraisal Report*, and *Sectoral Policy Paper* are restricted to the use of the World Bank's bureaucracy and its government negotiating teams. These documents are the most important primary sources for understanding macroeconomic and sectoral issues related to adjustment reforms of national economies, even though they are also designed to influence development theory and policy at the national level by propagating a particular approach to development problems and solutions. The recent World Bank policy on disclosure of some of its operational information indicates the increasing hegemony of the Bank over development literature and its ability to contain and coopt its critics. This strategy represents a partial liberalization of information. However, this new disclosure policy (which only became effective on 1 January 1994) is not retroactive and the release of many documents continues to depend on mutual agreement between the Bank and borrowing governments. There are many other *internal documents* that the World Bank did not and probably will not release or allow access to, particularly World Bank records concerning the deliberations of the board of executive directors. They are considered *sensitive*, and their release could undermine the progress of adjustment policies by revealing statistics or information that contradicts that published and propagated. Their release could also reveal the politics of decision making within the World Bank system, particularly the undemocratic nature of the *one dollar, one vote* principle upon which the balance of power between World Bank members is founded. Finally, it should be emphasized that the vast majority of (borrowing) government documents (particularly SAP economic diagnoses and development policies) are originally World Bank (IMF, Paris Club, and so on) documents that were formally altered (sometimes by simply changing the title) to make them seem like government-produced documents (for more details on this issue see policy formulation in chapter 4 and genesis of PREF in chapter 6). Indeed, a very small number of SAP documents could be attributed to the borrowing government, at least in the case of Mauritania.

One of the most important problems facing adjustment research today is its reliance on and satisfaction with *published* IMF/World Bank and government reports and studies, which are certainly important but not sufficient for a full understanding of how SAPs work. These publications are designed to make adjustment sound like the only possible, feasible, and desired solution for contemporary socioeconomic and political problems in developing countries. They propagate a highly optimistic assessment of adjustment policies and their impacts on economic growth and social development. But what these publications reveal is far less important than what is contained in other unpublished documents, such as diagnostic economic studies, economic and financial programs, policy framework papers, standby arrangements, Paris Club accords, Consultative Group summary of debates, minutes of proceedings of negotiating teams, texts of loan agreements, and supervision and project progress reports. Without these primary documents (upon which this work is primarily based), adjustment policies cannot be fully understood, and the recent disclosure of some of them will certainly inject new blood into adjustment studies in the coming years.

Theoretical Context of SAPs

Political, economic, and social restructuring of contemporary societies represents the focus of most development policy and research throughout the past fifteen years. Restructuring refers to a new strategy of capital accumulation. It reflects a transition from less to more efficient and more profitable forms of socioeconomic organization capable of bringing about higher capital returns. The transition involves great tension between "the increasingly global nature of economic relationships and the persistently national character of the system's main political units,"[4] that is, a global economy without a global state. Restructuring proper applies more to the kind of industrial changes taking place in the major industrialized countries where market-based planning systems have been in place for a long time. In developing countries, Eastern Europe, and the former Soviet Union, the transition is essentially a process of adjustment to the requirements of the above restructuring. To use a more commonplace terminology, restructuring represents a transition from command or regulated economies to free market or less regulated economies with a whole array of sociopolitical ramifications. This process of socioeconomic transformation fuels the restructuring debate, which has become a major research program whose "purpose is to elucidate the interaction between capital's strategies and the socio-spatial patterns of production and other social relationships."[5] As far as development policies are concerned, the restructuring debate provided a new context for raising old antagonisms between liberalism and Marxism, between modernization (i.e., Westernization)[6] and dependency theories, and even between universalism and particularism. Thanks to the influence of the political-economy perspective, geography has become "more directly oriented to social problems and it has achieved an awareness of politics"[7] and, because of this, has contributed significantly to the restructuring debate.

Geography's critical and theoretical contribution to the restructuring and adjustment debate has developed along two major lines of thinking. The first and probably the most influential is the uneven development school, which originated within the framework of the dependency school.[8] It seeks to investigate the geographic implication of capital accumulation.[9] This approach explains the dynamics of restructuring and adjustment by the continually frustrated search for "a spatial fix" that creates "distinct patterns of geographic unevenness through the continual seesaw of capital."[10] The second approach is the regulation school,[11] which focuses on state regulation of labor and capital arrangements. In this approach, the dynamics of restructuring/adjustment are analyzed within the framework of interactions between regimes of capital accumulation and modes of social regulation. Both lines of thinking (uneven development and regulation theory) continue to draw, though separately, on the Marxist fundamental articulation of contradiction, crisis, and change. For example, capitalist crises have always been (temporarily) solved through geographic expansion (uneven development) and/or the redefinition of capital-labor relations (regulation). However, given successive revolutions in the relationship between space and time, the current geographic expansion of the market (to solve the crisis of the decline of capital return) goes beyond the mere expansion into traditional Euclidian space by expanding into a new cyberspace. It implies new forms of socioeconomic organization that involve increased mobility of capital, particularly across international borders. For example, foreign direct investment by the United States, France, the United Kingdom, Japan, and Germany almost doubled from $1,000 billion to $1,949 billion between 1987 and 1992.[12] These rapid transformations have geopolitical consequences that are exacerbated by increased competition between localities, cities, regions, nations, and corporations.

One shortcoming of the above two schools of development is the separate tracks of their analyses of the process of restructuring. They do not systematically integrate the two issues of uneven development and social regulation in one approach capable of generating a thorough grasp of the various dimensions of restructuring. Uneven development and social regulation are two sides of the same coin. They constitute the backbone of restructuring, particularly its theoretical foundation in geography, and need to be combined in its analysis. This is so because restructuring is essentially a redefinition of, not a revolution in, social regulation at both the local and the global levels. That redefinition does not represent a radical transformation of capitalist relations because, after all, "we still live in a society where production for profit remains the basic organizing principle of economic life."[13] Restructuring at the national level is inextricably linked to the international level. One of the most visible manifestations of the current restructuring is the scope and speed of capital mobility across national borders. But this mobility is only possible and profitable thanks to the quasi-immobility of labor within national borders. Lifting restrictions on capital movement is often accompanied by tightening regulation on immigration. A second shortcoming of the two schools is their underestimation of the role of power and the geopolitics of North-South relations not only in launching the restructuring process but also in determining its trajectory. As a legacy of the early interpretation of historical materialism, where "materialist thought tended to denigrate action in favor of structure,"[14] the political-economy perspective continues to approach politics and power as an outcome of a more fundamental economic dynamic. While this might be the case, power itself can create economic dynamics.

Power can create wealth in many ways. Primitive accumulation (systematic use of violence and terror to extract wealth and labor from non-European regions) of the sixteenth and seventeenth centuries has nothing to do with the so-called law of supply and demand. Rather, power created primitive accumulation simply by the use of power. Today, major postmodern forms of accumulation such as currency devaluation, manipulation of the exchange rate, and credit allocation are based on power, not on the law of supply and demand. Market forces represent concrete social power relations that have become taken for granted to the extent that they may seem like metaphysical forces that are out of societal reach.

The issue of power is perhaps the point of junction of uneven geographic development and regulation of social relations. Spatial and social relations are in the final analysis power relations. Although poststructuralism and postmodernism do not propose (and probably do not have) any solution to the problem of power, their method of ontological deconstruction of theories to expose hidden power relations illustrates the omnipresence and importance of the problem of power. Post-Marxism too "is likely to attach itself to a general theory of power."[15] The worldwide drive for democratization (notwithstanding demagoguery) is also an illustration of the persistence of the problem of power and governance which constitutes "the prime political problem confronting human communities"[16] today. In short, the geography of power and geopolitics (traditionally misunderstood as the black sheep[17] of geography) must be called upon for any serious, thorough, and comprehensive analysis of restructuring and adjustment, which are both more of a restoration than a revolution. Sometimes what is needed is not only to track down changes but also to monitor the unchanged and often reinforced power relations. Beyond the structural integration of the uneven development and social regulation approaches, the geography of power and geopolitics attempts not only to pinpoint the various power foci and the major players behind the dynamics of adjustment but also to understand their structure and hierarchy. This approach is necessary because adjustment is above all a direct translation of domination relations between two partners of unequal power; one of them must adjust to the requirements of the other.

This process of adjustment represents a planned strategy whose real agents (the G–7 countries[18]) are often arbitrarily excluded from adjustment literature (in favor of the instruments of SAPs, such as the IMF, the World Bank, and the borrowing state), and their role has therefore escaped scrutiny. Another reason for adopting this approach is the nature of evidence that will be used in this work. That evidence is based on official documents covering most adjustment-related agreements that the Mauritanian government has signed with various partners of the international community of lenders and donors (the IMF, the World Bank, the Paris Club, the Consultative Group, and international NGOs). These primary source documents are crucial in understanding the dynamics of adjustment at the institutional (denationalization of the state), economic (internationalization of the economy), and social (sociopolitical fragmentation) levels. The impact of regulation and deregulation has even been an important theme in law and economics, as well as an increasingly important field of research in geography.[19] The presentation, discussion, reading, and analysis of regulation and deregulation texts represent a concrete form of analysis. Rather than ruminating on secondhand economic statistics in an apolitical approach, the emphasis here is on tracing the genealogy and determining the genesis of policy making and power relations. Before turning to the making of the global strategy of restructuring and adjustment in the next chapter, let us outline briefly the significance of SAPs during the past decade and the various approaches to their study, the importance of resource transfer from South to North despite the discourse of aid, and the overall economic failure of SAPs, particularly in sub-Saharan Africa, where the Mauritanian economy belongs.

Structural adjustment programs represent the hallmark of development policies in the Third World[20] (together with the post-*perestroika* Soviet Union and Eastern Europe) in the 1980s and 1990s. These programs constitute a concerted effort on the part of lender countries and institutions to deal with borrower countries on a case-by-case basis rather than as a group. They are articulated around a strategy of providing loans to developing nations and dictating development policies. In the early 1980s, heavily indebted governments of the Third World began to lose the option of doing business with foreign lenders on an exclusively bilateral basis. The seven major industrialized capitalist countries (the G–7) had already been working on a global strategy of coordination and cooperation on international economic and financial policies, particularly on debt and credit issues worldwide, since their first summit meeting in France in 1975. By 1982 they had succeeded in attaching strict conditionality[21] to any further provision of credits or rescheduling of debts through carefully designed structural adjustment programs. The developing nations were simultaneously seduced by foreign loans, frightened by their fiscal crises and balance of payments deficit, and haunted by the possibility of being declared insolvent by the Washington-based multilateral institutions, i.e., the International Monetary Fund and the World Bank. The formula of the strategy is that national economies must be adjusted so that they will automatically respond to the incentives and adapt to the imperatives of the global market in an attempt to homogenize the law of value worldwide,[22] even though this attempt at homogenization continues to produce differentiation because of the fundamental advantage of capital mobility across national borders compared to labor fixity. This strategy of adjusting national economies is based on the postulate that economic efficiency and rational management along the lines of market mechanisms should constitute the sole scale upon which all national considerations of production, administration and culture are measured. Efficiency (the new magic word) refers to the technical skill and political ability to allocate capital investment and reorganize labor to produce more output with less input, i.e., increase labor productivity, capital return, and profitability.

According to El-Naggar,[23] there are three methods of evaluating adjustment policies: a normative approach focusing on evaluation in relation to achievement of targets specified in adjustment, a historical method in which evaluation is made in relation to the situation prior to adjustment, and a hypothetical evaluation based on a hypothetical situation where there is no adjustment. Among these, the most common method of analysis and evaluation of adjustment programs is the historical one, which measures and compares key economic indicators (growth rate of GDP, level of foreign debts, budget deficit, inflation rate, and so on) at both the beginning and the end of each period and then draws conclusions regarding the positive and negative achievements according to available statistics. This is the classic before-after and control-group World Bank methodology of evaluating adjustment success. Although the importance of this approach and these indicators cannot be denied, they fall short of reflecting the real dimensions of these structural reforms. Quantitative data about the economy can vary a lot and can be intentionally manipulated[24] to support different claims, while qualitative ones are hardly accepted within the already quantitatively framed scientific community, whose obsession with facts and numbers makes it seem as though many of its members abide by the principle that "all policy implications drawn from economics are matters of faith."[25]

Another shortcoming of the quantitative approach is its inability to put as much emphasis on the South/North flow of resources as on the

North/South one, because the process of data production in many developing countries is designed essentially to show the inflow, not the outflow, of capital.[26] Even the balance of payments sheet (that governments publish annually) is structured in a way that is not helpful in determining precisely capital outflow. This is because capital outflow often exceeds capital inflow, which explains the chronic balance of payments deficit and embarrasses governments seeking to legitimize further borrowing from outside. Multilateral institutions are often more reserved about the transfer of resources from South to North, since their declared objective is "to raise standards of living in developing countries by channeling to them financial resources provided by developed countries."[27] However, Walter E. Fauntroy (chairman of a U.S. congressional committee) admitted that the only defense against a net capital outflow to the IMF is "the accumulation of arrears."[28] In 1987 alone, developing countries as a whole "repaid $6.1 billion more to the IMF than they received from it,"[29] and Africa's foreign debt service averages today some $27 billion a year.[30]

Estimates of net capital outflow from developing nations vary. But there is little doubt that donor grants and loans do not match transfer of remittances, as the huge and widening disparity between the rich[31] North and the poor South illustrates. Despite the generosity of the developed countries, the United Nations maintains that "financial resources are transferring from developing to developed countries."[32] One estimate is that net resource transfers from the Third World to the United States averaged $43.5 billion a year between 1982 and 1992;[33] another estimate is that throughout the 1980s, annual net outflow from the South averaged between $33 billion and $45 billion.[34] Between 1983 and 1988 net transfer of financial resources from the developing countries to the industrialized ones was estimated at $115 billion.[35] Capital flight from thirteen (mainly) Latin American countries jumped from $47 billion in 1978 to $184 billion in 1988.[36] These various amounts can be found and/or deduced from statistics published by international financial institutions but can hardly be inferred from analyses of official statistics published by individual governments. Capital flight represents a serious problem for accumulation in countries embarking on adjustment. Even the former Soviet Union is now experiencing this problem as it embarks on the adjustment process. But despite the difficulty of measuring accurately the transfer of resources from the South to the North, there is no question about its profusion, especially in Africa, where adjustment has worsened conditions.[37] The average annual GNP per capita growth rate in sub-Saharan Africa was -1.2 percent between 1980 and 1991, while it was 2.3 percent for Organization of Economic Cooperation and Development (OECD) members during the same period.[38] The inability of adjustment reforms to improve the standard of living of people in countries implementing them is well documented. In Latin America, the 1980s were "a disastrous decade,"[39] and in Africa they were a "lost decade," where adjustment led to the destruction of the continent through economic misery, political chaos, and environmental degradation, which, if not stopped, will "lead to a turbulent and unprecedented stage of development of underdevelopment in most regions of Africa."[40] Not a single African country or government escaped the current economic and political decay which made the 1980s "a decade of hardship for people in virtually every African country."[41] The only success in the continent was often attributed to NGOs, whose humanitarian and political influence over African states is really a sign of serious decline if we remember their role during the second half of the nineteenth century when they prepared the population for the subsequent military conquest of the continent by European powers. In the words of Latouche, "Official Africa has failed."[42] In 1989, the UN Economic Commission for Africa analyzed the efforts to implement adjustment policies in the continent and came up with this conclusion:

> in spite of all these efforts, the crisis remained unabated. Many African economies moved from stagnation to declining growth; food deficits reached alarming proportions; unemployment mounted; underutilization of industrial capacity became widespread; and environmental degradation threatened the very survival of the African people.[43]

Many Africanists and Third World analysts agree with the bulk of the above evaluation of SAPs. Susan George noted that the squeeze of SAPs not only is instrumental in the collapse and chaos of countries such as Liberia, Somalia, and Sierra Leone, but also is contributing to the destruction of tropical forests, desertification, urban pollution, hunger, and sickness. Paul Mosley and John Weeks came to the conclusion that there is little evidence that SAPs are leading Africa toward the road to recovery. Richard Sandbrook drew attention to how aid is offset by debt servicing and how the export-led growth model in Africa is inadequate in the long run because of protectionism in the industrialized countries, development of synthetic substitutes, and technological advances requiring less or different material inputs. This model is strengthening

Africa's dependence on the world market while eroding intra-African cooperation, which Adabayo Adedeji described as not only desirable but also imperative for lessening the impact of the economic crisis in Africa. John Ravenhill observed that in the second decade of SAPs, Africa is the world's most heavily indebted continent in terms of the ratio of debt to GNP and that "with current debt-servicing requirements much of the income from economic growth immediately flows back to the IFIs [international financial institutions] and Western donors." He and Thomas Callaghy warned that if the difficulties arising out of the implementation of SAPs are not learned and applied by IFIs and Western donors, "Africa will remain 'hemmed in.'"[44] In their various works on SAPs in Africa, these Africanists emphasized the debt problem, the decline of GNP per capita, and the increasing political instability and social disruption in the continent. Their works constitute an important contribution to Africa's experience with SAPs. However, in tracing the genesis and origins of SAPs, they often limit their analysis to the instruments of SAPs (IFIs and African states) rather than expand it to the real agents of SAPs, the Group of Seven, whose annual economic summits since 1975 carefully engineered SAPs as a global strategy of accumulation.

Another evaluation report by the members of a Staff Study Mission from the U.S. Congress who visited Britain, France, Senegal, Ghana, and Cote d'Ivoire in 1988 to assess adjustment impact on Africa noted that "structural adjustment has produced little enduring poverty-alleviation, and certain policies have worked against the poor."[45] The report pointed out that the price of groundnut in Senegal plunged from $1,000 to $550 per ton between 1985 and 1987 and poverty among urban Senegalese had been aggravated as a result of structural adjustment. Other assessments of adjustment in sub-Saharan African countries estimate that the collective GNP of the region has shrunk by 20 percent despite cash infusions of $100 billion.[46] In Mauritania, a 1990 World Bank evaluation report concluded that after six years of comprehensive adjustment programs, the Mauritanian economy is "far from achieving sustainable economic growth."[47] The negative impact of adjustment is also echoed in UN Development Program publications which had repeatedly pointed out the harshness of the social impact of adjustment and called for "human development" and "development with a human face." The bleak economic outlook and decline of the African continent is raising all sorts of new and old questions in the process of exploring all possible and imaginary means for stopping the decline of Africa, the *continent usé* (or worn-out continent) in the words of former Senegalese President Leopold Sédar Senghor.

In 1990, Nigerian President Ibrahim Babangida called on Western nations to pay compensation to Africa for damage done to the continent by the Atlantic slave trade, and in 1993 the Organization of African Unity appointed the Group of Eminent Persons to explore the modalities and strategies of an African campaign for compensation to Africa for damages caused by the Atlantic slave trade.[48] Although this might be a legitimate demand (for all ex-colonized and oppressed peoples) in the light of Germany's generous compensation for Jews following World War II and the opening of the U.S. Holocaust Memorial and Museum in April 1993, it addresses only the historical dimension of the problem but does not tackle the current adjustment process, whose exacerbation of the crisis is widely recognized. It is alarming that despite the failure of adjustment policies to bring about sustainable economic growth, the strategy of adjustment has not been abandoned. Indeed adjustment continues to expand in scope and scale, and this is despite the increasingly low priority given to sub-Saharan Africa since the disintegration of the Soviet Union.[49] The big question is why the implementation of adjustment policies continues unabated while the crisis they were supposed to solve continues to deepen as the "lost decade" of the 1980s seems clearly to be followed by "another lost decade" of the 1990s.[50]

The central argument made here is that structural adjustment programs are not actually aimed at either solving or aggravating the economic crisis in Africa, let alone in Mauritania. Adjustment was conceived outside Africa by the industrialized countries to expand their markets, increase their exports, and secure debt payments through a carrot-and-stick policy of providing loans to fiscally bankrupt Third World governments in exchange for fundamental reforms in their political economy. If structural adjustment programs fail, a senior World Bank official warns, "then it is a failure of *our approach to the economy*, a failure of *our institutions*, a failure of *our political will*, and there is no way that *we* will be able to say that it is just the failure of Africa. So *we* have a very, very big stake in this"[51] [italics added]. One objective of this work is to unpack and reveal both the intentionality and consciousness of the G–7 in engineering SAPs. The main objective of adjustment is not necessarily to solve the budget and balance of payments deficits of developing countries but to maintain an open world trade and payment system and prevent national governments from attempting to put further restrictions on capital movement and import of goods and services from the industrialized countries. From this perspective, adjustment is a success because nationalistic policies are for the most part reversed, resource transfer from the South to the North has accelerated, and liberalization policies are now sweeping the entire Third World, opening new markets and strengthening the umbilical cord between developed and developing countries through what many describe as the debt trap, where a nation seeks new loans to pay old ones. In short, SAPs succeeded in preventing any disruption in the world trade and payment system, which continues to transfer resources from developing to developed countries. To understand how SAPs were successful for some while unsuccessful for others, it is necessary to analyze the making and genesis of SAPs.

2

Globalization and Peripheral States

This chapter identifies and analyzes the main elements of global restructuring and adjustment and their implications for peripheral states.[1] It presents the international and geopolitical contexts within which SAPs were conceived and designed. First, it addresses the economic crisis of the 1970s, which opened the door to restructuring in the West and adjustment to that restructuring in developing nations. The main point made here is that the crisis developed out of a fundamental contradiction between nationalistic, protectionist policies seeking to achieve accumulation on a national scale on the one hand, and global policies working toward the destruction of all borders, barriers, and policies that might interfere with the free movement of capital worldwide, on the other hand. Second, adjustment is analyzed as a comprehensive Western strategy (with economic, political, military, and cultural dimensions) whose agents are the industrialized countries, particularly the Group of Seven, which has engineered, funded, and supported adjustment policies since 1980. The emphasis is on (1) the role of G-7 summits in conceiving and advocating SAPs, (2) the role of World Bank studies in discrediting nationalist models of development, (3) the role of military intervention and media propaganda in suppressing alternatives to SAPs, (4) the consolidation of the North/South divide in the aftermath of the Cold War, and (5) the identification of Islam as a new threat to the New World Order that emerged following the collapse of communism. Third, instruments and policies of the strategy will be examined, particularly the crucial role played by the peripheral state in the adoption and implementation of SAPs.

The Economic Crisis of the 1970s

The present crisis of accumulation (characterized by high inflation and massive unemployment) first began in the industrialized countries in the late 1960s and early 1970s and later began to spread to the rest of the world. The crisis "affected the center much more sharply than the periphery *as a whole*: whereas the annual growth rate by volume of OECD industrial production fell from 6.4 per cent before 1967 to 4.6 per cent and to 1.6 per cent between 1973 and 1978, the rate in developing countries rose, without a break in 1973, from 5 per cent to an average of 7.1 per cent since 1976."[2] Only later was the crisis "transmitted to the developing countries through the mechanisms of trade, capital flows, and aid."[3] The post–World War II blocs (West, East, and South) were structured on a nationally based form of capital accumulation where most states sought to achieve industrialization and economic growth via a policy of protectionism in which state apparatuses were highly involved in the production and distribution of goods and services. Protectionism here refers to the relatively inward-looking policies of Keynesianism that took place within the wider context of the Cold War, where imperialist expansion was temporarily checked and contained by the military balance between the NATO and Warsaw pact military alliances. Such inward-looking nationalist policies encouraged nations to subjugate their international relations to the imperatives of national sovereignty, independence, and industrialization.

Within the framework of the inward-looking nationalist strategy of development, the Soviet model of central planning and protectionism achieved an important industrial transition in communist countries and inspired nationalistic policies in the Third World, particularly after the Bandung Conference of 1955 inaugurated the mainstream philosophy of development. The objective of this development policy was to achieve industrialization via a series of nationalistic and protectionist policies aimed primarily at assuring accumulation at the national level. From the 1950s up to the mid-1970s, imperialism was strongly challenged in the Third World by revolutionary struggle, radical nationalism, and a growing solidarity between developing nations in the diplomatic arena.[4] At the same time, a wave of expropriations of foreign direct investment swept the Third World, with the aim of controlling natural resources via public ownership as exemplified by the nationalization of the Iranian oil industry and the Egyptian Suez Canal company in the 1950s and the Chilean copper industry in the 1970s. Many developing countries achieved significant rates of growth, moderate balance of payment deficits, and even the dream of graduation from underdeveloped status following a wave of nationalizations and strict control on capital movement across national borders. The GNP growth rates of developing countries averaged 6 to 7 percent between 1970 and 1980 compared to 1 percent between 1980 and 1988.[5] For example, Mauritania's GDP rate of growth reached 10.3 percent in 1974,[6] compared to 0.3 percent in 1990.[7] For sub-Saharan Africa as a whole (excluding South Africa), annual GDP per capita growth rates continued to rise up to the mid-1970s and then began to deteriorate, especially after the adoption of sweeping structural adjustment reforms as shown in table 1.

Table 1 Growth Rate in sub-Saharan Africa

1960–69	1970–74	1975–79	1980–84
1.6 %	2.9 %	-0.4 %	-4.1%

Source: Compiled from Sawyerr, A. "Les Politiques d'Ajustement: Problèmes Politiques," Conference Internationale sur le Facteur Humain dans le Redressement Economique et le Développement de l'Afrique, Khartoum, Soudan, 5–8 mars 1988, ECA/ICHD/88/29, 3.

The enforcement of protectionist policies in most developing countries, combined with semi-autarkic policies in the Eastern bloc, were probably one major cause of shrinking markets for industrialized nations, which were experiencing a postwar boom. Third World countries were implementing nationalist policies of accumulation through projects of industrialization and policies of nationalization that limited access to their markets and relatively protected local industries. On the other hand, the economic hegemony of the United States began to face challenges from new competitors in Japan and Western Europe following over two decades of reconstruction after World War II. These structural changes of the world economy and the attempt to contain them were partly reflected at the political level by increasing tension between West and East over the war in Vietnam and at the economic level by the collapse of the fixed rate of exchange between the dollar and gold in 1971. That collapse opened the door for a short period of protectionism and competition, especially among "the world Triad"[8] (the United States, Western Europe, and Japan), through manipulation of exchange rates. Such speculative trends were contained only when IMF leading members reached the Smithsonian Agreement of 18 December 1971, which provided for the realignment of industrial country currencies and an increase in the price of gold. The trend was further aggravated by the strong emergence of one Third World cartel, the Organization of Petroleum Exporting Countries (OPEC), and the first major rise of oil prices in 1973 and the subsequent recession in industrialized countries (even though most OPEC surplus was soon recycled to industrialized and newly industrialized countries). Developing nations went further and requested through the United Nations a New International Economic Order (NIEO).

First, Algeria proposed a special session of the UN General Assembly entitled: "Study of the Problems of Raw Materials and Development." The proposition easily obtained the required majority of states, and the sixth special session was held between 9 April and 2 May 1974. Within the framework of this conference, eighty-five developing nations drafted a proposal entitled: "Programme of Action on the Establishment of a New International Economic Order"[9] which was then passed as a UN resolution and whose preamble reads "We, the Members of the United Nations . . ., solemnly proclaim our united determination to work urgently for the establishment of a New International Economic Order based on equity."[10] The UN adoption of a declaration on the establishment of a NIEO addressed concerns of Third World countries over many development issues, particularly the stabilization of the terms of trade for countries that export mainly raw materials to and import finished goods from the industrialized countries. But above all, the UN resolution crystallized and codified the right of individual nation-states to pursue their own national strategies of accumulation and their corollaries of sociopolitical organizations. The resolution emphasized policies and strategies of accumulation at the national level and acknowledged the sovereignty of nations and the diversity of political and economic systems, something SAPs later denied by imposing a unidimensional world view based exclusively on liberal democracy and market capitalism. Excerpts from paragraph 4 of the UN resolution illustrate some of the principles upon which the NIEO is founded:

Para. 4(d) The right of every country to adopt the economic and social system that it deems to be the most appropriate for its own development and not to be subjected to discrimination of any kind as a result;

Para. 4(e) Full permanent sovereignty of every State over its natural resources and all economic activities. In order to safeguard these resources, each State is entitled to exercise effective control over them and their exploitation with means suitable to its own situation, including the right to nationalization or transfer of ownership to its nationals, this right being an expression of the full permanent sovereignty of the

State. No State may be subjected to economic, political or any other type of coercion to prevent the free and full exercise of this inalienable right;

Para. 4(g) Regulation and supervision of activities of transnational corporations by taking measures in the interest of the national economies of the countries where such transnational corporations operate on the basis of the full sovereignty of those countries;

Para. 4(j) Just and equitable relationship between the prices of raw materials, primary products, manufactured and semi-manufactured goods exported by developing countries and the prices of raw materials, primary commodities, manufactures, capital goods and equipment imported by them with the aim of bringing about sustained improvement in their unsatisfactory terms of trade and the expansion of the world economy;

Para. 4(s) Strengthening—through individual and collective actions—of mutual economic, trade, financial and technical co-operation among the developing countries mainly on a preferential basis.

The New International Economic Order, which emphasized parameters of the national economy, also represented a concerted Third World position in face of the danger of increasing internationalization of capital. In fact, by the 1970s, multinational corporations had been moving and relocating their investment around the globe and seeking advantages in labor costs and environmental regulations,[11] leading to the emergence of a small group of newly industrialized (and later indebted) countries (NICs). This phenomenon contributed to a trend of further internationalization of capital at a moment of increased protectionism. It is estimated that foreign investment by U.S. business increased sixteen fold between 1950 and 1980, while gross private domestic investment grew by less than half.[12] Regardless of the distribution of these investments among Europe, Japan, the NICs, or the other developing countries, they contributed to the establishment of a growing number of transnational corporations whose objectives of accumulation at a global scale often enter into conflict with state strategies of national accumulation. These developments began to trigger the so-called economic crisis of the 1970s[13] and, more important began to resuscitate strategies to manage and perhaps solve the crisis by spreading out its effects and designing new strategies to increase the rate of capital return. The first problem to tackle was protectionism. Restrictions on the movement of capital were widespread in the states of the Third World as a way of creating comparative advantages at the national level through state regulations. Third World economic cooperation was exemplified by the proliferation of Third World cartels[14] (not just OPEC). Diplomatic cooperation was also important, as illustrated by the active role of the

UN General Assembly at a moment when the Security Council was paralyzed by superpower rivalry. Developing nations succeeded in making their voices heard. For example, under their pressure the UN General Assembly passed a resolution in 1975 condemning Zionism as "a form of racism," despite strong Western opposition. Under the Bush administration's pressure, the same resolution was repealed by the same Assembly in December 1991, thus illustrating the changing balance of power between the West and the Third World following the triumph of the adjustment strategy. Compared to the 1970s, the Third World today is in serious disarray and the concept itself is increasingly questioned.[15] Moreover, the United States had never resorted to the use of its veto power in the UN Security Council prior to the 1970s and never suffered military defeat and international humiliation prior to Vietnam. U.S. reliance (for the first time) on the veto in the Security Council in the early 1970s indicates a defensive position in the face of diplomatic coordination among Third World nations, particularly on issues such as apartheid in Southern Africa and Zionism in the Middle East[16] that are intricately linked to the struggles for economic and political independence championed by the NIEO.

The economic crisis was so deep that the whole Keynesian formula was questioned. Its inability to solve the chronic stagflation gave rise to conservative movements in the West that began to brandish their classic formula of "back to the future," i.e, market economy. The trend was reinforced by the inability of the Soviet system to solve its problems or to continue to provide inspiration for Third World nations that were reluctant to fully open their markets to industrialized nations. Western nations were much more immune to the threat from the Third World in the 1980s than they had been following the first oil shock of the 1970s.[17] In this context, conditions were favorable for the conservative offensive of neoliberalism to preach free market policies as both the panacea for the crisis and the creed of the new strategy. The crisis was better reflected in the inability of state regulations to cope with the increasing volume of transactions taking place within the world economy. State regulations were more restrictive in countries of the East and the South where they have always been considered an indispensable comparative advantage in the face of the more competitive economies of scale in the West. Reopening new markets in the South and the East and reducing trade barriers among the "Triad" were to constitute the main pillars of the new strategy of global adjustment, which is actually "a process of forcing the capitalist transformation of colonial countries and their fuller integration into the world capitalist system in a subordinate position."[18] This strategy shifted the international balance of power away from developing countries and formerly planned economies in favor of foreign creditors and investors, international financial organizations, and industrialized countries, particularly the G–7 members.

SAPs: A Global Strategy

By the end of the 1970s, the Third World-backed New International Economic Order was collapsing because of strong opposition from the industrialized countries, the deepening trends of internationalization of capital, and the persistent difficulties of the Soviet system.[19] These developments opened the door for the new Western strategy of adjustment, which destroyed what remained of the NIEO and began to push toward the recompradorization of the Third World. This shift from the NIEO to the G–7 order inaugurated an era marked by the weakening of nationalist trends in the Third World and the ending of bipolarity in international relations, which both contributed to further shrinking the base of the pyramid of the international order and to the emergence of a complex global superstructure bringing together international financial institutions, lenders and donors, the state, and NGOs. Although this global superstructure remains short of a world government, it greatly expands the nest of world bureaucratic networks that link the process of decision making at the global, national, and local levels. It is within this global bureaucratic octopus that development policies are produced today, and therefore, should be analyzed.

Adjustment did not come out of unintentional developments of the world economy and did not develop from the pressure of domestic interest groups in developing countries. It was a relatively well-planned policy by the Group of Seven, whose regular summit meetings since 1975 "reflect a heightened recognition of the need for close cooperation as a result of the growing integration of the world economy and the globalization of financial markets."[20] Development research tends to blame (or praise) the IMF and the World Bank for adjustment. But this is often misleading since these institutions are mere instruments of a development policy that implements strategies decided by the industrialized nations, particularly the G–7 and their spearhead, the United States. This emphasis on instruments rather than agents has obscured and even confused our understanding of the genesis, the unfolding, the impact, and the implication of global restructuring and adjustment. In June 1995, Sandy Berger, the deputy national security advisor in the Clinton administration, summarized the mission of the G-7 as (1) opening and expanding the markets; (2) assisting the transformation of the former communist world into the mainstream market economies; (3) promoting economic reform in the developing world, where five-sixths of the population resides; and (4) promoting the process of reform of the international financial institutions to meet the new challenges of the global economy.[21] The first serious collective attempt to do something about the economic crisis of the early 1970s was discussed during the first G-7 summit in France in 1975. The Economic Declaration of Rambouillet[22] warned agains "a return to protectionism" and urged the trading nations of the world triad "to pursue policies which will permit the expansion of world trade to their mutual advantage" and to use "the IMF and other international fora in making urgent improvements in international arrangements for the stabilization" of developing economies. "We intend to intensify our cooperation on all these problems in the framework of existing institutions as in all the relevant international organizations." The declaration concluded with a thinly veiled warning to the Organization of Petroleum Exporting Countries that everything will be done "to secure the energy sources" needed for growth. During the next summit in Puerto Rico in 1976, U.S. President Gerald Ford expressed the determination of the G-7 to stabilize economies of developing nations "by agreeing on and working together to implement sound solutions to their own problems." At the time the main concern was to stabilize (rather than adjust) developing economies.

In 1977, U.S. President Jimmy Carter designated Henry Owen[23] as the president's special representative for summit preparations. This trusted advisor, with ambassador rank, was appointed to work on summit preparations on a full-time, year-round basis. The other G-7 members took similar steps. These advisors met formally on at least four occasions throughout the year preceding the summit.[24] During the same year, the G-7 began to spell out the strategy of lending money in exchange for structural changes (beyond mere stabilization) in economic policy and agreed in principle that additional resources should be provided for the IMF and the World Bank to permit their lending to rise in real terms. The G-7 declaration reads, "we commit ourselves to seek additional resources for the IMF and support the linkage of its lending practices to the adoption of appropriate stabilization policies."[25] Instructions were then given to these institutions to work together and consult with other developed countries in exploring how the details of this strategy could be best articulated. In 1978 the World Bank began publishing its well-known annual *World Development Report* series as the most distributed development study worldwide. Beyond providing ready analytical frameworks for development in general, the series began to shape the foundation of a new global strategy of adjustment. The 1978 *World Development Report* emphasized the growth of interdependence among nations and the necessity of taking this into consideration when designing development policies. The 1979 report began to develop what would be a systematic series of development scenarios and GDP growth rate projections focusing mainly on developing countries.[26] But it was the 1980 report that set the strategic agenda of development studies in the 1980s and strongly endorsed the findings of the Brandt Commission, which called for a North/South program of survival based on *bold* economic reforms. The first chapter of the report was entitled "Adjustment and Growth in the 1980s." The report also continued the slow-case-versus-fast-case scenarios of GDP growth projections. In 1980, the report stated, the number of people living below the absolute poverty line was approximately 780 million. With the slow case growth scenario (i.e., without adjustment), this number would actually increase over the 1980s to 800 million. With the fast growth scenario (i.e., with adjustment) the number could fall sharply to 590 million.[27] Yet the 1990 *World Development Report* noted that "it is estimated that in 1985 more than one billion people in the developing world lived in absolute poverty."[28] From the 1980 report on, the strategy of adjustment became a constant and straightforward argument of all *World Development Reports*. It was at the Venice summit of 1980 that the G-7 countries endorsed the new strategy of adjustment. The Venice Declaration reads: "We welcome the Bank's innovative lending scheme for structural adjustment."[29]

As the world recession began to spread in 1981 and 1982, particularly after Mexico's defaulted on its debt, the need to tighten lending standards increased.[30] Coordination among the G-7 on the adjustment strategy began to intensify when they designated the IMF and the World Bank "as the central authority for exercising the collective power of capitalist nations states over international financial negotiations."[31] The IMF managing director began to regularly report on the world economic outlook at the semiannual meetings of finance ministers and central bank governors of the leading industrial nations.[32] In this context, the U.S. Department of Treasury emphasized five policy tools (table 2) by which

Table 2   World Bank Political Leverage

---

1. The Bank's continuing dialogue on development policy issues with borrower-country nationals.
2. The Bank's country memoranda provide knowledge of the borrower and the basis for dialogue on national policy.
3. The Bank's process of project selection and execution provides the basis for policy dialogue at a micro level.
4. The Bank's use of the size and sectoral composition of the country lending program to influence policy.
5. The Bank's chairmanship of consultative groups provides further basis for influencing policy.

Source: Compiled from U.S. Department of Treasury, *United States Participation in the Multilateral Development Banks in the 1980s*, Washington, 1982, 31.

the World Bank could influence the process of development policy-making in borrowing countries, which are by and large developing countries. It is this strategy that shapes political economy in the African continent today. As Campbell put it, "not since the days of colonialism have external forces been so powerfully focused to shape Africa's economic structure and the nature of its participation in the world system."[33] It should be emphasized that the Bank is not just a financial institution. It "is basically a political institution"[34] that reviews the policies of all its major borrowers annually and all the others at least every three years. The World Bank "is, in fact, far more interventionist than the interventionist governments whose policies it seeks to transform."[35] It has an extensive country data base and a profound knowledge accumulated over the years from sectoral analysis and project work in most developing countries. In this way a permanent dialogue is taking place between the Bank and its borrowers. The policy dialogue combined with Bank missions for project identification, preparation, appraisal, negotiation, approval, supervision, and evaluation allow the Bank to influence borrowers' policies beyond the strict conditions specified in the provisions of individual loans. The dialogue allows the Bank a systematic assessment of the dynamics of local bureaucracies and the politics of economic policy-making within the borrowing government as well. Yet the Bank is widely perceived as an apolitical institution because Article IV, Section 10, of the Bank's agreement states that "the Bank and its officers shall not interfere in the political affairs of any member; nor shall they be influenced in their decisions by the political character of the member or members concerned."

Later, the strategy of adjustment was further spelled out by U.S. Secretary of Treasury Donald Regan in a hearing before a congressional subcommittee on 15 September 1983.[36] He stated that "a broad international strategy has been adopted." It has five elements: (1) adjustment in borrowing countries must be effective, (2) the IMF must ensure that the use of its resources is tied tightly to implementation of needed policy measures by borrowers, (3) governments and central banks of lending countries should provide a bridge financing in exceptional cases of systemwide danger, (4) commercial bank lending should continue for countries that are pursuing sound adjustment programs, and (5) protectionism must be avoided. Regan concluded his presentation by stating that "the IMF is a bank," and it "is the linchpin of our international strategy and much of the success that has been achieved is due to the IMF's effort to promote and support adjustment." Since 1982, the IMF has stepped in to alleviate the liquidity pressure that otherwise would have forced indebted developing countries to default, "defaults that would have threatened a collapse of international banking system."[37] In October 1985, U.S. Secretary of Treasury James Baker III reiterated his predecessor's strategy by insisting that the debt problem will not be solved unless three essential and mutually reinforcing elements (table 3) of the strategy of adjustment are adopted by developing countries. Beyond reiterating the Regan Plan, the Baker Plan encouraged the private banks to participate in investment since SAPs had eliminated during the previous five years the kind of business risk that private banks feared when Mexico suspended its international debt payment in August 1982.

Table 3 The Baker Plan

---

1. First and foremost, the adoption by principal debtor countries of comprehensive macroeconomic and structural policies, supported by the international financial institutions, to promote growth and balance of payments adjustment, and to reduce inflation.
2. Second, a continued central role for the IMF, in conjunction with increased and more effective structural adjustment lending from the multilateral development banks (MDBs), both in support of the adoption by principal debtors of market-oriented policies for growth.
3. Third, increased lending by the private banks in support of comprehensive economic adjustment programs.

Source: Quoted in Corbridge, S. 1993. *Debt and Development*. Oxford: Blackwell, 63.

Since the inception of the new strategy of lending money to developing countries on a large scale, the IMF quotas have been regularly increased. In 1981, the IMF quotas were raised by 50 percent to over $60 billion, and in addition the Fund borrowed $8 billion from Saudi Arabia. In 1990, IMF quotas were again increased by 50 percent, bringing the total IMF quotas to $137 billion and by April 1993 they reached Special Drawing Rights (SDR) 144.5 billion[38] (around $180 billion). It is important to note that an increase in the U.S. quota in the IMF does not involve U.S. Federal budget outlays. According to Regan, the United States borrows the money in the open market, lends it to the IMF, and has a gain or a loss on interest depending on the difference between borrowing and lending rates. In fact, between April 1980 and January 1991, the United States gained $7,537 million simply from transactions under the U.S. quota and U.S. loans to the IMF, while over 40 percent of the growth in the U.S. economy in 1990 was attributed to the increase in net exports of U.S. goods and services facilitated by the IMF export-led strategy.[39] With adjustment policies in their favor, the industrialized countries no longer needed credits from the IMF, while developing countries' demand increased dramatically. In 1977, the United Kingdom and Italy concluded major standby arrangements with the IMF, and in November 1978 the United States announced a drawing on the IMF; but from the early 1980s on, the IMF's clientele was reduced to its developing-country members.[40]

The establishment of the Multilateral Investment Guarantee Agency (MIGA) in 1988 represents a similar empowering of the World Bank that "has proved to be a cost-effective instrument for promoting the U.S. interest in integrating the developing countries into the international trade system."[41] Following the United States' recommendation, the World Bank adopted in June 1993 a detailed reform plan (of eighty-six specific policy actions) intended to "reorient the Bank culture toward more effective and consistent emphasis on the sustainable development impact of Bank-financed operations."[42] But empowering the World Bank and the IMF did not change the powerless position of developing nations within these global institutions that are unaccountable to them. No fundamental changes in the way the IMF and the World Bank operate can take place without an 85 percent majority of the votes that are based on quotas. The United States alone has a virtual veto power to block any change in the Bank's and Fund's lending system since its quotas are about 17 percent in the first and about 19 percent in the second. The process of decision making and resource allocation within these financial institutions continues to follow the predominant reasoning of the leading OECD members which asks: "How long would the capital of any bank last if it were run by borrowers?"[43] In this business area, like with the veto on the Security Council, democracy (one person, one vote; or one nation, one vote) is simply a taboo since the organizing principle within both the World Bank and the IMF is the so-called one dollar, one vote. Moreover, coordination between the IMF and the World Bank is increasing, particularly in cross-conditionality, since most loan conditions and performance criteria are specified in both Bank's loans and Fund's arrangements. The G-7 summit of 1988 expressed satisfaction with "the intensified process of policy coordination adopted at the 1986 Tokyo Summit and further strengthened at the Venice Summit," as well as with the overall success of adjustment policies and the way they had speeded up the globalization of markets and increased economic interdependence, "making it essential that governments consider fully the international dimension of their deliberations."[44] The Fund's and the Bank's control over credit and debt policies worldwide gives them the power to manufacture development research and policy. It therefore allows them to define the problems and design the solutions of development and, more significant, force other policymakers to adopt those policies as theirs.

Discrediting Nationalist Models

As mentioned earlier, the World Bank began the publication of its *World Development Report* series in 1978. Through such reports, the Bank attacked and discredited the main tenets of the statist and nationalist model of development as economically inefficient compared to the economically efficient model of adjustment. In addition, the Bank engaged in a large-scale production of economic and sector memoranda on almost all countries[45] and organized many national and international conferences and workshops that all propagate the same message, the free market. The Bank was also reinforced by the establishment in 1988 of the MIGA. The 1978 *World Development Report* emphasized the growth of interdependence. That focus was not a coincidence because one of the major obstacles that the adjustment argument has to overcome to be propagated beyond the small circle of government officials is the dependency argument, which was well established among large segments of the postcolonial elites in the Third World who believe that economic liberalization will abort any attempt at national accumulation, lead to more dependency, and drain resources out of the developing economy. This dependency argument provides a strong critique of the interdependence argument (of mutual benefits) that has always been favored among policymakers in the West, whose inspiration by Ricardo's Comparative Advantages and Rostow's Stages of Economic Growth continues unabated, though under new circumstances. That is why the theoretical argument of the new strategy of development aimed at (1) attacking the main tenets of the dependency school that dominated most development discourse at the time and (2) advocating the benefits of interdependency. Africa south of the Sahara represents a graphic example where the World Bank formulation of the crisis and its solution was so powerful that it developed a sense of crisis among African policymakers even though "there was no extraordinary sense of crisis among the population."[46] That sense of the crisis was instrumental in sensitizing African public opinion and focusing attention on the necessity of policy change, a change where "African governments have been obliged to submit to conditions which effectively remove their capacity to manage their own economies,"[47] particularly from the early 1980s on. One may even argue that the failure of development in Africa during the past decade is positively correlated to the extent and the degree of involvement of international financial institutions, since African countries complied with World Bank's policies more than any other developing countries.

In 1981, the World Bank published the famous Berg Report entitled *Accelerated Development in Sub-Saharan Africa: An Agenda for Action.* The report (as a diagnosis) attacked African government policies as the major causes of the economic crisis and laid down the basis for deep structural reforms that are "enormously tough and particularly sensitive, especially when the benefits are uncertain and in the future."[48] The report contributed to fostering the intellectual shift from the more militant dependency theory to the more passive concept of interdependency in international relations. Politicians, planners, and academicians were all reading and quoting from the Berg Report, which unleashed a controversy that ultimately detached African governments from the implementation of the 1980 Lagos Plan, which called for regional cooperation and coordination to achieve self-sufficient development. Many criticized "the report's overly self-confident style and tendency to instruct (or hector) rather than inform or advise Africans and African leaders."[49] Another implicit but central argument of the Berg Report was that African governments should not expect any change in the way the world market operates according to the ruthless market laws of competition and supply and demand. These represent constants with their own imperatives and requirements to which peripheral states and financial institutions must adjust. In other words, the international factor is taken for granted while the national and local factors are questioned. Since nothing can be done about the laws of the world market, governments must focus on their domestic policies as the only target for reforms. The report stated that the internal and external factors "impeding African economic growth have been exacerbated by domestic policy inadequacies," particularly the way "trade and exchange-rate policies have overprotected industry." This orientation in domestic policy is the main cause of the sub-Saharan crisis that "can only be surmounted by the joint efforts of African governments and the donor community." These two partners, the report concluded, "will surely work together to build a continent that shows real gains in both development and income in the near future."[50]

This cooperation between African governments and the donor community illustrates how local and national policies were being adjusted to the requirements of the global strategy of accumulation. It is this shift of power relations at the international level that is reflected in the intellectual shift within academia from dependency to interdependency discourse. The exogenous factors of development, especially the imperatives of the world market, were presented as a constant about which nothing can be done and everything must be done to adjust to it. For example, adjustment of the Mauritanian economy was based on a simple, but fundamental, assumption. The Economic and Financial Recovery Program (1985–88) states clearly in its introduction that "while the exogenous factors are beyond Mauritania's control, it is perfectly able to do something about the endogenous factors, especially poor management and the choice of investment with low returns." Implicit in this statement is a renunciation of the possibility of building a national independent economy whose external links and relations are nationally controlled. Hence, constant adjustment is *the only* possible and feasible option. In this way, the Berg Report established the intellectual and operational blueprint not only for subsequent Bank reports on sub-Saharan Africa but also for development policy in Africa and the Third World generally. This was so despite strong denial from Elliot Berg, the main writer of the report, who asserted that "the report is not a blueprint for Bank policy in the sense that it sets down a line of policy to be followed in every African country."[51] This kind of denial raises doubt about the real intention behind the World Bank report. Indeed, the foreword of the report emphasized that "the report offers no general prescriptions. The countries of Africa are too diverse—politically, culturally, philosophically—to attempt to define a single strategy."[52] By the same token, all World Bank presidents insist in their forewords to *World Development Reports* that these reports "do not necessarily reflect the views of the Board of Directors or the governments they represent." However, the Berg Report and subsequent Bank reports on sub-Saharan Africa represent comprehensive political platforms and hence contradict the Bank claim of political indifference and neutrality.

In 1983, the World Bank published a second report entitled *Sub-Saharan Africa: Progress Report on Prospects and Programs*. This report advocated solutions and programs along the lines of the previous diagnosis. The subsequent World Bank reports on African economic developemnt—*Toward Sustained Development in Sub-Saharan Africa: A Joint Program of Action* (1984), *Financing Adjustment with Growth in Sub-Saharan Africa, 1986–1990* (1986), *Sub-Saharan Africa: From Crisis to Sustainable Growth* (1989), and *Adjustment in Africa: Reform, Results, and the Road Ahead* (1994)—all focused straightforwardly on adjustment policies and thus set the stage for the sweeping adjustment movement of the 1980s and 1990s, where "there is no historical precedent for the extent and the degree of overt policy leverage now being exerted by multilateral agencies on African governments."[53] African leaders committed themselves to SAPs through the UN Special Session on Africa in 1986. As the decade of the 1980s came to a close, the 1989 World Bank report on sub-Saharan Africa again set the stage of African adjustment policies for the 1990s in more straightforward terms: "This report sketches a menu of options and ideas to guide the formulation of long-term development strategies" and constitutes a strategic agenda for the 1990s whose central argument is that "adjustment programs should continue to evolve."[54] The 1994 World Bank report on adjustment in Africa is even more categoric: "In Sub-Saharan Africa the road ahead for adjustment is clear: continue with the macro-economic reforms, complete the trade and agricultural sector reforms, restructure public finances, and provide an environment conducive to private production and provision of goods and services."[55]

The method of presentation and analysis followed by the Bank's reports is based on aggregate economic statistics used as a measure of decline of African economies and societies followed by further analyses explaining the causes of the decline and the appropriate policies to be followed if these problems were to be solved. The central argument made repeatedly by the World Bank in almost all of its *World Development Reports*, as well as in its regional reports on Africa, is that the main cause of economic decline is the role of the state in development, particularly its rigidity, its inefficiency, and its social welfare policy. The solution proposed by the Bank is to redefine and rethink the role of the state. "Put simply, governments need to do less in those areas where markets work, or can be made to work, reasonably well. In many countries, it would help privatize many state-owned enterprises."[56] The Bank advocates a pragmatic division of labor between the public and private sectors and points out that "while the invisible hand of the market is adept at dealing with this complexity [of industrializing economies], the visible hand of government needs to provide the rules of the game for markets to work." The range of public goods that only governments are in a position to supply adequately includes "national defense and internal security, money, and the provision of a legal system. Among the most important public goods is a legal and institutional system which reduces the costs and risks of transactions."[57] Each report also uses a method of grading the performance of selected countries that are considered successful in implementing structural adjustment reforms. The ones willing to comply with reforms are mentioned as good examples, while the unwilling ones are depicted as bad examples. In 1994, the Egyptian Country Portfolio Performance Review (CPPR) was disseminated by the World Bank as "the best practice example."[58]

World Bank reports destroyed confidence in the capacity of governments to manage the economy and developed the idea of "the sacred cow of free trade"[59] that few governments dare challenge. They provided the pro-adjustment forces in African governments with a powerful argument and a huge amount of statistics geared to support World Bank diagnoses and prescriptions for African economies. Techniques of persuasion such as simulation analysis based on those statistics would present future economic development (then up to the year 2000 and now up to 2025) in terms of various scenarios, of which the only possible and feasible one is the adjustment scenario. The Bank's scenario for Mauritania is a macroeconomic model illustrating the impact of adjustment policies on certain economic variables such as GDP growth rate, saving and investment, public finance, and balance of payments. The scenario predicts an annual GDP rate of growth of 2.7 percent between 1985 and 1993. The Bank warned that unless adjustment policies are implemented, the economic "situation will be aggravated considerably."[60] Such warning cannot be ignored by any government when it knows that "the Bank's reports are not designed to be discussed but to bring the States to accept the transnationals' strategies."[61]

As confidence in the role of government in the process of development declined, the lure of privatization soared. In the early 1980s the IMF was severely criticized by African governments as "a bad doctor that prescribes always the same medicine for all patients."[62] Later, their position on adjustment shifted to the more realistic and pragmatic attitude of "swallowing the bitter pill of the IMF." It was then clear that reports on Africa by the Economic Commission for Africa and by the Organization of African Unity (especially the 1980 Lagos Plan) were no longer able to influence the course of development set by adjustment. The media coverage of adjustment in Africa became an additional source of pressure on governments reluctant to adjust. The East African correspondent for *The Economist* wrote that since Kenya rejected (temporarily) the economic reforms demanded by the IMF, "even the trees have suffered."[63] In the 1980s, "36 sub-Saharan African countries initiated 241 adjustment programmes. Most have had multiple programmes, with 11 implementing 10 or more."[64] Yet sub-Saharan Africa's foreign debts increased from $84 billion (91 percent of the value of exports) in 1980 to $199 billion (237 percent of the value of exports) in 1993.[65] This trend culminated in the simultaneous dependence and marginalization of sub-Saharan Africa, both of which are of great concern to African peoples today.

The propagation and preaching of the central tenets of structural adjustment programs were not limited to sub-Saharan Africa. All over the Third World (and later throughout Eastern Europe and the former Soviet Union) the adjustment argument was being disseminated to displace other development discourses of nationalist development, economic independence, self-sufficient production, and son on. The reorientation of research grants toward economic restructuring and adjustment is a well-established trend of the 1980s and 1990s. In the words of Stanley J. Heginbotham, vice president of the Social Science Research Council, "internationally-oriented funders are coming increasingly to focus their programs around themes or problems associated with the challenges of building more effective social, economic, and political systems out of what now seem to have been misguided experiments with command economies and authoritarian political systems."[66] International financial institutions that advocate adjustment are recruiting within the ranks of intellectuals and planners and providing various forms of training (see policy formulation in chapter 4) articulated for the most part around the *political trial* of command economies and authoritarian politics once they are dead.

In 1987, the International Monetary Fund and the Arab Monetary Fund organized the first seminar dealing with adjustment policies and development strategies in the Arab world. Debates in the seminar turned primarily around the inward/outward development argument that lies at the heart of adjustment studies and policies. Said El-Naggar noted that there were two strains of thinking that animated the adjustment debate in the seminar. "The first can be described as a market-oriented, outward-looking approach to adjustment. The second is more inclined toward an interventionist, inward-looking approach."[67] The following year the IMF and the World Bank organized another international seminar on privatization and structural adjustment in the Arab world. Like the first one, it was held in Abu Dhabi, United Arab Emirates, and its papers were later published by the IMF in the form of a book.[68] Almost all the participants were high state officials or high-ranking IMF/World Bank officers. They all insisted on the necessity of pragmatism in privatization since most Arab economies used to have strong public sectors and interventionist states. Said El-Naggar noted that the transfer of all public enterprises to the private sector is neither politically feasible nor economically desirable. He suggested that public enterprises remain in oil and other forms of mineral wealth, in activities where considerations of efficiency require a single enterprise (railways, ports, tramways, telephones, and so on), and in areas where capital requirements and/or high technology go beyond the capability of domestic private enterprises.[69] However, Alan Walters insisted that the essence of privatization and deregulation is the reassignment of property rights from the state to the individual.[70] David Gill argued that transfer of ownership should include the transfer of control over the relevant business inputs and outputs and of operational management as well.[71] Ibrahim Helmy Abdel-Rahman and Mohammed Sultan Abu Ali argued that privatization does not mean the abolition of the public sector, which will stay regardless of ideology and the prevailing social system. To them the real question is: "Which activities should be private and which should remain public."[72]

Michel Camdessus, managing director of the IMF, in his foreword for the first edition of the report on the above seminar on privatization and SAPs in the Arab world, quotes from Ibn Khaldun's Muqaddima (d. 1406): "Other measures taken by the government, such as directly engaging in commerce or agriculture, soon turn to be harmful to the citizens, ruinous to the state revenues, and destructive to civilization."[73] Even though Camdessus was quoting from one of the seminar papers, he was actually trying to reach his Arab audience through Ibn Khaldun by asserting that government intervention in the economy has always been bad, while privatization has always been good. Another similar adjustment seminar was supported by the World Bank in Izmir, Turkey, in March 1988. It was attended by senior ministers from Algeria and high-ranking representatives from Morocco, Tunisia, Egypt, Jordan, Turkey, and Pakistan.[74] These and many similar seminars contributed throughout the 1980s to inculcating the adjustment strategy into the minds of Third World political and intellectual elites. In this way, the modernization thesis was resurrected and began again to replace the dependency argument. Development literature began to shift from an emphasis on the external causes of underdevelopment to its internal and institutional causes and imperialism almost disappeared from the analysis of policy choice in developing countries. This "shift of attention from the international to the national level supports the position of the Western donors"[75] that imperialist strategies have nothing to do with Third World economic, political, and social disarray. Rather, local conditions of "tropical environment" and "primitive cultures" are the real and eternal factors that impede development as modernization-inspired theories often claim.

But the strategy of adjustment could not have succeeded by just the power of its intellectual argument or by its worldwide dissemination. Political changes in the West and increased military interventions in the Third World went hand in hand with the direction of adjustment throughout the 1980s. Politically, the revival of the neoclassical theory of development (with its own version of representative, not direct, democracy) was reflected and reinforced by the victory of conservative parties over social democrats in the United States, the United Kingdom, Germany, and Australia during the late 1970s and early 1980s, a trend strengthened by the 1994 Republican victory in the U.S. Congress after forty years of Democrat control. Even France's Socialist Party (aligned with the Communists) began to adopt neoliberal policies as early as 1983. Economically, the United States also achieved a significant "success at breaking the commodity power of the Arab oil producers"[76] through an arrangement with Saudi Arabia, which agreed to pump a surplus of crude oil to bring down oil prices. The subsequent oil glut (Saudi Arabia steadily increased its oil production from 4.5 to 8.1

million barrels per day between 1984 and 1991) brought oil prices down from a peak of $37 a barrel in 1980[77] to less than $10[78] a barrel in 1986. Only Saudi Arabia (with proven oil reserves of 257 billion barrels) could sustain this production policy, which (1) brought down oil prices, (2) diverted Western technology from searching for a substitute to oil, (3) weakened the OPEC cartel, (4) increased dissension among OPEC members during the Iran-Iraq War, and (5) ultimately provided an excuse for Iraq to invade and attempt to annex Kuwait. Iraq's strategy of increasing oil revenues by decreasing oil production fundamentally clashed with Kuwait's strategy of increasing oil revenues by increasing oil production. "By having followed its own national oil-depletion agenda, Kuwait arguably contributed to the lowering of Iraq's early 1990 oil revenues by 20 percent compared to 1989 levels."[79]

Suppressing Nationalist Models

The direct role played by military power and the power of propaganda in suppressing alternatives to the adjustment strategy is largely absent from adjustment and restructuring literature. In my opinion, this is a serious intellectual shortcoming imposed by political considerations and the thinness of our knowledge of the military establishment, as well as by the traditional academic disdain for media and journalistic sources and styles. However, the role of military power in the success (i.e., spread) of adjustment worldwide should not be ignored, because without it, other development alternatives could have developed in many Third World countries.[80] The most important military strategy in this regard was the proclamation of the Carter Doctrine (centered primarily on the Middle East), which began with the establishment of the Rapid Deployment Force (later the Central Command), with bases on Diego Garcia, and in Oman, Egypt, Somalia, and Kenya. This military strategy was mainly designed to contain the 1979 Islamic revolution in Iran (which toppled the Shah regime, a long-time Western ally in the region) and the Communist take-over in Afghanistan. Throughout the 1980s, many landings and airborne maneuvers were conducted by the U.S. troops in several countries, including Somalia, Jordan, and particularly Egypt, where Operation Bright Star in 1987 and 1989 actually prepared U.S. troops for Operation Desert Shield and Operation Desert Storm in late 1990 and early 1991 in the Gulf. Carter's strategy was centered on Saudi Arabia and was intended to provide the military infrastructure necessary for an eventual rapid U.S. intervention in the Middle East. The cornerstone of the doctrine was a U.S.-Saudi agreement according to which the Saudis would pay for the building of an elaborate system of command, naval, and air facilities large enough to "sustain U.S. forces in intensive regional combat."[81] The doctrine was more than reaffirmed by President Ronald Reagan, who even went further by signing a Memorandum of Strategic Understanding with Israel that provided, among other things, for the prepositioning of U.S. military supplies in Israel[82] while surrogate U.S. military bases were built and equipped in Saudi Arabia, waiting for U.S. forces as the 1991 Gulf War later confirmed. In 1993, serious efforts were under way to make Haifa (Palestine/Israel) a military base for the U.S. Sixth Fleet at the same time that the U.S. Secretary of Defense had recommended (on 15 March 1993) the closure or realignment of over 130 U.S. military bases in the aftermath of the dismantling of the Warsaw Pact.

From the late 1970s on, the Middle East, Africa, and Latin America provided hot spots for U.S., British, and French military interventions to preempt a return to or an emergence of radical nationalism pursuing accumulation at the national level. The list of countries directly affected includes Zaire, Iran, the Falkland Islands, Lebanon, Grenada, Nicaragua, El Salvador, Chad, Libya, Panama, and, above all, Iraq and Kuwait. These violent forms of intervention continue today with the redeployment of NATO forces around the world under the cover of UN peacekeeping forces, the growing phenomenon of military humanitarianism,[83] and the enforcement of economic sanctions (in the Red Sea alone, the U.S. Navy searched some 1,700 ships during the first four years of enforcing sanctions against Iraq). This represented a strong warning to any Third World country reluctant to move along the lines of the new global strategy of adjustment and dependency. Today, only[84] seven countries have not fully complied with this *fundamentalist* strategy (of full compliance with the requirements of Western liberalism and capitalism) and they are facing a systematic combination of military threats, economic sanctions, and endless campaigns of defamation, just like the former Soviet Union. These are Cuba, Iran, Iraq, Libya, North Korea, Sudan, and Syria. In the U.S. State Department classification they are considered "states sponsoring terrorism" mainly because of their religious or secular nationalisms, which do not endorse U.S. policy in their regions, a policy that aims for the most part at placing these countries firmly in the hands of U.S. investors. Efforts to isolate and outlaw these nations are made easier today because of the changes in the balance of power within the UN system.

Even though Russia's veto power in the UN Security Council survived the disintegration of the Soviet Union, it no longer provides the balance of power upon which the stability and relative equity of the UN system were based during the Cold War. The growing marginalization[85] of the General Assembly and the increasing dictatorship and flagrant double standard of the Security Council have virtually transformed the UN system into a mere "rubber stamp"[86] that legitimizes U.S. actions and inactions in the world. Compare, for example, the feverish implementation of Security Council resolutions against Iraq with Israel's rejection of sixty-six Security Council resolutions plus twenty-nine others vetoed by the United States.[87] Moreover, the United States did not allow the United Nations to be involved in the current Arab-Israeli peace process, despite the fact that the conflict began originally with the UN partition of Palestine in 1947. While the UN is invited to mediate certain conflicts, it is deliberately kept away from others. Another example would be the Security Council's attitude toward Bosnia. The members not only stood by like spectators in the face of a three-year-long ethnic cleansing in Europe but also continued to enforce the arms embargo against Bosnia, thus encouraging the well-armed Serbs to continue or at least preserve their military conquest. The United Nations is being reconfigured and repositioned within a new global geopolitics where a few industrialized nations monopolize decision making at the world level. Its notion of a large world community of equal sovereign nations is being replaced by the more selective notion of "the international community" which "can best be located as residing somewhere between the [five permanent members of the] Security Council and the G–7."[88] These two international institutions represent a concentration of global power in which the military component remains important, particularly when nonmilitary means fail.

Reaganomics was not only a school of economics emphasizing reduction of taxes and social welfare spending but also a military school calling for qualitative and quantitative increase in military expenditures. During the eight years of the Reagan administration the Pentagon consumed an average of $1 billion every working day.[89] This huge defense spending made it impossible for the Soviet Union (which was already sinking in the mire of the war in Afghanistan) to keep up with the arms race and led to increased military intervention (for example, in Nicaragua and Grenada), which reversed the course of history in many countries by suppressing alternatives to adjustment. Does military intervention then constitute another (in)visible hand of the market?

Former U.S. President Richard Nixon argued that the United States must lead the world militarily because it has comparative advantage in that area. He emphasized the complementarity between Japanese economic performance and U.S. military performance.[90] In the words of Craig Murphy, the United States "may end up 'specializing' in building the coercive links of the North-South bloc(k) while Japan specializes in building North-South economic links, and the European Community specializes in 'Keynesian' assistance to Eastern Europe."[91] Such division of labor between capitalist blocs of states was largely materialized by the West's scramble for Kuwait during the 1991 Gulf War.

The Gulf War[92] allowed the United States to revive Teddy Roosevelt's uncompromising imperialist world view that "peace cannot be had until the civilized nations have expanded in some shape over the barbarous ones."[93] It reestablished a certain kind of military invincibility (lost during the Vietnam War) and a sense of both revenge and pride that President George Bush could not conceal when he said, "By God, we've kicked the Vietnam syndrome once and for all."[94] The Gulf War, however, accomplished more than just cleansing the American psyche of the Vietnam syndrome. According to Alain Lipietz,[95] the latest U.S.-led war against Iraq was "truly a war *for* oil" but also "a war for hegemony" of the United States. He argued that the United States is attempting to compensate for its inability to compete economically by trying to police the world through the "enforced sale of mercenaries," especially during the Gulf War, in which the United States "cashed in $41 billion from their backers for the loan of mercenary forces." The Gulf War could also be seen as one of those violent cyclical devaluations of capital or "constructive" destruction of assets and the creation of conditions for reconstruction, i.e., growth. Beyond the huge loss of human lives,[96] the war produced five million refugees (cheap labor) and created markets for multibillion dollar contracts in a region where the destruction and its economic ramifications were estimated at $620 billion[97] and where postwar reconstruction in Iraq alone was estimated at $100 to $200 billion.[98] In 1992, foreign debts of the Arab countries reached $153.5 billion,[99] and even Saudi Arabia is already deep in debt with a 20 percent cut in annual spending, something that raised fear within the U.S. industrial-military complex (which sold $30 billion dollars of U.S. military equipment to Saudi Arabia between 1989 and 1993) before the Saudis restored business confidence (after personal appeals from President Bill Clinton) by ordering up to $6 billion worth of U.S. made commercial liners from the Boeing company.[100] The role of the military-industrial complex was not only necessary in producing high-tech, deadly weapons that can nip in the bud any alternative to adjustment, but also crucial in the financial and economic recovery in the West, where arms exports played an important role.

Like military power, the role of propaganda in the success of the strategy of adjustment was often underestimated, despite the fact that propaganda did play an important role in vilifying alternatives to the Western strategy of development. It contributed to the rapid dissemination of American culture—indeed to the Americanization of the world—thanks not only to the shift from a bipolar to a U.S.-led unipolar world but also to technological breakthroughs in communication, which are triggering a worldwide process of rapid acculturation. The current worldwide explosion of American popular culture is "the closest approximation there is today to a global lingua franca, drawing urban classes in most nations into a federal culture zone."[101] But beyond these spontaneous cultural trends, there is systematic propaganda that has far more specific targets. From Radio Free Europe to Radio Free Asia to Radio Martí and Voice of America, the message is the same: free market![102] The increasing use of satellites to broadcast to other nations is even more effective than radio broadcasting. "Plain old American TV is more powerful than any military weapon. In fact, it should become our avowed way of making war."[103] Systematic propaganda, which aims at persuading and convincing people of real or imaginary issues, is very powerful in shaping perceptions and attitudes, which largely shape behavior. Comparing his perceptions in the 1950s with those of the 1990s, Bill Stoltzfus, a U.S. diplomat, noted that "the Holocaust—because of all the books and films and articles of recent years—seems a lot closer to us now than it was right after it happened."[104] The scope and the scale by which information is propagated today is increasing dramatically due to the technological revolution in communication. "The first word senior officials in Washington received about the Tiananmen Square massacre, Iraq's invasion of Kuwait, and the attempted coup against Mikhail Gorbachev came from CNN, not CIA."[105]

Propaganda against the Soviet Union reached a new peak in the early 1980s when the Iron Curtain concept was replaced by the Evil Empire stigma and détente was rejected in favor of the more expensive and challenging military program of Star Wars. In all the restructuring and adjustment literature I reviewed over the past two years these military and media events were often dismissed in favor of a more thorough analysis of the concepts of command economy and totalitarian state. The neoconservative and Cold War writer Francis Fukuyama exemplifies this dismissal when he insists that the intrinsic values of market and liberalism in general are behind the "triumph of the West" and the "end of history." As a Cold War warrior jubilantly celebrating Gorbachev's *perestroika* and *glasnost*, Fukuyama proclaimed ecstatically that "what we may be witnessing is not just the end of the Cold War, or the passing of a particular period of the postwar history, but the end of history as such: that is, the end point of mankind's ideological evolution and the universalization of Western liberal democracy as the final form of human government." In his attempt to explain the downfall of the Soviet system he invoked what he described as a virtual consensus among Soviet economists that "central planning and the command system of allocation are the root cause of economic inefficiency."[106] While economic efficiency or inefficiency are criteria that can better be observed at the workplace, Fukuyama seems to ignore Western military and propaganda pressures as having any impact on the Soviet system. For example, how much of the Soviet budget was allocated to thwart the external pressures of NATO? To what extent did this allocation of resources contribute to the decline of the Soviet economy? How and to what extent did Reagan's Strategic Defense Initiative (Star Wars) give the final coup de grace to the USSR?[107] How can efficiency (producing more with less) be accurately measured without taking into consideration the military nonproductive allocation of resources? Finally, did the Warsaw Pact members have access to resources outside their borders commensurate with what NATO members had access to in terms of raw materials and markets?

Since it is well established that military spending "penalizes the competitiveness of the *national* economy,"[108] I do not think that any serious and objective evaluation of efficiency at the work place can ignore the resource drain caused by the external military and propaganda threats, whose negative impact on the Soviet economy was probably not less important than the economic inefficiency of the command economy at the workplace. Moreover, why was so much money spent and so much blood shed on these events (military and propaganda) if they cannot make a difference? It can be argued that the unfolding chaos and confusion in the former Eastern bloc today arose not just from problems intrinsic to command communism but also from sustained and coordinated military, economic, and propaganda efforts undertaken by the West throughout the past four decades to destroy the Soviet system and penetrate the Iron Curtain, the unexplored market. President Clinton once noted that "the Soviet republics are rich in human and natural resources. One day, they and Eastern Europe could be lucrative markets for us."[109] Like the Western scramble for Kuwait in 1991, the current rush for Russia is serious if we believe repeatedly expressed Western concerns over the progress of market reforms in the former Soviet Republics. This concern is real and goes back to the G-7 support of Gorbachev's *perestroika*.[110] It continued through the G-7 plan to provide $28.4 billion[111] in aid for the former Soviet Union, as well as through Clinton's "present" of $1.6 billion to Yeltsin during the Vancouver Summit of April 1993 at a moment of serious concern about how to reduce the U.S. budget deficit. Western support for the promarket Russian President Boris Yeltsin continues unabated, despite the fact that he arbitrarily dissolved the Russian parliament and ordered soldiers to storm the parliament building in October 1993 and brutally crushed Chechnya's aspiration to independence and freedom in early 1995. Such unconditional support reflects Western determination to open Eastern European and Russian markets and gradually neutralize their countries' military capabilities. Despite its military might, Russia is increasingly playing the role of the "new sick man" of Europe. The January 1994 agreement between the United States and Ukraine on dismantling the latter's nuclear weapons (as well as U.S. smuggling of enriched uranium out Kazakhstan) and President Clinton's symbolic visit to a newly opened K-Mart department store in downtown Prague, Czech Republic, as well as the privatization in 1993 of some 7,000 Russian state companies,[112] finally "doing business with the enemy" by lifting the embargo against Vietnam, and delinking China's Most Favored Nation trade status from human rights considerations, all represent decisive steps in the same direction of opening up the world market. This is the essence of the current discourse of economic liberalization and political pluralism.

This Western offensive succeeded not only in reversing the post–World War II trend of nationalistic policies in the South and the East but also in launching a profound movement of restructuring in the West itself, where privatization, deindustrialization, plant (and later base) closing, and downsizing were under way as a means of reducing labor costs and maintaining an acceptable level of efficiency and profitability within the context of a feverish atmosphere of economic competition and financial insecurity. The fragility and insecurity of the world economy persist, as was demonstrated by the financial crash of 1987 and by the systematic layoffs going on in major multinational corporations today. Job loss is becoming a permanent feature of restructuring and adjustment and illustrates well the seriousness of the fragility of the economy and the insecurity of people within the economy. There are 30 million unemployed in the G–7 today.[113] On many occasions President Clinton warned his fellow citizens that the average American will be changing jobs seven times in his or her career, and his secretary of labor, Robert Reich, emphasized that "losing a job is part of a normal career today."[114] In the 1990s, robots are expected to displace 100,000 workers in the United States, and the use of word processors in the United Kingdom already reduced office staff in several companies by up to 50 percent.[115] During 1993 alone, 600,000 announced layoffs took place in the United States, and the process shows little sign of abating in 1994,[116] particularly with the emerging problem of overeducation and underemployment. But despite the problem of unemployment, adjustment policies contributed to the relative stabilization of the industrialized countries, while most developing countries went through unprecedented difficulties of payments, a process that further opens the door to more adjustment and more North/South contradictions, another issue obscured by the globalization of the economy and the rising discourse of a New World Order.

Consolidating North/South Divide

On the eve of the Gulf War, Andrei Kortunov, a Soviet analyst, predicted that the main contradiction between the East and the West is being replaced by the emergence of a new one, between the North and the South.[117] The end of the Cold War is "contributing to an onslaught of North against South and capital against labor."[118] Boutros Boutros-Ghali, the United Nations secretary-general, noted that despite improved West/East relations, North/South issues grew more acute.[119] A more critical view would say that the Cold War era was just one phase of the more fundamental North/South conflict. This trend has been confirmed following the military victory of the U.S.-led allied forces in the war against Iraq and the disintegration of the Soviet Union, as well as in the Pentagon plan for the future to fight simultaneously and win two major regional wars (for example, in the Middle East and the Korean Peninsula) rather than one world war. The East/West axis of conflict was replaced by the North/South divide between rich and poor nations, a trend exemplified today by increasing labor migration from the South, despite increased racism in Europe and violent attacks against migrants in Germany at a time of rising economic cooperation in the West (European Community and North American Free Trade Agreement) and the tightening of immigration regulations. This represents a clear indication of growing integration among the industrialized countries and disintegration among developing countries, as illustrated by the resurgence of ethnic strife and civil wars. These developments are accentuating the North/South contradiction and opening the door for increased South/North migration.

With the number of refugees worldwide jumping from 8 million in 1980 to over 16 million in 1991, policies of asylum are being reviewed in the United States and Europe. According to the Federation for American Immigration Reform, there is a national consensus to reduce immigrant and refugee numbers, and to do that "we must recognize the cost of these admissions, rationalize and de-politicize the selection process, tighten up the legal definition of a refugee, place permanent admissions under cap, and find a way to make so-called temporary admissions truly temporary."[120] Such a negative attitude toward migrants came about after the number of immigrants admitted to the United States, refugees excluded, jumped from 640,000 in 1988 to 1.5 million in 1990.[121] The increasing use of the metaphor "global apartheid"[122] is not an exaggeration of the explosive North/South relations, particularly in immigration matters where the North is pursuing an immigration strategy of "shutting out the South."[123] Most European countries are trying to prevent non-Europeans from migrating into their welfare societies.[124] In October 1991, "the Ministers of the Interior and of Justice of twenty-eight countries of Europe met for the first time in Berlin to discuss and find ways of controlling population movements."[125] In 1993, the French Parliament adopted bills that sought to achieve "zero immigration." These developments reflect a deeper contradiction of adjustment policies and regulations that impose the mobility of capital worldwide while they continue to discourage and even outlaw the mobility of labor across international borders, as illustrated by the current vigilance of Operation Gate Keeper on the U.S.-Mexican borders and the anti-immigration policies that the new Republican manifesto, *Contract With America*, might entail. But beyond the economic dimension of the issue of migration, the North/South divide is better reflected in military and security concerns in the West. Although such military and security concerns are clearly unwarranted given the magnitude of Western stockpiles of nuclear, biological, and chemical weapons and the determination of Western powers to prevent the proliferation of such weapons in the Third World, they can be used to justify military intervention to thwart any alternative to adjustment in developing countries.

In the early 1990s, policymakers in the United States began to locate "security threats" to the New World Order in the Third World. They expressed such security concerns at a moment when Soviet deterrence and influence were waning and thus facilitating "U.S. resort to violence and coercion in the Third World."[126] This is exemplified by U.S. Vice-President Dan Quayle and Presidents Bush and Clinton's repeated warning that the world is still "a dangerous place" even after the end of the Cold War. The United States continues to maintain hundreds of thousands of troops around the world and its global military commands remain almost intact.[127] Indeed, "America's 'Cold War' grand strategy is being reaffirmed today, rather than reexamined."[128] This is done by identifying and locating a new real or constructed enemy that justifies military spending at home and military intervention abroad. This policy of "relocating" threats was articulated by U.S. political and military leaders. President Bush declared in 1991 that the United States is now threatened by "the turmoil and dangers in the developing world," while General Alfred M. Gray, then U.S. Marine Corps commandant, virtually listed the possible excuses for military intervention when he said that the United States is "to have stability in these regions [of the underdeveloped world], maintain our access to their resources, protect our citizens abroad, defend our vital installations, and deter conflicts."[129] President Clinton could not have agreed more with his predecessors when he said "that retreating from the world or discounting its dangers is wrong for the country, . . . the collapse of Communism does not mean the end of danger."[130] He expressed continuity in foreign policy when he declared on 4 November 1992 that "America has only one president at a time . . . and even as America's administrations change, America's fundamental interests do not." There would be, he said, "essential continuity of American foreign policy."[131]

The same interventionist foreign policy was blatantly put by the director of the Central Intelligence Agency (CIA), James Woolsey, when he responded to the question of U.S. national security in the post–Cold War era during his confirmation hearings in the U.S. Senate by saying, "Yes, we have slain a large dragon, but we live now in a jungle filled with a bewildering variety of poisonous snakes. And in many ways, the dragon was easier to keep track of."[132] The jungle is Woolsey's euphemism for the Third World, including the Islamic world, which is "perceived by many Americans as the new focus of evil in the aftermath of the collapse of communism"[133] and more so after the arrest of Middle Eastern suspects (later convicted) in the bombing of New York City's World Trade Center in February 1993 and in the alleged attempt at bombing New York City's Federal Building, the United Nations, and both the Lincoln and Holland tunnels in June 1993. In this regard, the blind and diabetic Egyptian Sheikh Omar Abdel Rahman has been charged (later convicted) with "conspiracy to overthrow the U.S. government." This is a continuation of the Cold War era, during which the United States had suspicions about Third World nonalignment. According to former U.S. Assistant Secretary of State Charles William Maynes: "At least until the Reverend Jesse Jackson's campaign in 1988, any serious candidate for the White House has risked an electoral setback if he displayed too much sympathy for the Third World."[134]

Fabricating an Islamic Threat

Facing such a policy of defining and identifying real or imaginary foreign enemies to justify military spending at home and military intervention abroad, Third World fear of recolonization grew. President Raden Suharto of Indonesia warned during the nonaligned summit meeting in Jakarta in September 1992 that: "We must insure that the new world order to which leaders of the industrialized countries often refer, does not turn out to be but a new version of the same old patterns of domination of the strong over the weak and the rich over the poor."[135] Once the argument of the communist threat was lost following the disintegration of the Soviet Union, a new argument was developed to make Islamic fundamentalism (among other possible "isms")[136] the new evil of the post–Cold War era and the new regional threat to which the U.S. Central Command seems to be "preparing the next storm" in the Middle East.[137] This is a significant volte-face in U.S. foreign policy, since many Islamists from all over the Muslim world were recruited, financed, and trained by the U.S. Central Intelligence Agency as fighters against the Soviet occupation of Afghanistan.[138] This volte-face can easily be accommodated if one realizes the deep-seated prejudices in the West against Islam and Muslims. Former U.S. President Nixon reminds everyone that "no nations, not even Communist China, have a more negative image in the American consciousness than those of the Muslim world."[139] In the words of Rashid Khalidi, president of Middle East Studies Association, "Middle Easterners are the people many Americans love to hate, and they clearly think that they can do this with impunity."[140] These negative perceptions of the Muslim world developed out of a long history of confrontation between Islam and the West and the ramifications of the Arab-Israeli conflict over Palestine. Their virulence is positively correlated to the level of resistance of Muslim peoples to Western domination. Currently, Western policymakers perceive Islamism as a serious obstacle on the road to opening up the economies and cultures of Muslim societies, a strategic goal of liberalism in general and SAPs in particular.

Islamic militancy[141] as a new form of "religious nationalism" in Islamic countries could be viewed as a salient feature of a deeper North/South contradiction and seems to provide a portrait of the kind of "foreign threat" the West needs in the aftermath of the fall of communism. Throughout the 1950s, 1960s, and 1970s, secular nationalism in the Middle East was virtually declared by Western powers as the West's enemy and the strategic ally of communism. This form of nationalism was symbolized by Gamal Abdel Nasser in Egypt, Muhammed Mossadeq in Iran, Saddam Hussein in Iraq, and Muammar Qaddafi in Libya. But with the establishment and the crystallization of the Islamic Republic in Iran and the decline of communism, Western powers virtually declared Islamic fundamentalism as the new enemy. In July 1992, some 1,500 parliamentarians from Austria, Belgium, Britain, Canada, Denmark, France, Germany, Greece, Ireland, Italy, Luxembourg, the Netherlands, Norway, Spain, Sweden, and the United States declared their support for the secular nationalist People's Mujahidin Organization of Iran against "Khumeini's religious fundamentalism."[142] Within the Bush administration "the march of Islamic fundamentalism" was perceived as the most significant problem facing U.S. policy in Africa.[143] The Clinton administration's foreign policy is essentially a continuation of its predecessor and continues to define and view Islamic fundamentalism as a threat to U.S. interests. In the words of Robert H. Pelletreau, Jr., assistant secretary of state for Near Eastern affairs, "Certain manifestation of the Islamic revival are intensely anti-Western and aim not only at elimination of Western influences but at resisting any form of cooperation with the West or modernizing evolution at home. Such tendencies are clearly hostile to U.S. interests."[144] During his October 1994 tour of the Middle East, President Clinton used the opportunity to urge all heads of state in the region to crack down on the Islamists and promised U.S. support for such enterprise.

Other examples may further illustrate how Islamism is perhaps taken more seriously by Western powers compared to other potential challengers in the Third World. First, the ever-increasing U.S. support to Israel after the end of the Cold War ($11 billion in fiscal year 1993)[145] and Clinton's open partiality for and renewed commitment[146] to Israel even after signing the September 1993 Declaration of Principles ("a certain kind of peace," in the words of CNN) with the Palestine Liberation Organization (PLO) illustrate above all a general concern among policymakers in the United States and the Middle East over the growth of religious versus secular nationalism. Israel, by definition a fundamentalist state drawing its legitimacy from Old Testament legends, was used by the West to combat Soviet influence and Arab nationalism during the Cold War and is now being used to combat religious nationalism, i.e., Islamic fundamentalism. Secular nationalism has been seriously challenged in Egypt, Algeria, and among the Palestinians. It has even been overthrown in Iran and Sudan. From the perspective of modernist liberal elites in the Arab world, the "green threat" of Islam can now provide an argument that can be sold to the West with as much efficiency as the "red threat" was sold to the United States by Latin American authoritarian regimes during the 1960s.[147] From the viewpoint of Israeli leaders (who shape U.S. Middle Eastern policy in many ways), the new threat to the Arab world is no longer Zionism but fundamentalism. Raphael Israeli, one of the main Israeli writers about Islam, warns his Western audiences that "if the trend of re-Islamization continues, as the relatively free elections in Jordan (1989) and Algeria (1991) indicate, there is little doubt that the years ahead will be quite risky for both the West and Israel."[148] It is in this context that the new Western alliance with a weakened secular nationalism (beginning with the PLO) against the seemingly revived religious one (such as Hamas) provides a channel for preserving Western interests and, more important, a fresh source of legitimation for foreign intervention and continuous military buildup at a time of scarcity in defiant enemies.

Second, the "Islamic threat" may be to blame for the tacit tolerance of the Serbian/Christian ethnic cleansing against Bosnian Muslims in Europe. It is more so if we consider that the Bosnian government calls for a multiethnic and multireligious state where there should be no discrimination along ethnic or religious lines. Despite this and because of the "Islamic threat," Western powers would forgive ethnic cleansing and war crimes and accept a fascist Christian Greater Serbia rather than a tiny democratic Muslim-led Bosnia. A similar argument could be made for Western tacit support for Russia's brutal military intervention in Chechnya in January 1995 and subsequent massacres of Chechnya Muslims by Russian soldiers. Third, as part of the process of "making an Islamic threat," there is an increasing interest in the Rushdie affair, which has been a major source of cultural friction between the world of Islam and the West in recent years. Salman Rushdie's novel (*The Satanic Verses*) provoked Muslims' indignation around the world and was declared blasphemous. Rushdie was reportedly paid advance royalties of $1.5 million to parody Islam. Ali Mazrui commented that "Rushdie subordinates the anguish of Muslim believers to the titillation of his Western readers," and he described the novel as "A Satanic Novel."[149] In the beginning, most Western leaders were cautious about "Rushdie's affair" and were reluctant to appear with him publicly. But in March 1993 he was welcomed to France, and when he returned to the United Kingdom he was received warmly and officially by British Prime Minister John Major. By the same token, he was received by President Clinton on 24 November 1993. Only major defectors from the Soviet Union during the peak of the Cold War could have received such attention from Western leaders. The real or perceived "Islamic threat"[150] seems to be taken seriously by Western powers to the extent that they de facto oppose genuine multipartyism in the Middle East and North Africa, since it could bring to power the Islamists whose "ideological rigidities" and "non-Western cultural background" are considered a major obstacle to the progress of SAPs, which require not only economic liberalization but also the opening up of every facet of society, including the culture and the legal system where the Islamists continue to dominate in most Islamic countries. By constituting an obstacle to SAPs, the Islamists constitute an alternative. The "Islamic threat" also provides a rationale to justify military spending in the North as a prelude to military intervention in the South after the waning of the Soviet deterrence. The end of the Cold War brought nothing but "a dominant North and a dependent South."[151] As Noam Chomsky noted, with a new imperial age emerging at the end of the first 500 years (in the Columbus era), "the conquest continues" and "the South is assigned a service role: to provide resources, cheap labor, markets, opportunities for investment and, lately, export of pollution."[152] But all the mighty external forces of the North could not have marshaled SAPs without the close collaboration of states in the South.

The Crucial Role of the State

Before stressing the role of the state in the process of adjustment, let us outline briefly the two main pillars of SAPs: IMF stabilization and World Bank structural adjustment programs. Although adjustment refers to adjusting the balance of payments of a nation, it actually means adjusting national and local policies of development to the requirements of the functioning of the world market, which is controlled by the industrialized countries. This process involves comprehensive policies designed to achieve changes in internal and external balances, as well as changes in the structure of incentives and institutions. When these policies focus on balance of payments and budget deficits, they are labeled stabilization programs (budget austerity measures and currency devaluation aimed at demand management). When their goal is to reform policies, institutions, and the structures of economic incentive, they are labeled structural adjustment[153] (supply-enhancing policies requiring sectoral reforms and liberalization). Stabilization programs are supported by the IMF through a system of arrangements that allow the borrower to use a specific amount (depending on its quota) of the Fund's resources for a short period of time (usually one year) in exchange for the implementation of a series of monetary, fiscal, and other policies. Structural adjustment programs are supported by loans from the World Bank and can also be cofinanced by other lenders. Their macroeconomic objectives include IMF stabilization targets plus other structural and sectoral targets that are specified as conditions (for disbursement) in any Bank loan or credit agreement. Stabilization and structural adjustment combine quick-disbursing lending systems with explicit loan conditions requiring major policy changes. They illustrate the cross-conditionality of IMF arrangements and World Bank loans and credits. Unless a developing country follows an IMF program, it cannot borrow from the World Bank, and without a World Bank-endorsed investment program, the country cannot bring in international investors. So the IMF money unlocks the World Bank money, which unlocks international investors' money.

Adjustment policies are essentially aimed at reversing a set of nationalistic, protectionist policies that dominated development in the 1960s and the 1970s when the state used to intervene directly in the process of production and distribution of a variety of goods and services. These nationalistic policies were implemented throuhg a powerful public sector made up of state enterprises and agencies in which the state owned the means of production and controled much of the distribution process. This was the import substitution industrialization model. A direct consequence of this policy is state control over the price system, including the value of the national currency and its exchange rate. Adjustment policies work hard to systematically dismantle the above policies by reducing or eliminating direct state intervention in the process of production and distribution of most goods and services. The role of the state is to be limited to the creation of an adequate institutional and legal framework and an appropriate political environment for the promotion of private enterprises and the rehabilitation of public enterprises (that cannot be privatized) along the lines of efficiency and profitability. Privatization is not an end in itself since "the goal is to ensure—either by privatization or by management reform—that state enterprises respect the laws of the market."[154] However, it should be noted that the role of the state in reversing nationalistic policies is not less coercive than its role in establishing those policies in the first place. The role of the state was simply redefined to meet the challenges of the strategy of international accumulation. Privatization (or at least the separation of ownership and management in state-owned enterprises) represents the main instrument in redefining the role of the state in economic development and bringing about efficiency, i.e., producing more with less.

It is important to stress the central role of the state in all adjustment reforms. State deregulation in this regard is simply a form of reregulation that lifts restrictions on capital investment and transfer and prevents further nationalization, thus encouraging an internationally based form of capital accumulation rather than a nationally based one. This means that capital outflow is no longer restricted as was the case in the nationally based form of accumulation. Deregulation policies should be seen in the light of further national and international free movement of capital as one of the fundamental tenets of the new strategy of accumulation, which is based on a "theory of tendential dissolution of spatial heterogeneity and its replacement by homogeneous space of 'pure' market relations on a world scale."[155] State regulations are established or abolished according to a preconceived economic policy. In the case of adjustment regulations, they are designed to provide insurance and guarantees that the lenders will get their money back. The new regulations make it impossible for any Third World government to repeat Mexico's 1982 suspension of debt payment without facing formidable economic sanctions. But even though the global mobility of capital has limited the autonomy of the state, it could not have been achieved without the active intervention and mediation of the state.

Ambiguities surrounding the role of the state in adjustment stem from the state being at the same time a target and an instrument for reforms. The peripheral state has its own specificity vis-à-vis its relation to civil society. Rabah Abdoun argues that the state in the Third World is not the product of civil society, but the reverse. The state, he goes on, was integrated from its very inception into the international system, and it functions as the central instrument for mediating between the outside world and civil society.[156] With the growing internal and external market integration, the ability of the state to lead the process of economic development is widely questioned, and big business seriously challenges it,[157] even though it also needs it. This is more so in the peripheral state which Robert Jackson describes as a "quasistate" in contrast with the "real state" in the West.[158] Robert Cox cogently argues that the traditional role of the state as a bulwark or buffer protecting the domestic economy from harmful external influences is seriously undermined by its new role of transmission belt from world economy to domestic economy.[159] Samir Amin was probably the first to grasp the nature of the shift in the role of the peripheral state. He noted that the preadjustment state attempted to adjust its outside relations to the imperatives of its internal relations and structures, while the postadjustment state did the opposite.[160] A state that submits to external pressures for deregulation and liberalization is in fact a "denationalized state" whose hegemony over national policy and monopoly over the mediation between the outside and the inside are increasingly challenged by the mushrooming interactions between international capital and local interests within individual nation-states.

One might argue further that the state may be viewed as the superstructure of society, and when internal and external market transactions and commodity relations reach a point at which state regulations constitute bottlenecks and become obstacles to further development, then a crisis occurs and leads necessarily to a redefinition of state regulations and social relations in general. The ideological foundation of the nation-state resides in its ability to demarcate and if necessary dissociate itself from other states and from the world economy by asserting its full sovereignty over its citizens, its natural resources, and its territorial space. With increasing world integration, this option seems more and more difficult, and this is where really lies the crisis of the nation-state. The recent debacle of the Soviet state illustrates this restructuring, and, ironically, the classic Khaldunian[161] and Marxist analysis of the dynamic relationship between the infrastructure and the superstructure of society seems even more relevant in this regard. But the direction of change following the crisis is not absolutely predetermined since the specific nature of social alliance and opposition and the desired form of accumulation are the ultimate determinants of that direction. In this way the state represents a form and a synthesis of social relations, and consequently its role always shifts.

The denationalized state referred to here represents a state form that corresponds to the globalization of capital and the growth of international multilateral institutions. Christopher Chase-Dunn goes further: "I believe that a world state has become a necessity."[162] However, R. B. J. Walker insists that the claims of particularity, local authority, and unique identity will not go, nor will the states.[163] Gerald Helman and Steven Ratner observed the new phenomenon of nation-state failure and advocated an international system of conservatorship.[164] But their internationalist solution is at odds with their exclusively internalist diagnosis of the causes of nation-state failure or demise. The international forces working against any serious attempt at nation-state crystallization in the Third World were completely absent from their analysis. They totally ignored the obvious fact that the current demise of peripheral states is accompanied by a reinvigoration of core states, which are seeking to impose their will well beyond their traditional territorial jurisdiction, whether directly or through the UN and multilateral institutions. They also turned a blind eye to the role of imperialism and the growing evidence that "colonialism is even more active now in the form of transnational corporatism."[165] The persistence of imperialism today makes it not only the "highest stage of capitalism" but also the "permanent stage of capitalism."[166] The development and strengthening of international institutions under adjustment is bringing about a new form of multilateral imperialism that seems to tighten the grip around the national state on the one hand, and loosen direct control on internal groups and institutions on the other hand. This process threatens to tear apart peripheral nation-states, as the current worldwide strife of ethnic and other subnational identities demonstrates. In this regard, adjustment-related changes actually represent more of a restoration than a revolution. The process of global integration is releasing a variety of centrifugal forces working toward further national distingration. It is a process of recolonization of the former colonies very similar to what French Prime Minister Jules Ferry described in 1885 when he said that "colonial policy is the daughter of industrial policy" since the colonies represent "the most advantageous capital investment for the rich countries" and that "to found a colony is to create *un débouché*"[167] (i.e., openings and opportunities for jobs, markets, raw materials, and so on).

The opening up and decentralization of nation-states and the emergence of localities today as a new central focus for capital investment are easily understandable in the light of an almost complete centralization of money and credit worldwide by about a dozen international community lenders and donors. Therefore, decentralization at the national level is possible (even desirable) because centralization at the global level is completed and Northern control over global finance, technology, the mass media, and the military is greater today than at any time in the past. Developing nations cannot obtain new credits or reschedule their debts unless they are on good terms with the IMF and the World Bank, the twin policy instruments of the G–7. For peripheral states, the days of dealing bilaterally with individual governments or private banks are gone (at least for the time being). Within the framework of adjustment, a state must first secure a certificate of creditworthiness from these multilateral institutions before considering any bilateral or multilateral deal involving credit or debt relief. The colonial state in Africa created and shaped through intervention and regulation the markets of African countries. But now that those markets are structurally linked to the world market, the state as middleman is no longer the only instrument needed in market transaction matters. This is because economic incentives, need, and monetization of all commodities can make the system work according to the rationality of the market without necessarily having to rely exclusively on state coercion and direct regulation of transactions.[168] But in the final analysis, market forces are nothing but a series of taken-for-granted state regulations. The state remains the most important institution for the implementation of adjustment policies. Adjustment is not possible without a central government capable of imposing it. However, somewhere down the road, when market forces prevail, SAPs and state coercion will no longer be needed in integrating developing economies within the global economy because market forces will spontaneously do the job. Referring to the imposition of SAPs on African governments and perhaps anticipating the scenario that SAPs will soon no longer be needed to keep Africa integrated within the global economy, World Bank Vice President for Africa Edwards Jaycox was reported in 1993 as saying, "We are now insisting that the governments generate their own economic reform plans. We'll help, we'll critique, we'll eventually negotiate and we'll support financially those things which seem to be reasonably making sense, but we're not going to write these plans. . . . We're not going to do this anymore."[169] Such a shift will probably relieve the Bank of the charge of imposing SAPs and will lay bare most African governments as having no plans but SAPs.

So far, the state is the only credible partner for international capital, especially in countries where the private sector lacks the necessary financial means and technical expertise for dominating the national economy. At the same time, the state constitutes a problem for adjustment. The structural rigidity of its regulations, the inefficiency of its bureaucracies, and sometimes the ideological certainties of its leadership were the first targets of administrative reforms within the framework of adjustment. Its new role is to tune-up the internal market and play the transmission belt role between the domestic market and the world economy. To reflect the many changes brought about by adjustment to national economies, a new System of National Accounts (SNA 1993) was published by the IMF, the European Union, the OECD, the UN, and the World Bank. Many countries have already established timetables for conversion of their existing national accounts to the new SNA, which reflects many of the economic changes of the last twenty-five years. These changes emphasize the role of finance[170] in the articulation of national and international mechanisms and institutions within which the strategy of adjustment operates. At the international level, the IMF, the World Bank, the Paris Club, the Consultative Group, and NGOs produce policies and development programs and mobilize creditors to provide loans and technical assistance for the execution and monitoring of those programs. At the national level, the state ensures internal and public order, issues the necessary regulations, and sets up government structures and specialized administrative cells and units as ad hoc institutions working exclusively on the implementation, monitoring, and evaluation of the numerous programs and projects of adjustment. These government structures usually take the form of well-funded special cells or units within key ministries designed to centralize and monitor specific aspects of adjustment policies. They might take the form of an interministerial committee appointed to follow up specific programs of adjustment. In all cases they allow the lenders and the central government to occasionally circumvent the long and often slow bureaucratic process. Because of their influence and efficiency, they often operate as states within the state. These internal and external mechanisms operate through a careful combination and dosage of state intervention and market incentives and according to a sequence in which the political always comes first and the social last, i.e., a political decision is made first so that an economic measure can be implemented and later its social impact assessed and contained. As the Mauritanian case will demonstrate, the role of the state in the implementation of SAPs was crucial and was secured through a carrot-and-stick strategy of providing loans and grants to the government in exchange for a full restructuring of the political economy of the country.

3

The Mauritanian Context

This chapter provides a background to the Mauritanian context within which SAPs were implemented. It begins with an introduction to the historical geography of Mauritania and the circumstances that surrounded the creation of the country and the birth of the colonial state, as well as the evolution of the postcolonial independent state. It then describes briefly the main tenets of nationalist development planning that was adopted by the state throughout the 1960s and 1970s. The last section of this chapter introduces subsequent chapters by outlining a brief summary of the sequence of SAPs in Mauritania and their impacts on the state and the economy.

Historical Geography of Mauritania

Al-Jumhuriya Al-Islamiya Al-Muritaniya (the Islamic Republic of Mauritania) occupies a vast land area (1.03 million square km) of the Sahara and Sahel regions along the northwest African coast and has a sparsely distributed population of 2.2 million in 1994. The land area extends some 1,287 km from north to south and 1,255 km from east to west. It is bordered on the north by the Western Sahara and Algeria; on the east and southeast by Mali, on the south by Senegal, and on the west by a lengthy Atlantic coastline of 754 km stretching from the delta of the Senegal River to the peninsula of Nouadhibou and Guera. The country is a generally flat plain with occasional ridges and clifflike outcroppings. The highest point (915 m) is the peak of Kedyet Al-Jill near Zouerat. The current twelve administrative regions and the district of Nouakchott (see figure 1) developed out of five traditional geographic regions. The central region is known as Trab Al-Hajra, or country of stone, which corresponds to the Adrar and Tagant plateaus. Al-Gibla, or the south,[1] designates the Trarza and Brakna regions, which lay south of the Adrar, southwest of the Tagant, and north of the Senegal River. The Atlantic coastal region is known as Al-Sahel, or the coast. Al-Sahel also refers to the Western Sahara region. The southeastern part of the country is known as Al-Hodh, or the basin, which is surrounded by the overhanging cliffs of the Al-Assaba to the west, the Tagant to the northwest, and the Al-Dhar of Tichit and Walata to the north and east. The Al-Hodh region is also known as Al-Sharg, or the east. To the east of Adrar and to the north of Al-Dhar lays a vast empty quarter of barren sandy dunes described by Al-Bakri in the eleventh century as Al-Majaba Al-Kubra, or the Great Waste. The climate of the country is generally hot, dry, and dusty. In most of the country desert winds cause frequent sandstorms throughout the year, and desertification is giving rise to rapid mobility of sand dunes, which are threatening vegetation, human settlements, and the road system. The northern three-quarters of the country are dominated by the Sahara, with high temperatures and irregular rainfalls averaging less than 100 mm annually. The remaining fourth quarter to the south of the eighteenth parallel north is dominated by the Sahel (southern borderlands of the desert) climate, where annual precipitation during the rainy season of July to September averages above 100 mm and can even reach up to 600 mm in the extreme south along parts of the upper Senegal River valley. The wavy zones of intersection between the Sahara and the Sahel provide favorable conditions for extensive livestock raising, the backbone of the precolonial pastoral economy. On the eve of the French conquest at the turn of the twentieth century, the country was divided into independent emirates and tribal confederations: Emarit (Emirate) Trarza and Emarit Lebrakna in Al-Gibla, including the lower and middle parts of the Senegal River valley (since late seventeenth century); Emarit Ahl Hya Min Uthman in Adrar (since early eighteenth century); Emarit Idawish in Tagant and Al-Assaba including parts of the upper Senegal River valley (since the middle of the eighteenth century); and Shyakhit (Chieftain) Mashdhuf in most of Al-Hodh (since the middle of the nineteenth century).

Historically, the country represents a strong link between the Maghreb and the Sudan, particularly since the Almoravid (Al-Murabitun) movement unified the Berber Sanhaja[2] tribal confederations of central Mauritania in the eleventh century and swept north to conquer Morocco

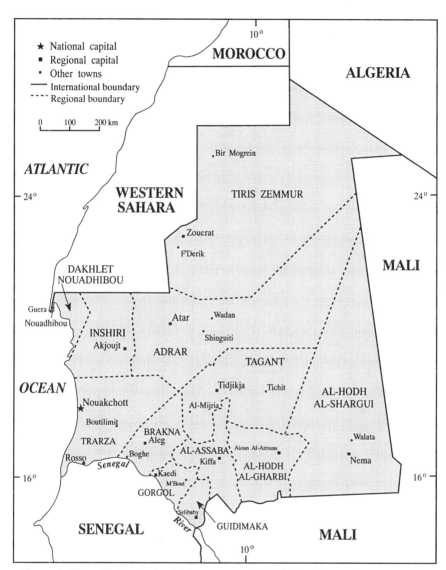

Figure 1 Map of Mauritania: Major towns and administrative regions

(1056), captured Ghana's capital (Koumbi Saleh) in 1076, and intervened in Spain, or Al-Andalus (1086), thus founding a short-lived (1053–1147) but vast trading and religious empire linking and bringing together the Sudan, the Sahara, the Maghreb, and Spain. They played a decisive role in the ultimate triumph of Sunni Islam (particularly the Maliki school of Islamic law, which was later strongly influenced by Sufi mysticism) over Shii and Khariji Islam in the entire Maghreb and the Sudan. Prior to the Al-Murabitun movement the Islamization of the Sanhaja tribes was superficial. It was under the teachings of Abdullah Ibn Yaseen (d. 1059) and the leadership of Abu Bakr Ibn Amer (d. 1087) and later his colleague, Al-Imam Al-Hadrami (d. 1096), that the Al-Murabitun succeeded in completing the Islamization of the country and establishing a traditional social structure dominated by warriors and marabouts (a sort of clergymen). Today, most Mauritanians refer to the Al-Murabitun as the founding fathers who completed the Islamization and started the Arabization of the country. Because of their movement, Islam became so deeply rooted that Mauritania is often described as "the only sub-Saharan country where Christian missionaries admit defeat beforehand."[3] With successive Arab migrations, Arabism too became as rooted in the country as Islam.

Although Mauritania experienced a slow but constant infiltration of Arabs and Arab influence from the late seventh and early eighth centuries on,[4] the process of ethnolinguistic Arabization of the country did not begin until around the thirteenth and fourteenth centuries, when many Arab tribes of Banu Maqil were pushed south to the Western Sahara by the Zenata Merinid dynasty in Morocco. The Maqil[5] were part of the massive Arab migration of Banu Hilal and Banu Sulaym who swept across North Africa in the eleventh century. These seemingly turbulent Bedouin tribes were used in support for, or in rebellion against, dynasties of the Abbasids in the Mashreq, the Fatimids in Egypt, and the Almoravids (the Ibn Ghania episode), the Almohads, and the Merinids in the Maghreb. They were originally "deported"[6] by the Abbasids from the Arabian and Syrian deserts following their support for the Shiite Ismailite Qaramita who attacked Mecca in 930 and carried off the Black Stone of the Kaaba and did not return it until 951. They were deported to Upper Egypt, where they settled temporarily between the Red Sea and the Nile River before the Fatimid Sultan, Al-Mustansir, encouraged them to migrate westward and reconquer Ifriqya (centered around Qayrawan in present Tunisia), whose leader, Al-Muizz Ibn Badis, had proclaimed his allegiance to the Abbasid Khalifate of Baghdad who the Fatimids of

Egypt sought to overthrow. Once in Ifriqya, they became involved in various power struggles, and many of them were later transferred westward by the Moroccan-based Almohads, while others migrated to various parts of the northern shores of the Sahara. By the fourteenth century, Ibn Khaldun gave a description of the positioning and location of various Arab tribes (Hassan, Mansour, Zughba, Riyah, and Sulaym) on the northern shore of the Sahara facing their counterpart Berber tribes (Gudala, Lemtuna, Messufa, Lemta, and Tuareg) on the southern shore.[7] As they penetrated further south, one branch of the Maqil, the Banu Hassan, progressively overwhelmed the already established Sanhaja tribes of the Sahara. By the seventeenth century, the Hassan tribes came to dominate all of what is now Mauritania, and their Arabic dialect (Klam Hassan or Hassanya) systematically replaced the Sanhaja dialect (Klam Aznaga). Most of the Hassan tribes formed the warrior class, while many of the Sanhaja tribes were reduced to a tributary class.

However, the original ethnic base of the above social structure dissipated gradually as the result of the Arabization of the Berbers through domination, social integration, disintegration, intermarriage, and the dynamism of social struggle, by which some Hassan tribes became tributaries and acquired the status of Aznaga while some Sanhaja tribes graduated from the tributary status and virtually became Arab by virtue of war or Islamic scholarship. Moreover, Sanhaja matriarchy gave way to Hassan patriarchy,[8] and the process of Arabization (facilitated by the early Islamization) deepened to the extent that today the majority of the Moors are of mixed Arab and Berber ancestry and almost all the original Sanhaja tribes reject strongly any Berber ancestry and claim Arab ancestry. Many of them claim even to be the descendants of the Prophet of Islam, Muhammed, or of his Companions of the Quraysh and Ansar tribes of Mecca and Medina in Arabia. This profound process of Islamization and Arabization constitutes the core of the Moorish culture, which continues to prevail over modernity by its myths, tales, and Arab poetry (Mauritania is known as the land of one million poets). It is this Arab Islamic culture that shaped the precolonial personality of the Moors and continued later to influence the postcolonial identity of the new Mauritanians. Harry Norris noted that "the Moorish Sahara is the western extremity of the Arab World. Western it certainly is, some districts further west than Ireland, yet in its way of life, its culture, its literature and in many of its social customs, it has much in common with the heart lands of the Arab East, in particular with the Hijaz and Najd and parts of the Yemen."[9]

In the early centuries of Islam, what is now Mauritania was known as Sahra Al-Mulathamun, or veiled men's Sahara. Its inhabitants, the Al-Mulathamun, were essentially Berber tribes who were pushed southward by a climatic shift toward increasing aridity in what became the Sahara, as well as by the Roman conquest of North Africa following the end of the Punic Wars in 146 BC. The Al-Mulathamun were certainly related to, if not the actual ancestors of the present day Tuareg of Mali, Algeria, Niger, and Libya. After its Arabization, the country became vaguely known as Bilad Shinguiti,[10] or the country of Shinguiti, a town in the Adrar region, and the Moors were known within the Arab and Islamic worlds as Al-Shanaguita. They were famous for their Islamic scholarship and Arab poetry, which were curiously preserved in nomad libraries[11] and widely propagated by the Mahadhra system (a sort of bedouin universities), where students spend a large part of their early lives moving from one center of learning (Mahadhra) to another and from one Aalem (plural Ulema or Muslim scholars) to the next. In this Islamic tradition of scholarship, the Moors were inspired by the famous Hadith of the Prophet Muhammed—"seek for knowledge, even in China"—and for many of them knowledge is an end in itself. Even today Mauritania continues "to export *qadis* [Muslim judges] to Saudi Arabia and the Gulf."[12] Moorish Muslim scholars, particularly sufi Sheikhs of the Kadiriya and Tijaniya sufi orders, were also instrumental in spreading Islamic mysticism in other parts of West Africa. The name Mauritanie was given to the country by the French at the turn of the twentieth century as a nostalgic way of reviving the names of some ancient Roman colonies in North Africa, especially in northwestern Algeria (Mauretania Caesariensis) and northern Morocco (Mauretania Tangitana). It is derived from the Latin (or Latinized) word Maurus, from which came the French Maures (Moors) which designates the dominant ethnolinguistic group in the country. The Moors call themselves Al-Bidhan or "the Whites," in juxtaposition to the Al-Sudan or "the Blacks" of sub-Saharan Africa.[13] They are Arabic-speaking and are predominantly of Arab and Berber descent. The Moors also include a substantial number of blacks, or Haratin, who are the descendants of black slaves but who have been Arabized and tribalized to the extent that they never identified with the non-Arabic-speaking black Africans. The Moors are found in all of the Western Sahara and in parts of southern Morocco, southwestern Algeria, and northern Mali. Precolonial "ethnic nationalism"[14] among the Moors was essentially based on real or ideologically reconstructed Arab genealogies, a form of representation that is increasingly superseded today by a postindependence fervent pan-Arabism often colliding with black nationalism of the non-Moor Mauritanians, as well as with the dominant francophone culture in West Africa.

There are no reliable statistics on the exact number of the Muslim but non-Arabic-speaking black minorities of Mauritania. Officially, they are believed to form some 20 percent of the total population. UN documents confirm this estimate.[15] However, certain leaders of these minorities reject this estimate as too low. They belong to three black African ethnic groups living along the Senegal River valley (even though they are found since independence in significant numbers in Nouakchott and Nouadhibou) and known collectively today among the Moors as Lekwar (singular Kewri). The Pulaar-speaking ethnic group is the largest one and includes the Toucouleur and the Peul who inhabit the middle river valley, particularly in and around the towns of Boghe and Kaedi. The Soninke represent numerically the second group and live in parts of the Guidimaka region of the upper river valley. The Wolof, the smallest group, live in the lower river valley. The Toucouleur, Peul, and Wolof ethnic groups are found in Senegal, while the Soninké are found mainly in Mali. It is believed that centuries ago some of these groups could be found as far north as Tijirit to the west of Adrar.[16] They probably migrated or were pushed south by North African Berbers as the Sahara dried up. At the time of the Portuguese exploration of the West African coast in the middle of the fifteen century, the Senegal River (or at least its mouth) was already dominated by the Sanhaja tribes when the European explorers named the river after them, the "Zenega River" which later became the Senegal River. During the nineteenth century, the number of Toucouleur, Peul, Soninké, and Wolof north of the Senegal River was insignificant, but it "increased under the protection of the French administration"[17] during the first half of the twentieth century to reach 17 percent of the total population in 1953, according to Paul Dubié, *administrateur en chef de la France d'outer-mer* (chief administrator of the French overseas territories).[18] Their number increased disproportionately within the administrative structures of the postcolonial state, which needed French-educated cadres in the early years of independence. Because of their geographic location and cultural orientation, they were able to turn out (relatively) more graduates from the French education system during the period of colonization than the Moors, whose attachment to Arabic and Islamic education never abated. In contrast with the Moorish society, the black African society of Mauritania turned out to be "more francophile, more francophone, frequented more assiduously French schools and later found itself in a position of domination" within the state administrative system,[19] despite its minority status.

Traditional social structures are similar among the Moors and the black ethnic groups. Warriors and religious literates make up the two poles of an aristocracy whose hegemony is based on the power of the *Ktab* and the *Rkab* (the book and the stirrup or the turban and the sword),[20] respectively symbols of ideology and violence. "At the top of the social hierarchy"[21] of the precolonial Moorish society, there is a warrior class (Arab or Hassan), whose power is essentially based on the capacity to raid rivals and protect allies in a nomadic setting characterized by a great deal of spatial mobility and environmental uncertainty. They are followed closely by the literates among the marabouts (Zouaya or Tolba), whose religious teaching, numerical superiority, and role in the organization of the pastoral economy (often via the use of a servile labor force) made them the second dominant class within precolonial Moorish society. However, this order of domination is inverted among the Halpulaar ethnic group, where the warriors (cebbé) "are considered inferior"[22] to the literates (Toroodo) who—unlike the Zouaya of the Moors, whose revolt against Hassan warriors failed in the 1670s—defeated the Peul warriors during the Islamic uprising of 1776. Among the Moors, the tributaries (Lahma or Aznaga) and casted groups (Maalmin and Iggawen) are followed by black slaves (Abid whose free descendants formed the Haratin). Domestic slavery was widespread among all ethnic groups. In Moorish society it is "probably as old as the Moors themselves,"[23] and its residues and vestiges are still visible today throughout the country. Although Article 1 of the Mauritanian Constitution of 20 May 1960 ensures equality among citizens regardless of race, religion, and social condition, it was actually Ordinance 81–234 of November 9, 1981 that abolished and brought a complete end to slavery in rural areas, where the state used to have little control over local structures. Among the black African ethnic groups of the Senegal River, the proportion of slaves reached near half of the population at one time.[24] The Peuls' slave-based state (1512–1776) in the middle valley was overthrown by the Toroodo Islamic revolution, which actually stopped the Atlantic slave trade[25] in most of the river valley, but domestic slavery continued until it was abolished by the French colonial administration and the postcolonial state.

Although the essentials of the foundation of the above social structure go back to the Al-Murabitun, its finished form in Al-Gibla was firmly established in the aftermath of a (civil) war during the seventeenth century, when a coalition of the already established Zouaya tribes declared their own Imam, Nasser El-Din, and sought to implement the Islamic Sharia in political and economic matters in an open act of rebellion against the dominant and newly arrived Hassan tribes. Nasser El Din's unsuccessful rebellion actually attempted (though it failed) to repeat the enterprise of power conquest undertaken by the Al-Murabitun movement of the eleventh century. The revolt (known as the war of Shurbubba or Shar Bebba in the 1670s) failed and further crystallized Hassan power, particularly among the Trarza and Brakna. According to the terms of settlement of the Shurbubba war, the Zouaya tribes were to renounce the bearing of arms, to pay a water tax or water tribute (known as the third of water), and to accept other levies such as free lodging and transportation for Hassani travelers. As part of its colonial strategy of strengthening the weak in order to weaken the strong and as a prelude to imposing a general tax system (Al-Ushr, literally the tenth), the French colonial administration gradually abolished these and other forms of tribute[26] paid to the emir and other Hassanis and restricted or abolished slavery in most parts of the country. However, under French colonization, the social structure was somehow preserved. Generally, the French first disarmed Moorish warriors as a sign of submission and then rearmed and reorganized them as auxiliary *goums*[27] (*goums supplétifs*), a sort of native desert police. For example, when the former dissident emir (Ould Deid) of Trarza surrendered to the local French colonial administration, they nominated him emir by Order no. 364/AP of 11 July 1930. His newly defined duties include commanding and training auxiliary *goums*, supervising tax collection, and implementing French administrative orders.[28] This institutionalization of an emasculated emirate system was "the only alternative to direct rule"[29] since the bulk of the central colonial administration was located outside the country in Saint Louis in Senegal.

The precolonial economic history of the country was dominated primarily by nomadism and long-distance trade. Nomadism is a form of landuse highly "adapted to the scarcity and fragility of natural resources in the Sahelian-Saharan environment."[30] It is characterized by extensive livestock raising and a high mobility over space. The predominant animals reared in this environment are sheep, goats, cattle, and camels, which all ensure the bases for the self-sufficient precolonial economy by providing important products from milk and meat to hides, sandals, cords, and hair to weave tents, the nomads' shelters. Large-scale nomadism involves a great deal of spatial mobility in a regular back-and-forth movement from South to North, following the annual rainfall pattern. In their constant search for better pastures and water, nomads can cross hundreds, sometimes thousands, of kilometers every year, a characteristic that earned some of them the nickname Oulad Al-Mezna (sons of the cloud). Flood-recession and rain-fed agriculture were important in the Chemama (the flood plain along the Senegal River), while irrigated agriculture developed on a small scale in the Saharan oases, where date palms grow. Fishing was essentially confined to meeting the subsistence needs of small communities living along the Senegal River and in a few villages on the Atlantic coast.

Long-distance trade involved an important trans-Saharan caravan trade, where products such as gold from the Sudan, salt from the Sahara, and fabrics from the Maghreb were exchanged. This trade favored the emergence and even the florescence of oasis-towns (Walata, Tichit, Wadan, and Shinguiti) along the trans-Saharan trade routes that used to cross most of the interior of the country. Contrary to the image of today, the Sahara linked rather than divided the peoples on its shores. These towns represented important caravan routes and Islamic centers and strong bridges linking the Sudan kingdoms and empires of Mali and Songhai to their counterparts in North Africa and the Mediterranean region. These trade patterns began to decline as soon as the Atlantic trade patterns began to develop, particularly when Portuguese traders began to divert the gold trade from the Saharan oasis-town of Wadan to the Atlantic coast in 1443, when they took control of the Arguin island, about halfway between Nouadhibou and Nouakchott on the Atlantic coast. During the sixteenth century, the center of gravity of world trade began to shift from the Mediterranean Sea to the Atlantic Ocean. Consequently, the center of gravity of the country was moved gradually from the oasis-towns of Walata, Tichit, Wadan, and Shinguiti in the heart of the Sahara to the Senegal River and the Atlantic coast regions, where contact with European traders began as early as the fifteenth century. For a long time, these contacts were limited to the search for the sources of the gold imported from the Sudan. One important demographic consequence of this great shift was the gradual migration of many Moorish tribes from the northern and central parts of the country to the Al-Gibla, Tagant, and Al-Hodh regions. From the eighteenth century on, the Moors' trade with the Europeans involved exclusively gum arabic as a commodity wanted in Europe for textile finishing and inks, pharmacy, confectionery, and the manufacture of adhesives.

This trade was particularly important in the Al-Gibla region where "the emergence and consolidation of the Emirates owe much to the European companies"[31] seeking control of the Arabic gum trade. In fact, competition between European powers (the Dutch, the English, and the French) for control of the trade of this commodity led at some point to the so-called gum war between the British and French navies in the eighteenth century[32] and enabled the Moors (particularly the Trarza, the Brakna, and the Idawish) to maintain their independence and even to extract annual payments (*la coutume*) from the French in exchange for allowing the gum arabic trade to take place. Such extraction led a Frenchman, le Chevalier Boufflers, to portray the Trarza Emir in 1787 as *un roi mendiant* (a beggar king).[33] It should be noted, however, that these Moorish "kings" were approached by their followers as sheikhs (tribal chiefs) who were nothing but the first among equals. Actually it was the French annual payments to these tribal chiefs that allowed certain dominant Moorish lineages to rise above their followers, to enlarge their scope of patronage, and overall to stabilize the office of the emirate and regularize succession to the office of the emir.[34] Gum arabic and *la coutume* paid to the emir were actually the two economic and political instruments by which the Moors were integrated into the French colony of Senegal and the European-led world economy in general.

Following the Treaty of Paris (1814)[35] and the Congress of Vienna (1815), French intentions north and south of the Sahara were clearly expressed. During the 1810s they reestablished their control over the town of Saint Louis (lost earlier to the British) at the mouth of the Senegal River, and in 1830 they conquered Algeria. These developments were sufficient to make Mauritania fall into the French sphere of influence and geopolitics, especially after the 1885 Berlin Conference, in which European powers agreed to partition the African continent. French explorers and spies, often disguised as Muslims,[36] began to penetrate the Sahara to assess the environmental, political, economic, and social conditions as a prelude to military conquest. In the 1850s, the French succeeded (through a series of battles) in driving the Trarza Moors out of the left bank of the Senegal River, while the Spanish began in the 1880s in the north to carve the borders between what would become the Western Sahara and Mauritania. In 1891, France and Spain concluded a draft agreement on the delimitation of their possessions in the peninsula of present Nouadhibou and Guera. Article 1 of the document reads:

The boundary between the Spanish possessions and the French possessions depending on the colony of the Senegal will follow a line which, starting from the point indicated on the map annexed to the present agreement, on the west coast of the peninsula of Cabo Blanco between the extreme point of this cape and Bahía del Oeste, will continue to the middle of this peninsula, dividing the peninsula in half so far as the terrain permits, and will then be drawn northward up to the point of intersection with the parallel 21° 20' north, and will continue along this parallel to the interior.[37]

In 1898, the Trarza and the Brakna accepted a French arbitration of a conflict (some say a civil war) between two of their tribes, Oulad Ebyeiri and Idjeidjba. This arbitration virtually ended the emirs' credibility and sovereignty over their subjects and prepared the French for direct military intervention north of the Senegal River, where between 1902 and 1904, they and their *tirailleurs Sénégalais* (Senegalese riflemen) crossed the river in tacit agreement with the Trarza and Brakna emirates. Their penetration in Mauritania during this period was led by Xavier Coppolani, a French national from Corsica who spent his childhood in Algeria, where he learned the Arabic language and Islamic theology, two instruments that prepared him for the difficult *mission civilisatrice* in the Sahara. He was assassinated in Tidjikja in 1905 by northern-based resistance movements thhat were spiritually guided by Shaykh Ma Al-Ainin, a native of Al-Hodh who is considered a hero of resistance to colonization in Mauritania, Western Sahara, and Morocco. The Tagant and Adrar emirates, which opposed French penetration, were conquered, and their emirs (Bakar Ould Sweid Ahmed and Ahmed Ould Aidda) were killed in action against the French military penetration. Resistance among the northern Moorish tribes (particularly the Rguibat) of the Western Sahara was not effectively suppressed, however, until 1934, when the process of military conquest or "pacification"[38] of *le pays de la poudre par excellence*[39] (the true country of gunpowder) was completed. The French strategy was to prevent any rival European power from occupying what they called the *grand vide* (great emptiness) separating France's two major colonies in Africa at the time: Senegal and Algeria, which represented the mothers of all French colonies in the continent.

Within the framework of French imperial policy, Mauritania was conceived from the beginning as a *trait d'union* (literally a hyphen, here meaning a transition zone joining two distinct regions) state between the Maghreb and the Sudan. But Morocco's strong opposition to Mauritania's independence on 28 November 1960 further pushed the country into West African geopolitics. Though ethnically the Moors share the Arabo-Berber heritage of the Maghreb, they were administratively integrated by the French into francophone West Africa for decades. This policy put Mauritania on the margin of two interlinked but distinct cultures and civilizations: the Arab world and black Africa.[40] To outsiders, "Mauritania is a country which is divided, or rather which bridges two worlds, two civilizations and two cultures," while to insiders it "is a reflection of Africa as a whole, with an Arab north and a black African south."[41] The postcolonial state in Mauritania has at the same time enjoyed and suffered from this unique position of a geographic and cultural transition zone. In the words of Baduel, Mauritania experiences *l'epreuve de la frontière*[42] (the ordeal of the frontier), and the country continues to suffer from the artificial nature of its international borders. The lengthy northern and eastern boundaries of the country cut across Moorish tribes in the neighboring Western Sahara, Algeria, and Mali in much the same way southern boundaries cut across black African ethnic groups on both banks of the Senegal River. Because of this special geopolitical location, the country was affected by the Western Sahara war from the mid-1970s and the presence of substantial numbers of Sahrawi refugees. From the mid-1980s, Arab and Tuareg rebellions in northern Mali brought more than 50,000 refugees to eastern Mauritania, while dissidence and opposition among black Mauritanian southerners led finally to the 1989 political crisis between Senegal and Mauritania, which brought about the sudden repatriation of some 250,000 to 500,000 Mauritanians or Senegalese of Mauritanian origin and the deportation of some 50,000 to 60,000 Senegalese or Mauritanians believed to be of Senegalese origin. Most of these border, ethnic, and political problems are far from being solved and will continue to besiege the Mauritanian state for the foreseeable future as they have done since the beginning of political reforms toward statehood and nationhood in the 1940s when the eastern region of Al-Hodh was detached from the French Sudan (Mali) and united with the rest of Mauritania. The nature of the future settlement of the conflicts in the Western Sahara and Northern Mali will certainly have a lasting impact on the Mauritanian state.

During the period of colonization, Saint Louis (known locally as N'Darr) at the mouth of the Senegal River was the capital for the French colonial administration of Mauritania. The French administered the country indirectly making it "a kind of hinterland" and a sort of "economic appendix"[43] for the French colony of Senegal. At the time of independence (1960), there was no modern infrastructure left by the

French in the country, not even a capital city. The postcolonial state transferred the central administration of the country from Saint Louis to the newly designated capital city, Nouakchott, originally a small village on the Atlantic coast where the Sahel and Sahara regions meet around the eighteenth parallel north. It is sometimes argued that French colonial impact on the country and the people was marginal compared to the imprint left by France on the neighboring states of Algeria, Senegal, and even Morocco. But compared to the precolonial period, the country and the people changed in many ways. Philippe Marchesin argued that beyond the introduction of a mercantile economy and of Western state institutions, "the most important impact of French colonization on Moorish society was the decline of the warrior aristocracy and the rise of the middle class Marabout."[44] Another important impact of French colonization was the incorporation of Moors and non-Moors into the Mauritanian state, even though the French referred only to the Moors when engineering the name Mauritanie. This incorporation created and developed an always latent and sometimes explosive politics of ethnicity that is reflected in a dual national identity where the Moors perceive themselves as an integral part of the Arab world while the non-Arabic speaking black ethnic groups consider themselves an integral part of sub-Saharan Africa. This dual national identity between "*arabité et africanité*"[45] was often centered on the use of Arabic and French languages and made the national unity of the country an always urgent and constant concern in Mauritanian politics since the early political moves toward independence following World War II.

The first political reform of French colonial policy in Mauritania began in the aftermath of World War II when the Mauritanian *Territoire d'Outre-Mer* (French overseas territory) was allowed to elect a representative (*deputé*) to the French National Assembly. During the first elections, Yvon Razac (a French national of Arab-French descent, probably brought from Algeria), the candidate proposed by the French colonial administration to represent Mauritania, was defeated by (Ahmedou Ould) Horma Ould Babana, a native Moor, who became Mauritania's first representative to the French National Assembly from 1946 to 1951 and who was also a member of the French Socialist Party for some time. Unhappy about the outcome of this election, the French organized a local opposition to Ould Horma within the framework of the Union Progressiste Mauritanienne (UPM), a pro-French party rallying together the main traditional tribal and regional chieftains of the country in 1948. In 1950, Ould Horma reacted by creating a new party, the

Entente Mauritanienne, and sought (but did not get) support from the French Socialist Party, from which he withdrew later accusing its leadership of sympathy with the Zionists. In 1951, he was defeated in the elections by the pro-French UPM candidate, Sid El Mokhtar N'Diaye (of Wolof and Moorish descent). The second postwar reform in French colonial policy came in the aftermath of the French defeat in Vietnam and the launching of the Algerian revolution in 1954, which both forced France to rethink its colonial strategy. In this context, Morocco and Tunisia obtained their independence in 1956, while in West Africa the *Loi-Cadre* Defferre called for the election of territorial assemblies in the colonies. Mokhtar Ould Daddah (one of the first Mauritanian university graduates) ran on a list of the UPM and was elected *conseiller territorial* of Adrar in March 1957. He was nominated vice president of the Council of the Government in May 1957 and subsequently became the first president of the Islamic Republic of Mauritania, a young state caught from its inception between Arab and black nationalisms whose confrontations have often blurred class relations in favor of ethnic or racial ones.

The ethnic political cleavage began to develop on the eve of independence when two political parties expressed their different nationalisms. On the one hand, radical elements of the Rabitat Al-Shabab Al-Muritany (Association of Mauritanian Youth, established in 1955) founded Hizb Al-Nahda Al-Wataniya Al-Muritaniya (Mauritanian National Renaissance Party) in 1958 as an incarnation of Arab nationalism strongly inspired by the unfolding of the Egyptian Revolution (particularly the overthrow of the Egyptian monarchy in 1952, the rise of Nasser following the nationalization of the Suez Canal in 1956, and the unification with Syria in 1958), the launching of the Algerian Revolution in 1954, and the independence of Tunisia and Morocco in 1956. The Renaissance Party opposed integration within French West Africa, and some of its members wanted and worked for a federation with Morocco that claimed that Mauritania is part of "Greater Morocco," stretching from Tangiers on the Mediterranean Sea to Saint Louis on the mouth of the Senegal River. On the other hand, the Union des Originaires du Sud[46] (Union of Natives of the South), created in Dakar, Senegal, and the Bloc Démocratic du Gorgol (Democratic Bloc of the Gorgol region), founded in 1957, wanted a federation within the framework of *l'Afrique Occidentale Française* (French West Africa). In 1958, Mokhtar Ould Daddah (then prime minister) declared in this regard that "if we were to choose between a federation with the Maghreb or a federation with French West Africa our preferences go to the Maghreb."[47] Seemingly there was no choice since the French wanted an independent Mauritania rather than a "Greater Morocco." Backed by the French, Ould Daddah was able to work a third way between Arab and black nationalisms. He co-opted first, then later eliminated the progressive wing of the Nahda (Bouyagui Ould Abidin, the founder of the movement, and Ahmed Baba Ould Ahmed Miske, the general secretary), while several other members or sympathizers of the Nahda (such as Ahmedou Ould Hourma, Mohamed Fall Ould Oumeir, Mohamed El Mokhtar Ould Bah, and Dey Ould Sidi Baba) chose self-exile in Morocco. At the Congress of Aleg in May 1958, Ould Daddah worked toward the dissolution of the two major political parties (Union Progressiste Mauritanienne and Entente Mauritanienne) and founded the Parti du Rassemblement Mauritanien. After independence, Ould Daddah founded the Hizb Al-Shaab Al-Muritany (the Mauritanian People's Party) as a sort of compromise between the extremes, Arab and African nationalisms. It was also a compromise between the power of the traditional tribal chiefs and the aspirations of the modernist "Young Turks." The compromise worked relatively well because the state was at the time facing a serious external threat (Moroccan rejection of Mauritania's independence), which was instrumental in galvanizing a unified internal front as well as institutionalizing the ideological foundations of the single-party rule for the following two decades, despite Moroccan attempts at destabilization.

The day of the proclamation of Mauritania's independence from France on 28 November 1960 was declared a mourning day in Morocco.[48] With full support from all the Arab countries (except Tunisia), Morocco rejected the independence of Mauritania and opposed its admission to the United Nations by mobilizing a Soviet veto in December 1960. The Soviet Union vetoed Mauritania's UN membership in retaliation for Western powers' support for Nationalist China's veto of Outer Mongolia's UN membership. But the newly independent West African countries (manipulated by France) pressured Nationalist China (by threatening to recognize the People's Republic of China) and made it easier for France to engineer a superpower bargain in which the UN admitted simultaneously Mauritania and Outer Mongolia.[49] But Morocco continued throughout the 1960s to veto Mauritania's membership within the League of Arab States, and this strengthened further Mauritania's relations with France and former French West Africa, where it played an important role. It was a founding member of the Organization of African Unity (OAU) and was active in the Non-Aligned Movement. During this period, Mauritania followed an all azimuthal cosmopolitan foreign policy whose subtle vestiges may be discerned today in the naming of many streets of Nouakchott after world leaders of the 1960s, such as Abdel Nasser (Egypt), Kennedy (United States), General de Gaulle (France), Gandhi (India) and Lumumba (Congo/Zaire). Such policies were successful in establishing a temporary sort of *trait d'union* identity, which was strongly challenged during the late 1980s, particularly following the April 1989 ethnic clashes in Mauritania and Senegal, after which *arabité* prevailed in Mauritania, and when the 1991 Constitution dismissed French and established Arabic as the national language of the country.

Nationalist Development Planning

The above brief historical geography of Mauritania provided the background and context for the birth of the state and its subsequent pursuit of a nationalist and statist development planning between 1963 and 1984. Such a development model was based on (1) unification and control of the national market, (2) protection and promotion of local industries and production (import substitution-industrialization), (3) strong regulation of foreign trade and a rigid exchange rate system, (4) nationalization of foreign capital, and (5) international coordination to protect the price of raw material exports (cartels). In Mauritania the statist and nationalist model aimed at developing the current four major economic regions of the country. These are the northern region of Tiris Zemmur, where important iron deposits are located; the eastern region of Al-Hodh, where the bulk of livestock is raised; the southern region of the Senegal River, which provides conditions for both flood-recession and irrigated agriculture; and the northern parts of the Atlantic coast, which are adjacent to some of the richest fishing grounds in the world. Development planning for the exploitation of these resources began with the First Plan for Economic and Social Development (1963–67), whose focal point was the building of the infrastructure necessary for a modern state. During this period, basic infrastructure was built including important construction works in the new capital, the construction of a wharf in Nouakchott, and two roads linking the latter to the southern and northern regions of the country. Also during the same period, MIFERMA (Mines de Fer de Mauritanie), a French-led multinational mining company, completed its infrastructure, including a 650 km railroad, a mining town (Zouerat), and its port (Nouadhibou) for exporting iron ore. The strategy of development followed during the first decade of independence was essentially centered around extraction and export of iron ore, which began in 1963. The priority of mining was expressed in the first plan, which reads that "in a country where agricultural resources are limited and where the development of pastoralism is handicapped by the problem of pastures and the lack of water, economic growth can be sought through the exploitation of mineral resources."[50] This export-led strategy aimed at earning the necessary cash for importing consumption goods for the growing administrative apparatus and the necessary equipment for the construction of infrastructure: ports, airports, water supply, electricity, education and health services, and, above all, roads, which were important in integrating the different regions of a vast and sparsely populated country into a unified national market.

The Second Plan for Economic and Social Development (1970–73) was launched amid a period marked by a great deal of disruption in the pastoral economy, which was deeply affected by successive years of drought. In fact, between 1968 and 1973 a severe drought hit the entire region of the Sahel, and Mauritania was probably affected more than any other Sahelian country because of the fragility of its environment (with three-fourths of its land area falling into the Sahara) and the predominance of extensive livestock raising and traditional food cropping in the economy (with over 80 percent of the population involved in those activities at the time of the drought). It was estimated that 30 percent of the livestock was lost and a large proportion was sold by owners to avoid further loss. One major consequence of this drought was a dramatic acceleration of rural-urban migration on an unprecedented scale, with many nomads turning to sedentary life. In 1965, the population was distributed between nomads, 78 percent; rural sedentaries, 15 percent; and urban dwellers, 8 percent. In 1988, the distribution was nomads, 12 percent; rural sedentaries, 41 percent; and urban dwellers, 47 percent; and the trend continues.[51] Moreover, this dramatic urbanization was very uneven, and the capital Nouakchott is one of the fastest-growing cities in the world. Its population increased from 5,000 in 1960 to 40,000 in 1970; 134,000 in 1977 to 387,802 in 1988 and 581,238 in 1991.[52] This phenomenon of rapid and chaotic urbanization without real industrialization virtually transformed "a largely nomadic society into a society of environmental refugees"[53] and established a serious spatial disequilibrium where nearly 30 percent of the total population lives in one city, the capital Nouakchott, where political power and hence economic power are concentrated. The population growth and distribution by administrative regions are shown in table 4. The concentration of political and administrative power, the distribution of foreign food aid, and the lack of important urban centers in the country in the past all made Nouakchott the most attractive urban center for rural migrants hit by successive cycles of drought.

Table 4 Evolution of Population Distribution

Administrative regions	1977	1988	1994
Nouakchott	134,704	387,802	683,272
Al-Hodh Al-Shargui	156,721	208,386	243,078
Brakna	151,353	185,883	206,881
Gorgol	149,432	179,718	198,843
Trarza	216,008	200,592	192,316
Al-Assaba	129,162	161,307	182,726
Al-Hodh Al-Gharbi	124,194	152,329	169,535
Guidimaka	83,231	116,676	139,310
Dakhlet Nouadhibou	23,526	61,799	103,638
Adrar	55,354	60,633	63,598
Tagant	74,980	65,255	60,594
Tiris Zemmur	22,554	33,741	41,714
Inshiri	17,611	13,635	11,931
Total	1,338,830	1,827,756	2,297,53

Source: Compiled from Tableau 1, Annex I of "Schema National d'Amenagement du Territoire" (SNAAT), Bases de Representation, OTRACI Janvier 1990, Ministère de l'Interieur, des Postes et Telecommunications, Nouakchott. The 1994 figures are based on the projections of the growth rate (natural increase plus in and out migration) of the 1977–1988 period.

These transformations led (among other things) to a growing number of young unemployed people roaming the streets of the major cities, especially Nouakchott and Nouadhibou. There are no estimates for the number of these young unemployed, who were locally known as *Tekusu*, or *Al-Kawasa* (the wandering unemployed), but the magnitude of the phenomena was substantial enough to constitute the social basis for an increasing political opposition turning to leftist political movements (Al-Haraka Al-Wataniya Al-Dimukratiya and Hizb Al-Kadihin Al-Muritaniyin), particularly after 1968 when the government brutally crushed an uprising of mining workers in Zouerat, where the multinational company MIFERMA extracts iron ore. The combined effects of drought, rural-urban migration, and political opposition brought sufficient pressure on the government to embark on new reforms. In June 1972, Mauritania began a process of negotiations with France aimed at the revision of a series of economic, financial, and technical agreements that kept Mauritania's relations with France close throughout the 1960s. Between November 1972 and June 1973, it withdrew from the French-dominated monetary Franc Zone (the Communauté Financière Africaine), created a national currency, the ouguiya (*Al-Awqiya*, UM), and a central bank, the Banque Centrale de Mauritanie (BCM). In December 1973, it became a member of the Arab League after Morocco dropped officially its claim over the country as a preliminary step to raising a stronger claim over the then Spanish colony of the Western Sahara. Another important reform was the nationalization of MIFERMA in November 1974. Other reforms included the Mauritanization of most positions in the state bureaucracy and an increasing Arabization of the education system. President Mokhtar Ould Daddah explained to Jean Audibert, president of MIFERMA, that the youth opposition (Hizb Al-Kadihin) forced him to adopt "extreme solutions" such as the nationalization of MIFERMA.[54] However, the reforms enabled him also to fatally divide Hizb Al-Kadihin and co-opt some of its leaders (the so-called Kadihin Mariem) as he did a decade ago with the then opposition party, Hizb Al-Nahda.

   These reforms affirmed further the national identity of the country with more balanced relations between West and North Africa. But perhaps more important, they established the framework for a statist and nationalist development strategy involving a growing public sector, which was reinforced by the Third Plan of Economic and Social Development (1976–80) and particularly fostered by an important flow of external resources coming mainly from Arab OPEC members. Between 1973 and 1977 the flow of external resources amounted to $880 million and provided support for the balance of payments and the state budget.[55] This amount represents the equivalent of $160 per capita, roughly half the GDP per capita at the time.[56] However, Mauritania's alignment with Morocco in its war against the Frente Popular de la Liberación de la Saguia Al-Hamra y de Río de Oro (POLISARIO)[57] from late 1975 to mid-1978 was devastating for the economy as a whole and particularly for the mining sector, whose extracting and exporting points were located within the war zone. Also the war came at a time when recession in the West led to a crisis in the European steel industry, a major importer of Mauritanian iron ore. Consequently, a severe fiscal crisis of the state encouraged the military in 1978 to overthrow the single-party civilian regime in power since 1960. In 1979 the new military government negotiated and signed a peace treaty with the POLISARIO according to which Mauritania gave up all claims to and withdrew from the Western Sahara. The new government also adopted a stabilization program in conjunction with the International Monetary Fund aimed at strict control of the salaries of government employees, an improvement of tax collection, and an important rescheduling of foreign debts. At the same time, the government launched the Fourth Plan of Economic and Social Development (1981–85) and opened the Société Nationale Industrielle et Minière (SNIM) to international capital through a new mining project (Guelbs Project) that aimed at replacing the nearly depleted site of high-grade ores (64 percent iron) in the Kedia site (near Zouerat) with the larger but lower grade ores (38 percent iron) of the Guelbs site 30 km north of Zouerat.

Throughout the 1960s and 1970s, a process of nation-state building was taking place in Mauritania amid the ideology of national independence and economic development, which began to spread out from the first meeting of the Non-Aligned Movement in Bandung in 1955. The aim of this process was to develop a sovereign, independent, and modern state, having relations with the rest of the world but clearly demarcated from it. The underlying assumption was that international trends of economic interdependence could be controlled politically and economically at the national level through the preservation of national sovereignty and the pursuit of protectionist economic policies. Political centralization of the state and spatial, economic, and cultural integration of society were cornerstones of this process of statehood and nationhood building, a process of asserting a national identity. Environmental changes (drought) and socioeconomic transformations (rural-urban migration) of the late 1960s and early 1970s in Mauritania accelerated the crystallization of the project of an independent national state and an autocentric development through a series of reforms and nationalizations. These led to the emergence and growth of an important public sector, which, in the late 1980s, was composed of over eighty public enterprises providing jobs for 25 percent of the modern sector workforce and contributing 25 percent of the GDP of the country.[58]

Although internal social forces and environmental changes were the primary agents behind the reform movement of the 1970s, the external relations of the state were the main target of almost all these reforms. Political movements pushing for reforms were concentrating on the external relations of the state as the major source of contradiction.[59] They criticized the government on the grounds of its tight relations with France, its inability and unwillingness to control MIFERMA, and its monetary dependence on the Franc Zone. For them, political independence was meaningless without economic independence and complete control of national resources. Thus, the reforms of the early 1970s attempted to establish more control over the external relations of the state and to subjugate them to some explicit or implicit norms and standards of nationhood, independence, and sovereignty. For example, membership in the Arab League, revision of a series of technical and financial agreements with France, withdrawal from the Franc Zone and the creation of a national currency, and nationalization of MIFERMA illustrated the importance of the external relations of the state and the centrality of the issue of dependence for the political agenda of both the government and the opposition. These reforms strengthened the national identity of the country with more balanced relations between the Maghreb and West Africa and gave the state greater control over the national economy.

This attempt at nation and state crystallization was seriously challenged by a chronic fiscal crisis of the state in the second half of the 1970s, a crisis that was exacerbated by the burden of Mauritania's involvement in the war in the Western Sahara from 1975 to 1978. The crisis was further accelerated by a recession in the steel industry in Europe, where most Mauritanian iron ore is sold. Under the combined effects of the Western Sahara war and recession in the European steel industry, Mauritanian exports of iron ore dropped from around 12 million tons in 1974 to about 6 million tons in 1978. Drought also was often blamed for bringing about the crisis. Between 1973 and 1978 the live-stock and the grain production of the country declined by 8.5 percent and 44.9 percent, respectively.[60] Whatever the actual individual contribution of each one of these factors, the crisis was so severe that the civilian government was overthrown in a bloodless coup by the military in 1978 and a series of coups and countercoups[61] continued until 1984, when a new military government adopted, without hesitation or ambiguity, a full-scale adjustment program in close collaboration with the IMF and the World Bank. The military coup of 1984 was widely and officially publicized as *le mouvement de la restructuration*[62] (the restructuring movement), a euphemism for the sequence of SAPs in Mauritania. The next section presents a brief outline of the sequence of adjustment programs in Mauritania and their impacts on the Mauritanian state and economy as a preliminary summary of the detailed arguments that will be developed in subsequent chapters.

Sequence of SAPs in Mauritania

The military coup of 12 December 1984 represents a watershed in the history of adjustment policies in Mauritania. Three days after the coup, the president of the new ruling Military Committee of National Salvation received an IMF delegation in the presence of the minister of finance and commerce and the governor of the central bank. A few days later a World Bank mission arrived in Nouakchott to resume the policy dialogue suspended earlier. It was then that the new military government embarked on the full-scale adjustment program (proposed by the IMF and the World Bank) that had been rejected partly by the previous government.[63] This political change inaugurated a shift from government policies aimed (with little success) at managing the fiscal crisis of the state without completely renouncing state control over national economic policy to a new government strategy of trading economic policies for foreign loans and aid, a process that made the Mauritanian government progressively lose its hold over the national economy.

Economic liberalization or the process of opening up the national economy actually began with the launching of the Economic and Financial Recovery Program, the Programme de Redressement Economique et Financier (PREF), for the period 1985–88. The initiation of drastic reforms met little resistance in the beginning because it took advantage of the political mood created by the coup (liberation of political prisoners and blaming the former government for economic failure). The government agreed with the IMF on a short-term standby arrangement of $12 million signed in Washington, D.C., on 12 April 1985. The World Bank Group also provided several sectoral loans, including a $20 million loan (signed on 27 January 1986) for the restructuring of SNIM. The Paris Club met on 27 April 1985 to reschedule Mauritania's foreign debts, and the Consultative Group for Mauritania gathered in Paris (25–27 November 1985) to discuss the $540 million external financing requirement under the PREF covering the period from 1986 to 1988. This adjustment program was laid out in a first policy framework paper (PFP)[64] that was reviewed by the executive directors of both the IMF and the World Bank in September 1986. The second phase (1987–88) of the PREF program was supported by a structural adjustment loan (SAL 1) of $50 million approved by the World Bank board on 2 June 1987, with cofinancing from the Kingdom of Saudi Arabia ($4.8 million) and the Federal Republic of Germany ($2.8 million). This program also received additional financing of $19.6 million from the African Development Bank.

This pattern of partnership between the Mauritanian government and the above multilateral institutions continued systematically during the second phase of consolidation of the reforms (the Economic Consolidation and Growth Program 1989–91), when the government signed in 1989 the third policy framework paper. The IMF approved on 24 May 1989 a three-year arrangement equivalent to SDR 50.85 million for Mauritania under the enhanced structural adjustment facility (ESAF). The Paris Club held a meeting on 19 June 1989 for the third rescheduling of Mauritania's foreign debts. Then the Consultative Group for Mauritania gathered in Paris for the second time (25–27 July 1989) to discuss the $604 million public investment program under the Economic Consolidation and Growth Program 1989–91. The third adjustment program (1992–94) was adopted between late 1992 and early 1993 when the fourth PFP was signed, the fifth IMF arrangement was agreed upon, and the fifth Paris Club debt rescheduling was arranged. The government was the only partner in Mauritania working officially with these multilateral institutions. It was deeply involved in the implementation of adjustment policies and played a crucial role in handling their internal social and political ramifications. However, the government played a minor role in the conception, funding, monitoring, and evaluation of these policies.

The initiation of the strategy of adjustment in Mauritania began when a severe financial crisis induced the government to approach the IMF and the World Bank for assistance. These institutions do not accept government diagnoses of the economy they are going to assist. They have their own trained experts, their own methodology of analysis, and their own solutions for what they see as problems of development. Their intervention begins at the level of diagnosis, prescription, and formulation of policy. In this context, the World Bank produced a major report on the Mauritanian economy in May 1984, but the government did not endorse the findings until after the military coup of December 1984. This is the most important political step of adjustment because once the diagnosis and prescription of the World Bank are adopted by a government, the rest becomes essentially a matter of procedure and technical implementation. The next step is the establishment of a PFP based on the above diagnosis. It is widely publicized that there is no economic planning under adjustment—only market forces working at their optimum. But a careful analysis of adjustment policies leads to the conclusion that PFPs' economic planning is more rigorous than planning within the framework of the classic Plan of Economic and Social Development. The actual transition is from a national state-centered economic plan to a world-centered economic planning system, perhaps a new global command economy. According to the IMF,

The PFP is a forward-looking document, updated annually on a three-year rolling basis, that identifies the country's macroeconomic and structural policy objectives, the strategy of the authorities to achieve these objectives, and the associated financing requirements. The specific policy undertakings for the first year and general indications of policies to be pursued in the second and third years of the program are described in the PFP. The document also discusses the country's public investment program and financing requirements and outlines the likely social and environmental impact of policy changes, along with steps that can be taken to cushion the poorest segment of the population from any adverse effects. Potential creditors and donors—that is, members and multilateral organizations that may provide external assistance in support of adjustment programs—may be consulted informally in the preparation of PFPs and often draw on completed PFPs as a reference in making their own decisions about financial assistance. The PFPs are reviewed by the Fund's Executive Board and by the Committee of the Whole of the Executive Board of the World Bank.[65]

Within the framework of the PFP, the government, the IMF, and the World Bank agree on implementing a set of major policies for a period of three years. The details of those policies are then stated in separate agreements between the government, the IMF, and the World Bank. When these steps are taken, the government signs a standby arrangement with the IMF and then applies for a rescheduling of its debts before the Paris Club, where Mauritania's creditors meet under the chairmanship of the French Treasury to assess the financial situation of the country in the light of its progress in implementing adjustment policies. Once an accord is signed with the Paris Club, the government begins bilateral negotiations with its creditors on the details of the terms and procedures of rescheduling certain debts. At the same time, the World Bank works on establishing a Consultative Group for Mauritania, where international investors meet in Paris under the chairmanship of the World Bank and thoroughly analyze and assess opportunities provided by Mauritania's investment program. Each investor selects to finance partly or wholly certain development projects of certain economic sectors in certain regions of the country. Once the economic policies are defined in the policy framework paper, the terms of debt rescheduling are agreed upon with the Paris Club, and financing is provided through the Consultative Group, then the process of implementation of adjustment policies begins. Disbursement of funds for individual projects is then tied to a matrix of detailed policy measures that the government must implement in a given sector by a specified deadline. Throughout the period of project execution, the Bank (on behalf of international investors) undertakes a systematic monitoring of progress in all investment projects by a series of supervisory missions. They issue numerous mission reports that are processed at the Bank's headquarters in Washington before being presented officially to the government as binding documents. These reports assess government progress in executing the matrix of policy measures agreed upon with the creditor(s) in the loan agreement document. They either congratulate or warn the government on either progress or delay in the execution of policies. This is how the state and the government are literally robbed of their sovereignty and national prerogatives by playing a less and less important role in the conception, funding, monitoring, and evaluation of development policies. The international financial institutions take the reins of the state when they take the reins of the economy and vice versa. At this stage of adjustment, the state is denationalized and the process of devaluation of the economy can begin with little effective resistance.

Systematic and consecutive devaluations of the national currency have been the number one policy measure in adjustment programs and everywhere they have direct repercussions on the comparative advantages of nations. To my knowledge, there was no single case in which the IMF required overvaluation or appreciation of a Third World national currency: always and only devaluation and depreciation. As Sandro Sideri noticed, "International exchanges are determined less and less by natural and given comparative advantages, but increasingly by rapidly evolving man-made advantages."[66] Devaluation is based on the assumption that the national purchasing power is overvalued with regard to the world market and because of this, national exports are not competitive in the world market. To solve this problem a nation must devalue its currency to make its exports cheaper. When this takes place it is assumed that the volume of exports will increase and compensate for the loss in price caused by devaluation. But these are assumptions, not facts, especially in the context of economies based on the export of one or two major commodities. These assumptions represent a set of prepared rationalizations aimed at impressing and convincing peripheral states' bureaucrats, who often have little background in economics since their nominations have more to do with their allegiance to the political system in place than to their economic expertise. Many Third World countries export similar commodities, and any simultaneous increase of production and export of a given commodity in different countries following currency devaluation brings about a market glut and then a decline in world prices of that commodity.[67] In the 1980s, the prices of the principal commodity exports of developing countries have fallen by one-fifth and earnings by one-third, thus creating a loss of $120 billion.[68] Bringing down the export prices of Mauritanian iron ore or fish makes them competitive only if other worldwide producers of iron ore or fish are not following the same strategy, which is not the case. Therefore, exporting more and getting less represent the typical deterioration of the terms of trade that follows devaluation. This self-reinforcing cycle of producing more and getting less is the essence of the debt problem and better explains the puzzling absence of any significant accumulation at the national level despite the infusion of billions of dollars in the borrowing country. In addition, devaluation contributes, with inflation, to a dramatic decline of the purchasing power of all people because it devalues their production (export) and overvalues their consumption (import). The effects of huge amounts of grants and loans by the international community are nullified by devaluation.

Devaluation is a sophisticated economic measure that allows the international community of lenders and donors to turn the apparent flow of resources to developing nations into a net outflow from the South to the North. It is sophisticated because it is done through an overnight political decree that significantly reduces the value of all goods and services in an entire country and contributes to a major redistribution of wealth between a nation and the rest of the world. An example from Mauritania illustrates how devaluation offsets external aid. Total external aid (grants, loans, and technical assistance) to Mauritania was estimated by the UN Development Program at $245 million[69] for 1989, and around 50 percent of this amount is constituted by loans that will be paid back as principal plus interest. Mauritania's GDP in 1991 was estimated at $1.1 billion[70]. On 4 October 1992 the Mauritanian ouguiya was devaluated by 42 percent[71] after lengthy negotiations between the government and the IMF and the World Bank. Overnight, Mauritania's GDP was devalued by about $462 million in relation to the dollar, an amount that nullifies external aid for years. Moreover, many economic operators transfer a great amount of their assets to other currencies on the eve of each devaluation and keep them in foreign banks. This is capital flight, which is another form of capital outflow. Besides the obvious loss of assets following any devaluation, the financial environment it creates encourages capital flight. Capital inflow cannot match capital outflow resulting from such systematic devaluation, even if we assume that all external aid is constituted only of donations and grants. Among all adjustment policy measures, devaluation explains best the magic by which the international community of lenders and donors is able to keep a huge capital flow to Mauritania with little accumulation results in the country. That is one reason why adjustment continues unabated despite its failure to achieve its declared objectives. According to a preliminary version of a World Bank study on aid and debt in sub-Saharan Africa, Public Aid for Development finances more than 50 percent of imports in Mali, Somalia, Burkina Faso, Tanzania, Burundi, Central African Republic, Mauritania, Malawi, and Rwanda.[72] Devaluation is the extraordinary monetary policy by which such a generous foreign aid can be transformed into a lucrative business in a seemingly simple, but actually complex, system of exchange in which the seller provides cash for the buyer. Devaluation is above all a political measure requested by the international community of lenders and taken by states that are increasingly more responsive to international pressures than to domestic demands. Such states are defined in this work as denationalized states, i.e., fully unpacked states, more open to foreign influence and less in control of the process of conceiving, designing, and monitoring economic policy. Based on a detailed analysis of the geopolitical economy of the restructuring of the Mauritanian state, the next chapter addresses why and how the national state is becoming a multilateral state, that is, a denationalized state.

Denationalization: From National to Multilateral State

This chapter begins with a brief conceptualization of "denationalization" as a way of situating the analysis within the larger theoretical context of the current debate over the restructuring of peripheral states within the framework of SAPs. The rest of the chapter demonstrates how and to what extent the Mauritanian state is being denationalized. The emphasis is on how the internal relations and structures of the state are being adjusted to the imperatives of its relations with the outside world. The influence of international forces in shaping state policy is shown through a thorough examination of the power interplay between the government and international financial institutions. This is done through a detailed analysis of the geneses and processes of (1) formulation of public policy; (2) articulation of development strategies; (3) engineering of fiscal policy; (4) management of foreign debts; and (5) design of public investment programs. In all these various aspects of public policy, the role and agency of the state remain important yet secondary to the role of multilateral institutions.

Concept of Denationalization

The essence of adjustment in Mauritania (and elsewhere) is the reversing of a set of policies that aimed during the 1960s and 1970s to achieve two objectives: (1) securing a stronger position within the international system of states while constantly attempting to subjugate the external relations of the state to some imperatives of its internal relations and social structures, i.e., adjusting the "outside" to the "inside," and (2) assuring maximum political centralization and socioeconomic and spatial integration through state institutions and government policies, i.e., centralization. These two objectives constitute the backbone of state and nation building. To illustrate the genesis and the process of denationalization, I describe and analyze the role of the Mauritanian state and the international financial institutions in reversing this process of nation and state building through two sets of policies: (1) subjugating the internal relations and social structures of the state to the imperatives of its external relations, i.e., adjusting the "inside" to the "outside;" and (2) pursuing a certain degree of political and economic decentralization at the national level when centralization of wealth and power is completed at the international level. These two sets of policies represent what I refer to as denationalization and embody the shift from national to international accumulation. Because of the dialectical relationship between adjustment and denationalization of the state, the state is at the same time an instrument and a target for most adjustment reforms. State regulations were perceived as "symbols of all rigidities."[1] But deregulation of the state and expansion of market forces also need a strong state.[2] Even though the state constitutes a structure for initiating and consolidating adjustment, the agency for that initiation and consolidation is located outside the state structure, i.e., within a complex set of international forces among which the state is a partner at best. The Mauritanian case shows that the state played an important role in adjustment. But adjustment was not an initiative of the state even if we take into consideration the fact that adjustment reforms began first with a change of government in Mauritania (the bloodless coup of December 1984). The state debate needs to be guided and enlightened by the fundamental contradiction between national politics and global economics and geopolitics. Otherwise, it will face the danger of slipping toward some form of fetishism where the state is perceived as an entity beyond control of the government that is operating it. Most of the discourse of the state debate tends to divert us from focusing on the government in charge, the policies at stake, the social forces in motion, and the ways in which these effect and are being effected by events and actions outside the jurisdiction and political space of the nation-state. The debate is further confused by the problem of where to draw the line between the state and the government, between the national and the international, and between the economic and the political. But even though these different scales, structures, and agencies seem (technically) to operate separately, they work simultaneously within and without the Mauritanian state to produce adjustment policies that virtually rob the state of its sovereignty over national economic policies. As David Morris noted,

> the story of the late 20th century is massive centralization of economic power. This rush toward globalism makes the concept of political self-determination hollow. Ethnic or cultural "nations" may be allowed to retain their colorful native garb or even their religiously based moral codes. They will not, however, be allowed to control their own resources or manage their economies. They will be forbidden to nurture or even protect their domestic productive capacity.[3]

The ascendance of the international financial institutions involves a substitution of their own power for significant aspects of the traditional power of the state. In a way, the new power relations between the peripheral state and the international financial institutions are similar to the power relations between a client and his or her bank. Even though the bank depends on its clients, the latter (taken individually) have no control over the former. Because of their control over credit policy and their close cooperation and coordination, international financial institutions have the advantage of capital mobility while the peripheral state does not. The nature of such a relationship is actually of "a fixed state to a globally mobile capital."[4] The process of denationalization of the state referred to here includes but goes beyond the mere privatization and denationalization of public enterprises. As a profound restructuring of the state, denationalization seems to be the prevailing solution to the "increasing contradiction between the transnationalization of capital and the persistence of the state system as the exclusive political pattern in the world."[5] Susan George identified the following prerogatives lost by the state to the international financial institutions:

1. Control over the currency. Indebted countries must devalue when instructed to do so. This is supposed to make exports more competitive, but the effects are often negligible because so many countries are devaluing at once.
2. The fixing of macro-economic policy. The framework is set by the structural adjusters; only the details are left to the government.
3. The choices of foreign policy. The classic case is the carrot/stick approach applied to Egypt during the Gulf War.
4. The "monopoly of legitimate violence." At the Bank-Fund annual meeting in Bangkok in October 1991, the managing director of the Fund, Michel Camdessus, for the first time made clear that his institution would henceforward look much more closely at the military expenditures of its "clients." In his view the cessation of cold war hostilities made such expenditures obsolete. While we may welcome any measures leading to disarmament anywhere, the ability to make war and peace and

to defend itself have always been essential to the nature of the state.[6]

I show in the following sections how the Mauritanian state is losing control over fundamental tenets of sovereignty such as the formulation of policy, the articulation of development strategies, the engineering of fiscal policy, the management of foreign debts, and the design of public investment programs. A great deal of my evidence relies on the presentation, discussion, reading, and analysis of agreements and texts involving the Mauritanian government and its various partners in the international community of lenders and donors. This approach and the level of detail are crucial to understanding state restructuring and policy change. The balance of power between the state and international forces can be better evaluated by reading carefully agreements specifying duties and rights of each party under those agreements, a method often overlooked by previous research,[7] which relies heavily on secondary sources and economic statistics.

Genesis of Policy Formulation

Formulation of economic policy is a primary function of the state and an important element of planning. Policies are often solutions to some problems that are singled out following certain diagnostic studies that are themselves based on a great deal of data collection and analysis. Although Mauritania was a planned state during the 1960s and 1970s, actually the state planning system was not a rigid one. For example, we read in the second plan 1970–73: "This plan will essentially be a framework plan. Consequently, it will deal more with defining a broad general policy and sector policies than with the presentation of all the projects to be achieved during the four coming years."[8] This was so because the government did not have a precise data base and did not have the financial means for the execution of most of the projects. Indeed, the lack of a precise data base for planning convinced the government in 1978 to agree with the United States Agency for International Development (USAID) that it should carry out a comprehensive study of the rural sector and human resources in Mauritania to prepare the fourth Plan of Economic and Social Development (1981–85). The project, known by its English acronym, RAMS, engaged fifty-five specialists for varied periods of time over twenty-eight months and came up with forty-four formal studies and reports beside numerous other special inquiries and investigations requested from time to time by the services of the Ministry of Planning. This major study was the first one to criticize the strategies of development followed by the Mauritanian government since independence and to point out that weak planning in some areas and absence of it in others played an important role in the failure of development projects. The study also argued that the appropriate way to correct these failures is to create a sustained mechanism of planning and coordination that ensures discipline in planning and prevents the different ministries from following their own interpretations of development matters within their respective departments.[9]

The RAMS study also sowed the seeds for the subsequent strategy of adjustment in Mauritania and its market-oriented philosophy of development. Its findings constituted at the time the only comprehensive investigation dealing with a whole range of development issues (from environmental problems to government and politics) and providing an important data base and a market-oriented analysis, which were rapidly disseminated within influential circles of planners, politicians, academicians, and researchers. The American functionalist approach to sociology (emphasizing descriptive ethnography rather than class analysis) was largely applied to the overall study of the Mauritanian society, which was accordingly divided into six ethnic groups. The two major studies of sociological profiles were revealing in this regard with their carefully selected titles: *"Les Maures"* and *"La Mauritanie Négro-Africaine."* It is difficult to measure with precision the impact of these studies on the ethnic consciousness and ethnic strife that later plagued Mauritania. But these studies were the first to directly emphasize subnational identities, which the nationalist state had never acknowledged because of their potential danger for national unity and interethnic cohesiveness and coexistence. The study also set the direction and agenda for further market-oriented socioeconomic analyses and prepared the ground for subsequent systematic World Bank economic diagnoses. It should be noted that the RAMS study followed the guidelines of the Country Development Strategy Statement (CDSS) for Mauritania prepared by the USAID in January 1979. The CDSS document strongly criticized the development strategies of the previous regime as based on:

a policy of extensive state interference in the determination of the satisfaction of individual and collective wants, reflecting a collection of independent but nevertheless mutually reinforcing factors: (i) an ideological flirtation with socialist type state control of economic activity by some elements of the society; (ii) a French colonial legacy that favored centralized direction of economic activity; (iii) the tendency for

the new bureaucracy to have a vested interest in state control; and (iv) in some cases
the movement of the urbanized upper income class to social orientations that viewed
state control, or at least certain forms of it as the best means to satisfy their wants
at the expense of the masses of the people in the field of health and education, for
example.[10]

The development strategy put forward in the CDSS document
represents actually the mother of all development policies in Mauritania
from 1981 on. It preceded and paved the road for World Bank and IMF
structural adjustment programs. This illustrates the organic linkages
between USAID Country Development Strategy and World Bank
Country Memorandum. During the adjustment process the production of
socioeconomic data and analyses and the formulation of policies on their
basis were exclusively done by consultants of the World Bank, by
independent consulting firms[11] approved by the Bank, or within the
framework of workshops directly or indirectly arranged by the Bank.
Formulation of development policies has been an important part of
adjustment programs. Howard Wolpe (chairman of the Subcommittee on
Africa in the House of Representatives of the U.S. Congress) put it this
way: "Not only are the Bank and the Fund leading participants in the
international response to Africa's economic crisis, but they are also
furnishing the analysis and policy recommendations behind the aid
programs of bilateral donors including those of our own
Government."[12] The increasing marginalization of borrowing
governments in matters related to the formulation of their own national
policies was also observed by a Staff Study Mission of the U.S.
Congress visiting some African countries in 1988. The mission found
that "while the programs are almost always jointly designed by
international donors and recipient governments, it is recognized that the
local government role has been 'weakest' in sub-Saharan Africa."[13]
Local governments implementing adjustment policies have always
adopted World Bank diagnoses and prescriptions and often disseminated
them as "their" own diagnoses and prescriptions. This is the source of
a great deal of confusion about the real agency and dynamics of power
within and without the state apparatus. To assess the actual power
relations between the state and the multilateral institutions, it is necessary
to understand the genesis and the process of policy formulation.

In June 1979 the World Bank released a major report entitled "Islamic
Republic of Mauritania: Recent Economic Trends and Needs for Foreign
Capital." This study (similar in its approach to the RAMS study)
constituted the basis upon which a first stabilization program was adopted

by Mauritania in 1979 in collaboration with the Bank and the Fund. Although the Bank carried out several other studies dealing mainly with economic sectors, the major study upon which the first comprehensive adjustment program was initially conceived and carefully tailored was a comprehensive one entitled *"Memorandum Economique, République Islamique de Mauritanie,"* released on 10 July 1985. This study was initiated by a World Bank mission whose members stayed in Mauritania during April and May of 1984. A second mission came in December 1984 to update the findings of the first mission in the light of the military coup of 12 December 1984. The members of the first mission were Kathryn Larrecq (head of the mission and main writer of the study), Peter Boone, consultant (food and agriculture, projections), and Janvier Kpourou-Liste (foreign debts). The mission was assisted in the field by Rudolf Hablutzel, chief economist, Programs II Department, Regional Bureau of West Africa. The findings, conclusions, and recommendations of the study were discussed with the Mauritanian government on 1–6 June 1985. The problems diagnosed and the solutions proposed in this study constituted the framework for subsequent economic policies in Mauritania and their formulation within the framework of structural adjustment programs.

But however decisive economic policies are, they need an appropriate political, administrative, and legal environment for their implementation. Institutional and economic policies could not be implemented without the state. As Louis Emmerij put it, "The role of the state is essential whatever the ideology of the day may say."[14] Defining the exact role of the state in the adjustment process is crucial. "It is not whether the state has a role, but what the role is."[15] The government and the Bank have agreed that the economic and financial reforms could not succeed without an institutional and administrative reform since the state is involved in all development activities. They even acknowledge that one root cause of the country's economic predicament stems essentially from weak public sector management. The World Bank diagnosis focused not only on economic management but also on state institutions and the necessity to reform the administrative system and make it an efficient instrument of policy implementation and a safe environment for capital investment.

One of the most important instruments for the restructuring of the Mauritanian state was the Project of Institutional Development and Administrative Reform, better known by its French initials: PDIAR. It is a sort of joint venture that shows clearly the nature of partnership between the Mauritanian government and the World Bank in reforming the public administration from within. This is a concrete example of power sharing between the Bank and the government in restructuring state institutions in a way that makes them fit the need of economic adjustment. The project unleashed a new conceptual framework of governance and administration that continues to animate and fuel the entire operational process of institutional reforms in Mauritania. According to the *coordinateur* (coordinator) of the PDIAR, Moustapha Ould Khalifa, the project received one-fourth of the total funding provided by the World Bank for institutional reforms in Africa in 1986 and this, he said, demonstrates that the Bank finances, via this project, more research studies for new methods and procedures applicable in institutional reforms in other regions of the world.[16] The project illustrates the genesis of decision making and the growing influence of international forces within the state apparatus.

This project went through several phases from its inception to its implementation. It was first identified and conceived by a mission of two experts from the World Bank, Louis de Merode and Mireille Guigaz, who stayed in Nouakchott between 12 September and 4 October 1985. They produced a preliminary diagnosis of the Mauritanian government system. Their study was finalized and adopted by the headquarters of the World Bank in Washington, D.C., on 9 December 1985, and later presented to the Mauritanian government in the form of a sixty-five–page document.[17] The conclusions and recommendations of the study emphasized that the stage of the general diagnosis is now over and it is the duty of the Mauritanian authorities to take the next step in terms of political commitment and operational readiness. The document was then discussed and adopted by the Cabinet Council of the Mauritanian government in March 1986. Later, on 25 December 1986, two government structures (proposed by the study) were established by the government for the preparation and implementation of the project.

The first government structure was a consultative body, the Commission for the Institutional and Administrative Reform, created by Decree 86.213/PCMSN/PG. The commission is chaired by the minister of the civil service. He is assisted by a state controller and three advisors for the president. The other members include a representative from each ministry, the president of the University of Nouakchott, the director of the National School of Administration, a representative from the General Union of Mauritanian Employers, and a representative from the Union of Mauritanian Workers. These two latter representatives are nominated by the members of their unions, but the minister is entitled by the decree to accept or reject their membership in the commission. The members have no deputies or substitutes and their job is to formulate advice and recommendations on any question submitted by the minister and related to the institutional and administrative reform. The secretariat of the commission is held by the second government structure, labeled the Structure for Institutional and Administrative Development of the Reform, or simply the Coordination (of the project).

The Coordination (better known in French as *la coordination*) was created by Decree 86.214/PCMSN/PG. Its role is to coordinate the preparation and implementation of the reform among and within the different ministries and particularly to check the coherence of all bills that translate in legal or administrative terms any decision taken by the government in relation to the reform. It provides periodical evaluations of the project according to a schedule established by the minister of the civil service and the World Bank. The Coordination is consulted by the different ministries involved in the reform and can exchange correspondence directly with the Bank. The head of this structure is a coordinator appointed by the Mauritanian government. He manages the funds of the project and centralizes correspondence related to the project between the Mauritanian authorities and the Bank. He organizes the Bank missions in Mauritania and participates in their discussions. The Coordination represents an important articulation among the government and the Bank and a well-equipped cell[18] within the Ministry of the Civil Service. In fact, one recommendation from the World Bank study insisted that the Mauritanian government should demonstrate its commitment to the project by first appointing a coordinator who will be the representative of the World Bank in all the phases of the project.

The next phase in the implementation of the PDIAR was the dissemination of the World Bank diagnosis among the higher staff of the state at both the central and regional levels according to a well-designed trickle-down process of social learning. The Coordination attached a two-page introduction (dated 5 April 1987) to the original World Bank document and circulated it within the different ministries and among selected high state bureaucrats, including the members of the Commission for the Institutional and Administrative Reform. The introduction urges the reader to make sure that the World Bank "diagnosis and recommendations become Mauritanian, by Mauritanians" and welcomes suggestions and comments, which, it is said, will assist the Coordination in preparing a workshop for further discussion of the document and help the government in the forthcoming negotiations with the World Bank. On the other hand, the Coordination (in collaboration with the Bank) began organizing a general mobilization and preparation for state officials within the framework of a major workshop held in Nouakchott between 25 July and 5 August 1987. This workshop brought most high-ranking state officials from both the central and regional administrations together for learning about and discussing the World Bank diagnosis and prescription for reforming the Mauritanian administration. It was labeled "Days of Thought and Information for the Starting of the Administrative Reform." Introducing the workshop, the minister of the civil service, Mohamed Mahmoud Ould Deih, said, "The World Bank diagnosis should be corrected and completed by the Mauritanian cadres themselves, this is the objective of these days of thought and information."

The summary report emerging from the workshop was so similar to the early World Bank report that one wonders why the workshop was organized in the first place except perhaps to provide some feedback for the Bank's diagnosis. Discussions in the workshop were framed along the lines of the diagnosis and the recommendations of the World Bank document. The Bank's usual methodology of listing the objectives, identifying the constraints and selecting the means to overcome them, and taking advantage of opportunities was adopted by the workshop and followed by the two working groups dealing with the central and regional administrations. The actual goals of the workshop were to disseminate and propagate the diagnosis and prescription of the World Bank among state officials and employees and to set the stage for further professional training along those lines. In this regard, the Bureau Organisation et Méthode of the presidency was reorganized as was the *Journal Officiel*, which publishes government legislation and regulations. Along the same lines, a center for documentation and a cell for training civil servants were created within the National School for Administration, with which the Coordination signed a convention of cooperation on 5 November 1989. The convention stipulates in Articles 5 and 7 that the National School for Administration will put its faculty and its didactic and administrative experience at the disposal of the cell for training civil servants. Between 1988 and 1990, the Coordination of the project organized fourteen seminars in Nouakchott dealing with various aspects of the administrative reform and providing retraining for some 442 civil servants from all ministries and professional categories and ranks. At the same time, forty-seven cadres of the administration received higher training abroad in France, the United States, Canada, the United Kingdom, Morocco, and Tunisia.[19] These adjustment-trained cadres facilitated in many ways the implementation of policies and the propagation of the World Bank's desired approach to administration and economic management.

The conception, dissemination, and implementation of this and many other projects of economic management and administrative reform demonstrate that the Mauritanian state is losing the initiative in the process of policy formulation. It is the World Bank, not the government, that did the diagnosis and prescribed the solution in the economic and institutional arenas. The Mauritanian state issued the necessary decrees and regulations and set up the appropriate government structures, units, and ad hoc committees for the implementation of economic and institutional reforms that are based on studies and evaluations conducted by international consulting firms approved by the World Bank. All development projects within the framework of adjustment are identified and implemented in this way, which leaves an auxiliary role to the government in terms of policy formulation. By losing the ability to formulate policy, the state lost an important tenet of sovereignty and statehood. The economic and sectoral memoranda allow the World Bank to maintain a continuous dialogue with government officials and further penetrate the state bureaucracy to formulate policies and ultimately to shape the strategy of development at both the central and sectoral levels.

Articulation of Development Strategies

Prior to the adjustment program, the Mauritanian state adopted strategies of development within the framework of National Plans for Economic and Social Development laid out by specialized government structures occasionally assisted by foreign consultants selected by the government. With adjustment, the state followed a strategy of development stated in a policy framework paper laid out in close collaboration with the World Bank and the International Monetary Fund. This change placed the state in a position of less control over the conception of development strategies. Planning in Mauritania began in 1963 when the Commissariat Général du Plan was established and attached to the Office of the President. Four plans for economic and social development were adopted throughout the 1960s, 1970s, and early 1980s. Even though these plans were highly dependent upon external financing, each plan was centered around a strategy of development (laid out by the central government) and an investment program (often over 30 percent of GDP) proposed by the different ministerial departments. Overall, planning was not as centralized and rigorous as it is now under the adjustment program. The government institution in charge of planning was moved twelve times among different ministries throughout the 1960s and 1970s. It was even curiously attached to ministries and government departments such as urbanism and tourism, civil service, foreign affairs, rural development, handicraft and tourism, and mining and fishing.[20] The process of selection of development projects was flexible and the follow up was sometimes poor. For example, among the 157 planned development projects within the framework of the Second Plan (1970–73) only 48 were completed by 1976.[21] Such a poor record in state management of development projects was used by lenders and donors as a leitmotif for change in the volume and management of investment programs.

Within the adjustment program the strategy of development is laid out in the PFP that is developed by the Bank and the IMF in collaboration with the Mauritanian government. The idea of PFP was endorsed and developed by the executive directors of the Bank and the Fund following U.S. Secretary of State James Baker's initiative in 1985. According to James W. Conrow (deputy assistant secretary for developing nations, U.S. Department of Treasury), Baker proposed that the Bank and the Fund first coordinate their intervention through a three-year policy framework paper negotiated and agreed upon with the borrowing country, then they "negotiate independent, but related policy-based lending programs consistent with the overall framework."[22] The first policy framework paper for Mauritania (covering the period from July 1986 to July 1989) was reviewed by the executive directors of the Bank and the Fund in September 1986. It represents a political commitment of the government to implement a development strategy based on a careful management of demand (stabilization) and a dynamization of supply (structural adjustment) through a wide range of specific financial and economic policies. The declared objectives of the first PFP included: (1) 4 percent annual growth rate of GDP; (2) lowering the inflation rate from 7 percent in 1986 to 5 percent in 1990; and (3) reducing the deficit of the external payments account to zero by 1989–90.

The strategy of development in the first PFP represents a departure from the previous plans. The public investment program was reduced from 32 percent of GDP in 1984 to around 20 percent of GDP over the period covered by the first PFP. A greater amount of investments (42.1 percent of the total investment program) was allocated to rural development. The main reforms focused on economic policies in four areas: (1) management of public finance and administrative reform, (2) rehabilitation of public enterprises, (3) restructuring of the banking system, and (4) management of the external sector. The second PFP[23] was adopted in 1987 as a document that lays out and reviews the first PFP 1986–89 by presenting development and progress accomplished during the first year and identifying actions of economic and financial policy to be pursued during the period from July 1987 to July 1990. The main areas of reform continued to be public finance management, public enterprises, banking, agriculture, fishing, and the legal and regulatory frameworks. The main factors of growth were identified in agriculture, fishing, and small and medium enterprises. Over 150 measures of economic policy were originally scheduled in the first and second PFP, but a record of 176 measures had already been implemented by 1989.[24]

The third PFP (1989–91)[25] was reviewed by the executive board of the Fund and the Bank on 12 May 1989. It was preceded by discussions between a seventeen-member delegation of the Mauritanian government headed by the minister of economy and finance, Mohamed Ould Nani, and a twenty-one member joint delegation from the IMF and the World Bank in Washington on 13–22 February 1989.[26] Its declared objectives were: (1) 3.5 percent annual growth rate of GDP; (2) reduction of annual rate of inflation from 7 percent in 1987 to 4.5 percent in 1991; and (3) reduction of current account deficit from 11.8 percent of GDP in 1987 to 3.5 percent in 1991. The government made a commitment to take all necessary measures to achieve these objectives. Ninety measures of economic policy were specified and annexed to the thirty-seven-page PFP for implementation between 1989 and 1991. They fall within ten major policy areas that encompass all aspects of political economy in the country as shown in table 5.

Table 5 PFP Scope of Policy Reforms

1. Agricultural policy	6. Management of public sector
2. Industries, fisheries, energy	7. Public finance policy
3. Public enterprises	8. Monetary and credit policy
4. Banking sector	9. External sector
5. Price policy	10. Human resources

Source: Compiled from "Matrix of economic and financial measures" of the third PFP.

The fourth PFP (1990–93) was drafted in 1990.[27] We can read in paragraph 10 of that draft: "despite some progress achieved in the framework of previous PFPs, the Mauritanian economy is still fragile and its prospects in the long run are uncertain." Negotiations between the government, the Bank, and the Fund on the fourth PFP were completed in 1990, but the governor of the Mauritanian central bank sent a letter to the IMF on 17 July 1990 requesting certain modifications of some economic policy measures agreed upon in the PFP document. His request was rejected by the Fund and the Bank in a conjoint reply, which reads:

> we have already informed our services of the positive conclusion of our consultations with the Mauritanian authorities on all points in the PFP except the issues related to the *Banque Nationale de Mauritanie* (BNM) and the *Union des Banques de Développement* (UBD). We would like to draw your attention to the fact that some of the modifications you are suggesting tend to reduce the significance of the reforms we agreed on and run the risk of weakening the process of adjustment in which your country engaged itself.[28]

The invasion of Kuwait by Iraq in August 1990 and the subsequent U.S.-led Gulf War in 1991 delayed negotiations between the government and the Bank because the United States (with its well-known influence over the Bank and the Fund) did not accept Mauritania's sympathy with Iraq. In hearings before the U.S. Congress held three months after the end of the war, one member of the panel noted: "In Mauritania, the U.S. has really few ties. We have ended our bilateral aid program and it seems that we are on the way to ending support for the multilateral aid program to Mauritania"' because of its pro-Iraq position in the Gulf War even though it is now "seeking ways to get back into the world's good grace."[29] Negotiations of the fourth PFP resumed again in Nouakchott in March 1992 and continued in Washington, D.C., where the PFP document was finally signed on 13 November 1992.[30] The long negotiation process was partly due to the reluctance of the Mauritanian government to accept the devaluation of the ouguiya by about 42 percent, especially in the immediate aftermath of the 1992 presidential and parliamentary elections, during which the adjustment program was harshly criticized by the public and the press. Although the two main presidential candidates carefully avoided talking about adjustment throughout their campaigns in order not to alienate the international financial institutions and/or the voters by raising controversies about liberalization policies (see in the next section why adjustment policies did not constitute the major issue of the electoral campaign).

When comparing the PFPs with previous planning processes, one comes to the conclusion that adjustment represents actually a very rigid system of planning of the whole economy and its different sectors. While most preadjustment planning was done at the national level, most postadjustment planning is done and coordinated at the global, national, and local levels. It is not an exaggeration to speak of a new *global command economy*. The state has little control over the articulation of development strategies. The three-year PFP is systematically revised and updated before the third year and no economic policy measures can be taken outside the framework stipulated in the PFP. In the plans, the statement of goals and means are established by the government. The implementation is done by various government departments and agencies that are supervised by the central government and the politburo of the single party. Within the framework of PFPs, the Bank and the Fund are responsible for most of the conception of economic policies, while the government's role is essentially to facilitate and guarantee the implementation of these policies. The plans were mainly commitments from the government to itself, while the PFPs represent commitments from the government to the Fund, the Bank, and beyond them to the international community of lenders. The state is not only losing control over the planning of the overall strategy of development but also over other important tenets of detailed economic policy, particularly fiscal policy and the control of money supply and credit allocation.

Engineering Fiscal Policy

Regulation of money and allocation of credit represent important functions within the state system. Control of money and credit is the first means of regulation of the state.[31] The central bank plays a "pivotal role"[32] within the state system and represents the instrument through which government policies determine the amount of money to be printed, the rate of exchange with other currencies, the amount of credit to be allocated, and the priorities and procedures of such allocation in accordance with a predetermined strategy of development. Mauritania created its own currency, the ouguiya (UM), and central bank in 1973, and continued to perform the above functions prior to the adjustment programs. But from 1985 on, special binding arrangements between the government and the IMF began seriously to challenge the ability of the state to perform these functions independently. The IMF interference with credit and monetary policies illustrates the far-reaching process of denationalization, since money issuing is perhaps the last tenet of state sovereignty. To the central bank of Mauritania, the IMF became simply what the central bank of Mauritania is to the primary banks in Mauritania. Although the IMF seems always as an apolitical institution dealing exclusively with money and finance, it has strong political leverage on small states. One of the first international figures to visit Mauritania following the 1992 presidential and parliamentary elections was Michel Camdessus, managing director of the IMF, who came to pressure the government for a 42 percent devaluation of the ouguiya. Speaking to the press in Nouakchott, he noted, "I came to see how the President, the Premier, and the Opposition see the future of the country."[33]

In 1990, the IMF had a membership of 155 countries. But as adjustment expands and the process of debt and credit centralization worldwide continues, more countries are scrambling to get membership in the IMF. As of June 1993, membership reached 178 countries.[34] Mauritania has been a member since 10 September 1963 and has a quota of SDR 47.5 million in 1992. This represents about 0.03 percent of the SDR 144.5 billion quotas of the IMF since 1993 and gives Mauritania virtually no voting power. The value of the Mauritanian currency (the ouguiya) is determined in relation to a basket of currencies—on top of which is the U.S. dollar—but under obligations of Article IV, 1(iii) of the Second Amendment of the Articles of Agreement of the IMF (30 April 1976) members shall avoid manipulating exchange rates to gain competitive advantage over other members. Section 2(b) of the same Article IV also gives full authority to the IMF to "exercise firm surveillance over the exchange rate policies of members." This obligation and the firm surveillance of the IMF do not leave room for Mauritania to manipulate fluctuation in the value of currencies, rather it must adjust its exchange rate to those fluctuations. The lack of full control over the exchange rate is aggravated by the systematic devaluation of the ouguiya (agreed upon officially from time to time by the government and the IMF) and its almost annual depreciation following the adoption of a flexible exchange rate policy, i.e., adjusting the value of the ouguiya to fluctuations of certain world major currencies instead of manipulating those fluctuations to maintain the value of the ouguiya. In 1981, one U.S. dollar could purchase only UM 48.3, while in 1994 one U.S. dollar could purchase UM 128.3. The depreciation of the ouguiya was even worse in relation to the French franc (France is still the first trading partner of Mauritania). To better illustrate how the Mauritanian state is losing control over its financial policy, I will describe and analyze the balance sheet of the second and the proposal of the third standby arrangements as typical examples of the six arrangements that the government has so far signed with the IMF between 1985 and 1992. The emphasis will be on how these arrangements systematically limit the ability of the state to pursue sovereign decisions in matters of money, credit, and other crucial economic and financial policies.

The third standby arrangement was signed on 5 May 1987.[35] It was prepared by the members of an IMF mission who stayed in Nouakchott between 8–24 February 1987.[36] The mission helped the government to draw up the Letter of Intent and the Memorandum of Economic and Financial Policy that were reviewed and accepted by the executive board of the IMF in May. The Letter of Intent is dated 24 February 1987, cosigned by the minister of economy and finance, Mohamed Salem Ould Lekhal, and the governor of the central bank of Mauritania, Dieng Boubou Farba, and addressed to Michel Camdessus, the IMF managing director. It documents the progress the government has accomplished in the implementation of the previous IMF arrangement of 1986 and its operational readiness and political commitment to implement further policies within the framework of a new arrangement with the IMF in 1987. Moreover, the minister and the governor made it clear (paragraph 3) that the government is ready to take additional policy measures (beyond those specified in the Memorandum of Economic and Financial Policy) if requested to do so by the IMF managing director. The measures of economic policies requested by the IMF and implemented in one year by the government under the 1986 IMF arrangement are summarized in table 6. They were comprehensive and virtually put the Mauritanian economy under siege for twelve months to meet the IMF realization criteria. Whether these arrangements are called standby, structural adjustment facility (SAF), or enhanced structural adjustment facility (ESAF), or any other successor program, they all represent "an effective vehicle for formulating macroeconomic policies and structural reforms"[37] in developing countries.

The IMF evaluation of the implementation of the above balance sheet reads: "the IMF Services congratulate the Mauritanian authorities for their commitment to increase the role of the private sector in all aspects of economic activity," particularly their commitment to review (in 1987) all restrictions on imports in order to implement further liberalization policies. The performance of the government in executing the IMF program of 1986 constituted enough evidence for the IMF board to trust

Table 6   Balance Sheet of IMF Program in 1986

Policy measures required by the IMF	Government implementation
A. Budgetary policy 1. Reduce budget deficit from 4.6% of GDP in 1985 to 3% of GDP in 1986 2. Bring about surplus in Treasury operations equivalent to 1.5% of GDP 3. Increase tax on commercial/industrial profits and wages; reduce customs duty 4. Freeze personnel expenditure and stop hiring except in the ministries of education and health	Deficit reduced to 2.5% of GDP Surplus reached 1.1% of GDP Measures implemented Ceilings on personnel expenditure and hiring
B. Money and credit 1. Increase internal banking credit by only 5.5%; increase credit to non-governmental sector by 7.1%; freeze credit to the state 2. Rehabilitate the banking system	Measures implemented (credit to the state decreased) Measures implemented
C. Price and marketing policy 1. Reduce list of goods subjected to price control 2. Increase agricultural prices 3. Limit free distribution of grain to 50,000 tons	Implemented Implemented Implemented
D. Public enterprises 1. Accelerate rehabilitation of public enterprises 2. Improve the financial situation of the company for distribution of petroleum products (SMCPP)	Implemented (tariffs on electricity increased) Implemented
E. Public investment program 1. Implement public investment program for 1986 in consultation with the World Bank 2. Establish an investment budget for 1987	Implemented 1987 budget adopted
F. External sector 1. Continue the policy of flexible exchange rate 2. Negotiate a debt rescheduling with the Paris Club and the other official lenders	Implemented (the ouguiya was depreciated in 1986) Agreement with Paris Club on 16 May 1986 (negotiations completed with lenders except Brazil and Netherlands)

Source: Compiled from IMF Document EBS/87/73, April 1987.

Mauritania to implement another program for 1987. Table 7 presents a summary of the economic policy measures that the government committed itself to implementing under the 1987 IMF arrangement. They are similar in many ways to those of 1986 and provide a tight frame for fiscal policies for another twelve months. Paragraph 29 of the Memorandum of Economic and Financial Policy particularly emphasizes the following performance criteria that must be met: (1) ceiling on total internal credits, (2) ceiling on banking credits to the state, (3) commitment of the government not to accumulate any internal or external arrears, (4) commitment of the government not to contract or guarantee any loans except within the framework of debt rescheduling, and (5) commitment to tighten restrictions on government and bank indebtness *except for import credits*. Throughout the period of an IMF arrangement, Mauritania cannot impose restrictions on payments and transfers relating to international (current) transactions or institute dealings of multiple exchange rate or impose restrictions on imports. These three conditions represent the essence of any stabilization program. Their real goal is not necessarily to solve the budget and balance of payment deficits but to maintain an open world trade and payment system and prevent the government from putting restrictions on the transfer of capital and/or the import of goods and services, these being the policy measures that really attack directly the balance of payment deficit but at the expense of international trade and capital mobility.

So far six arrangements have been signed between Mauritania and the IMF within the framework of adjustment. They prevent the state from exercising full control over the money and credit systems and many other macroeconomic and sectoral policies that the state used to control prior to the adjustment program. Without signing such arrangements, the state will not obtain the right to purchase millions of special drawing rights from the IMF to continue payment for its imports on the one hand, and the Paris Club will not agree to reschedule Mauritanian debts on the other hand. The conditions specified in the IMF arrangements are also similar to those specified in all World Bank loans. If they are not met by the government, the Bank will immediately suspend loan disbursements. Finally, if Mauritania does not comply with IMF conditions, it will be declared an insolvent country and will not be able to import goods and services from the world market, and the international community of lenders will not invest in or provide loans for Mauritania. Such developments lead often to shortages of food and inadequate supply of the market, something that can trigger riots and eventually the overthrow of the government. This scenario always haunts the government. Even though many state officials see clearly the negative impacts of IMF arrangements, they do not dare to publicly criticize them because they would lose their jobs. Many of them are convinced that given the narrowness of the internal market and the concentration of economic power, free market by itself cannot stimulate economic, social, and cultural development for the majority of the people.[38] That fear is combined with the fact that state officials and politicians (whether from the ruling or opposition parties) do not see any alternative policy that will preserve their privileges and at the same time solve the internal and external deficits, even in the short run.

The opposition was legalized only from late 1991, well after structural adjustment policies became a fait accompli. Its leader (Ahmed Ould Daddah, former minister of finance and half brother of the first Mauritanian president, Mokhtar Ould Daddah) was himself working as a consultant for the World Bank while an economic advisor for the government of the Central African Republic before he returned to Mauritania and ran for the presidency in January 1992. He lost the elections and could not have won them, not only because he had been away from the country for years, but also because he underestimated the power of the military, the appeal of Arab nationalism, and the depth of the ethnic fissure following the events of April 1989 between Mauritania and Senegal. He was perceived by many Mauritanians (partly under the effect of the ruling party's propaganda) as even more likely to go further with adjustment policies if he got elected. The other two 1992 presidential candidates (Moustapha Ould Mohamed Salek, a former Mauritanian president, and Mohamed Mahmoud Ould Mah, a Nouakchott University professor of economics) who vehemently criticized and condemned adjustment obtained together less than 4 percent of the votes. The bulk of the population did not make a direct link between the decline of their standard of living and the implementation of adjustment austerity programs. On the one hand, politicians could make a more effective appeal to voters by raising other issues such as cultural identity, ethnic affiliation, Arab nationalism versus francophonism, and pro-West, anti-West[39] than by raising adjustment policies, which are too complex to be easily understood and more difficult to articulate in a way that can make an effective appeal to the general public. On the other hand, many politicians consider SAPs a necessary evil and carefully avoid raising them, and when pushed to do so they easily find ways to mislead people about these policies. In this

Table 7 Policy Measures of IMF Program in 1987

A. Budget policy
1. Increase budget surplus from 636 to 1,400 million ouguiya in 1986–87.
2. Increase budget revenues by 15.4% in 1987 by reforming investment code, import license, and tax system.
3. Limit increase of budgetary expenditures to 11.2% in 1987; limit the growth wage bill to 8.6%; freeze the personnel to its level of December 1986 for all ministries, except the ministries of education and health.
4. Limit investment expenditures for public sector to 12.5 billion ouguiya.
5. Do not accumulate public arrears.

B. Money and credit
1. Limit the growth of total credit to 6.5% and redirect it exclusively to the nongovernmental sector (including public enterprises) and limit banking credit to the state to its level of the end of 1986.
2. Promote mobilization of saving by encouraging the creation of a network for collecting deposits in the rural areas and abroad.
3. Improve the distribution of credit for the agricultural sector.
4. Complete the rehabilitation of the banking system by merger by increasing participation of foreign capital and the private sector, and by strengthening surveillance of the central bank.

C. Public enterprises and price policy
1. Implement the rehabilitation program of the mining company (SNIM) and of the company for the distribution of petroleum products (SMCPP); strengthen the rehabilitation of the power and water distribution company (SONELEC).
2. Liberalize marketing of petroleum products.
3. Abolish subsidies for consumption of butane gas.

D. Agricultural policy
1. Limit the role of the food security agency (CSA) in marketing grains and encourage the participation of the private sector in the activities of marketing and transforming grain products.
2. Sell rice mills to the private sector.
3. Adjust rice prices.
4. Intensify the Food for Work program.

E. External sector
1. Maintain a flexible exchange rate.
2. Liberalize exchange regulation for exporters and review import licenses.
3. Negotiate with Paris Club and other lenders external financial aid.
4. Do not contract new (short term) external borrowing except for imports.
5. Do not accumulate external arrears.

Source: Compiled from IMF document ESB/87/73, 7 April 1987.

regard, the policy of currency devaluation could easily be interpreted by naive public opinion as resulting from market fluctuations (a sort of modern metaphysics) about which nothing can be done. Such metaphysical representations continue to influence even the most sophisticated liberal economist today, let alone the public.

Moreover, adjustment policies and particularly the details of IMF arrangements were never known by the public, and few state officials have ever seen or read an IMF standby agreement. Such documents are always labeled as confidential, and their first page reads "IMF Document, Do Not Communicate to the Public."[40] With the process of democratization and its free press, the confidentiality and sensibility of adjustment-related documents became even more officialized and the number of state officials having access to those documents and participating in high-level negotiations with the IMF and the World Bank was limited to the ministers of planning and finance, the governor of the central bank, and the director of the budget. During negotiations of the fourth PFP in Nouakchott in March 1992, the Mauritanian delegation was composed of four members, compared to seventeen members in 1989 during negotiations of the third PFP in Washington, D.C. Information dealing with adjustment became so centralized that only one or two persons have access to it in an entire ministry or institution. For example, at the central bank only two persons (the governor and the director of credit) have access to the text of standby arrangements. When I wrote several times to the governor of the central bank requesting access to those documents, I received four months later a letter saying that they cannot be communicated because they are confidential.[41] The secrecy and taboos surrounding such fundamental policies contribute to a great deal of confusion about the actual political economy of adjustment and seem to open the door for a variety of erroneous interpretations, extrapolations, and mere speculations, which can easily lead to the fact that people generally cannot relate their successes or failures to policies they do not understand correctly. This political economy of ignorance is crucial for further confusing SAP's victims, at least during the early shock of an unpopular economic policy measure. For the government, an agreement with the IMF provides temporary cash for the payments of imports and, more important, constitutes a sine qua non condition for rescheduling Mauritania's foreign debts within the framework of the Paris Club, another international forum that has more and more leverage on the Mauritanian state through the centralization and management of foreign debts.

Management of Foreign Debts

One leitmotif of the adjustment process in Mauritania is the debt problem. In 1984 the outstanding foreign debt of the country was $1.7 billion and the debt service $88 million (28 percent of export earnings). In 1988, with three consecutive debt reschedulings (1985, 1986, and 1987), the outstanding debt reached $1.806 billion, while debt service soared to $182 million (36 percent of export earnings). In 1990, the outstanding debt reached $1.9 billion, or about $1,000 per capita. Prior to adjustment the Mauritanian state was able to do business with its creditors on an exclusively bilateral basis. Foreign aid (loans, grants, and technical assistance) averaged $270 million annually between 1979 and 1984, something equivalent to $170 per capita[42] (approximately 40 percent of GDP per capita). Within the adjustment program, particularly its rescheduling component, Mauritania deals with its creditors on a multilateral basis within the framework of the Paris Club. Case-by-case dealings with Third World debts have been decided and reiterated in several G–7 summits. Originally the Paris Club represented an informal group of the finance ministers of the ten wealthiest member states of the International Monetary Fund (the Group of Ten). These are: Belgium, Canada, the Federal Republic of Germany, France, Italy, Japan, the Netherlands, Sweden, the United Kingdom, and the United States. While the London Club (of banks) deals with nonofficial and nonofficially guaranteed debts, the Paris Club (of governments) deals exclusively with government or government-guaranteed debts. As the debt crisis deepened in the developing nations throughout the 1980s, the Paris Club became an institutionalized forum where requests from developing nations for debt rescheduling are formally presented to a World Bank-led gathering of international creditors. The club meets monthly in Paris under the chairmanship of the French Treasury. Debt rescheduling within the framework of the club can take place only if the country requesting it maintains a standby arrangement with the IMF and commits itself to implement a set of carefully specified policies. In the following I will describe and analyze four reschedulings of Mauritania's foreign debts within the framework of the Paris Club. This will demonstrate the declining bargaining power of the state when facing the international community of lenders organized in the Paris Club. It should be noted that almost all Mauritanian debts are guaranteed by the government. Like the text of each PFP document, the text of each Paris Club agreement is signed page by page as a rigorous method of commitment not only regarding the content but also the wording of the agreement.

The first rescheduling of Mauritanian foreign debts took place in Paris on 26 and 27 of April 1985[43] following the signature of an IMF arrangement in Washington two weeks earlier. The creditors present at this meeting were representatives from the Federal Republic of Germany, Austria, Spain, the United States, France, Kuwait, the Netherlands, and the United Kingdom. Also present were observers from the governments of Finland and Japan, from the International Monetary Fund, the International Bank for Reconstruction and Development, the secretariat of the Conférence des Nations Unies pour le Commerce et le Développement (CNUCED), and the Organization of Economic Cooperation and Development (OECD). The Mauritanian delegation presented the economic and financial difficulties facing Mauritania and expressed the firm determination of the government to solve the financial and economic disequilibria and to reach the goals stated within the framework of the latest standby arrangement. The IMF delegation presented a description of the economic situation in Mauritania and the main points of the adjustment program that was implemented in the country and supported by a standby arrangement covering the period from 12 April 1985 to 11 April 1986. The delegation emphasized the precise commitments of the government in economic and financial policies. The representatives of the community of lenders noted the policy measures undertaken by the government within the adjustment process. They underlined how important the regular and full implementation of the program was, particularly the revitalization of the productive sectors, the improvement of public finances, and the efficient management of the country's external earnings. Following these presentations the representatives of the creditors decided to recommend to their governments or organizations a rescheduling of certain categories of Mauritania's foreign debts according to the specific terms of rescheduling outlined in table 8. The categories of debts targeted were commercial credits and loans (contracted for more than a year and prior to 31 December 1984) guaranteed by the governments or appropriate organizations of the creditor countries participating. Ninety percent of principal and interest from those categories was rescheduled to be reimbursed in ten semestrial payments between 1990 and 1994.

The Mauritanian government committed itself to seek rescheduling of its debts according to the Paris Club terms and accepted to provide an equal treatment for foreign creditors (public and private) and not to make any discrimination between them. Debts less than SDR 500,000 were not

Table 8   Terms of Debt Rescheduling in 1985

1. Definition of debts targeted: a) commercial credits, guaranteed or ensured by the governments or appropriate organizations of the creditor countries participating, contracted for a period of more than one year and signed prior to 31 December 1984. b) Loans from governments or appropriate organizations of the creditor countries participating, contracted for a period of more than one year and signed prior to 31 December 1984.
2. Terms of rescheduling: a) 90% of principal and interest (from the above loans and credits) due from 1 January 1985 to 31 March 1986 will be rescheduled or refinanced. Reimbursement by the government of Mauritania will be made in ten semestrial payments which are equal and consecutive, the first being on 1 January 1990 and the last on 1 July 1994. The remaining 10% in principal and interest will be paid as follows: One-fourth on 31 March 1986 One-fourth on 31 March 1987 One-fourth on 31 March 1988 One-fourth on 31 March 1989 b) 90% of principal and interest (from loans and credits mentioned in paragraph 1) due on 31 December 1984 will be rescheduled or refinanced. Reimbursement by the government of these rescheduled debts will be made in eight semestrial payments which are equal and consecutive beginning 1 January 1989 and ending 1 July 1992. The remaining 10% in principal and interest will be paid as follows: One-third on 31 March 1986 One-third on 31 March 1987 One-third on 31 March 1988 Interest rates and conditions of the above rescheduling will be determined bilaterally between the government of Mauritania and the government (or organization) of each creditor country participating on the basis of appropriate market rates.

Source: Compiled from "Procès verbal agreé relatif à la consolidation de la dette de la RIM," Paris, 26–27 April 1985.

included in the provisions of this agreement and had to be paid no later than 31 September 1985. The participating creditors informed the government that they would communicate to each other a copy of their bilateral agreements with Mauritania in application of the present agreement. Each participating creditor was to inform the president of the Paris Club about the date of signature of its bilateral agreement with Mauritania, the interest rates applied, and the amount of debts rescheduled.

By the same token the government would inform the president of the Paris Club of the contents of its bilateral agreements with the other creditors and would pay to participating creditors and observers all its other debts not included in this agreement as soon as possible, but not later than 30 September 1985. Moreover, the government was to take all necessary administrative measures to allow private Mauritanian debtors to pay to the central bank of Mauritania the equivalent of their debts in the local currency. Last but not least, the provisions of this agreement were to be applicable only if the Mauritanian government continued to maintain an agreement with the IMF and made sure that all agreements to be signed with banks and other creditors conformed to the conditions specified in this debt rescheduling agreement. Written reports concerning bilateral debt rescheduling agreements were also to be sent on a regular basis to the president of the Paris Club.

The second agreement between Mauritania and the Paris Club was signed on 16 May 1986. The participating creditors were the Federal Republic of Germany, Austria, Brazil, Spain, France, Morocco, the Netherlands, and the United Kingdom. Observers from the United States, Italy, Japan, the International Monetary Fund, the International Bank for Reconstruction and Development, the secretariat of CNUCED, and the OECD were also present. The agreement was very similar to the first one: 95 percent (instead of 90 percent in the first agreement) of the same category of debts was targeted for rescheduling or refinancing. The reimbursements were to be made in ten semestrial payments that were equal and consecutive beginning 31 March 1991 and ending 30 September 1995. The remaining 5 percent was to be reimbursed in two equal payments on 31 March of 1987 and 1988. The third agreement for debt rescheduling was signed on 15 June 1987. Beside the above creditors, new ones were present at this meeting. They included Belgium, Canada, Sweden, Switzerland, and the Commission for European Communities. The creditors took note of Mauritania's "chronic problems of balance of payments aggravated by important debt services and a very low per capita income." The same category of debts as in the second agreement was targeted for rescheduling or refinancing, i.e., certain commercial credits and government loans. Ninety-five percent of principal and interest in those categories was rescheduled to be reimbursed in twenty semestrial payments that are equal and consecutive beginning 1 April 1993 and ending 31 October 2002. The remaining 5% was to be paid no later than July 15, 1987.

The fourth agreement was signed on 19 June 1989. The participating creditors took note of the durable and structural problems of the balance of payments and debt service of the Mauritanian government combined with a very low per capita income. Because of this and since Mauritania was implementing an important adjustment program, the creditors saw that Mauritania's debts deserve "an exceptional treatment." The debts targeted in this rescheduling include not only certain commercial credits and government loans but also the reimbursement of principal and interest resulting from the 1985 and 1986 reschedulings. The French and the Japanese did cancel certain Mauritanian debts and rescheduled others. The other creditors rescheduled the payments to a period ranging from 1997 to 2014. The latest debt rescheduling accord between Mauritania and the Paris Club was signed in early 1993,[44] but I have been unsuccessful in getting access to its text.

The Paris Club allows the creditors to coordinate their policies in debt matters. This coordination provides to each creditor the needed information on debts. Mauritania cannot bargain separately with the creditors and cannot discriminate between them. It must deal with the creditors as a well-organized international financial group. This strategy of dealing with debt issues on a case-by-case basis was emphasized in many G-7 meetings, especially in Venice in 1987 and Houston in 1990.[45] This is why a debtor cartel could not take place and why developing nations have not been able to put together a collective strategy that will force the creditors to make concessions on debt issues. The coordination between creditors is not limited to debts but also to credit and investment policies, another important tenet of national sovereignty lost by the state to the international community of lenders and donors.

Design of Public Investment Programs

Within the framework of adjustment, the public investment program of a borrowing nation is presented to the Consultative Group, which is a formal gathering for international lenders seeking to invest in a particular country. It was conceived by the World Bank as an instrument for monitoring public investment programs and centralizing loans and other forms of investment that are not provided directly by the Bank or the Fund. It also provides an insurance for creditors that their money will be used within the framework of an investment climate and procedures that will guarantee their money back with enough profits. By 1982 dozens of Consultative Groups were already formed to oversee investment in dozens of developing countries, and in June 1988 the Multilateral Investment Guarantee Agency was created as an instrument within the World Bank Group that "ensures private foreign investment in developing countries against non-commercial risks such as expropriation, civil strife, and inconvertibility."[46] Almost all Consultative Groups are chaired by the World Bank. The first Consultative Group for Mauritania gathered in Paris on 26-27 November 1985 to examine the investment program of Mauritania for the period 1985-88. The second meeting took place on 26-27 July 1989. In this section I will describe and analyze the latter meeting based on its minutes of proceedings dated 12 August 1989.[47] It is an example of further coordination between international lenders and a testimony of the inability of the Mauritanian state to control or finance its investment program. The meeting was held in Paris and chaired by Michael Gillette, director of the Sahel Department at the World Bank. The twenty-five-member Mauritanian delegation was headed by the minister of planning and employment, Moustapha Ould Abeiderrahmane. The other delegations were composed of thirty-nine members of bilateral and multilateral lenders from seven countries and ten banks and development organizations.[48]

Opening the meeting, chairman Gillette stated that the forum offers an opportunity for Mauritania to present its development program for 1989-91 and its related public investment program and to indicate and explain the impacts of recent civil strife (of April 1989) and ask for assistance in establishing a reinsertion program for Mauritanians repatriated from Senegal. He also underlined the significance of the recent Paris Club meeting in which Mauritania's debt was rescheduled. Discussions within the Consultative Group were centered essentially around the following four themes: (1) implemented government policies from 1985 to 1988 and planned programs for 1989-91; (2) reinsertion program for Mauritanians repatriated from Senegal; (3) implementation of land reform; and (4) public investment program for 1989-91. In his presentation, the Mauritanian minister of planning[49] summarized the objectives achieved within the framework of the Economic and Financial Recovery Program 1985-88, which was supported by the IMF, the World Bank, and other lenders. He then reaffirmed the commitment of the government to continue the process of adjustment through the implementation of the Economic Consolidation and Growth Program 1989-91 as defined in the third policy framework paper, which was reviewed by the IMF and the World Bank in May 1989. He reminded the lenders that Mauritania's foreign debts represent 180 percent of its

GDP and the investment program under consideration represents only 16.6 percent of GDP, compared to over 30 percent prior to adjustment.

Some participating creditors commented on the government program and approved what had been done and suggested what should be done. The IMF representative expressed support for the government adjustment program and emphasized that Mauritania needs further financial aid for its medium-term program. He informed the Consultative Group that the IMF board had recently approved a three-year structural adjustment facility program of SDR 50.85 million for Mauritania. Several members of the group noted that despite earlier progress, the external financial situation of the country remains fragile due mainly to the burden of foreign debts. Other members expressed reservations on issues such as budgetary discipline, social dimensions, environment, reform of the banking system, and execution of public investment programs. They expressed satisfaction about the size and composition of the public investment program for 1989–91, but they recommended more rigor in the process of selection and execution of productive projects.

The Mauritanian minister of planning presented the reinsertion program, which was initially prepared in collaboration with an interinstitutions team led by the UN Development Program. The program aimed at solving the many problems created by the sudden repatriation from Senegal of hundreds of thousands of Mauritanians who had been living in Senegal for decades and who lost all their properties there, estimated one time by the government at some CFA (Communauté Financière Africaine) franc 1,500 billion,[50] or the equivalent of $4.6 billion (clearly an overestimation since the GDP of Mauritania is four times smaller than this amount). The program includes two phases: a relief program aimed at providing food and other needs during the first six months and a two-year program aimed at training and job creation. In presenting the report, the minister noted that the government encouraged the reintegration of the repatriated within the traditional framework of solidarity (i.e., extended family, tribal solidarity, and so on) to avoid establishing camps that would need long-term public aid and hence budget outlays. Most refugee camps for repatriated Mauritanians, particularly in Nouakchott, were dismantled by the government and integrated within regional and tribal social structures.[51] The costs of the first phase of the program were estimated at $18 million, while the costs of the second phase of training and job creation were estimated at about $42 million.

The representative of the UN Development Program announced that the

UN General Secretariat would submit soon the report of the interinstitution mission to all donors at the UN seeking their assistance. Many creditors expressed their concern about the additional burden imposed on the Mauritanian government following the unexpected arrival of the repatriated and declared their intention to participate in the relief program by providing food, financial resources, and other aid. For the second phase of the program, aid was also provided in terms of training and credit. However, certain donors wanted further clarification on the institutional procedures of the program. Others wanted further details about certain components of the program. It was also noted that the training activities could be adapted in a way that encourages the private sector to participate in the program, especially in economic sectors where the state has to withdraw in accordance with the adjustment program.

In general, the Consultative Group saw that the components of the insertion program should be harmonized with those of the social dimension of the adjustment program. Many donors noted with satisfaction the government decision that allows access to training and credit for all needy people and not just the repatriated. Although a small number of those repatriated was to be settled in the irrigated agricultural zones, several donors recommended that Mauritania proceed cautiously with the program given the uncertainties related to the situation in the Senegal River valley.[52] All participating members welcomed the idea of creating a temporary governmental structure in charge exclusively of implementing the insertion program when the government announced the creation of an interministerial working group and invited all interested donors to participate. This group aimed at defining the main features of the reinsertion program in close collaboration with the UN Development Program. The president of the Consultative Group suggested to the participating members to hold a separate meeting during the annual gathering of the IMF and the World Bank in Washington, D.C., at the end of September 1989 to examine the revised program. This proposition was accepted and it was decided that financial contributions to the program be examined at that time. The reinsertion program for Mauritanians repatriated from Senegal was thoroughly discussed by the Consultative Group because of its humanitarian, economic, and political significance.

In his presentation of the development program for the period 1989–91, the Mauritanian minister of planning and employment insisted particularly on the necessity of accelerating the development of the agricultural sector. In this regard he emphasized the determination of the government to implement land reforms that were recently approved within the context of the project of adjustment of the agricultural sector that would be supported by the World Bank and other lenders. He pointed out that the policy measures agreed upon were implemented on time and confirmed that the subsequent measures would also be implemented as scheduled. He invited all donors interested in the implementation of land policy to join the World Bank missions in charge of supervising the project of adjustment of the agricultural sector. Several creditors and donors who contributed to irrigation projects in the Senegal valley expressed their concern about the impact of the conflict with Senegal; certain projects were seriously affected by the departure, following the trouble, of some of those who were supposed to have benefited from them. They also expressed reservations about the future of projects already under way. All agreed that reducing tension between Mauritania and Senegal was essential for reestablishing favorable conditions for an orderly improvement of irrigation potential in the Senegal valley. The Mauritanian delegation agreed on this and noted that progress of the Mauritanian economy depends largely on establishing good relations with its neighbors, pointing out the willingness of the government to intensify regional cooperation. Moreover, the government indicated that any Mauritanian national displaced following the recent events could return and further departures would be avoided. Many donors encouraged the government to continue the implementation of its land reform and welcomed its decision to invite other donors to participate with the Bank in the supervision of the project of adjustment of the agricultural sector. Several donors noted that the implementation of land reform will be watched not only by the creditors but also by other African countries because it constitutes one of the first regional attempts at an extensive land reform in which the traditional collective ownership of land would be replaced by a system of private ownership based mainly on capital investment. The socioeconomic ramifications of this land reform are partly responsible for the exacerbation of the crisis between Mauritania and Senegal, as well as within the Senegal River valley region.

Concerning the last point on the agenda of the meeting, the government presented its strategy of public investment based on the objectives of the reform program and centered around rural development, fishing, mining, and human resources as the productive sectors of the economy. The proposed public investment program amounted to $604 million (approximately UM 45.3 billion) of which 93.7 percent was provided by the community of lenders and donors, while only 6.3 percent was to be funded by Mauritania. It represented a decline of investment from 30 percent of GDP in 1984 to 16.6 percent in 1989.[53] All delegations expressed their support for the development program of Mauritania, even though some of them thought that the investment program was perhaps too large. Nevertheless, certain donors indicated that they would probably increase their financial support for the development of Mauritania, but the exact destination of their contributions would be decided later during bilateral negotiations with the government. They were pleased by the commitment of the government to continue adjustment programs, but they expressed concern about the repercussions of the crisis between Mauritania and Senegal on the implementation of the agricultural reform on the one hand, and on the budgetary implications of the return hundreds of thousands of repatriated Mauritanians on the other hand.

The Consultative Group for Mauritania is another international forum where the Mauritanian state has to present and explain "its" policies, especially policies of investment. How much to invest, where to invest it, in which sector, what are the priorities of investment, and so on, are all important decisions in which the Mauritanian state is a partner among many others. The investment program is based on "a strict selection of projects"[54] and is defined within the context of a strategy of development specified in a policy framework paper prepared in close collaboration between the government and the services of the IMF and the World Bank. The priorities in investment among regions (projects supporting export-related activities) and sectors (the agricultural sector has potential for strengthening the private sector) is determined following diagnoses and recommendations of consultants and experts funded and cleared by international creditors and multilateral institutions. The state is coordinating actions of lending and investment among all these actors. In all those meetings and discussions in Washington, Paris, and Nouakchott, the state is one voice among many others. But the state is not only facing serious challenges from multilateral institutions and donor countries within the framework of international forums, it is also facing strong competition from lender missions and NGOs working in its own backyard.

5

Denationalization: Lenders and NGOs within the State

Introduction

The Mauritanian state is losing control over much of its national and international policy, particularly the formulation of economic policies, the laying out of development strategies, the engineering of fiscal policy, the management of debts, and the design of public investment within the adjustment process. Even though the state is responsible for the implementation of these policies, it is strictly supervised and monitored by multilateral agencies in putting them into effect. The functions of identification, preparation, supervision, monitoring, and evaluation of adjustment policies and related development projects are always done by missions of experts from the community of lenders, particularly the World Bank. The lenders do not trust the ability and willingness of the state in articulating efficient development projects, even though the government is strongly committed to implementing those projects. The Bank designed a system of continuous monitoring through tranching loan disbursement and policy actions to be taken prior to negotiations of loans. The role of supervising missions is to make sure that policies are implemented in the right place and at the right time and to penetrate the state's influential circles and the economic sectors through a systematic dialogue with government officials. In the following sections, I will examine how the state is also losing control over the above aspects of its internal policy. The focus will be on the ability (or inability) of the state to monitor the implementation of policy and the execution of development projects. I will analyze the ways in which missionaries from the international community of lenders (World Bank missions) and donors (NGOs) are scrambling for the conception and implementation of national and local development projects and therefore competing with the state in its own backyard. I will give specific examples of the preparation and implementation of one structural adjustment loan and one sectoral adjustment loan and the subsequent division of labor between the government and the community of lenders within the framework of SAPs.

Lender Missions and Government Committees

Lender missions and government committees represent the fora where both political and technical measures of SAPs are negotiated in detail. It is estimated that African countries conducted some 8,000 separate negotiations with international creditors between 1980 and 1992.[1] Any correct understanding of the African political economy today requires a correct understanding of the division of labor between these government committees and international lender missions, particularly what Matthew Martin has referred to as the bargaining processes between Northern creditors and Southern debtors.[2] Their conjoint work and close collaboration on SAPs represent a new parameter of the emerging *multilateral state*, since they constitute the fundamental articulation between the state and international financial institutions. In the case of Mauritania, it is clear[3] that government committees were often impressed by the power, wealth, prestige, and know-how of the international financial institutions, while the latter were astonished by the weakness, lack of initiative, and acquiescence of these government committees. State officials and World Bank consultants compete with their fellows to be nominated as members of these committees and missions. Members receive important financial and prestigious rewards, and, in some cases, personal interest between members seems to have developed. In others cases, criticism of a government committee by an international lender mission has led to Cabinet reshuffles. In all cases, the bargaining power of lender missions is greater than that of government committees, as will be indicated through the detailed analysis of the various stages of conception, implementation, and supervision of the first structural adjustment program in Mauritania.

The first structural adjustment loan (SAL 1)[4] for Mauritania covers the period from June 1987 to December 1988 and emphasizes policy reforms in six areas: public administration, banking and public enterprise reforms, energy, food policy, fisheries development, and private sector promotion. According to the World Bank Program Completion Report of January 1990,[5] seventy-seven out of ninety-nine monitorable policy actions had been fully implemented in the above reform areas, nineteen were under way in December 1988, and nine had not been implemented. These sweeping reforms complemented others taken in 1985 and 1986 within the framework of the Economic and Financial Recovery Program (1985–88) and opened the way for many more in the subsequent Economic Consolidation and Growth Program (1989–91). To better understand the division of labor within this project between the government and the lenders, I will examine the identification, preparation, negotiation, financing, monitoring, and evaluation of this major program by World Bank missions (see table 9).

Table 9   World Bank Missions for SAL 1

Mission Objective	Month/Year	Number of Persons	Date of Report
Preparation	January 1986	7	January 1986
Preappraisal	March 1986	7	March 1986
Appraisal	June 1986	15	September 1986
Supervision I	November 1987	8	December 1987
Supervision II	February 1988	3	March 1988
Supervision III	May 1988	4	July 1988
Completion	December 1989	1	December 1989

Source: Compiled from World Bank, Country Operations Division, Sahelian Department, Africa Region, "Islamic Republic of Mauritania, Structural Adjustment Program, Program Completion Report, 12 January 1990," Annex I.

The program was initiated by a World Bank mission of seven specialists who stayed in Mauritania during the month of January 1986 for the preparation of the project, especially the initiation of a policy memorandum on the basis of which the government was to draft its Letter of Development Policy. In March 1986, a preappraisal mission assisted the government in drafting the Letter of Development Policy and defining the major elements of a structural adjustment program, particularly the establishment of conditions for tranche releases. The appraisal mission included fifteen specialists and stayed for two weeks in Nouakchott in June 1986. It finalized with the government the Letter of Development Policy, which identified monitorable policy actions to serve as tranche release conditions. The following prenegotiation mission in March 1987 updated the Letter of Development Policy and finalized the elements of discussion on the first structural adjustment loan (SAL 1) program, particularly the banking-sector reform component. Finally, SAL 1 was negotiated in May 1987 and approved by the executive board of the Bank on 2 June 1987.

Monitoring the program began with the first supervision mission in November 1987. The mission noted progress in some areas (public expenditure management and investment programming) but reported delays in others (banking reform, energy policy, and public enterprises). It pointed out the "lack of commitment of the concerned authorities." The World Bank Completion Report stressed that the decision-making process was almost paralyzed due to a power struggle within the military, an aborted coup, social unrest, and a financial scandal that resulted in the incarceration of the minister of finance, the minister of fisheries, and the governor of the central bank. The second supervision mission of February 1988 noted progress in economic management, energy policy, and fisheries policy, but it criticized delays in reforms related to food policy and the restructuring of public enterprises and the banking system. The blame for these delays was put on "the exceptionally weak economic team which was in place in late 1987 and early 1988."[6] Following this supervision mission, several ministerial reshuffles were undertaken and the Bank Completion Report noted that between November 1987 and December 1988, the World Bank task manager of SAL 1 met with four different ministers of economy and finance and three different governors of the central bank. The report of the third supervision mission of May–June 1988 expressed satisfaction about the "new government team, which was more dynamic and more committed to the adjustment effort."[7] However, the report noted certain delay in the restructuring of the banking system and public enterprises, even though the reasons for the delay were described as "beyond the government's control."[8] Nonetheless, the mission recommended that tranche release be deferred until October 1988. Negotiations to release the second tranche of the structural adjustment loan continued later in Washington, D.C. After a series of discussions, the World Bank delegation insisted that disbursement would take place only if the conditions in table 10 were met. These conditions concern (1) price and marketing policy of grains and the restructuring of the Food Security Agency (Commissariat à la Sécurité Alimentaire [CSA]); (2) restructuring of the banking system; (3) personnel training for the unit in charge of maritime fishing surveillance; and (4) the implementation of the new investment code. As the details in table 10 illustrate, the Bank was so inquisitive in its conditions that it did not leave to the government even the margin of selecting its wording and style in writing "its" regulations.

The last mission was a completion mission that took place during the month of December 1989 and involved one specialist (Miguel Saponara) from the World Bank. It concluded that "the predominant influences on the performance of the economy during the PREF and SAL periods were world market prices for Mauritania's principal exports (fish and iron ore) and imports and also external factors such as weather, but not necessarily the effects of adjustment."[9] But even though the SAL 1 program did not play a major role in the performance of the economy, it was perceived by the Bank mission as a success since the Mauritanian economy became more decentralized and market-oriented because of the SAL program. Delays in reforming the fisheries, agriculture, and the banking system retarded the momentum of adjustment. Another problem noted by the Bank report is the difficulty for the government to reach consensus, even though the success of the overall program was explained by the "firm commitment of the President and economic teams in place at the time."[10] The first structural adjustment program prepared the ground for the more detailed sectoral adjustment programs.

Another major adjustment program that illustrates the division of labor between the government and the Bank and more precisely between government committees and lender missions involved the process of preparing and monitoring the agricultural sector adjustment loan (AGSECAL), better known by its French acronym, PASA. Even though Mauritania is well known for its arid climate, agriculture continues to be a major focus for international investment, and its share of total investment programs has steadily grown with adjustment mainly because of its potential for strengthening the private sector and market mechanisms.[11] The weakness of the public sector in agriculture is another good reason for the Bank to concentrate on this sector. Thus, adjustment of the agricultural sector represents a priority for the Bank, as well as for the government, which has often been criticized for its systematic neglect of agriculture over the past decades. The project was

Table 10   Conditions for Second Tranche of SAL 1

A. Concerning price and marketing policy of grains, the following measures must be completed: (1) issue a decree concerning food policy. The decree should include the following comments: (a) *Article 12*: the content of this article will be specified in a ministerial decision stipulating: (i) that CSA will reduce its purchases of locally produced rice from 20,000 to 8,000 tons between 1988/89 and 1990/91; and (ii) that CSA will take all necessary measures to purchase annually 6,000 tons of locally produced rice from small producers receiving assistance from SONADER; (b) *Article 18*: change the second sentence of this article with the following specification: a progressive withdrawal (of CSA) from the secondary marketing centers as early as 1990 and whenever the private sector shows a minimum of efficiency and moderation in speculation; (c) end decree by: "all previous provisions and clauses contrary to this decree are abrogated;" (2) sign sale contracts for ricemills to the private sector; (3) sign a management contract for CSA garage to the private sector; (4) the provisions described in Article 12 should be publicized by all media; (5) other measures: (i) publish a ministerial decision creating a committee for annual food programming that includes foreign lenders and donors; (ii) produce a report on CSA purchases of locally produced rice (paddy).

B. Concerning bank restructuring, the following measures are to be taken or to be completed: (1) recover bank loans, (2) merge SMB and BIMA into one bank, the Banque Nationale de Mauritanie (BNM), open 30 percent of shares in the new BNM bank to the Mauritanian private sector, and keep the current manager of the BNM until a technical partner or other satisfactory form of management such as a foreign manager is found, and (3) sign agreement plans between the central bank and all primary banks.

On the other hand the World Bank would like to have the following documents: (a) balance-sheets of UBD and SMB/BIMA before and after audits of accounts with a detailed description of the way the audit was conducted and how much did the state take responsibility for, (b) updated schedules of bank audits in accordance with those of 1988.

C. Concerning personnel training for the unit in charge of maritime fishing surveillance, the government must take all necessary measures in order to begin the technical training of the personnel by the end of March 1989.

D. Concerning the implementation of the new investment code and its ministerial decision of execution, the Bank wants some clarifications and specifications to be made at the time of preparation of the draft decision dealing with the procedure of approval of investment projects.

Source: Compiled from "*Procès verbal des discussions entre the Gouvernement de la RIM et la Banque mondiale sur les conditions de deboursement de la 2eme tranche du credit d'ajustement structurel, le programme d'investissement 1989–1991, et le cadre macro-economique, le 28 février 1989*," World Bank, Washington, D.C.

prepared by a World Bank mission[12] composed of many specialists on all aspects of rural development. They began by organizing subgroups within different ministries to make the task easier and also to mobilize the administration from within by creating connections and inculcating new methods of teamwork within the Ministries of Rural Development and Interior. Land reform is not just a technical and financial matter since it involves social problems related to expropriating landowners and displacing communities. It also involves dramatic changes in property rights since it abolishes collective ownership of land and establishes individual ownership. In Mauritania, the situation is further complicated by ethnic conflicts over land along the Senegal River. It is important to note that those conflicts over land were quite minor in the past decades, but in recent years they became serious due to important investments made by international lenders in the area, particularly after the completion of two major dams (Manantali and Diama) along the Senegal river within the framework of the Organisation de la Mise en Valeur du Fleuve Senegal (OMVS), which includes Mauritania, Mali, and Senegal. They led partly to the April 1989 crisis between Mauritania and Senegal and the repatriation and insertion problems discussed in the previous chapter.

The mission first set a schedule of operational actions[13] for the project and identified a series of thirty-two policy actions that had to be taken immediately in several areas such as irrigation, land reform, price and marketing, agricultural credit system, organization of the Ministry of Rural Development, livestock, research and training, and environmental protection. It took the government about eight months to complete the paperwork and implement the recommended policy measures. One of those measures was the creation of the Technical Support Committee (Comité Technique d'Appui) for the day-to-day execution of of the adjustment of the agricultural sector. This committee came to reinforce the already existing planning cell within the Ministry of Rural Development, which is financed for the most part by the main lenders and which actually represents a ministry within the Ministry of Rural Development. All services and institutions within the Ministry of Rural Development and the Direction of Planning were placed permanently at the disposal of the committee for any information, investigation, and control that is deemed necessary for monitoring the adjustment program of the agricultural sector. Other policy measures that were to be taken immediately include the promulgation of a code for irrigated perimeters, creation of a National Land Commission, preparation of a decree liberalizing the grain market, and conclusion of an agreement between the Union des Banques de Développement (UBD) and the rural development agency (Société Nationale pour le Développement Rural [SONADER]) to provide loans for peasants.

As soon as the preparation of the project was completed, a new World Bank prenegotiation mission arrived in Nouakchott.[14] The mission report congratulated "the government for the excellent progress it had made so far in implementing the sectoral adjustment program"[15] and informed it that the Bank had invited all lenders to participate in the cofinancing of the project and that the French Caisse Centrale de Cooperation Economique and Ministry of Cooperation, the Federal Republic of Germany, and the World Food Program had already expressed their interest in cofinancing the project. The mission recommended that, before negotiations, the government enter into official contact with these foreign lenders to set the terms and define the details of their participation in financing the project. Given the progress already made in the preparation of the project, the mission came up with a schedule of operations that shows how the Bank is able to put government committees to work within the framework of strict deadlines and tight procedures.[16]

Thanks to this mission, the government finalized and sent its Letter of Development Policy to the Bank on 12 April 1989. It committed itself to restructuring the agricultural sector along the lines of the strategy laid out in the different PFPs, standby arrangements, and individual loan agreements. First, there must be encouragement and incentives for private investment in the agricultural sector through efficient policies in land matters, prices, marketing, and the credit system. Second, efficiency of public services in the agricultural sector should be improved through the progressive transfer of their commercial activities to the private sector and the concentration of their efforts on planning and organizing the appropriate environment for improving land. Third, a new land and environmental policy must be defined by taking into consideration the conclusions of the post-dam study for the Senegal River region and the promotion of river crops. In all these programs, priority was to be given to the integration of livestock raising and to environmental protection in all development activities. To ensure an effective implementation of the adjustment in the agricultural sector, the strengthening of interministerial coordination was to be assured by the minister of rural development assisted by a technical committee headed by the director of planning and including representatives from the Ministries of Rural Development,

Interior and Post and Telecommunications, and Hydrology and Energy. Finally, the agricultural sectoral adjustment loan was signed on 26 February 1990 by the government and the Bank. The International Development Association (IDA) provided SDR 19.4 million, while the Federal Republic of Germany, the Caisse Centrale de Cooperation, and the World Food Program provided 3.5 million Deutsche Marks (DM), 50 million French francs (FF), and $1.3 million, respectively.

Supervision of the project was conducted by missions led by the World Bank and included members from the other cofinanciers of the project. One of the conjoint general supervision missions took place between 28 May and 13 June 1990 and was composed of specialists from the World Bank, the Caisse Centrale de Cooperation Economique, and the French Ministry of Cooperation. The mission stressed the role of the Technical Support Committee in mobilizing state institutions for implementing the agricultural adjustment program. In particular, a national mobilization campaign was to focus on state officials, the private sector, and the peasants; the coordination, follow-up, and supervision would be systematic and would not be undertaken only by the Technical Support Committee but also by the ten subgroups that worked in close collaboration with the Bank during the initial preparation of the project and during this mission. The mission recommended that these groups meet monthly to review the progress of adjustment in their subsectors and every three months a complete review report should be presented to the Technical Support Committee for review and sent to the lenders. It also reiterated one recommendation of a previous mission (December 1989) that invited the government to take into consideration the rights (in land ownership) of particular Mauritanian groups that were displaced following the conflict between Mauritania and Senegal in April 1989. The mission recommended a timetable of operations (see table 11), which shows how the lenders are organized as a group quite capable of holding accountable not only the government but also its different technical departments and agencies in executing specific policies. The Cabinet Council, the Ministry of Rural Development, the Ministry of Interior, and the Rural Development Agency all are responsible and individually accountable before the lenders for taking particular policy measures and meeting specified deadlines. This level of leverage and penetration fragments the authority of the government among a growing number of committees often working separately with lender missions. It also marginalizes many government institutions that are not directly involved in the adjustment process. This occurs when adjustment units or cells are established within certain ministries and endowed with generous financial resources and the best and most qualified staff as exemplified by la Cellule de Planification, which represents a ministry within the Ministry of Rural Development. The process of decentralization of state institutions and administrative procedures are actually providing new windows for a well-coordinated intervention by lenders and donors. While the government is decentralizing its institutions and chain of command, the lenders are increasing their centralization and coordination of the conception and supervision of development projects. For example, the Ministry of Rural Development does not centralize all information related to the PASA project, but the lenders do.

Table 11 Timetable of Operations for AGSECAL

Policy Actions to be Taken	Accountable Institution	Deadlines
Meet conditions specified in the CCCE loan	Government	--
Send to the lenders minutes of meetings of the Technical Support Committee of the Project	Ministry of Rural Development	15 July 1990
Every three months, send to the lenders minutes of meetings of the ten subgroups	Technical Support Committee	15 July 1990, 15 October 1990, etc.
Begin the implementation of land reform in Trarza East once the necessary new structures are established in Nouakchott and Rosso	Ministries of Interior and Rural Development	1 September 1990
Send to the lenders a report on the progress in the implementation of the recommendations of the roundtable held for restructuring SONADER	Rural Development Agency (SONADER)	31 December 1990
Lenders's second supervision of the Project	Lenders	December 1990
Implement policy measures to release the second tranche of the loan	Government	6 December 1990

Source: Compiled from Banque mondiale, Caisse Centrale de Cooperation Economique, and Ministère Français de la Cooperation, "Aide-memoire, mission de supervision du Projet d'ajustement agricole et amelioration de l'irrigation, 28 mai au 13 juin 1990."

The next conjoint mission of supervision issued its report in July 1991. The report congratulated the government for the progress in implementing the matrix of policy measures.[17] In particular, the report stressed progress in four areas: (1) the reorganization of land administration, the setting up of the necessary technical assistance, and the publication of laws and regulations relating to the reform; (2) the launching of the operation of land regularization in Trarza-East; (3) the establishment of a new and autonomous framework for agricultural credit within the UBD bank and the definition of new procedures for granting loans; and (4) the abolition of the monopoly practices in rice import by the Société Nationale d'Import et Export (SONIMEX). The mission reminded the government that some policy measures were not implemented and that the release of the second tranche of the loan would depend upon their implementation. Other measures were in the process of implementation but they were not at the stage that would have allowed the mission to recommend the release of the second tranche of the loan. These include (1) improvements in debt recovery from agricultural loans, (2) acceleration of the restructuring of SONADER, (3) implementation of land reform in Trarza-East, and (4) changing the Decree no. 91–093 of 5 June 1991 to make it more adaptable to liberalization of rice imports. On the other hand, the mission was satisfied with the government decision to reserve half of the agricultural land for eventual returnees from Senegal. Government compliance on this issue was requested repeatedly by previous World Bank missions and constitutes a major concession to the lenders on what is considered a sociopolitical domestic problem. The main concern for the Bank (which represents other creditors) is the possibility of social conflicts that can jeopardize current and future investments in the only major agricultural region of the country. This concession raises other questions since the Mauritanian government had always maintained that those expelled to Senegal were Senegalese, not Mauritanians.

It should be noted that World Bank missions are highly informed about detailed social and political conflicts within the country. They have a huge data base about Mauritania in the headquarters of the Bank in Washington and an important team of country specialists and advisors that includes some Mauritanian nationals. They also have had an important resident mission in Nouakchott since 1985, and it provides them with the necessary logistic and infrastructure for conducting a thorough analysis on any aspect of the political economy of the country. Mission reports are first presented to the government at the end of the mission, but they become official reports only when they are read and processed in the headquarters of the World Bank in Washington, D.C. For example, the above report (July 1991 mission) became official only when the Bank sent the following telex from Washington on 13 August 1991 to the ministers of rural development, planning, and interior:

> We are honored to confirm the conjoint report issued by the International Development Association, the French Ministry of Cooperation, and the *Caisse Centrale de Cooperation Economique* on July 10, 1991, with the following amplifications.

These amplifications stressed two points. The first is the lender insistence on protecting the rights of groups and individuals displaced during the conflict between Mauritania and Senegal in April 1989. Some of these groups were living for decades in villages in and around the agricultural area of the project. The Bank wanted the government to send to it the detailed administrative and political measures already taken and the future intentions of the government in solving this problem. The telex emphasized that providing such information would help discussions of these issues in September when Katherine Marshall, director of the Sahel Department at the World Bank, was scheduled to visit Mauritania. The Bank's insistence on the politically sensitive issue of the deportees had a lot to do with its real and potential use as an effective and embarrassing way of pressuring the government for more concessions on adjustment policies in general. In this regard, Katherine Marshall sent a letter to the Mauritanian president on 30 October 1991 in which she insisted that progress in land reform and related social problems was the main stipulation for continuing aid to Mauritania. The second point was the Decree no. 91.093 of 5 June 1991. The Bank stated in the telex that "the text of the decree is incompatible with the objectives of the project"[18] and therefore should be changed.

It is clear from the above that the primary functions of supervision and monitoring of major adjustment policies and development projects are no longer in the hands of the state. Lender missions of supervision are working at all levels and within all sectors to make sure that policies are implemented in the field as they were stated in the government letters of intent and in the matrix of policy measures attached to all loans. The role of the state does continue to be crucial in providing the necessary legal framework and political environment for the foreign consultants to do their job within the country. The state is becoming a mere local partner and a law enforcement agent for a well-organized international community of lenders entwined together primarily by the World Bank Group. I have provided examples above in which loans from different countries (Germany, France, Saudi Arabia, and so on) are managed by the Bank within Mauritania. The International Development Association, which is considered the "soft window" of the World Bank Group, reviews annually its projects in all sectors of the Mauritanian economy and communicates directly with different ministries. Its review report of the fiscal year 1991 summarized the problems encountered by the different World Bank missions in Mauritania and urged the ministers to "solve these problems in order to promote the growth of the private sector which is the main objective of development in Mauritania."[19] The significance of the role of the state in providing security and safety for organized international capital is likely to diminish in the long run since all development projects are giving rise to local interest groups that are in the process of being systematically and organically tied tightly to international interests to such a degree that the state will not be able (even if it is willing) to effectively interfere with or sever the growing complex of connections and linkages between the local and the global. Much of the current crisis of the peripheral state lies in its inability to fully mediate and regulate the overflowing interactions and transactions between the global and the local while retaining its sovereignty and national character. But even though the state is still a necessary partner for lender missions within the country, its bargaining power and legitimacy are further undermined by increasing interactions between NGOs and local communities.

Government and NGOs

Before discussing NGO involvement in Mauritania, I would like to mention that the concept and practice of NGOs can be questioned inasmuch as NGOs often represent instruments of pursuing state interest and political influence by means other than those of the state apparatus. Some of the international NGOs operating in Mauritania receive as much as 80 percent of their funding from their governments. Even though NGOs provide indispensable humanitarian relief to millions of needy people, their apolitical nature may be questioned, particularly on the ground of their active role in working with the state and local communities. One can even argue, without being cynical, that the role played by contemporary NGOs in the developing world is not so much different from the role played by Christian missionaries in the second half of the nineteenth century when they were preaching Christianity while they were preparing the natives for direct colonial rule. In response to great catastrophes and tragedies caused by wars, famines, and natural disasters during this century, NGOs were able to provide significant humanitarian assistance on a large scale. With the adjustment programs of the 1980s, NGOs became systematically and permanently involved in local development and their political leverage increased as states became denationalized. As public expenditure was dramatically reduced by SAP austerity programs, vulnerable social groups were facing a deterioration in their already low standard of living. It is in this context that NGOs began to champion assistance to these vulnerable groups, especially at the community level where state power is at its lowest. In other words, the growing influence of NGOs indicates the increasing weakness and bankruptcy of peripheral states and their inability to provide relief for a significant proportion of their citizens, as the Mauritanian case illustrates.

Throughout the 1970s only three international NGOs arrived and began operating in Mauritania: the Catholic Church–based Organisation Caritative Internationale (1972), the American–based Catholic Relief Services (1973), and the Switzerland–based Lutheran Federation (1974). All came as relief organizations focusing mainly on food relief and environmental protection following the severe drought that hit the Sahel region in the late 1960s and early 1970s. Following the open-door policy of adjustment in the 1980s, the number of Western NGOs operating in Mauritania increased rapidly and their development activities went well beyond food relief and environmental protection to include a variety of socioeconomic projects in various sectors, particularly agriculture, health, housing, water, children and mother care, as table 12 illustrates. Other semi-NGOs dealing with local communities arrived, too. The number of U.S. Peace Corps volunteers in the country increased from 35 in 1984 to 60 in 1985.[20] By 1992, some 600 American Peace Corps volunteers had served in Mauritania,[21] with an overwhelming majority coming after 1984. Beyond their obvious humanitarian relief efforts, NGOs stimulate private enterprise and establish direct links with local communities. Through their small-scale development projects, they enhance market mechanisms, and through their assistance to the poor, they contribute to the containment of political dissent and the overall social peace necessary to the development of free enterprise. It can even be argued that NGOs constitute one of the instrumentalities of adjustment and play a crucial role in cushioning the social shock of economic and financial austerity measures.

Table 12 Western NGOs in Mauritania

Name of NGO	Nationality	Arrival	Activity
CARITAS Mauritanie	Catholic Church–based	1972	Relief and development
Catholic Relief Services	United States	1973	Relief and agriculture
Federation Lutherienne Mondiale	Switzerland	1974	Environment protection
SOS Sahel	France	1983	Water
Medecins sans Frontiere	France	1983	Child care
World Vision International	United States	1984	Health and agriculture
Terres des Hommes	Switzerland	1984	Mother and child
Eco Operations 66	France	1984	Housing
Association Volontaires du Progres*	France	1984	Small projects
Africa 70	Italy	1985	Urban problems
Oxfam	United Kingdom	1986	Spatial planning
Centre de Transfert de Technologie*	France and others	1986	Computer tech. transfer
Community Doulos	United States	1987	Mother and child
Freres du Tiers Monde	Belgium	1987	agricultural perimeters
Helen Keller International	United States	1987	Small rural projects
Association Aide au Developpement*	France	1987	Integrated projects

Source: Compiled from Ould Mohamed Lemine, M. "The Impact of NGOs on Development in Mauritania." Unpublished memoire in Arabic, University of Nouakchott, July 1992. *Name of NGO was shortened for space purpose.

World Bank/NGO cooperation and coordination began as early as adjustment itself and developed to the extent that today NGOs collaborate in more than a third of World Bank–supported projects. In 1980, the World Bank and NGOs held a workshop in Paris on small enterprise development, and in May 1981 an NGO/World Bank Committee[22] was founded and began its work under the umbrella of the World Bank and the International Council of Voluntary Agencies (ICVA). The NGO/World Bank Committee meets once a year, and its NGO members constitute a specialized working group within the ICVA structure. It is cochaired by the chief of the Bank's Strategic Planning and Policy Review Department and an elected NGO member and includes eight senior World Bank staff members and twenty-six representatives of NGOs. The NGO/World Bank Committee is 100 percent financed by the World Bank. Within the framework of cooperation between the World Bank and the International Council of Voluntary Agencies, NGOs are assigned the job of bringing their experience, local knowledge, perspective, priorities, and institutional alternatives to the attention of the World Bank to help it in the formulation of country programs and policy choices, as well as to participate in the implementation and/or monitoring of Bank-financed programs that involve the poor. Both the World Bank and NGOs have interests in promoting such cooperation. Promotion of private enterprises is the raison d'etre of NGO/World Bank growing coordination and cooperation in small-scale development projects. While Bank-financed development programs are implemented and channeled through state institutions, NGO-financed projects are channeled directly to local communities and local governments, and this is where the complementarity between the Bank and NGOs lies within the framework of SAPs. The World Bank is now working on a new lending strategy designed to provide *microloans* to local groups and even local individuals. Such move demonstrates the Bank's intention to further circumvent the state and penetrate localities. At his first press conference in Washington, D.C., on 1 June 1995, the newly appointed president of the World Bank noted that his future visits to countries implementing SAPs will not be limited to meetings with state officials. In his words, "those visits will not be state visits. I will, of course, see the governments in the countries but it is my expectation that I will visit projects, that I will talk with project managers, that I will walk the streets, that I will meet with the locals, that I will go and have a beer at night after dinner in good Australian fashion."[23] Even though at some point certain NGOs (for example, Oxfam) have spoken harshly against

SAPs (see chapter 9), the overall NGO strategy of integrating local communities into the world economy through small-scale local projects founded on the principle of free enterprise is consistent with the interests of the World Bank in integrating the world economy at the global, national, and local levels. The moral and material impact of NGO projects ensures the impossibility of any break away from the world economic and value system. In this regard, minorities and marginalized groups represent the first target for NGO humanitarian assistance, since these groups are often the first to be hit by SAPs. The NGOs' strategy of focusing on the poor, the marginalized, and minorities earns them a social basis that can be embarrassing for the state whose failure to provide assistance for its needy citizens will always provide the leitmotif and justification for NGO intervention as the welfare state continues to shrink, thus forcing the poor to fend for themselves while SAPs expand.

As adjustment policies opened the door to NGOs in Mauritania, the state began to design policies aimed not only at encouraging NGOs but also regulating and controlling their activities. On the one hand, NGOs wanted direct contact with local communities, particularly those marginalized by state policy; on the other hand, the state was concerned about the close collaboration between NGOs and local communities because of their potential for discrediting the state as unable to feed, educate, and take care of its citizens. Although the state and NGOs are competing and any success for one might be a failure for the other, they nevertheless continue to cooperate with a great deal of mutual respect and suspicion, and many NGOs still intervene only at the request of state officials such as government ministers, regional governors, and city mayors.[24] With the beginning of SAPs, the government issued a decree creating the NGO Coordination Committee under the trusteeship of the permanent secretariat of the Military Committee for National Salvation. The committee became the official interlocutor between the government and any NGO desiring to work in Mauritania. A general agreement must be signed first between the committee and the NGO as an approval of its activities within the country. By registering through this agreement, NGOs obtain a legal status allowing them freedom of movement and work within the country. Once this step is completed they can initiate agreements with ministerial departments or local governments to provide specific assistance or execute particular projects of development. Under the guise of such regulations, the government is trying to make sure that NGOs remain under control and do not go too far without giving credit to the state. NGOs expressed some frustration when going through all these required administrative procedures, and some of them were not happy about the political climate marked by monolithic military rule. Others were influenced by the struggle between the government and the opposition, as well as by the ethnic divide in the country. This was the case for certain Christian missionaries who erroneously and continuously believe that "there may be secret [Christian] believers among the Islamized African peoples of southern Mauritania," a temptation demonstrated by the fact that "Protestants have on several occasions attempted to begin activities in Mauritania but without success."[25] In 1987, four major NGOs withdrew from Mauritania: Catholic Relief Services, Cooperative for American Relief Everywhere (CARE), Helen Keller International, and Medecins sans Frontière (Doctors without Borders). It should be noted that CARE and Catholic Relief Services are U.S.-based and received 83.5 percent and 84.3 percent (respectively) of their total funds from the U.S. government in 1987.[26] Within government circles, it was widely believed that these NGOs were supporting the opposition against the government in a way that undermined the peaceful interethnic relations in the country, and some of them were even accused of engaging in subtle anti-Islamic activities.[27]

The government also created two technical cells to stimulate NGO operations. In 1987, the Cell for Support of Small Projects was created under the trusteeship of the Mauritanian Red Crescent and in collaboration with the United Nations Development Program (UNDP). Its goal is to stimulate and provide technical support for all development projects at the local level. Also in conjunction with the UNDP the government created under the trusteeship of the food security agency (CSA) another cell labeled Food for Work. This project undertakes small-scale development actions throughout the country using funds raised from selling international food relief. A typical example of development action carried out by the Food for Work project would be to provide a specific amount of grain (per person per day) for a couple of dozen unemployed poor people and in return they clear a road of sand or collect garbage, and so on. The government went further in inducing NGOs by organizing an international conference in Nouakchott on 27 February 1987 entitled "Relations between Cities and NGOs." The conference increased NGOs' awareness about the growing needs of people experiencing the austerity effects of the adjustment program. It provided them with the opportunity to organize and the possibility to lobby inside and outside the state apparatus to build structural relations with local communities. In 1988 the Federation of NGOs working in Mauritania was created in response to the government Committee for NGO Coordination. Membership of the Federation grew rapidly to include ten Western-based NGOs in 1990.[28] With the process of democratization and the emergence of elected local municipal councils, NGOs found an opportunity to work closely with local communities through local governments.

The election of mayors in urban municipalities in 1986 and rural municipalities in 1988 and the subsequent decentralization of the administrative system constituted important outcomes of adjustment. Privatizing the economy led to the rise of various interest groups and particularly to the emergence of local governments, in which NGOs found a more appropriate interlocutor, but the state attempted again to mediate relations between NGOs and local governments. In 1989 the Cell for Support of Small Projects organized the First National Seminar on Rural Municipalities, NGOs, and Development.[29] The seminar provided a forum for the state and NGOs to present their cases. The participants in the seminar advocated the need for financial resources for municipalities and pointed out the lack of coordination between rural municipalities, NGOs, and foreign donors. They criticized the existing legal framework within which they have to work. They also came up with a series of recommendations that reflected the contradictions and competition between the state, NGOs, and local governments in the process of influencing or even controlling events at the local community level. The state does not want NGOs to have direct access to local communities without some sort of state mediation. One resolution of the seminar recommended that the Cell for Support of Small Projects (not the state) should be the sole structure of coordination between NGOs and local communities. This is because the cell is under the trusteeship of the Mauritanian Red Crescent, which is at the same time an NGO (it represents the International League of Red Crosses) and a government institution (its president is nominated by governmental decree). In this way, a subtle state mediation between NGOs and local communities was created. The Association of Mayors emerging from municipal elections and embodying the power of local governments requested to have a representative within the national Committee for NGO Coordination so it could lobby at the central government level. It also recommended a decentralization at the regional level of the Cell for Support of Small Projects so it could fall within the association's jurisdiction. NGOs also wanted more decentralization of the cell so they could have more leverage at the local level. The participants in the seminar requested more power sharing within the Cell for Support of Small Projects by recommending the creation of an executive board headed by the national Committee for NGO Coordination and including representatives from (1) the Association of Mayors, (2) interested ministries, (3) the Ministry of Interior, (4) NGOs, and (5) foreign donors or lenders. This power-sharing mechanism was to be further reinforced by changing the existing legislation (related to NGOs), particularly the 1964 and 1973 laws, which gave the state too much control over initiatives from individuals and small groups of people. New legislation was to be enacted to encourage NGOs and was to be drafted by the authorities in close collaboration with the different services dealing with NGOs. At stake in all this are the local communities and how the state, local governments, and NGOs compete to reach them and have credit for assisting them.

International NGOs succeeded in awakening local NGOs and reducing state pressure on their movement and the procedures by which they can receive authorization to operate within the country. They were able to do so by increasing their cooperation with local governments, especially after the establishment of rural municipalities. According to an investigation made by the Cell for the Support of Small Projects in 1989, the Federation of NGOs in Mauritania channeled the equivalent of $5 million of aid to Mauritania in 1989. This amount represented 2 percent of total foreign aid received by Mauritania during the same year. It was a small proportion of foreign aid compared to neighboring Mali, for example, where in the same year the contribution by NGOs represented 10 percent of total aid, and where about 400 NGOs were operating. But more significant was how this $5 million was giving rise to dozens of small projects throughout ten out of the thirteen administrative regions of the country. The mushrooming of these small-scale and local community-based projects is invigorating private initiative and market relations on the one hand, and connecting all corners of the country with different regions of the world on the other hand. These small-scale projects include providing small loans for a variety of local associations of women, artisans, small farmers, and so on, to help them produce and market their products. Such small enterprises are leading the transition from a self-sufficient form of production involving little exchange of goods and services to a market-based and monetized system of production, exchange, and consumption. They constitute the nucleus of market economy in regions and sectors that would have otherwise remained outside the global economy for at least another generation.

Table 13 is an example of how major Western NGOs in Mauritania are operating a variety of these small projects in almost all regions of the country, thus further contributing not only to the overall process of denationalization of the state described in this chapter but also to the internationalization of the economy and the fragmentation of society, as the following chapters attempt to explain. The denationalized state represents the appropriate instrument of regulation for an internationalized economy. Such a state is no longer sovereign according to Anthony Giddens's definition:

A sovereign state is a political organization that has the capacity, within a delimited territory or territories, to make laws and effectively sanction their up-keep; exert a monopoly over the disposal of the means of violence; control basic policies relating to the internal political or administrative form of government; and dispose of the fruits of a national economy that are the basis of its revenue.[30]

Table 13 NGO Operations in 1989

NGOs	Regions	Objective	Budget
AFVP	Al-Assaba, Guidimaka, Gorgol	training local craftsmen, well sinkers, and health workers	$524,048
CARITAS	Adrar, Al-Assaba, Brakna, Nouakchott, Gorgol, Inshiri, Tiris, Trarza	food aid, micro-projects, women promotion, market-gardens, education, social services, rural development, small projects	$813,416
DOULOS	Nouakchott	mother/child care	$964,433
FLM	Nouakchott, Al-Assaba	research, women and social action, basic health care, rural development	$740,000
Oxfam	Trarza, Al-Hodh Al-Gharbi	rice decorticators, rural development	$246,381
TDO	Nouakchott	mother/child care	$366,667
WVI	Nouakchott, Al-Assaba	health education, mother/child care	$524,000

Source: Compiled from Ould Mohamed Lemine, M. "The Impact of NGOs on Development in Mauritania," unpublished memoire in Arabic, Department of Geography, University of Nouakchott, July 1992. See also Federation des ONG en Mauritanie, "Bulletin d'Information Inter-ONG, January 1990."

6

Globalization and Devaluation of the Economy

Introduction

The previous chapter analyzed how the process of structural adjustment in Mauritania led to the denationalization of the state. It examined the transformation from a national to a multilateral state where the formulation of development policy, the articulation of development strategies, the engineering of fiscal policy, the management of foreign debt, and the design of public investment programs have all been conceived, funded, and supervised by a series of international financial institutions and mechanisms, leaving the role of implementation to the state. This chapter analyzes the scope and extent of the economic restructuring and the internationalization and devaluation of the Mauritanian economy following the denationalization of the state. It examines how successive stabilization and adjustment programs in Mauritania have in part ceded the reins of the national economy to a complex network of international economic operators whose control over policy design and project financing turned the state into an executor[1] of World Bank/IMF development policies and a guarantor of international loans. Although these economic operators invested significant capital in the form of grants or loans to Mauritania, the policies of systematic currency devaluation and free profit repatriation offset this apparent capital inflow, as the problem of foreign debt constantly reminds us. In fact, the volume and importance of international capital flows have grown enormously in recent years[2] as a consequence of the global strategy of adjustment and the process of denationalization of peripheral nation-states. Despite fanfares surrounding recent trade blocs (the North American Free Trade Agreement [NAFTA] and the European Union [EU]), "there can be little doubt that such arrangements have diverted attention away from multilateral efforts to liberalize the world trading systems."[3] Reducing trade barriers and freeing capital movement represent two major goals of SAPs. As more and more local processes of production and styles of consumption are linked to the world market, dependency (or interdependency) deepens. The increasing use of economic sanctions[4] as a formidable weapon against nations reluctant to accept global adjustment illustrates not only the integration and interdependence of the world economy but also the growing centralization of its mechanisms by the G-7 countries and the widening economic disparity between them and the rest of the world. While the per capita income gap between the richest and the poorest countries was 2 to 1 at the beginning of the nineteenth century,[5] it is today 420 to 1 when comparing the highest GNP per capita in Europe with the lowest in Africa.[6] World economic integration created export-led systems of production and increased exchange faster than production. International economic exchanges have increased far more rapidly than domestic production,[7] and during the last decade alone "the rate of world foreign direct investment has grown four times as fast as world output."[8] The reduction of barriers between nations was further accelerated by technological breakthroughs in communication, where the costs of transmitting and processing information have been falling dramatically. The round-the-clock and round-the-globe trend of fast trade and exchange reflects the destruction of geographic constraints and ultimately of any national construction that may constitute a geographic constraint. The trend seems so irreversible that concepts such as "the end of geography"[9] and "the collapse of space and time"[10] are now commonplace. Some observers have pointed out that the national economy is a myth and the capitalist world economy is now so thoroughly integrated across national boundaries that an autonomous national economic strategy is no longer possible and that the contemporary global economy is no longer state-centered.[11] Others have gone even further by arguing that national borders "have effectively disappeared and, along with them, the economic logic that made them useful lines of demarcation in the first place."[12]

    At the July 1993 economic summit in Tokyo, the G-7 countries confirmed the trend when they agreed to eliminate trade tariffs on eight manufacturing sectors and reduce them on many others, a move described as the biggest tariff cuts in history. The trend was also confirmed by the 15 December 1993 General Agreement on Trade and Tariffs (GATT), which has called for further cuts in import duties while bringing trade in agriculture and services under the GATT regime for the first time. During the July 1994 economic summit in Naples, the G-7 (G-8 since Russia was admitted in this session) committed itself to ratifying the world trade pact by 1 January 1995, a step short of President Clinton's trade initiative, called Open Markets 2000.[13] This increasing liberalization of trade regimes and the internationalization of capital markets have serious implications for peripheral economies whose main comparative advantage was based on protectionist regulations. According to a September 1993 study by the OECD and the World Bank, it is estimated that Africa as a whole could lose as much as $2.6 billion annually between 1994 and 2002 as a result of the December 1993 GATT, while the annual gains of the leading industrialized countries from the same agreement could be as high as $135 billion.[14] Therefore, not all economies benefit from the process of global economic integration advocated by the current strategy of adjustment, which systematically dismantles protectionist regulations, thus leaving peripheral economies at the mercy of global competition in which the "fixed" national state struggles and offers concession after concession to attract an increasingly mobile international capital.

SAPs in Mauritania

The process of economic adjustment in Mauritania was articulated around three distinct, but strongly interlinked, sets of policies: (1) stabilization measures, (2) structural adjustment policies, and (3) sectoral adjustment programs. Stabilization and adjustment are designed conjointly by the Bank and the Fund, whose cooperation in Mauritania has been close, with continuous consultation and participation of IMF staff in economic and sectoral missions of the World Bank. This collaboration is reflected in the growing cross-conditionality between the two institutions. However, the Bank has a broader interest and a more profound knowledge about the country and has had a resident representative in Nouakchott since the beginning of adjustment in 1985. Stabilization policy measures in Mauritania were engineered by the IMF as the first component of the overall adjustment program. They consist of temporary use of IMF's special drawing rights (SDRs)[15] in exchange for the implementation of carefully selected economic and financial policies. They are aimed at reducing total demand and ultimately bringing down or even eliminating the external account deficit, which was diagnosed as the source of the financial crisis. For this objective, a set of austerity policy measures was designed within the framework of successive IMF programs (table 14) agreed upon with the Mauritanian government between 1985 and 1994.[16] These programs are essentially articulated around a platform of austerity involving particularly deep cuts in public expenditure, reduction of the money supply, restriction and reorientation of credit flows, and devaluation of the national currency. They represent short-term measures that are more visible and more observable than the long-term structural reforms and because of this they are politically more explosive. But since they are renewed almost annually, they actually constitute a long-term strategy of austerity that continuously paves the road for sweeping structural reforms sponsored by the World Bank.

Table 14 IMF Programs in Mauritania

Type of IMF arrangement	Period of arrangement	SDRs in millions
Standby arrangement	April 1985 to April 1986	12
Standby arrangement	April 1986 to April 1987	12
Structural adjustment facility	September 1986 to September 1989	21.5
Standby arrangement	May 1987 to May 1988	10
Enhanced structural adjustment facility	May 1989 to May 1992	50.85
Enhanced structural adjustment facility	December 1992 to December 1994	33.9

Source: Compiled from *IMF press release* (5 May 1987, 9 November 1987, and 29 May 1989) and *IMF Survey*, 5 April 1993.

Structural and sectoral adjustment programs are designed by the World Bank as a set of medium-to-long-term macroeconomic and sectoral policies that affect the structures of incentives and price mechanisms of the economy. Prior to adjustment, World Bank operations in Mauritania focused more on project lending, such as the two International Bank for Reconstruction and Development (IBRD) loans ($66 million to MIFERMA in 1960 and $60 million to SNIM in 1979) for iron ore mining operations, which constitute the most important export sector in the country,[17] and several IDA credits for projects in agriculture, transport, and education. These operations were essentially of an investment nature and did not require a substantial change of policy. With adjustment, the Bank introduced a new policy-based lending system where the Bank's comparative advantage lies in supporting policy formulation as a form of long-term political investment. This strategy of trading loans for policy change aims at changing institutional structures, economic management, investment planning, and project implementation. When these kinds of policy changes are sought on a macroeconomic level they are labeled structural adjustment, and when they focus on specific sectors they are labeled sectoral adjustment. Between 1985 and 1992 Mauritania implemented many World Bank adjustment programs through IBRD loans and/or IDA credits (see table 15). The four most important adjustment projects, which have far-reaching impacts on the entire economy, are: the first structural adjustment loan (SAL 1) of 1987 and the three sectoral adjustment loans designed to restructure the sectors of public enterprises, agriculture, and mining. Almost all the other socioeconomic sectors were also restructured by the Bank. These include small-scale irrigation, industrial and artisanal development, administrative reform, education, and health and population policy reform. The distinction between IBRD loans and IDA credits is essentially based on the interest rate, which is higher in the former than in the latter. Also, IBRD loans are repayable over a shorter period of time compared to IDA credits. The long-term strategic objective of World Bank projects is to rally all economic sectors along the single criterion of economic efficiency and ultimately to make the economy a safe place for profitable investments since many international investors are cofinancing these development projects side by side with the World Bank.

The identification, preparation, financing, and monitoring of these projects allow the World Bank to firmly control the reins of the Mauritanian economy. The analysis of the genesis of the first economic and financial recovery program (PREF) will illustrate how the Bank actually sets the stage for reforms by undertaking a series of economic and sectoral diagnostic studies. These studies were then used as an instrument for keeping open a permanent dialogue with various government policymakers and bureaucrats, who would ultimately adopt

Table 15 World Bank Credits and Loans

Credit/Loan Number and Date of Approval	Project Title and Purpose	$ million
IDA Credit 1567–MAU, March 1985	Public Enterprise Technical Assistance and Rehabilitation	16.4
IDA Credit 1571–MAU, March 1985	Small-Scale Irrigation	7.5
IDA Credit 1572–MAU, March 1985	Industrial and Artisanal Development	5.25
IBRD Loan 2643–MAU, December 1985	SNIM Rehabilitation Project	20
IDA Credit 1658–MAU, April 1986	Second Livestock Project	7.6
IDA Credit 1812–MAU, June 1987 plus a Special Africa Facility Credit	First Structural Adjustment Program	42.4
IDA Credit 1865–MAU, December 1987	Institutional Development and Administrative Reform	10
IDA Credit 1943–MAU, August 1988	Education Sector Restructuring	18.2
IDA Credit 2093–MAU, February 1990	Agricultural Sector Adjustment and Irrigation Improvement	25
IDA Credit 2166–MAU, June 1990	Public Enterprise Sector Adjustment Program	40
IDA Credit 2167–MAU, June 1990	Public Enterprise Sector Institutional Development and Technical Assistance Project	10
IDA Credit ?–MAU, September 1991	Health and Population Project	21.3

Source: Compiled from IDA President's Reports no. P–4550–MAU and P–5293–MAU of 11 May 1987 and 30 May 1990, respectively. See also *Lettre du Directeur (par interim) du Département du Sahel à la Banque Mondiale addressée au Ministère Mauritanien du Plan en date du 9 Décembre 1991.*

the Bank's diagnosis and prescription as their own for reasons such as: (1) a national government should be able to produce diagnoses and prescriptions for its national economy, otherwise its credibility and legitimacy would be seriously damaged; (2) without accepting the diagnoses and adopting the prescriptions of the World Bank, there would be no loans, grants, or any other assistance from the international community of lenders and donors; and (3) for many state officials the World Bank diagnoses and prescriptions are intellectually challenging, reliable, and convincing. According to the president of the International Development Association, Barber B. Conable, the government has no choice but to take on board the World Bank prescriptions because "it is fully aware of the country's strong dependency on foreign assistance for overcoming its financial imbalances and implementing a viable economic and social development strategy. That assistance will be forthcoming only if the country continues to demonstrate a strong commitment to austerity and reform."[18] The strategy of social learning combined with loans and grants encourages the government to be a wholehearted defender of economic liberalism as the only choice for countries willing to modernize their economies. The Mauritanian prime minister seems to have assimilated this strategy when he said: "We have been working on structural adjustment programs with the World Bank, the IMF and all our development partners since 1985, aiming to modernize the Mauritanian economy, eliminate dysfunction and ensure greater economic rationality. . . . We in Mauritania are convinced that economic liberalism is now the only choice."[19]

Genesis of the PREF

All the above mentioned stabilization measures, structural adjustment policies, and sectoral adjustment programs were actually conceived and tailored on the conclusions and recommendations of a 1984 World Bank economic memorandum on Mauritania. The study provided a diagnostic analysis of the economy and advocated an economic and financial recovery program. It stated that while exogenous factors (world economic recession, drought, and war) contributed significantly to the deterioration of Mauritania's economic and financial situation, their impact was aggravated by weak economic management, particularly the selection, funding, and execution of public investment programs[20] and the weakness of the contribution of the private sector to the formation of the GDP resulting from the overpowering role of the state in the economy. Since Mauritania cannot influence these exogenous factors, its only option is to change its domestic economic policy. It was this line of reasoning that provided the rationale for adjusting the local and the national to the imperatives of the global/international. The recovery program involved a series of economic policies designed to curtail demand and boost supply. On the demand side, government expenditures and public investment were to be reduced as part of a comprehensive restructuring of the public sector. On the supply side, the government was to improve the institutional and political framework of the economy by giving a greater role to the private sector. The World Bank Action Pogram, which spans the entire Mauritanian economy, is summarized in table 16. The three areas of policy reform (public sector, resource management, and sectoral policy) correspond more or less to stabilization measures, structural adjustment policies, and sectoral adjustment programs, respectively. The Action Program provided the blueprint for all subsequent IMF arrangements and World Bank structural and sectoral adjustment programs. It set a long-term strategy of development that continues today to frame economic policy in the country.

On the basis of the above World Bank Action Program, the government drafted the Economic and Financial Recovery Program (1985–88) (known by its French acronym, PREF), which was nothing but an attempt to give the Bank's program a Mauritanian facade (see policy formulation in chapter 4). The declared objectives of the PREF were to maintain an annual rate of real GDP growth that is higher than the population growth rate of 2.7 percent, to bring down the ratio of public investment to GDP from over 30 percent to below 20 percent, to bring the government budget into balance by 1986 and achieve budgetary savings that could reach 15 percent of public investment by 1988, and to reduce the current balance of payments deficit to less than 10 percent of GDP by 1988. The government was very enthusiastic about and rigorous in the execution of the PREF because it released quick disbursements of foreign loans and grants. By government decree (no. 85.213 of 13 November 1985), the interministerial Comité de Suivi (follow-up committee) was established as a sort of mini-government (which includes the ministers of finance and planning, a chief advisor to the president, and the governor of the central bank) in charge of the coordination and supervision of a fast implementation of the PREF. Beyond some sixty policy measures already implemented within the framework of the April 1985 IMF arrangement, the government expressed its commitment to further implement a matrix of some ninety[21] measures of economic and

Table 16 World Bank Recovery Program 1985–88

A. Public sector	B. Resource management	C. Sectoral policy
1. Budgetary policy	1. Exchange rate and price	1. Mining sector
a. improve tax collection	policy	a. reduce costs of
b. tax fish export	a. adjust internal prices	SNIM and improve
2. Public spending	and eliminate subsidies to	productivity
a. freeze government	propagate the effect of	b. improve market
wage bill and eliminate	devaluation	analysis of iron ore
redundant posts	b. eliminate price control	2. Fisheries
b. eliminate subsidies	for basic goods and	a. evaluate sector
and reduce scholarships	services and introduce	resources
c. budget foreign debt	tariffs on public services	b. formulate a
beginning 1986	2. Banking system	strategy for fish
3. Foreign debt	a. recover bank arrears	processing in
a. implement the Paris	and improve credit risk	Mauritania
Club accord of April	evaluation	c. upgrade
1985	b. increase interest rate	Nouadhibou Port and
b. do not contract short-	c. follow restrictive	give incentives to
term foreign debt	monetary and credit policy	small and medium
c. specify government	to reduce budget and	private enterprises
guarantees for parastatal	balance of payments	d. encourage
and commercial	deficits	traditional and
borrowings	d. increase private	industrial integration
4. State companies	shareholds in banking	3. Agriculture
a. liquidate or privatize	capital	a. increase cereal
nonprofitable public	3. Public investment	prices and reduce free
enterprises	a. define sectoral	food distribution
b. establish performance	investment strategy,	b. establish fund for
contracts between	particularly for irrigation,	food aid sales
government and public	water supply, and power	c. restructure the
enterprises	generation	rural development
c. maintain strong	b. establish precise criteria	agency (SONADER)
government support for	for project conception and	4. Human resources
reforming three public	selection	a. consider population
enterprises: SNIM,	c. enact better planning	increase in economic
SONELEC, and EMN	procedures, such as the	planning
d. accelerate reforms of	establishment of planning	b. restructure
OPT, CSA, and SMCPP	units within ministries	education system

Source: Summary of paragraphs 6.11 to 6.19 of "Banque mondiale, RIM, Memorandum Economique," 1985.

other development policies between 1985 and 1988 to achieve the goals of the PREF. These were prepared and discussed in close collaboration with the Bank before their presentation to the first meeting of the Consultative Group for Mauritania in Paris on 26–27 November 1985. They included both stabilization and structural adjustment policies focusing on a series of austerity and restructuring measures such as a flexible exchange rate policy; a restrictive monetary and credit policy favoring the private sector; continued austerity in public finance; decontrol of prices; rehabilitation of public enterprises; an investment program giving priority to the mining, fisheries, and agriculture sectors; and development of training facilities tailored to the needs of these economic reforms.

By endorsing the Bank's strategy for the country, the government fully opened the national economy to international capital. That opening and the subsequent liberalization policies were welcomed by the international community of lenders because of the export opportunities they opened up. Such welcome was echoed in a 1985 *Business America* commentary on Mauritania, which stated that "prospects for U.S. exporters are promising in the areas of mining, fishing and fish processing, and modern farming equipment and techniques."[22] These are the three productive sectors in the country around which adjustment reforms were articulated. In 1993, a U.S. congressional delegation toured eight sub-Saharan African countries (Mauritania, Senegal, Nigeria, Congo, Cameroon, Central African Republic, Uganda, and Kenya) with a declared objective of assessing human rights in those countries, but its members were actually exploring African markets for U.S. agricultural exports. Speaking candidly on his return from the trip, U.S. Senator Larry Pressler had this to say: "One of the main missions of my recent trip to Africa was to continue my efforts to promote South Dakota agricultural exports. . . . In 1991, total United States agricultural exports to Africa totaled $1.9 billion. In 1992 that total had risen to $2.6 billion—a 35 percent increase. Africa represents one of our fastest growing agricultural markets. U.S. agricultural exports to all developing countries are expected to reach a record $17.7 billion in fiscal year 1993—nearly 43 percent of all U.S. agricultural exports."[23] It should be noted that Mauritania's foreign trade deficit with the United States began to grow in the 1990s following these liberalization policies, as illustrated in table 17, even though the United States was never among the major trading partners of Mauritania. This example illustrates that even though the IMF stabilization programs were designed theoretically to curb demand, they actually created a trade environment that encouraged imports by removing restrictions on them.

Table 17 Mauritania's Trade Deficit with the United States (U.S.$ million)

Year	Mauritania's imports	Mauritania's exports	Trade balance
1990	14.4	26.3	+11.9
1991	21.5	12.7	-8.8
1992	58.4	9.6	-48.8
1993	19.1	7.2	-11.8

Source: Compiled from National Trade Data Bank, U.S. Department of Commerce, Bureau of the Census, U.S. Merchandise Export Trade, Country by Commodity, "Exports to Mauritania" and "Imports from Mauritania," July 1993 and April 1994.

A more systematic international support of Mauritania's liberalizing policies came within the framework of the Consultative Group, where major international creditors meet periodically to assess Mauritania's business climate and the overall progress of the adjustment process. At the first Consultative Group for Mauritania (see chapter 4), the government requested and was, for the most part, granted three types[24] of external assistance to finance the three-year recovery program (PREF): (1) direct official assistance in the form of food aid and technical assistance amounting to $170 million, (2) financing of new public projects through loans and grants amounting to $520 million, and (3) debt rescheduling amounting to $397 million for fiscal years 1986, 1987, and 1988. It should be noted that this high level of foreign assistance remains, however, lower than what Mauritania was able to mobilize on a bilateral basis prior to adjustment. Bilateral aid used to finance much of Mauritania's balance of payments deficits without any policy change. To be eligible for further assistance, particularly in debt relief, the government solicited and was granted the status of a Less Developed Country and proposed that the donors meet regularly to track the investment program and monitor its execution. The government also emphasized that even though the implementation of the program "will be particularly hard socially," the policy measures will be applied with the same rigor as was deployed in the implementation of the stabilization program agreed with the IMF in April 1985. The Consultative Group session on the overall investment program was followed by sector meetings to examine the strategies, action programs, and projects pertaining to investment in each sector.

Structural Reforms

In April 1986, the government concluded a second stabilization program with the IMF and signed a second accord with the Paris Club. Four months later the government obtained from the IMF a loan in the form of the first structural adjustment facility (SAF) and Mauritania's development strategy was laid down in the first policy framework paper (PFP), which was reviewed by the executive directors of both the Bank and the Fund. Government implementation of the two stabilization programs in 1985–86 (the first phase of PREF execution) was described by the president of the International Development Association as "impressive."[25] Consequently, the government obtained on 4 May 1987 a third IMF standby arrangement for the period from June 1987 to May 1988 and the Bank board approved the first structural adjustment loan (SAL 1) in Mauritania on 2 June 1987. These operations were designed to support the second phase (1987–88) of the PREF. The SAL 1 program was financed by an IDA credit of $15 million equivalent, a Special Facility for Africa credit of $27.4 million equivalent, and a Special Joint Financing Facilities of $7.6 million equivalent from the Kingdom of Saudi Arabia and the Federal Republic of Germany. An additional parallel financing of $19.6 million from the African Development Bank (ADB) was also provided for the program. These credits (excluding the ADB one) were estimated to finance about 7.5 percent[26] of the merchandise import bill of the country for the 1987 and 1988 calendar years. Such credits are typical of SAPs since they are crucial for sustaining both lender exports and government imports, the two strategic goals around which SAPs are constructed and administered. In exchange for them, the government committed itself to implement some 156 policy measures in the areas of macroeconomic policies, public sector management, banking sector reform, energy sector rehabilitation, agriculture and food policy, fisheries sector development, and private sector promotion. These policy measures were classified by the World Bank report[27] into five categories: (1) far-reaching policy changes, such as the liberalization of the pricing and marketing system of cereals, private incentives reform, and tax reform; (2) institutional reforms, such as a new organization structure for the Ministry of Economy and Finance and the CSA, and preparation of a legal framework for supervision of the consolidated budget; (3) intermediate actions, such as the increase of water and electricity tariffs; (4) prerequisite actions related to policy intent, such as government declarations on energy policy and discussion and agreement on the Food for Work program; and (5) studies and reports, such as the studies on fringe benefits, promotion of artisanal fisheries, and data collection.

Credits from SAL 1 were disbursed in two tranches. Each tranche was released after the government had taken specific policy measures. For example, the government implemented fifty-seven policy measures during the preparation stage of the program and prior to its presentation to the IDA board of executive directors of SAL 1 as conditions for release of the first tranche. The release of the second tranche was scheduled for February 1988 but was delayed until October 1988 because two World Bank supervision missions (February and June 1988) noted delays in the implementation of certain reforms related to the banking sector and public enterprises. Conditions for disbursement of both tranches are summarized in table 18. The bottom line of these conditions is that the government of Mauritania must follow a well-defined development policy that is satisfactory to the IDA. A cornerstone of that policy is the liberalization of both domestic and foreign trade as well as the adoption of a flexible exchange rate of the ouguiya. This actually means increasing food prices and interest rates, reducing the protection of import-substitution industries, encouraging industries to turn to foreign markets in accordance with their comparative advantage, eliminating import quotas, reducing import duties, and depreciating the national currency. The World Bank evaluation[28] of SAL 1 found that the program achieved its objective in the sense that it brought about a more decentralized and more market-oriented economy, and the structures of the economy were no longer as regulated as they were prior to the program, especially after most quota import restrictions and price controls were removed. These structural changes, the report says, made the Mauritanian price system adjust and respond to shifts and fluctuations in the global system of supply and demand. This is perhaps the major success of the program since it represents the real objective of SAPs.

A careful examination of the PREF reveals that it was based on two components: (1) an investment program and (2) a set of economic policy measures. The balance sheet of investment in development projects was mediocre. By 1988, the rate of disbursements for the investment program was only 55 percent[29] of what was planned. The rates of achievement were 48.4 percent for the rural development sector; 82 percent for mining, fisheries, and energy sectors; 24.2 percent for infrastructure; and

Table 18 Conditions for Disbursement of SAL 1

Conditions for disbursement of the first tranche
1. approve legislation for a consolidated budget (October 1986)
2. adopt investment program for 1987 acceptable to IDA (December 1986)
3. initiate studies to strengthen economic management
4. create a special unit to prepare an administrative reform
5. strengthen central bank control on debt recovery and credit allocation
6. open the Société Mauritanienne de Banque (SMB) and the Banque Internationale de Mauritanie (BIMA) to private investors (March 1987)
7. merge and restructure the Banque Mauritanienne pour le Développement et le Commerce (BMDC) and the Fonds National pour le Développement (FND) (April 1987)
8. agree with IMF on strengthening BCM as agreed with IDA (April 1987)
9. adopt a coherent strategy for the energy sector (November 1986)
10. introduce price for petroleum products agreed with IDA (April 1987)
11. liberalize import procedures for petroleum products (April 1987)
12. establish fund for projects financed by food sales (November 1986)
13. submit an action program for CSA agreed with IDA (April 1987)
14. adopt a strategy/action program for the fisheries sector (April 1987)
15. reduce fishing permits in 1987 (April 1987)

Conditions for disbursement of the second tranche
1. agree with IDA on investment program for 1988–90 before December 1987
2. adopt investment budget for 1988 satisfactory to IDA by December 1987
3. make reforms satisfactory to IDA to strengthen the Ministère de l'Economie et des Finances (MEF) before March 1988
4. conclude agreements satisfactory to IDA for bank privatization (October 1987)
5. set electricity tariffs in a way satisfactory to IDA (January 1988)
6. agree with IDA on restructuring the Société Mauritanienne pour la Commercialisation des Produits Pétroliers (SMCPP), the Société Mauritanienne pour la Commercialisation du Poisson (SMCP), the Société Nationale d'Eau et d'Electricité (SONELEC) (December 1987)
7. agree with IDA on cereal pricing and marketing policies by October 1987
8. adopt an organization structure and management procedures satisfactory to IDA for CSA by November 1987
9. agree with IDA on an investment program for the fisheries sector, and submit an action-program satisfactory to IDA to: (1) enhance the control of fishing activities; and (2) formulate a training program for the fisheries sector by December 1987
10. enact a revised investment code satisfactory to IDA before December 1987
11. enact revised tax regulations satisfactory to IDA for fisheries operations, small businesses, and SNIM before the end of 1987.

Source: Compiled from IDA President's Report (P–4550–MAU), 11 May 1987, paragraphs 81 and 82.

6.4 percent for human resources. This rate of performance in planned investment projects was lower than the 58 percent and 78 percent[30] rates achieved within the framework of the second (1970–73) and third (1976–80) Plans for Economic and Social Development, respectively. Different sorts of technical delays and lack of financial resources were cited as causes for this poor performance. But the main reason resides in the fact that the PREF was primarily an austerity program designed to bring down the ratio of public investment to GDP. Its focus was on the implementation of a series of economic policy measures, and it succeeded well in this regard. Between 1985 and 1988 the government implemented 176 policy measures (see table 19) required by the international community of lenders. This was the essential element of achievement in the PREF program[31] during which Mauritania's economic situation improved markedly according to the UN Development Program (UNDP).[32] The success attributed to PREF resides essentially in the austerity program it has imposed. Such austerity had grave consequences for the productive system as a whole. Reduction of public investment led to the deterioration of infrastructure and lowered productivity in the long term. For example, the continuous deterioration of the road system in the country's capital city, Nouakchott, and the negative impact of this on many productive activities illustrate how a dramatic reduction of the budget deficit may constitute a marked success at the expense of vital infrastructure. Reduction of the public investment is easier politically because few political interests would lobby for long-term investment in infrastructure compared to very vigilant groups of employees and students affected by direct cuts in public spending. Reduction of the money supply, setting a ceiling for credit to the public sector, and reorientation of credit to the private sector weakened the material base of the state, which then sought more foreign loans and grants with more conditionality. The circle is vicious: state bankruptcy leads to a search for foreign loans whose conditionality puts further limits on the material base of the state by reducing its ability to borrow locally from the banking system at a time when it is borrowing heavily from international financial institutions.

Cuts in state expenditure were actually designed to stop the growth of the public sector as a way of downsizing the entire administrative system to balance the budget and save resources for foreign debt service. For this purpose, the World Bank produced a diagnostic study of the Mauritanian administration and concluded that the 183 services in the administration should be reduced because they "actually" correspond to

Table 19 Policy Measures Implemented 1985–88

Sector or subsector	Number of policy measures	Major issues addressed by policy measures
Public finances	26	systematic budget cuts, fiscal and management reform
Money and credit	6	restriction and reorientation of credit and increase of interest rate
External sector	10	devaluation, tariff reduction, and import liberalization
Rural sector	14	deregulation of prices and marketing of agricultural products
Fisheries	16	definition of a sectoral strategy, surveillance, infrastructure
Mining	9	increasing SNIM productivity and servicing its debts
Industry	7	state divestiture and promulgation of a new investment code
Energy	12	reform of SONELEC and creation of the Société Mauritanienne de Gaz (SOMAGAZ)
Housing/urbanism	9	sectoral studies, water supply, transportation
Infrastructure	8	sectoral studies, maintenance of existing infrastructure
Education	16	reduction of education costs, reform of education system
Health sector	4	deregulation of medical and pharmaceutical professions
Banking sector	13	strengthen BCM, reform primary banks, issue a new banking law
Parastatal sector	26	privatization of thirty enterprises and rehabilitation of seventy others

Source: Compiled from "Bilan d'exécution du PREF 1985–88," 17–37.

a civil service of 120,000 employees, but Mauritania's civil service was only one tenth of that.[33] Although some selective layoffs took place, the government/Bank strategy was to begin with a freeze on hiring state employees and civil servants. Only retired, deceased, or departing civil servants were to be replaced by new recruits, i.e., no new positions were to be created for the period 1986–88. For example, the education sector was the subject of a sectoral adjustment program to reduce its demands on public finances. These measures froze or even decreased the wage bill in real terms and freed substantial funds that would have covered current expenditures of new recruits and new services added each year. Another important measure of austerity was the reduction of subsidies for public services (particularly for public enterprises) and the increase of tariffs for their services. Although state subsidies were reduced as part of budget cuts, the problem of subsidies was dealt with radically within the framework of the sectoral adjustment program, particularly the public enterprise sector, where only a small number of public establishments was to continue to be supported by the state budget, while the others were to become profitable or face privatization or liquidation. Stabilization programs paved the way for structural adjustment programs, which paved the way for sectoral adjustment. The first adjustment program (1985–88) focused on stabilization and structural adjustment, while the second adjustment program (1989–91) focused on the adjustment of the three productive sectors: public enterprises (which include SNIM), the fisheries sector, and the agricultural sector. Between 1989 and 1992, structural policy measures continued to be comprehensive but with a special focus on public sector management, public enterprise restructuring, and public finance reforms as shown in table 20.

Table 20   Policy Measures Implemented 1989–92

Fiscal policy	External sestor	Agriculture policy
Fiscal policy 1. Revenue Introduction of new customs tariffs; completion of tax reform study, and harmonization of turnover tax rates on domestic products and imports; improvement of tax collection; recovery of arrears on SNIM wage taxes. 2. Expenditure Control Strengthening monitoring procedures. 3. Government Budget Further improvement in the preparation and monitoring of budget. **Banking system** 1. Restructuring banks, enacting new banking law, reinforcing supervision and control, privatization of the financial structures. 2. Creating money market 3. Establishing detailed lists of outstanding loans (March 1992) and a list of largest debtors. **Fishing sector policy** Preparation of a letter of intent for fisheries. **Environmental policy** Presentation of an anti-desertification plan to donors' meeting.	**External sestor** 1. Elimination of import licenses. 2. Liberalization of foreign exchange. **Public enterprises** 1. Restructuring SONELEC. 2. Liberalization of petroleum, drug, and transportation sectors. 3. Abolition of SMAR insurance monopoly. 4. Abolition of SONIMEX monopoly. 5. Participation of private sector in marketing activities of SMCP. 6. Audit, restructuring, privatization, and liquidation of selected public enterprises. 7. Rehabilitation of SNIM. 8. Liquidation of six public enterprises. 9. Plan to reduce outlays in services by SONELEC and OPT. 10. Settlement of government arrears to SONELEC. **Monetary policy** 1. First step toward the liberalization of interest rates. 2. Setting of reserve requirements on deposits.	**Agriculture policy** 1. Reforming pricing and marketing systems. 2. Reducing the role of CSA and reorganizing SONADER. **Domestic trade** 1. Abolition of the fixed margin system and *prix homologués* 2. Reduction of number of products subject to price control. **Public sector** 1. Preparation of a three-year rolling investment program. 2. Civil service census. 3. Elimination of 159 "irregular" employees from the payroll and implementation of retirement policy. 4. Communication to IDA of conclusions of the second phase of the civil service study. 5. Establishment of coherence between civil service payroll and civil service register. 6. Improving management of external debt. 7. Institution of prior clearance requirements by BCM on all external financing agreements. 8. Implementation of a new accounting system.

Source: Compiled from the fourth policy framework paper, 13 November 1992, Appendix II, table 2.

Sectoral Reforms

Public Enterprises

The rehabilitation and restructuring of individual public enterprises began as early as 1985. The key enterprises targeted at the time were the iron ore mining company (SNIM), the power and water utility company (SONELEC), the postal and telecommunications agency (OPT), the port of Nouakchott (PANPA), and the rural development agency (SONADER). For example, SNIM's rehabilitation led to 1,000 layoffs in March 1987 and consequently a reduction of 30 percent in overhead costs.[34] The early restructuring of individual companies smoothed the way later for a comprehensive restructuring of the entire sector. The Public Enterprise Sector Adjustment Program (better known by its French acronym, PASEP) was first identified by a World Bank mission in April 1988 as a sectoral adjustment project aimed at extending and deepening earlier sectoral reforms of 1985 and the structural reforms initiated within the framework of the first structural adjustment loan of 1987–88. Project preparation, appraisal, negotiation, and presentation to the World Bank board took place between January and June 1990. The project focused specifically on a fundamental modification of the legal and institutional framework governing public enterprises to facilitate their privatization, ensure their autonomy vis-à-vis the state, improve their financial management, and assure their profitability. In the Government Sectoral Policy Letter, the minister of planning and employment, Moustapha Ould Abeiderrahamane, explained (by way of apology about previous nationalization laws) to the World Bank that "after independence, the government had to take over several economic activities, deviating from its traditional field of action, to meet certain pressing needs that the embryonic and deficient private sector at that time could not satisfy."[35] To correct this deviation from the "true" role of the state, the government agreed with the World Bank to implement a deep restructuring program for the public enterprise sector. The specific actions to be taken under this program include: (1) modification of the legal and institutional framework with the objective of eliminating state monopolies and facilitating private sector participation; (2) a program of divestiture aimed at reducing the number of enterprises in the sector; and, (3) financial restructuring programs for key enterprises remaining in the sector, particularly SNIM, which is by far the largest company in the country, and SONELEC. Many ordinances, government decrees, and ministerial decisions (see table 21) were passed to restructure the sector along the lines of privatization of ownership and/or management. Moreover, a special unit (Cellule de Rehabilitation des Entreprises Publiques) was created to oversee, coordinate, and speed up the restructuring of public enterprises. This unit actually represents something like a "donor ministry" within the Ministry of Planning, as well as a sort of mastermind for public enterprise reform, as is the Cellule de Planification within the Ministry of Rural Development.

Table 21 Texts Reforming Public Enterprises

1. Ministerial Decision R–194 of 21 September 1987 establishing a Special Commission for Reform.
2. Ordinance no. 90.09 of 4 April 1990 establishing a status for public enterprises and their relations to the state.
3. Decree no. 90.154 P/CMSN of 22 October 1990 reclassifying public enterprises into new categories.
4. Decree no. 90.118 of 19 August 1990 establishing executive boards for public enterprises.
5. Decree no. 89.046 of 13 March 1989 reorganizing the National Commission for Investment.
6. Amendment of Ordinance no. 91.017 of 20 July 1991 ending monopoly of the insurance company (SMAR).

Source: Texts of these regulations, and *Foreign Broadcast Information Service*, NES, 27 November 1992, 19–20. These are by no means all regulation texts reforming the public enterprises, just examples to illustrate the point.

The strategy of encouraging the private sector and discouraging the public sector was developed through a policy of deindustrialization, where credits to industries declined from 28.4 percent of total credits in 1985 to 10.8 percent of total credits in 1990.[36] This policy was recommended in 1984 by the World Bank economic memorandum on Mauritania, which criticized the country's industrialization policies in the 1970s, particularly the creation of large industrial projects for processing oil and sugar.[37] The deindustrialization policy was also strongly advocated by a UN Industrial Development Organization (UNIDO) seminar on industrial development strategies in Mauritania held in Nouakchott in 1985. The conclusions of the seminar recommended that the state should intervene in the industrial sector activities only if (1) they necessitate an important volume of investment that the private sector cannot mobilize and/or (2) the intervention is justified economically or socially but without jeopardizing profitability.[38] Large strategic companies such as SNIM or SONELEC were to be rehabilitated, which means leaving the ownership structure intact if necessary, but introducing new management reforms based exclusively on rentability. Other companies were to be liquidated or privatized. On the eve of adjustment, the government withdrew from ten[39] out of an estimated ninety enterprises owned and run by the public sector. By the time the sectoral adjustment program was presented to the World Bank in May 1990, over thirty public enterprises had been either liquidated, privatized, restructured, or reclassified.[40] During the 1970s the public sector experienced rapid growth, but it began to decline in the 1980s following the reduction of the volume of investment programs and the privatization of ownership and/or management of many public enterpises within the framework of SAPs. In 1986, the private sector shares of the national added value and workforce were estimated at 62.5 percent and 71 percent, respectively (see table 22). In 1990, public enterprises were providing jobs for 25 percent of the modern sector workforce and contributing 25 percent of the GDP of the country. Since all public sector employees are classified within the modern sector, the percentage of public sector employees (25 percent) in 1990 is lower than their percentage (29 percent) in 1986. The overall reduction of the role of the public sector in the national economy represents the major objective for spending millions of dollars on the Public Enterprise Sector Adjustment Program. The heart of this sectoral adjustment program was the rehabilitation of public enterprises through the privatization of their ownership and/or management.

Table 22 Private Sector Share in 1986

Economic sectors	Private sector share of added value in UM million and (%)	Private sector share of workforce in thousands and (%)
Primary sector	14,255 (87)	275 (87)
Secondary sector	5,233 (43)	17 (43)
Tertiary sector	9,309 (52)	53 (40)
Total	28,797 (62.5)	345 (71)

Source: Compiled from "Etude du Climat d'Investissement et Enquête sur le Secteur Privé," International Science and Technology Institute Inc./USAID, Nouakchott, août 1986.

The required financing for the adjustment of the public enterprise sector was estimated at $159 million distributed as follows: $119 million (excluding the African Development Fund's participation) for the financial restructuring of SNIM, $25 million for restructuring other public enterprises, $8 million for the settlement of government arrears to public enterprises, and $7 million for social costs, i.e., severance pay for laid-off employees. It was estimated that the total credit was to meet some 16 percent of Mauritania's external financing gap during the credit's three-year disbursement period from July 1990 to July 1993. Various international lenders expressed their willingness to contribute to the financing of the PASEP project (see table 23). However, some of these commitments were not fulfilled following the 1991 war against Iraq, during which major donors suspended their assistance to Mauritania following its nonendorsement of the war.

Table 23   Cofinancing of PASEP

Lenders	Amount	Lenders	Amount
IDA	$50 million	German government	$4 million
Japanese government	$50 million	Arab funds	$50 million
Spanish government	$5 million	African Development Fund	UCF 15 million

Source: Compiled from IDA President Report no. P-5293-MAU, 30 May 1990, Annex VI; and Accord de Prêt entre la RIM et le FAD en date du 30 juillet 1991.

The IDA credit for the restructuring of the public enterprise sector was arranged to be disbursed in three tranches, provided that a series of conditions are met by the government (see table 24). Three tranches rather than the usual two represent a new step toward tighter and closer supervision of state implementation of adjustment. These conditions are designed to weaken state control over public enterprises, reduce their financial burden on the government budget and the domestic banking system, and free resources for foreign debt payment, among other things. As table 24 illustrates, certain conditions were aimed at liquidating or privatizing certain public enterprises, while others were aimed at reducing staffing levels in public enterprises by approximately 1,550 workers. This represents over 11 percent of the total workforce of the

Table 24 Conditions for Disbursing PASEP Loan

Conditions for disbursement of the first tranche
1. Revise the public enterprise law to improve the legal and institutional framework of the sector
2. Liquidate the only sugar factory (450 employees) in the country
3. Liquidate five other defunct companies in the textile and fishing sectors
4. Agree with IDA on an action program to reform Air Mauritanie, PANPA, SMCP, and SMCPP
5. Dismiss 255 employees on the payroll of PANPA and privatize PANPA stevedoring activities
6. Remove the government monopoly on the insurance sector
7. Fully liberalize the petroleum products distribution sector
8. Change the technical management of the Guelbs plant
9. Cap the operating costs of the state monopoly on fish exports
10. Sell all of SMCP's fishing boats to the private sector
11. Approve a cross-debt plan for settling arrears
Conditions for disbursement of the second tranche
12. Liquidate or privatize one half of nonprofitable enterprises
13. Achieve efficiency and production targets in SNIM reform
14. Finalize a M'haoudat development plan satisfactory to IDA
15. Implement the financial restructuring for SNIM and Air Mauritanie, including signing of a performance contract with Air Mauritanie and PANPA and action plans for SONELEC and SMCP
16. Reduce by 50 percent government arrears with public enterprises
17. Make adequate provisions in the budget for payment of services of SONELEC, SMCPP, and OPT and for the surveillance of fishing waters off the coast of Mauritania
18. Remove SONIMEX's monopoly on rice imports
Conditions for disbursement of the third tranche
19. Liquidate or privatize the remainder of nonprofitable enterprises
20. Achieve efficiency production and restructuring objectives by SNIM, including further reduction of long-term debt if SNIM's financial situation permits
21. Eliminate the remaining government arrears
22. Make adequate provisions in the budget for services provided by SONELEC, SMCPP, and OPT and for surveillance of fishing grounds
23. Remove SONIMEX's monopoly on the remaining products
24. Sign a performance contract with OPT based on the action plan agreed with IDA

Source: Compiled from IDA President, Report No. P–5293–MAU, 30 May 1990, paragraphs 74–77.

public enterprise sector and 48 percent of the workforce of the concerned industries and 40 percent of their combined wage bill. The expected distribution of the affected workers was estimated as follows in 1990: (1) some 150 lower level managers or supervisors, (2) some 700 skilled workers, and (3) some 700 unskilled workers.[41] To smooth these drastic policy measures, the government and the lenders proposed an indemnification of twelve to eighteen months of salary for laid-off workers.[42] This form of indemnification proved to be successful in pacifying the laid-off employees (at least in the short term), as was the case with the massive layoffs of SNIM workers in March 1987. In many cases the laid-off workers used their unemployment indemnifications to start up small private enterprises, a trend that further strengthens the development of the private sector and market mechanisms.

Mining Sector

Mining was restructured through SNIM, the largest public enterprise in the country. From 1963 to 1974, Mauritanian iron ore mines were operated by MIFERMA, a multinational corporation owned by French, British, German, and Italian interests. The company extracted iron ore from deposits around Zouerat and transported them by a two-kilometer-long train via a 650 kilometer railroad to Nouadhibou, from where they were exported to Italy, France, Belgium, the United Kingdom, the United States, and Japan. MIFERMA was a powerful multinational corporation feared by the Mauritanian government, which did not hesitate to use live ammunition against MIFERMA workers on strike in 1969. In 1974, MIFERMA was nationalized and operated subsequently by SNIM, a state-controlled corporation. In 1979, SNIM opened its shareholdings to international capital and became SNIM-SEM (Société d'Economie Mixte), and in 1984 it transferred its headquarters from Nouakchott to Nouadhibou, where the port for exporting iron ore is located. SNIM's share capital in 1990 was as follows: the Mauritanian government (70.9 percent); Kuwait Foreign Trading, Contracting, and Investment Company (9.6 percent); Arab Mining Company (7.6 percent); Iraq Fund for External Development (6.2 percent); Bureau de Recherches et de Participations Minières of Morocco (3.1 percent); Islamic Development Bank (2.4 percent); and Mauritanian private shareholders (0.2 percent). Between 1979 and 1987 SNIM received millions of dollars as either equity share or loans from international lenders for the financing of the Guelbs Project and the 1985 Rehabilitation Program (see table 25).

SNIM again became an international corporation whose lenders and shareholders meet regularly in Paris to discuss its plans for long-term viability.

Table 25 SNIM Lenders and Shareholders 1979–85

SNIM Lenders and Shareholders	$ million	share (%)
Kuwait/Arab Funds	90.8	14.6
International Bank for Reconstruction and Development	80.0	12.9
SNIM Retained Cash Generation	79.1	12.7
Saudi Fund	65.0	10.5
CCCE, France	61.3	9.9
European Investment Bank	42.5	6.8
KFTCIC, Kuwait	40.0	6.4
Arab Mining Company	28.0	4.5
Iraq Fund for External Development	22.0	3.5
African Development Bank	22.0	3.5
European Commission	20.0	3.2
Abu Dhabi Fund	20.0	3.2
BRPM, Morocco	20.0	3.2
OECF, Japan	16.0	2.6
Islamic Development Bank	10.0	1.6
OPEC Fund	5.0	0.8
Total	621.7	99.9%

Source: Compiled from IDA President Report (P–5293–MAU), 30 May 1990, Annex 8, Appendix I.

The internationalization of SNIM deepened its indebtedness (see table 26). In 1990, the outstanding debt of SNIM reached $487 million (25 percent of total Mauritanian foreign debts and nearly half of the GNP), and it increased substantially in 1991 following new loans for the

M'Haoudat Project,[43] which was designed to enrich the low-grade iron ore located in M'Haoudat site. During the same year debt service paid to SNIM lenders amounted to $45 million, while disbursement of loans amounted to only $26 million. Moreover, SNIM annual imports from the world market are estimated at $50 million a year.[44] SNIM indebtedness is simply the result of a structural unequal exchange in which the value of exports (despite the increase in the volume of exports) cannot keep up with the value of imports because of currency devaluation and the reduction in national labor costs following the various austerity programs and the wage control policy. On the sectoral level, the rehabilitation of SNIM made iron ores cheaper through layoffs of over a quarter of the labor force. On the macroeconomic level, devaluation made iron ores even cheaper, as it did for fish, the other major Mauritanian export.

Table 26 SNIM Indebtedness

SNIM indebtedness	1989	1990
Outstanding debt (million dollars)	354	487
Average interest rate on debt (%)	5.7	5.8
Debt service (million dollars)	45.5	45.1

Source: Direction de la Dette Exterieure, Ministère des Finances "Rapport SNIM, Realisation de 1990."

Fisheries Sector

Since the 1980s, fisheries have provided the largest source of foreign exchange for the Mauritanian economy. Mauritania's waters are known to be among of the best stocked in the world because of favorable oceanographic conditions, particularly the presence of the Canary Island cold current along the northwest African coast. Annual potential fish harvest within the exclusive economic zone of Mauritanian waters is estimated to be as high as 600,000 tons. The sector has always been dominated by foreign fishing fleets, but the deepening fiscal crisis of the state encouraged the government in 1979 to adopt a new fisheries policy aimed at optimizing economic and budget returns of the sector. The policy led, among other things, to a growing fleet (owned by Mauritanians) that accounted for about half of the production in the fisheries sector in 1987.[45] Yet corruption, foreign control, and capital flight remain among the major problems of the sector. The sectoral adjustment of the fisheries began in July 1985 when one World Bank consultant prepared a report in which he identified a set of preliminary studies deemed necessary for the articulation of a sectoral strategy. These basic studies and their related feasibility studies were financed essentially by the Kuwait Fund with small cofinancing from the World Bank and the French Caisse Centrale de Cooperation Economique (CCCE). The findings and recommendations of these studies were adopted by the government in April 1987 as a sectoral strategy that establishes the level of fishing capacity and type of fleet appropriate to Mauritanian waters. The maximum fishing quotas were lowered because the level of overfishing had been reached for many species. Once the sectoral strategy was adopted by the government, five donors (Kuwait Fund, Arab Fund, CCCE, Food and Agriculture Organization (FAO), and the World Bank) agreed in March 1987 to finance the necessary preparatory studies for the donor sector meeting that was scheduled for early 1988.[46]

Within the framework of the overall restructuring of the fisheries, the French CCCE provided FF 53 million for repairs of the quay of Nouadhibou Port,[47] from which fish are exported. Along the same strategy, the European Economic Community (EEC) is planning to build fisheries facilities in Mauritania where fish can be processed, using cheap labor, before it is exported. Manuel Marín, vice president of the EEC Commission, described the new agreements between Mauritania and the EEC in this regard as "accords of second generation," where fish processing could take place in Mauritania and thus increase the added value of the sector. But Marín warned that if Mauritania wants to benefit from EEC capital investment, it must make itself "more attractive and more seductive." He added "I cannot put a pistol on European investors' temple and order them to go to Mauritania."[48] One effective policy to attract and seduce international capital is through cheap labor, which is possible through devaluation of the national currency, as well as through socially indifferent labor policy and environmental regulation. The government has reportedly adopted and presented to its creditors in Brussels, Belgium, on 24 March 1994, a new development program for the fisheries sector. One must assume that the new program responds to creditors' concerns over cheap labor and relaxed environmental policy.[49] This internationalization of the sector is further illustrated by an important number of joint ventures with many countries and by the fact that 80 percent of the sector foreign exchange earning is spent abroad.[50] The development strategy underlining the restructuring of both the mining and the fishing sectors is based on an export-led policy aimed at reducing the prices of iron ore and fish, while the strategy for other sectors is essentially based on their potential role in strengthening the private sector, as is the case for the rural sector, or on reducing budget expenditures, as is the case for the education sector.

Rural Sector

The rural sector (agriculture and livestock) was given priority under adjustment because of the real and potential role of private enterprises in this sector. Most agricultural and all livestock activities are in the hands of the private sector,[51] a preexisting condition that made SAPs more interested in projects in agriculture despite (or because of) the arid climate of the country. About 42 percent[52] of the first public investment program (1985–88) under adjustment was allocated to the rural sector. This is a fourfold increase compared to an average of 10 percent of total public investment that was allocated to the rural sector between 1975 and 1980.[53] Credits to agriculture and livestock increased from 0.4 percent to 2.2 percent of total credits between 1985 and 1990.[54] While restructuring the mining and fisheries sectors aimed at increasing export volume and reducing export prices, the restructuring of the rural sector aimed essentially at reducing the budget deficit (abolition of subsidies), promoting the private sector (through land reform), and expanding the potential imports of farming equipment, veterinary drugs, and animal feeds (these are rapidly integrating subsistence farmers and nomads into the world economy). The project was prepared by a World Bank mission (May-June 1988) and in 1989 a follow-up committee (ministerial Decision no. R 020 of 4 January 1989) was established to monitor and accelerate the restructuring of the agricultural sector. The secretariat of the follow-up committee was in the hands of the planning cell within the Ministry of Rural Development, which is largely funded by the lenders. One of the most important elements of the agricultural restructuring was the liberalization of cereal production, marketing, and import. Mauritania imports most of its cereal consumption, and food aid is declining while commercial imports are rising as a consequence of the lender strategy to enlarge windows for their exports through a careful management policy of food aid and food imports. While "the sharp hikes in the consumer prices for imported cereals are the direct result of the IMF's pressure on the government," major food aid donors also pressured the government to raise the selling price of food aid "so that it will have reached parity with import prices by 1987."⁵⁵ Similarly, subsidies are taken away from local agriculture to make it less competitive than heavily subsidized agricultural imports from industrialized countries. "In West Africa, Oxfam has seen how heavily subsidized exports from the USA and the EC destroy domestic markets for local producers, reduce household incomes, and discourage investment in agriculture."⁵⁶ In the 1980s, Mauritania's cereal production averaged 47,000 tons a year while its cereal imports averaged 147,000 tons a year.⁵⁷ The agricultural sector was further liberalized and privatized when Decree no. 89.056 of 17 April 1989 on cereal policy was issued. Article 1 of the decree states that every person (physical or moral) of public or private status can produce, collect, transform, and market all cereals and all cereal products. Article 8 states that retail and wholesale prices of cereals produced locally are unregulated. These policy measures reinforced the already strong private enterprise system within agriculture and the well-established trading culture of Mauritanian business. Liberalization and privatization also meant internationalization of the sector. Loans for the financing of the project of agricultural restructuring came from: International Development Association (SDR 19.4 million), Germany (DM 3.5 million), the CCCE (FF 50 million), and a grant from World Food Program ($1.5 million).

Livestock is an agricultural subsector that has always been completely controlled by the private sector. It was restructured through a separate project. The second livestock project was developed not only to reinforce private enterprise in the sector but also to integrate it within the world economy. This is pertinent given the long history of subsistence and self-reliance of the livestock subsector. The cofinancers of the livestock project are the International Development Association (SDR 7.2 million), African Development Bank ($6.3 million), OPEC Fund ($2 million), and Norway (Nkr 14 million). The objectives of the project include the establishment of some fifteen pastoral cooperative associations throughout the country; the establishment of the necessary conditions for the import, distribution, and sale of veterinary drugs and animal feeds; strengthening of livestock services and rehabilitation of existing infrastructure, and design, construction, and operation of a new abattoir in Nouakchott. These measures were designed to transform an essentially subsistence and self-sufficient form of production and consumption into a market-oriented system of production and consumption structurally linked to, and dependent on, the world market. It is the only economic sector where Mauritania is self-sufficient, particularly in the production of red meat (from cattle, camel, sheep, and goats). Mauritanian pastoralists have already begun importing veterinary drugs and animal feeds from the world market in the same way agriculturalists have been importing farming equipment and techniques. One can say that Mauritanian agriculturalists and pastoralists are perhaps among the last self-sufficient producers to be fully incorporated into the world economy through the livestock sectoral adjustment program.

Education Sector

Like the other sectors, the project of restructuring the education sector is based on the diagnoses and recommendations of a World Bank mission,[58] which stayed in Mauritania in January and February 1988. The project aims essentially at reducing the costs of education, particularly the costs of secondary and higher education. This objective is achieved by increasing expenditure on primary education to reduce it on secondary and higher education. For example, one policy measure of the education reform froze the annual government budget for scholarships in secondary (in the training of teachers) and higher education to its 1987 level of UM 584 million.[59] This latter measure triggered a general student strike at the University of Nouakchott in January 1992. Although the strike continued for months, it failed to change the policy measure, which ultimately proceeded as planned. Another objective of the restructuring is to adjust the education system to the requirements of economic reforms. In other words, the burden of the education system on the government budget should be reduced and the system should produce the kind of skills needed for the management of the kind of projects financed by the international community of lenders and donors. The salient feature of the restructuring of the education system remains the control of expenditure. In this regard, the government committed itself to providing the World Bank with the education budget for every fiscal year, as well as the investment budget of the education sector for the next three years. This government commitment is all what the World Bank needs to closely monitor the education budget, determine the level of expenditure, and influence education policy so it serves the goals of the adjustment program. The financing of the project is distributed as follows: International Development Association ($18.2 million), African Development Bank ($17 million), government ($0.7 million), and local communities ($1.6 million).

Health and Population

The health and population project aims at (1) developing regional health services, (2) reinforcing the Ministry of Health and Social Affairs so it can provide support for regional health services, (3) defining a national population policy and an action plan for its implementation, and (4) promoting the status of women. The project intends to improve efficiency through the implementation of (1) the master plan for the health sector, (2) the cost recovery system, (3) the essential drug distribution system, and (4) staff redeployment. The two central elements and the long-term objectives of reforming the sector are the politics of demography and the marketing of medicines. It was specified in the development credit of the project that by 31 December 1994, the Mauritanian government must adopt a national population policy and an action plan for its implementation. Both measures must be judged satisfactory to the World Bank. The national population policy is likely to be articulated around family planning and includes an important component on ways to integrate women into the process of economic and social development by the adoption of a national strategy and an action plan entitled Women and Development. The project was financed by a development credit from the International Development Association (SDR 11.8 million), and grants from United Nations Fund for Children ($2.4 million), United Nations Population Fund ($3 million), and the (German bank) Bundesministerium fur Wirtschaftliche Zusammenarbeit ($2.3 million). The project is expected to be completed by February 1998, and the details of its implementation are being worked out closely between the Ministry of Health and Social Affairs and the International Development Association.

Banking Sector

The restructuring of the banking sector aims essentially at achieving better control of credit and its reorientation toward the promotion of the private sector in general. The banking reform under the PREF focused on (1) reforming credit policies and banking regulations, (2) strengthening the central bank, and (3) restructuring four (government owned) of the seven commercial banks (see table 27). In 1988, a new banking law was enacted (Ordinance 88.50/CMSN of 20 April 1988) in which the banks and financial institutions were required (Article 20) to publish each year a balance sheet showing a profit or a loss and this must be published in the *Journal Officiel de la Republique Islamique de*

Mauritanie. At least once a year, all banks and financial establishments must submit (Article 21) their accounts to an external audit. Also, the governor of the central bank issued a series of regulations establishing a series of prudential ratios[60] (for example, a minimum ratio of liquidity and risk sharing) that all primary banks must rigorously apply in their financial and credit management. Overall, the central bank's supervisory function over the primary banks was reinforced, particularly through the establishment of the *performance contract*, which codifies the responsibilities and rights of each primary bank in its dealing with the central bank. For example, the performance contract signed between the central bank and the Union des Banques de Développement (UBD) on 13 July 1989, stated that within forty-eight hours of each meeting of the UBD Credit Committee the minutes of proceedings must be sent to the director of credit at the central bank. The 1988 banking law included also a specific list of new disciplinary actions (Articles 33, 35, and 41) that can be taken against banks and/or their directors in case of violation of banking law. These seem to represent much stronger deterrents than previous regulations.

,During the first stage of the adjustment of the banking sector, the state share of banking capital was reduced from 55 percent to 42 percent and the number of banks dropped from seven to five, as shown in table 28. A second stage in the deepening of the restructuring of the banking system began when the 1988 banking law was abrogated in December 1991 and replaced by a new one (Ordinance no. 91.045 of 30 December 1991). Article 22 of the new banking law strengthened credit screening procedures by having bank boards determine the volume of credit that bank directors can authorize. This stage of banking reform is taking place under the third adjustment program (1992–95) and aims at further privatization and internationalization of the banking system. In this context, the central bank is requesting commercial banks to increase their capital on the basis of the 1991 audit of their financial accounts. Such request for increase is also an opportunity for opening up the banks so that state shares can be bought by international capital. As the last step of state withdrawal from this sector, the government decided to sell to the private sector its minority shares in the Banque Nationale de Mauritanie (BNM) (46 percent), the Banque Arabe Mauritanienne Islamique (BAMIS) (10 percent), and the Banque Mauritanienne pour le Commerce International (BMCI) (10 percent). At the same time the government stopped all lending operations of the UBD, the only majority state owned bank.[61] Both decisions are nothing but a prelude to the internationalization of the entire banking system, a policy that is facilitated by the increasing liberalization of exchange. If the private sector is not able to acquire the privatized shares, all the doors are open to international capital to fill in the vacuum. This is one example in which adjustment policies establish the conditions for international capital to recompradorize national institutions of capital formation.

Table 27 Pre-SAPs Structure of Banking Capital

Banks	Capital in UM million	Shareholders	%
BIMA	500	Mauritanian state Banque Internationale de l'Afrique de l'Ouest	91 9
BAMIS	500	Group Al Baraka (Saudi Arabia) Private Mauritanians Mauritanian state	50 40 10
BMAA	500	International Arab African Bank Private Mauritanians Mauritanian state	50 40 10
FND	400	Mauritanian state	100
BMDC	300	Mauritanian state Societe Tunisienne de Banque	93 7
BALM	200	Libyan Foreign Bank Mauritanian state	51 49
SMB	150	Mauritanian state Other banks	55 45

Source: Direction du Controle des Banques, Banque Centrale de Mauritanie, Nouakchott.

Private national capital is already playing an auxiliary role for international capital as is exemplified by the Saudi-dominated BAMIS, the largest bank in the country, where the six major Mauritanian shareholders control only between 1 percent to 3 percent each.[62] Privatization of the banking sector is also leading to a growing concentration of capital in few hands. In 1991, the BMCI was 90 percent controlled by the Mauritanian private sector, and 89 percent of its capital was controlled by six shareholders.[63] Several pockets of sporadic accumulation are developing mainly in connection with import/export activities. But even if one may call these trends the early stages of national capital formation, they do not necessarily constitute a serious trend of capital accumulation at the national level. Such patterns of capital accumulation have been occurring in almost all peripheral states over the past 500 years without bringing about sustained capital accumulation. On the contrary, these patterns facilitated capital drain out of peripheral economies. But even if we assume that there was indeed significant capital accumulation, devaluation is a new threat hanging over the process of national capital formation. If kept in the country, capital will be devalued. If flown outside, it will lose its national character. As Dharam Ghai and Cynthia de Alcantara[64] noted, these segments of (national) capitalists are too much associated with transnational capital, and their way of life is international rather than national.

Table 28 Banking Capital Structure in 1992

Banks	Capital in UM million	Shareholders	%
BAMIS	1000	Groupe Al Baraka (Arabia)	50
		Private Mauritanians	40
		Mauritanian state	10
UBD	800	Mauritanian state	97
		Société Tunisienne de Banque	3
BMCI	750	Private Mauritanians	90
		Mauritanian state	10
BALM	520	Foreign Bank (Libya)	51
		Mauritanian state	49
BNM	500	Private Mauritanians	54
		Mauritanian state	46

Source: Compiled from data of Banque Centrale de Mauritanie and BAMIS.

Devaluation of the Economy

The bottom line of stabilization and adjustment policies is devaluation of the national currency, which represents the cornerstone policy of actually devaluing the national production of most developing countries on the ground of making them more competitive. It is an advanced form of banking on the poor by simply issuing an overnight government decree aimed at reducing the prices of exports while increasing the prices of imports in a given country. As a financial measure, it is one of the (technically) easiest adjustment policies a government can adopt. The World Bank acknowledged how governments are good at rewriting financial claims when it noted that "unlike the problems of industry, those of finance are not frozen in bricks and mortar, plant and machinery. Financial claims, together with the all-important 'rules of the game,' could be rewritten overnight by government decree."[65] In Africa, even the franc of the Communauté Financière Africaine (CFA)—the currency for fourteen former French colonies in Africa—was finally devalued by 50 percent in January 1994.[66] For decades the CFA franc had fixed parity with the French franc and that protected it against devaluation. Pressures from France, the IMF, and the World Bank have finally imposed the devaluation of the CFA franc (without the devaluation of the French franc), a measure that led to "strikes, deaths in clashes with police and a ban on demonstrations in Senegal and Gabon in February" 1994.[67] As a reward for this disastrous measure, the international lenders promised a financial aid tactic of some $7 billion in debt cancellation and adjustment loans for the fourteen affected countries.

Through currency devaluation, international lenders give by one hand less than what they take by the other hand. The best example of this "give and take" was illustrated by the January 1995 financial package (of up to $40 billion) prepared by the Clinton administration and intended to "rescue" the Mexican economy in the aftermath of a depreciation by 35 percent of the Mexican peso against the dollar in three weeks. Such devaluation "has underscored the fragility of the exchange-rate strategy that Mexico pioneered and much of the rest of region imitated."[68] Involved in the issue of devaluation is efficiency or productivity, regardless of how adversely it might affect people's purchasing power (see the discussion of devaluation in chapter 2). For example, the restructuring of SNIM was all about increasing productivity, that is, producing more output with the same input or producing the same output with less input. In other words, worker productivity could be increased by lowering the ratio of worker wages/volume of production. This could be achieved either by reducing worker wages while keeping the same level of production or by keeping the level of wages while increasing the level of production. In SNIM's case, this was achieved by making people work more for the same wage: production per employee improved from 1,690 tons of iron ore per year in 1986 to 2,650 tons in 1989,[69] especially after layoffs of 27 percent of the company's employees.

Indeed, the IDA President's Report mentioned that detailed figures about reduction of production costs in the company were available but were not disclosed by the Bank at SNIM's request since they will reveal an even greater deterioration of the purchasing power of SNIM's workers. Even though the above objective of increasing production was achieved through sectoral policies in the process of rehabilitation of SNIM, it was also achieved within the framework of the macroeconomic policy of currency devaluation, since the real value of wages would be reduced while the overall level of production would be preserved. This is how macroeconomic and sectoral policies reinforce each other.

Productivity in SNIM's mining activities was increased by the depreciation of the production itself through the devaluation and depreciation of the ouguiya in relation to G-7 currencies. Between 1984 and 1994, the Mauritanian national currency, the ouguiya (UM), lost 100 percent, 184 percent, and 238 perceent of its value in relation to the dollar, the IMF special drawing right (SDR), and the French franc, respectively, as table 29 illustrates. Devaluation was the most important policy measure that contributed to bringing down export prices and increasing import prices, the twin policy objectives of SAPs. It nullified any comparative advantage of the country. Devaluation is a tricky financial maneuver because it dissociates local cost of production (measured in ouguiya) from sale prices measured in dollar or other G-7 currencies. Iron ore exports increased in volume (from 6.2 million tons in 1978 to 11.1 million tons in 1989) but measured in constant 1977 terms, its prices dropped 45 percent from $16.9 per ton in 1977 to $9.3 per ton in 1989.[70] Devaluation also depreciated the value of fish, the other major Mauritanian export. According to Prime Minister Sidi Mohamed Ould Boubacar, the general trend in the fisheries sector in 1993 is that the increase in the volume of fish exports is accompanied by a decrease in their value.[71]

Table 29   Devaluation of the Ouguiya

Year	1984	1986	1988	1990	1992	1995*
UM/SDR1	65.9	90.6	101	110.7	158	195.5
UM/$1	64	74	75	80	87	125.3
UM/FF1	7.1	11	12.4	14.9	18.6	26

Source: IMF, *International Financial Statistics*, various issues. * As of March 1995.

The rationale of making exports competitive through devaluation is a rather vicious economistic and intellectual argument aimed at confusing public perception of price changes. It is a poor rationale used to create the illusion that the decline of export prices following devaluation can be offset by increasing the volume of exports. Worldwide producers' competition to compensate price loss by increasing the volume of sales leads to a market glut which tends to drive prices further down. Hence, the need to increase the volume of production is driven by the constant loss of value of the production following devaluation and underpricing. This is one of the most important economic tools in the hands of the industrialized nations today, since it allows them to create artificial comparative advantages through the systematic manipulation of exchange rates worldwide. Devaluation is a sine qua non condition for any dealing with the IMF, and without it a developing nation can be isolated from the international community of lenders. No developing country can afford economic isolation given the level of economic interdependence and the degree of centralization of money and credit worldwide by a few international financial institutions that abide by the policies of the G–7 countries. Winning the confidence of international lenders became the cornerstone policy of any government willing to do business with the world market. Explaining (to a Western journalist) the rationale behind the October 1992 devaluation of the ouguiya (which led to a riot followed by a curfew in Nouakchott), the governor of the Mauritanian central bank gave the reasons why the Mauritanian government had taken this devastating measure of devaluation after two years of negotiations with the World Bank and the IMF:

> You don't devalue light-heartedly. . . . We expect this decision to put us back in the international financial community. We also think we can restore the spirit of confidence so as to create the sort of investment capacity which will get growth established. There is no point in balance for balance's sake. How can we restore confidence and, particularly, attract external investments through partnership? Restoring confidence, first and foremost, means guaranteeing freedom of enterprise. We have also proposed some varied but practical incentives. Everyone must be able to repatriate his profits and no longer be cramped by a scarcity of foreign exchange.[72]

The impact of devaluation on import prices is devastating for the purchasing power of all, rich and poor. Most consumer and capital goods in Mauritania are imported, and their prices are immediately affected by devaluation. Selected retail price increases in table 30 reflect the periodical devaluation and annual depreciation of the ouguiya following the adoption of a flexible exchange rate policy. The commodities selected here are among the least affected by devaluation because their prices were somehow government regulated (*prix homolgués*). These substantial price increases were not compensated for by any comparable increase in wages. With devaluation, exchange between the national economy and the world market will always be unequal. Without currency devaluation, there is no reason to believe that the prices of fish and iron ore could have been brought down to where they are today.

Table 30 Price Changes in Nouakchott January 1985–January 1994

Selected Commodities	January 1985 Prices = 100	May 1992 Prices (%)	January 1994 Prices (%)
Rice	100	+245	+272
Wheat flour	100	+156	+160
Bread	100	+145	+181
Coca Cola	100	+178	+275
Cement	100	+203	+212
Electricity	100	+123	+192
Water	100	+150	+227
Gasoline	100	+160	+180

Source: Compiled from "Fonds monetaire International, Bureau des Statistics, Rapport de Mission en Mauritanie, etabli par Michel Le Marois, 20 mars 1986;" author's field work in Nouakchott in 1992; and Mohamed Ali Ould-Mey's field work in Nouakchott in January 1994.

In the long run, devaluation guarantees a constant reduction of the prices of raw materials coming from developing economies and a steady increase of the prices of finished goods imported from developed countries. As the trade of goods and services became more and more liberalized worldwide, financial and monetary policies became important in terms of creating advantages by playing out the difference in the mechanisms of articulation between national monetary policies and exchange rate fluctuations. In this regard, each devaluation is a redefinition of the national economy vis-à-vis the economies of countries whose currencies are used as a reference in determining the value of the ouguiya. This is how devaluation actually transforms the apparent net capital inflow into a net capital outflow from an increasingly globalized and denationalized economy. With the exception of devaluation (which demarcates the economy from other economies), all other economic adjustment policies concentrate on the globalization and internationalization of the Mauritanian economy. With the state being denationalized, most economic activities are in the process of being informalized and integrated into the overall global economy, where informal economic activities of street vendors in Africa are formally linked to the world market.

Globalization of the Economy

This section summarizes the previous arguments with an emphasis on (1) the increasing dependence of the economy on Western lenders and donors; (2) the leadership of the World Bank in entwining these lenders/donors; (3) the growing leverage of these lenders and donors over budget allocation, food policy, and so on; and (4) the mediocre performance of the economy during the past ten years of intensive adjustment. Throughout the 1970s and early 1980s Mauritania was able to mobilize substantial amounts of foreign aid (grants and loans) from bilateral sources, particularly from the Arab oil-producing countries. Between 1973 and 1983 foreign aid averaged $200 million a year. During the 1979–81 period it reached $250 million annually, and in 1982 it peaked at $340 million. Foreign aid sometimes contributed over $170 per head, or 40 percent of GNP per capita.[73] Mauritania's membership in Arab, Islamic, and African regional organizations explains this unusual access to a variety of sources of international aid. Prior to adjustment, this foreign aid was mobilized and managed on a bilateral basis, without international coordination. Loans and grants were negotiated bilaterally between the government and individual donors. The government was solely in charge of allocating these resources according to its national priorities, which were determined conjointly by the different ministerial departments working within the framework of a national plan of economic and social development.

Adjustment inaugurated an era in which international economic cooperation began to shift from bilaterally centered to multilaterally centered relations. Although the World Bank's 1985 Action Program promised to reduce the external dependence of Mauritania,[74] it actually internationalized the economy and put it at the mercy of a complex multitude of international investors. With adjustment, foreign donors and lenders improved the coordination of their investment and debt policies within the framework of international institutions such as the Consultative Group, the Paris Club, the IMF, and the World Bank. What used to be considered as purely domestic policies, such as formulating development strategies, designing public investment programs, and managing external debt, became international matters (see chapter 4) bringing together the Mauritanian government and a variety of other governments and multilateral organizations led by the World Bank and bound together by the driving desire to engage in profitable and safe business. This internationalization of the Mauritanian economy is further illustrated by the fact that economic diagnoses are no longer conducted by the government. World Bank experts regularly and systematically prepare macroeconomic and sectoral memoranda upon which they (in collaboration with the government) draft the Letter of Intent, which is used by the Bank and the Fund to establish the policy framework paper, which determines all economic policies every three years. But the internationalization of the Mauritanian economy is unbalanced since it is dominated by a few Western lenders and donors. Total foreign aid to Mauritania in 1989 reached $245 million, representing $130 per capita, or 27 percent of the country's GNP per capita. The grant/loan distribution of the aid was half/half and the sectoral allocation was as follows: technical cooperation (24 percent), investment (48 percent), aid program and support for budget and balance of payments (19 percent), food aid (7.7 percent), and urgent relief (1.3 percent). Mauritania's major donors/lenders used to be the Arab countries and Funds to whom Mauritania owed 40 percent of its foreign debt as of December 31, 1988 (see table 31). But as adjustment progresses OECD countries and organizations took the lead in Mauritania's debts. In 1989 grants and loans to Mauritania came from OECD (56.2 percent), Arab countries and Funds (14.4 percent), African Bank and Fund (12.2 percent), UN system (10.4 percent), China and USSR (5 percent), and NGOs (1.8 percent).[75]

Foreign aid is structurally linked to foreign trade, which is dominated by the industrialized countries as table 32 illustrates. Also the proportion of multilateral debts seems to be increasing compared to bilateral debts. It increased from 27.2 percent in 1983[76] to 33.9 percent in 1988. This multilateralization of foreign aid is further reflected in the fact that many bilateral loans and grants are administered and monitored multilaterally by international financial institutions, particularly the World Bank, which is providing more and more security for foreign investors through the Multilateral Investment Guarantee Agency (MIGA). Foreign trade partners of Mauritania are also the major food aid donors who, in 1993, included: Spain, Japan, Saudi Arabia, Norway, Canada, Germany, France, Switzerland, China, Italy, the United States, Qatar, South Korea, the World Food Programme, the European Union, the United Nations Development Program, and the United Nations High Commission for Refugees.[77]

Table 31 Foreign Debt 12/31/1988

Official Creditors	$ million	Official creditors	$ million
Bilateral creditors	1,170	Multilateral creditors	601
Kuwait	216	International Development Association	148
Saudi Arabia	183	Arab Fund for Economic and	
France	130	Social Development	96
China	109	International Monetary Fund	80
Algeria	99	International Bank for	
Libya	88	Reconstruction and Development	53
Austria	76	Arab Monetary Fund	51
Iraq	57	African Development Fund	37
Spain	41	European Investment Bank	37
Morocco	39	Islamic Development Bank	31
Netherlands	36	African Development Bank	25
Brazil	29	Organization of Petroleum	
Japan	28	Exporting Countries	24
United Kingdom	11	International Fund for	
Qatar	8	Agricultural Development	11
Germany	7	Arab Organization of Petroleum	
United States	7	Exporting Countries	8
Italy	5		
North Korea	1		

Source: Compiled from a letter of the director of external debt to the minister of economy and finance, Nouakchott, July 1990.

Even though Mauritania has since its independence been strongly dependent on diversified foreign assistance, the level of internationalization of its economy and the degree of its dependence on the West is deepening with the proliferation of Western donors and projects in the country. In 1989, over fifty donors were committing nearly a billion dollars for financing some 290 projects in almost all sectors of the national economy (see table 33). The implication of this

Global Restructuring and Peripheral States

proliferation of foreign donors is the unprecedented leverage of a complex multitude of international economic operators who are influencing every aspect of the Mauritanian economy, from budget allocation to food policy. This is part of the worldwide increase of foreign direct investment in recent years, as the nationalization of foreign affiliates during the 1950s, 1960s, and 1970s was reversed by the privatization of state-owned enterprises in the 1980s and 1990s. At the beginning of the 1990s, there were 37,000 parent transnational corporations (92 percent from developed countries) controlling some 170,000 foreign affiliates worldwide.[78] The trend is certainly growing since the adoption of the Guidelines on the Treatment of Foreign Direct Investment (GTFDI) by the World Bank in 1992. These guidelines provide a (still) voluntary framework for the treatment of foreign capital, from admission procedures, general standards treatment, transfer of capital and revenues, expropriation and compensation, and settlement of disputes between host countries and investors. It should be noted that while these guidelines contain detailed prescriptions to government host countries on how they should treat private foreign investors, they do not deal with the obligations of foreign investors, except in general terms.[79]

Table 32 Mauritania's Foreign Trade ($ million)

Exports	1990	1992	Imports	1990	1992
Japan	93	138	France	149	166
Italy	62	58	United States	24	67
Spain	38	49	Spain	24	48
France	48	46	Italy	6	42
Belgium-Luxembourg	94	39	Germany	30	37
Others	133	177	Belgium-Luxembourg	32	29
Total	468	507	Total including others	338	581

Source: The Economist Intelligence Unit, *Country Report 4th Quarter 1993: Senegal, The Gambia, Mauritania*, London: EIU, 38.

Table 33. Development Projects in Progress in 1989

Donor/Lender Institutions	Sectors (# of Projects, Amount in $ million)
GTZ, UNDP, FAC, DGCS	Management (6, 5)
GTZ, UNDP, UNPF, AFESD, AGFUND, IDA, FAC, SDF, USAID, KFW,	Administration (24, 62)
UNICEF, UNDP, FENU, UNSO, AFESD, FAC, KFAED, IDB, ADF, EIB, CCCE, SDF, EDF,	Mining, waterworks (28, 142)
UNDP, CARITAS, UNPF, IDA, FAC, IDB, ADF, SDF, USAID, SOATC, MATC, EACT, TATC, CHATC, IDRC, DGIS, CAID, GTZ, IQDF, AFVP, WFP	Human resource (32, 73)
CCCE, UNDP, GTZ, FAO, LWF, DGIS, AFESD, IDA, WFP, FAC, ADB, SDF, IFAD, AGFUND, AAFED, USAID, OPEC, EDF, IDRC, DGCS, AFR70, ITAPIANTI, CHNCEE, DGIS, WFP,	Agriculture and and fishery (61, 171)
KFW, GTZ, UNDP, LWF, CARITAS, OXFAM, DGIS, AFESD, ILO, FAC, KFAED, USAID, UNICEF, EDF, TECPLAN, AFR70, Others	Regional development (25, 139)
JICA, UNDP, AFESD, IDA, KFAED, ADB	Industry (7, 17)
CCCE, UNDP, AFESD, FAC, ADB, EIB, EDF	Energy (16, 55)
UNDP, EDF, ADF, SDF, FAC	International trade (5, 58)
UNDP, KFW	Internal trade (4, 6)
CCCE, FAC, UNDP, KFAED, IDB, EDF, CHNCEE, AFESD	Communication and transportation (18, 63)
GTZ, LWF, WV, UNDP, DOULOS, FAC, KFAED, SDF, EDF, CHNCEE	Social development (14, 16)
TDH, UNPF, UNICEF, ZOA, GTZ, UNDP, LWF, WV, AFVP, DOULOS, AFESD, FAC, ADF, SDF, DGCS, USAID, WHO, SOATC, CHATC, EDF	Health (27, 98)
CARITAS, IDA, FAC, ADB, FAO, USAID, UNHCR, EDF, DGCS, DGIS, CHNCEE, CCI,	Humanitarian relief (23, 71)
All Donors/Lenders	All sectors (290, 976)

Source: Compiled from UNDP, "Mauritanie, Rapport 1990," Novembre 1990.

Thanks to the adjustment strategy and to the coordination and planning provided by international financial institutions and mechanisms (the IMF, the World Bank, the Paris Club, the Consultative Group, and international NGOs), these foreign investors are increasingly in a position to influence and even determine the trajectory of economic policy in developing countries, particularly in Mauritania, where their leverage is now overwhelming at all levels of the state apparatus and in all sectors of the economy.

Budget allocations for several sectors are determined conjointly by the Bank and the government. For example, as part of an agreement between the Bank and the government for the restructuring of the education sector, the latter has had to present the annual education budget to the Bank on 30 October of each year from 1989 on.[80] It must also present the education budget for the subsequent three years, and the amount proposed by the government can be accepted or rejected by the Bank. Moreover, food policy in the country is decided by a Food Programming Committee (Ministerial Decision no. 0073 MEF/MDR, April 1989) whose membership is half national and half international. The committee's members are: minister of rural development, minister of economy and finance, minister of industry and mining, minister of commerce and transport, commissioner of food safety, World Food Program, European Economic Community, the United States, France, and Germany. The role of the committee is to provide a permanent follow up of the evolution of agricultural production, foresee and solicit food aid, and identify and program food imports. One more example that illustrates further the process of internationalization of the economy is that Mauritania has no control over proceeds from its iron ore sales. These are paid exclusively into a designated account of a French institution (Societé Générale pour favoriser le Développement du Commerce et de l'Industrie en France). Then Societé Générale is instructed by SNIM lenders to transfer certain (set aside) funds to a trust account, where the trustee is irrevocably instructed to pay to SNIM lenders all due principal, interest, and other charges. SNIM gets only leftovers of proceeds from its own sales.[81] Despite the increasing internationalization of the Mauritanian economy, one cannot overlook the uneven weight of the various international economic operators. For example, the World Bank leads by far all the others not only in putting together and designing development policies but also in financing them as illustrated in table 34.

Table 34 Cofinancing of SAPs

Projects	Lenders/donors	Amount committed
First Structural Adjustment	IDA African Development Bank Kingdom of Saudi Arabia Federal Republic of Germany	$42.4 million $19.6 million $4.8 million $2.8 million
Agricultural Sector Adjustment and Irrigation Improvement	IDA Federal Republic of Germany France World Food Program	$25 million DM 3.5 million 50 million FF $1.5 million
Public Enterprise Sector Adjustment Program	IDA Arab funds Japan Spain Germany African Development Fund	$40 million $50 million $50 million $5 million $4 million 15 million UCF
Education Sector Restructuring	IDA African Development Bank Mauritanian government Local communities and private sector	$18.2 million $17 million $0.7 million $1.6 million
Health and Population Project	IDA United Nations Population Fund United Nations Children Fund Germany	$16.5 million $3 million $2.4 million $2.3 million
Second Livestock Project	IDA African Development Bank Organization of Petroleum Exporting Countries Norway	$7.6 million $6.3 million $2 million Nkr 14 million

Source: Texts of various World Bank loans and credits.

Following a decade of IMF stabilization programs and World Bank structural adjustment policies, the national economy has been substantially devalued and is now in the hands of a complex multitude of international economic investors whose control over resource allocation and management is growing. However, with the increasing dependence on the world market, the steady decline of living standards continues for the majority of the population. Using IMF statistics, the French-based Moniteur du Commerce International estimated Mauritania's GDP growth rate in 1990 at -1.9 percent.[82] The World Bank gave an estimate of 0.3 percent growth rate the same year.[83] The United Nations Development Program's *Human Development Index* of 1991 noted that the structure and level of underdevelopment of Mauritanian society did not change much after a decade of adjustment. The report placed Mauritania 147th out of the 160 countries covered. The mortality rate among children under five is 214 per 1,000 live births, life expectancy is forty-seven years, adult literacy is 35 percent, the combined primary and secondary enrollment ratio is 35 per cent, and the portion of the population with access to health services stands at 30 percent.[84] More alarming is that two years after launching adjustment, Mauritania acquired the status of Less Developed Country and at the beginning of the 1990s, it "slipped from its World Bank classification as lower middle income to low income status."[85] Yet the prime minister and the ministers of finance and planning insist that Mauritania is rich in natural resources and has a small population and that "the issue now is management of these resources . . . and we believe we have made the right choices in terms of economic orientation."[86] There is near consensus among the elite that the major economic problem is economic mismanagement or corruption and, the magic solution is to get "the right man in the right place." Notwithstanding the scale and scope of corruption within the Mauritanian state, this naive management economic philosophy is widespread among the major political parties and illustrates the ideological impact of ten years of learning and assimilation of the World Bank approach to the problem and solution of development.

The two major political parties (the ruling Democratic and Social Republican Party [PRDS] and the opposing Union of Democratic Forces [UFD]) do not have any original economic program and exhibit little difference in their economic thinking. In the words of one journalist, the opposition/government fight is nothing but "a snake biting its tail."[87] Both avoid any criticism of adjustment policies. The PRDS abides strictly by the tenets of liberalism. The spokesman of the PRDS explains that the party's economic philosophy is based on liberalism and priority to rural development and on the postulate that, in economic matters, the state should play the role of a referee.[88] The leader of the UFD, the main opposition party, always emphasizes his belief in economic liberalism and the necessity to privatize or liquidate state companies and to limit the role of the state to regulation of economic activities and settlement of problems. In 1993 he noted, "I am sorry that my compatriots all too often make the same mistake as the ruling party and shift too much responsibility onto the shoulders of the funders, the World Bank and the IMF."[89] The complete absence of any original economic platform from the agenda of both the government and the opposition and their submissiveness to the *diktat* of SAPs make the intensity of social struggle shift toward politics, culture, identity, and other forms of representation amid an economic crisis and a process of social fragmentation. Since economic relations are taken for granted because of the triumphant (imposed) market economy, sociopolitical relations became the focus of politics and conflicts. In the words of Abdelali Doumou, "The particular status of the 'economic' makes it impossible to assume 'commodity fetishism' in the peripheral social formations since, despite a dominance of commodity relations, 'the economic' is not a 'fetish' insofar as it does not constitute the exclusive system of behavior and representation of social life."[90] This shift of representation from economics to politics is better reflected in the shift from the preadjustment buzzword of *development* to the postadjustment buzzword of *democratization*.

7

Social Dimension of SAPs

Adjustment began as a Western strategy of development conceived by the G-7 and implemented for the most part by the World Bank and the International Monetary Fund in close collaboration with Third World states. At the core of this strategy are economic and financial reforms designed to further open Third World markets for exports of goods, services, and capital from the industrialized countries. This objective was mostly achieved through the processes of denationalization of the state and globalization of the economy analyzed in the previous three chapters. As noted earlier, one of the most salient features of these structural reforms is the adoption of a series of austerity programs designed to reallocate resources away from the public sector. This shift from the welfare-state system had adverse effects on employment and negative repercussions on the general standard of living of most people. It also triggered various forms of resistance to these reforms and consequently induced the government and the lenders/donors to incorporate a social policy component into SAPs to cushion their impact and perhaps alleviate the social costs for less-favored groups. The interplay between government austerity programs, the resistance of many social groups, and the social policy of adjustment all brought about deep sociopolitical adjustments, the most dramatic of which remains the process of democratization and sociopolitical fragmentation, which will be addressed in chapter 8. This chapter analyzes the origins, processes, and outcomes of social policy and social differentiation under adjustment.

Social Dimension of Adjustment or Global Information System?

In the early SAP packages, the World Bank did not include a social policy component. One of the main concerns of the Bank at the time was to draw attention of the borrowing government to the specter of widespread unemployment arising out of SAPs and its potential for sociopolitical destabilization. The Mauritanian adjustment program of 1985 included an "employment promotion policy" rather than a "social policy." But strong criticism of SAPs began to emerge and spread in the mid-1980s, particularly from United Nations Children's Fund (UNICEF) when it published the famous and pioneering work entitled *Adjustment with a Human Face*,[1] which emphasized the issue of the negative social consequences of SAPs, particularly on children and their mothers. UNICEF's report noted that during the first half of the 1980s, there was an annual average of forty-seven developing countries, each with an IMF adjustment program, and most of these "programmes did not reverse the adverse developments in the conditions of children"[2] and "in many cases it appears that stabilization and adjustment policies were themselves neglecting the nutrition and health of the most vulnerable."[3] At the same time, the World Health Organization "calls on Member States to ensure, in cooperation with international financing institutions, that the health and nutritional status of the most disadvantaged social groups are protected when economic adjustment policies are designed and implemented."[4]

Along the same line of concern about the social dimension of adjustment, the United Nations Development Program (UNDP) undertook an assessment of the social impact of SAPs in sub-Saharan Africa[5] and drew attention to the negative social impact of adjustment. Strong criticism came also from the United Nations Economic Commission for Africa which questioned the narrow economic and financial focus of SAPs and their neglect of the social and historical roots of Africa's problems.[6] Even the European Community, a strong advocate of SAPs, acknowledged the tremendous social problems caused by SAPs, and in response to that it began spending significant funds within the framework of the first financial protocol of the Lomé IV Convention to contain SAPs' social problems and perhaps give a "more human face to adjustment."[7] Moreover, a 1992 study by the United Nations Research Institute for Social Development came to the conclusion that "despite problems of data and interpretation, there appears to be sufficient evidence to warrant the generalization that these processes and policies [of SAPs] have contributed to a significant redistribution of income and wealth from the poor to the rich both nationally and internationally."[8] Other analysts of SAPs, particularly in Africa, drew attention to their negative social impacts on specific groups affected by cuts in public spending, abolition of subsidies, and devaluation of the national currency which further aggravated the already deteriorating "day-to-day reality of life in Africa: crumbling roads, growing unemployment, clinics without medicines, schools without teaching materials—a reality of diminished prospects, especially for the poor."[9] Ultimately, widespread social suffering caused by SAP austerity programs combined with strong political criticism of SAPs at the local, national, and international levels encouraged lenders and governments to incorporate a new "social component" or "social policy" into otherwise socially indifferent financial and economic programs.

It was in 1987 and in response to widespread criticism of the negative social impacts of SAPs that the World Bank (in collaboration with the UN Development Program and the African Development Bank) launched an initiative called Social Dimension of Adjustment (SDA). This innovative initiative was proposed and designed to protect the poor against negative impacts of SAPs on the one hand, and integrate them into SAPs on the other hand. The above three multilateral institutions provided a modest amount of $10 million for this ambitious SDA program and the World Bank was in charge of its execution. An SDA unit was created within the World Bank as an instrument for designing a social policy to be integrated into structural adjustment programs. The SDA program was further strengthened when several donors joined it and provided further assistance. These include: the International Fund for Agricultural Development, the European Economic Community, Canada, Germany, Norway, Sweden, Switzerland, the United Kingdom, and the United States Agency for International Development. Later, the World Bank, along with the African Development Bank and the United Nations Development Program Regional Bureau for Africa, developed an agenda for SDA to address the growing hardship and poverty resulting from the implementation of SAPs. Since then the organic linkage between poverty and adjustment has continued and led the World Bank to convene a symposium on Poverty and Adjustment involving some seventeen countries, the IMF, development agencies, and researchers.[10] By 1990, some thirty-two countries had begun implementing SDA in an attempt to give a "human face" to often inhumane social ramifications of economic and financial reforms. (Similar developments led the World Bank later to incorporate an environmental policy into SAPs).

The SDA initiative concentrates on four areas: (1) improved management of macro and sectoral policy, (2) social action programs and projects to help vulnerable socioeconomic groups, (3) strengthened national information systems to enhance policy and program formulation, and (4) institution building and training to integrate social dimensions into the ongoing policy-making and implementation process. It particularly facilitates policy analysis and coordination in the overall process of administering SAPs at the macro as well as micro levels. In this regard, "the SDA Unit has proposed a framework that explicitly recognizes the links and processes that transmit changes in macro strategy to the actual behavior and decisions made at the micro or household level." The SDA agenda is based on the fact that "the poor themselves constitute a large part of Africa's human capital stock, and their activities are a major component of national output." They are so numerous that they cannot be ignored politically or economically and therefore must be incorporated into SAPs. The real dilemma, however, is to do something or to pretend to do something for the chronic poor as well as for those impoverished by SAP policies without any substantial concession on the rigor and timetable of SAPs' economic and financial reforms. "The key policy problem is therefore how to assist these poor and vulnerable groups without causing distortions in economic mechanisms that would threaten the maintenance of macroeconomic discipline."[11] The 1990 *World Development Report* came to the conclusion that there is a two-part strategy for any rapid and politically sustainable improvements in the quality of life for the poor. "The first element of the strategy is the pursuit of a pattern of growth that ensures productive use of the poor's most abundant asset—labor. The second element is widespread provision to the poor of basic social services, especially primary education, primary health care and family planning."[12] These two objectives are often set on a collision course.

To grasp the real social dimension of SAPs, two aspects need to be pointed out. First, there is an obvious contradiction between the austerity regime advocated by SAPs and the range of welfare measures and spending proposed by SDA. Whenever this contradiction appears, however, SAPs prevail. SDA programs "must be compatible with the theoretical and ideological foundations of adjustment programs in general and specific policy measures taken by each country in particular."[13] This fundamental observation came out of an international conference (held in Khartoum, Sudan, in 1988) on the human factor in SAPs. It raises the paradox of SDA: providing financial and economic assistance to vulnerable groups (the chronic poor as well as the new poor) within the framework of SAPs, which themselves call for cutting the same financial and economic assistance within the framework of budget cuts and austerity programs. The incompatibility of these two objectives necessitates that one of them prevail at the expense of the other. Actually SDA programs never delay or alter the design of SAPs. Even though social policy under adjustment is designed to soften and cushion the austerity measures of adjustment, it must above all conform to adjustment objectives in terms of financial and economic policies. Second, the apparent search for a social policy of adjustment hides the perhaps more serious objective of the World Bank to establish a *global information system* on the micro level of household and informal sectors via SDA programs. Even though most national information systems of most developing countries provide a quantifiable measure of socioeconomic indicators at the macro level (national census, GDP, balance of payments, foreign debts, budget deficit, and so on), they rarely provide reliable data on household incomes and expenditures. The World Bank information system, which is based for the most part on national information systems, was often weak on socioeconomic data at the micro level, and the design of SAPs was exclusively based on data at the macroeconomic level. Thus SDA programs came to provide much-needed data on household incomes and expenditures. They were articulated around the concept of poverty, defined as "the inability to attain a minimal standard of living."[14] Such conceptualization of poverty in absolute terms rather than in terms of inequality sets the agenda of most SDA systems of data collection: measurement of standards of living through measurement of household incomes and expenditures per capita, which constitute the backbone of SDA research. While certain social actions of SDA may provide an immediate relief and a political anesthetic for the poor amid the turmoil of SAPs, their statistics component seems to be a more important element of the World Bank strategy of building an information system at the global, national, local, and household levels.

The primacy of the statistics component (rather than the social one) in SDA programs is revealed by the following example. In 1990, an evaluation of the SDA program was conducted by an independent team selected by the Central Evaluation Office of the UNDP Bureau for Program Policy and Evaluation (BPPE) after an extensive consultation with the World Bank and the African Development Bank. On the positive side, the evaluation report found that the SDA project had "succeeded in developing guidelines for the establishment of an information system on the social impact of adjustment programs." On the negative side, the report revealed that there was "an overemphasis on data gathering" with no links to the social action components of the project. It also revealed that "the World Bank appeared to have used the SDA project as a condition for disbursing other loans" and that a "significant proportion of resources were being used to produce theoretical documentation." The report recommended that "if SDA is continued, the World Bank should no longer be the sole executing agency."[15]

It can be concluded that the SDA project represents a series of experiments and measures aimed at containing the sociopolitical ramifications of economic and financial reforms while gathering vital data at the household and informal sector levels for a *global planning system*. The SDA project "is a useful figleaf, but a figleaf nonetheless."[16] Preparation of microeconomic data on consumption and income are useful for stabilization programs and other economic policies.[17] In addition, the World Bank maintains that statistics generated from the SDA program can and should be recycled again within the next generation of SAPs and, more important, can help the government show that the standard of living of the majority of the poor did not decline. This technique of persuasion is based on the purposeful selection and manipulation of statistics and the use of variance between sectors, social groups, and countries to emphasize the *mixed* result of SAPs and therefore pacify SAP critics. This persuasive strategy of emphasizing the mixed results of SAPs has provided the central argument in all World Bank self-evaluation studies, as well as in most friendly assessments of the adjustment process, as illustrated by many SDA studies and research sponsored by the OECD (see the previous note). SDA programs constitute a by-product of economic and financial reforms, not an original and genuine social policy. Above all, they constitute instruments for ensuring the success of economic and financial reforms amid a discourse of "social policy" and "poverty alleviation" which themselves were never used seriously as the yardstick against which SAPs are assessed and judged. SDA was not developed with the early SAPs, rather it was later incorporated as a reaction to the worsening social impact of adjustment and the growing criticism of SAPs. The Mauritanian case demonstrates that it developed out of an attempt to cushion the social impact of SAPs and contain their political critics.

PREF Employment Policy

The first structural adjustment program in Mauritania (PREF 1985–88) had direct negative impacts on most of the population since it was centered around an austerity program. It was a shock program in which budget cuts curtailed government expenditure and recruitment of personnel, the restructuring or downsizing of public enterprises led to massive layoffs of employees, the abolition of subsidies raised prices and tariffs of public services, and the currency devaluation and price policies contributed to a deterioration of the purchasing power of the population in general. During each phase of the adjustment process the government and the World Bank developed policy measures initially designed to mitigate the above negative impacts of SAPs. Under the first adjustment program, the predesigned policy response was labeled employment promotion policy since the Social Dimension of Adjustment did not exist at the time. Under the second adjustment program (PCR 1989–91) these policy measures were renamed "the Social Policy of PCR" and led to the establishment of a Social Policy unit within the Ministry of Planning similar to the SDA unit created within the World Bank. During the third adjustment program (1992–95), the social policy of adjustment continued under the name of "National Poverty Alleviation Strategy."[18] The following presents a more detailed analysis of how employment policy under the PREF was the forerunner of what will be Mauritania's SDA programs.

The PREF employment promotion policy was designed to mitigate the shock created by layoffs in the public sector and public enterprises. It was obvious that government budget cuts and the restructuring of public enterprises, which constitute the linchpin of the PREF program, would also increase unemployment. A set of policy measures (table 35) were conjointly adopted by the government and the World Bank hopefully to create jobs in the private sector for those losing jobs in the public sector. Among these policy measures, the Fonds d'Insertion et de Reinsertion dans la Vie Active (FIRVA) constitutes the most tangible one. It is a reinsertion fund that is supposed to provide loans for specific categories of job seekers negatively affected by SAPs, particularly young graduates and former civil servants. But the economic impact of this project is rather insignificant in terms of job creation, since the number of those who actually get loans is infinitely small compared to those who are eligible. The significance of the project lies perhaps in its political impact. First, it is widely publicized by the government as a serious and genuine enterprise dealing with unemployment in a way that seems to ensure an equal opportunity for everyone. Even those who were not successful in getting loans through FIRVA may think that others got the loans. Second, the few who got loans are often the most active politically and not necessarily the most dissatisfied with their unemployment or the most in need of assistance. For example, retired state officials were often more successful at getting FIRVA loans than young graduates or immigrant workers, who usually lack the necessary government and bureaucratic connections. The unemployed who have government connections represent the activists whose pacification and cooptation is a political objective for FIRVA. The others would not be able to disturb or delegitimize SAPs. The process of competition and selection involved in a loan application creates a sense of fairness, while the actual outcome is not necessarily fair given the importance of corruption in the state apparatus and the level of nepotism among a still tribalized society.[19] Eligibility to apply for FIRVA loans does not guarantee getting a loan, and being in one of the categories of job seekers is a necessary, but not a sufficient, condition for obtaining loans. Moreover, when FIRVA was set up in 1985 it was not simply a policy designed to cushion the social impact of adjustment. It actually supports and strengthens the grand objective of SAPs in creating and promoting the private sector through the firm establishment of market relations. Beyond its political and psychological impact, FIRVA encourages the creation of small individual enterprises by young graduates, retired civil servants, and former immigrant workers. These small private enterprises (growing out of FIRVA loans) are considered to be the backbone of a market economy whose building is the raison d'etre of SAPs.

However, FIRVA and other job-creation policy measures did not prevent unemployment from rising. Employment in the "social ministries" of education (where 43.6 percent of total civil servants work) and health decreased by about 10 percent during the first year of adjustment in 1985.[20] By the end of the PREF program in 1988–89, the rate of unemployment in Mauritania was estimated at 35 percent,[21] and remained the same in 1993. The situation further deteriorated with the massive and sudden influx of some 250,000 to 500,000 Mauritanians and Senegalese of Mauritanian origin who were dispossessed and expelled from Senegal after thousands were killed[22] following the crisis between Senegal and Mauritania in April 1989. This crisis was the most devastating socioeconomic disruption in the country since the 1940s, when the combined effects of drought and World War II led to a famine in several regions of the country. Prior to the crisis, hundreds of thousands of Mauritanians were depending on remittances sent by family members working in Senegal. In less than two months, the large Mauritanian immigrant community in Senegal was virtually destroyed. The white book report of the government noted that "the moral and material harm undergone by the Mauritanian community in Senegal, after the genocide carried out against its existence, is immeasurable and not easily repairable."[23] The Moorish community was well established in Senegal for decades. By the 1930s, it already had tens of thousands of people and in Medina (a city neighborhood in Dakar) 130 out of a total of 150 stores were owned or run by the Moors.[24] After the crisis of 1989, Mauritania demanded from Senegal compensation amounting to CFA 300 billion, while Senegal claims a loss of CFA 60 billion.[25] All this came at a time when the process of adjustment of public enterprises was about to begin, with some 1,550 workers scheduled to be dismissed in 1990.[26] The social impact of rising unemployment was further accentuated by a new food policy that discourages free distribution of foreign food aid.

Table 35 PREF Employment Policy

(a) Channeling of public investment toward productive sectors (particularly agriculture) that create jobs.
(b) Establishment in 1985 of a fund for job market entry and reentry (Fonds d'Insertion et de Réinsertion à la Vie Active—FIRVA) to enable retirees, former immigrant workers, and certified graduates to carry out projects that create jobs.
(c) Revitalization of the informal sector through better access to credit, marketing, and supply, and the organization of various occupational groups into production cooperatives.
(d) Start of labor intensive works programs which will be supported by the expansion of Food for Work projects made possible by food aid, and an ILO-sponsored project involving community activities (well drilling, construction of dams and other works, and reforestation).
(e) Incentives for companies (seeking approval under the investment code) to create jobs.
(f) Introduction of plan to replace technical assistance in areas where national one exists.

Source: RIM, Economic and Financial Recovery Program 1985–88, paragraph 79.

Free distribution of foreign food aid was a well-established social policy following successive droughts from the late 1960s on. But the economic rationale of SAPs worked against free distribution of food aid, which actually dropped from 74,000 tons in 1985 to 13,000 tons in 1989.[27] The rationale behind reducing free distribution of foreign food aid was presented as a strategy aimed at creating hardship and hence increasing incentives for work among the poor who, allegedly, were discouraged from working because of the availability of occasional food relief and the traditionally dominant system of values, which disdains manual labor. More important, food aid was questioned by major donors because it was said that it competes with local crops. Based partly on this rationale, "the United States cut bilateral aid to Africa by more than a third during the 1980s, a decade which saw 3.5 million Africans die of hunger or hunger-related illnesses."[28] Free distribution of foreign food aid in Mauritania was replaced by the Food for Work program which was prepared by technical ministries in cooperation with local communities and interested NGOs. In this way, the state withdrew gradually from its social policy and responsibility of providing food relief for the poor, leaving them at the mercy of what is often referred to as fending-for-oneself liberalism. Most of these social policies and responsibilities were actually transferred to the elected local authorities (of the communes established in 1986 within the framework of decentralization), which were then encouraged to develop local projects (for example, basic preventive medicine) in close collaboration with international NGOs, since the central government does not want to commit itself to a social policy that generates rising expectations and crises,[29] particularly amid continuous budget cuts. In this regard, a new division of labor between the state and local government emerged: the central government coordinates and collaborates with international financial institutions in terms of national policies, while local governments do the same thing with international NGOs in terms of the social and economic needs of local communities. This policy continued under the Economic Consolidation and Growth Program (PCR).

Social Policy of PCR

As the government and the Bank launched the PCR (1989–91), they acknowledged the worsening employment situation and the "alarming outlook due to diverging trends of job openings in the formal modern sector and the number of job seekers turned out by the educational system."[30] In the third policy framework paper (1989–91), the government, the Bank, and the Fund were well aware of the negative social impact of SAPs. They acknowledged that "the adjustment program would require sacrifices from the Mauritanian people. In particular, higher prices and tariffs for currently subsidized public services would have repercussions on the purchasing power of the population, while budget austerity and public sector reforms would adversely affect employment in this sector."[31] The fundamental components of the social program of the PCR represent a continuation of policies initiated under the PREF. They were articulated around food aid policy, budgetary allocation to social sectors, and data collection and studies on the social situation in the country. The following policy measures and actions were to be carried out on the social aspects of adjustment: (1) collection of statistical data on income distribution, on the standard of living of families, and on social and economic indicators using the household survey that began in December 1987; (2) review of the social effects of adjustment and the social situation in the country; and (3) implementation of a set of priority actions revolving around the extension of the informal sector, the development of the FIRVA program, and the reinforcement of the economic role of municipal councils on urgent health-oriented actions.[32]

It is hard to imagine how the first component (Food for Work) of this policy could contribute to alleviating poverty, since free distribution of food declined dramatically and the Food for Work program (at least in Nouakchott) did not go much beyond providing a few kilograms[33] of grains (rice, wheat, etc.) per person per day to a relatively small number of no-income people following hours of collecting garbage and/or clearing sand-blocked roads. By the same token, resource allocation to the social sectors of education and health actually declined. Although the 1989 PCR document discusses "a significant increase of budget credits allocated to health and education compared to previous years,"[34] this is simply an exaggeration if we take into consideration the devaluation and depreciation of the ouguiya, often articulated vaguely as inflation (a term that reveals more about what is a price increase than about who caused it). The PREF total investment program between 1985 and 1988 amounted to UM 55.1 billion of which 8 percent (UM 4.4 billion) went to the education and health sectors. The PCR total investment program between 1989 and 1991 amounted to UM 45.3 billion of which 10.1 percent (UM 4.5 billion) went to the human resources sector. Although the share of resource allocation to the education and health sectors seems to have slightly increased in absolute terms (by 2.2 percent) from UM 4.4 to UM 4.5 billion between the PREF period (1985–88) and the PCR period (1989–91), actually the overall public investment declined in absolute terms (from UM 55.1 billion to UM 45.3 billion), and the exchange rate between the ouguiya (UM) and the IMF's special drawing right deteriorated for the former by 32 percent between 1985 and 1991, making UM 4.4 billion in 1991 equivalent to UM 3 billion in 1985 prices. Applying the exchange rate between the SDR and the UM, the apparent slight increase in resource allocation to the education and health sectors actually represents a decline in their budget expenditures. This trend of restricting expenditures is also accompanied by an increase of taxes. One major objective of such austerity is to free resources for the payment of foreign debts. In 1993 (1 January to 30 November) the government budget achieved a surplus of UM 2.245 billion.[35]

Social policy under the PCR was not genuine or serious in terms of either food aid policy or the increase of budget allocation to social sectors. These were mentioned to camouflage the decrease in both food aid distribution and budget allocation to education and health. The real focus of social policy under the PCR was data collection and studies on the social situation in the country. From the poor's perspective, this component of social policy does not make much difference. Whether or not one collects data on income and consumption in a poor household or an informal sector activity does not by itself change their conditions. It makes a difference only for government policymakers, who are then able to determine which group might be a source of discontent to plan the appropriate strategies of containment. The permanent household survey was designed to improve the information and the data base which are used to identify vulnerable social groups and monitor socioeconomic indicators of their standard of living. Social policy within the third adjustment program 1992–95 represents a continuation of SDA programs under the PCR. It is coordinated by the Social Impact unit established within the Ministry of Planning. The World Bank was to assist the Social Impact unit in using household surveys conducted in 1988 to construct a poverty profile, which will be used to determine the national poverty alleviation strategy. Other surveys would be conducted to assess the social situation and economic needs of specific groups, notably nomadic populations and retrenched civil servants.[36] Again, these measures are more likely to strengthen the government's and Bank's information systems than to provide any short-term relief for SAP victims. SDA programs have little impact on the growing social disparity exacerbated by SAPs. Perhaps a better assessment of SDA came from a U.S. Congressional Evaluation Commission, which found that

As international donors slowly began to pay more attention to poverty-alleviation, their initiatives also suffered from an absence of grass-roots input. For instance, the World Bank's Social Dimension of Adjustment Project included national living standard surveys to be conducted in several countries, including Ghana and Senegal, over several years. These surveys were promised to help fill an enormous gap in information about the impact of adjustment on the poor. But, as one leading expert on African economic development pointed out, the surveys were partially based on dubious assumptions that participants in the underground informal sector would speak candidly about their incomes to government pollsters and that household expenditures could be regarded as a single unit rather than separated out by gender. Moreover, the project might have made greater use of "rapid appraisal" sampling techniques that could provide relevant information for policymakers before the 1990s. In these respects, the surveys appear to be another Western, bureaucratic, high technology development project that would have greatly benefited from the input of representatives of poor Africans.[37]

Social Differentiation

SAPs are often perceived as a set of economic and financial measures, but their sociopolitical dimensions cannot be overlooked since they clearly challenge the interests of many social groups while they promote the interests of others. In their sociopolitical unfolding, adjustment policies represent a compromise between constraints imposed by economic and financial austerity programs and the power of various interest groups supporting and or resisting those programs. Even though these social groups sometimes have succeeded in delaying the implementation of certain programs, they were never able to reverse them. Social sectors negatively affected by SAPs include various groups that benefit from protectionism, groups affected by reduction of expenditure on education (for example, students whose scholarships were reduced or suspended) and health in rural areas, and urban informal sectors experiencing a decline in sales to modern sector employees who were particularly hit by devaluation. Women and children too were hurt by SAP policies, despite the appointment of a woman to the cabinet. Adjustment-related efficiency measures may also work against some of the family benefits that women received before adjustment. By law, men and women in Mauritania must receive equal pay for equal work. Women have three months of maternity leave and upon their return to work after giving birth they are allowed one hour of leave per day to nurse their child. The shifting of resources from public to private hands and the decline of the purchasing power[38] of wage earners represent the most significant example of the decline of the middle class, which was enjoying relatively stable purchasing power thanks to the nationalistic, protectionist policies of the 1960s and 1970s. In the words of the president of the International Development Association, "the immediate social effects" of SAPs "are triggering growing tensions among the population, particularly urban public employees and young graduates, who perceive reduced public sector employment opportunities."[39] At the same time, an international class is emerging and improving its connections worldwide, while the large rural and urban masses are experiencing rapid impoverishment and marginalization. At the level of representation, antagonism between these two groups is partly expressed in the frictional cultural encounter between Al-Asala or Al-Turath (tradition) and Al-Hadatha (modernity), which the Islamists are attempting to turn into a real political debate expressing the struggle for social power framed into abstract literary and religious discourse.

Groups negatively affected by SAPs react in different ways. General strikes represent the favorite response by public employees, students, and wage earners in the modern sector. Although this method succeeded in delaying the implementation of certain policy measures, it was not able to thwart them. While students went on strike several times, wage earners in both the public and private sectors feared losing their jobs and being replaced by others waiting among the growing number of unemployed. The graduate unemployed are the boldest in expressing their dissatisfaction since they have nothing to lose. On one occasion, a group of unemployed graduates "besieged the Presidency" demanding jobs and condemning the phenomenon of holding several public offices or salaries while other people still are unemployed.[40] It is important to note that it is not the decline of unionism among workers and students which made them unable to sustain a confrontation with the authorities over a long period of time. Rather, it is the failure of unions and union leaders to protect their members from layoffs in public enterprises and from declining purchasing power following the devaluation of the national currency that actually discredited and brought about the decline of unionism in general. Not being able to organize any real collective resistance, wage earners resorted to individualist competition and the search for a second occupation (the part-time or second job phenomenon) to compensate for the decline of purchasing power. This strategy of individual response led to a general decline of productivity in the public sector, where many civil servants became de facto part-time, even though they are paid as full-time employees. This in itself led to the fulfilling of the old prophesy that claims that the public sector is unproductive. Low-income urban groups, often with no leadership from the middle class, resorted to riots but were violently suppressed (from the late 1970s and throughout the 1980s "bread riots," triggered by liberalization policies, have been frequent in many Third World cities).[41] One such riot took place in Nouakchott in October 1992 following the devaluation of the national currency by 42 percent and another one took place in January 1995 following the abolition of state subsidies for bread. Business groups responded by engaging in massive capital flight, as reported by endless tales in Nouakchott about the growing Mauritanian business community in Las Palmas, Canary Islands, especially following the closure of the borders with Senegal in 1989. Other groups resorted simply to emigration as another form of response to problems and opportunities arising out of SAPs.

The dynamics of SAP resource allocation policy creates rapid social mobility with more movement down into poverty than movement up out of poverty, opening up new chances for a few while pushing the majority deep down. The measure often cited by the government and the Bank as an example of equitable redistribution of income is the substantial increase in agricultural producer prices.[42] While this measure benefited a few businessmen who transferred some of their assets from trade to agriculture, it did not change much in the conditions of the wage earners who work in the fields and whose earned wages continue to suffer from continuous currency devaluation and depreciation. Moreover, the increase in agriculture producer prices reflects the abolition of subsidies and the fact that when these domestic prices increase their potential for competing with imported agricultural commodities decrease, particularly when restrictions on imports are being lifted. Economic and financial policies that fuel the overall social shake-up include layoffs in restructured public enterprises, higher prices and tariffs for public services after abolition of subsidies, impacts of budgetary austerity and public sector reforms on employment, and above all deterioration of the purchasing power of the majority following systematic devaluation and depreciation of the national currency. The combined impact of these policy measures led to a general decline of the standard of living of most people. Only a very small number of state officials, businessmen, and speculators who have access to the credit system moved up. During the early years of SAPs, the Mauritanian government provided important *fonds speciaux* (special funds amounting sometimes to 100 percent increase of annual income) and luxury Mercedes cars for high-ranking state officials in response to the declining purchasing power brought about by SAP policies, particularly the devaluation of the national currency. This policy co-opted state officials and made them more inclined to support SAPs anyway. It also accelerated the process of social differentiation under adjustment.

While the small elite in the government and business community was enjoying the positive impacts of SAPs, the purchasing power of the majority was going down, unemployment in the cities was going up, and widespread cases of malnutrition were visible in the poor districts of Nouakchott, where free distribution of international food aid had been systematically declining. Social and spatial differentiation was obvious in Nouakchott before SAPs but was exacerbated and accelerated by SAPs. Social disparity in Nouakchott is well illustrated by the geographic contrast between the relatively rich northwestern residential areas and the generally poor southern neighborhoods of the city. This disparity began to emerge in the mid-1970s, particularly during Mauritania's involvement in the Western Sahara war (1975–78). One outcome of the war was the acceleration of the emergence of the two poles of the city of Nouakchott. Tevragh Zeina emerged as a wealthy neighborhood for the nouveaux riches (successful businessmen, high-ranking state officials, top army officers, and *new* religious sheikhs), while El-Kebbe emerged as a collection of squatter settlements where rural population fleeing the drought took refuge. Since then the gap between the two forms of settlement has grown, giving a special morphology to the spatial organization of the city and illustrating the new social stratification, based more and more on income. The housing stock differences and contrasts in the city represent a stark illustration of disparity in income and standard of living, even though the symbolic world of representation of tribal and familial solidarity continues simultaneously to express vertical tribal solidarity and camouflage horizontal social tensions of class formation. Generally, economic and social disparity are successfully contained by complex forms of tribal and/or ethnic representation, which tend to reinforce clientelism as a function and a consequence of unequal access to power and wealth. Exploitation and domination are somehow made anonymous through a growing expansion of commodity relations combined with complex forms of social identity based mainly on ethnicity, tribalism, and various types of regional and religious brotherhood.

The general pattern of social differentiation brought about by SAPs in Mauritania is similar to what Dharam Ghai has observed and analyzed in other developing countries going through the process of adjustment. He noted that "there has been a shift of power in favor of capital, especially that linked with the international economy, and away from the organized working class and to some extent the middle class."[43] The growing social disparity is reflected in the rise of a comprador international class, the decline of salaried and wage earners in the middle class, and the homogenization of a class of urban and rural poor engaged in various strategies of survival in the informal sector, including crime activities whose rate increased in Nouakchott in 1993.[44] The international class is structurally linked to Al-Kharij (the outside), which is increasingly becoming synonymous with power, prestige, and wealth, a phenomenon paralleled only by the decline of urban and rural masses of Al-Dakhil (the interior), which increasingly connotes poverty, weakness, and marginalization. Access to Al-Kharij became the obsession of the international class, whose members are often irritated by preadjustment regulations and restrictions such as those repeated by the announcer just before landing in the airport of Nouakchott: "It is prohibited to take photos of the airport; it is prohibited to import alcohol; it is prohibited not to declare the amount of hard currency in your possession."[45] The new international class constitutes the linchpin of the postnationalist bourgeoisie, a class that has totally accepted its comprador status and no longer aspires to national independence. However, social differentiation, as well as the social shake-up and tension brought about by SAPs, continues to be somehow diffused by the process of democratization, a process full of hope as well as illusions about freedom and equality.

8

Political Implications of SAPs

Democratization: The Post–Cold War Buzzword

The concept of democracy and the process of democratization are very much in intellectual and political fashion today, particularly with regard to Third World politics.[1] "Everywhere in the world today, West, East, and South, *democracy* has become the principal and most universal political rallying cry."[2] For some, the new rise of liberal democracy represents the "end of history" while for others it is "the reference point for the construction of a new left,"[3] whose shift away from socialist to democratic discourse is noticeable. Like the use of the concept of *development* following World War II, the concept of *democracy* became simultaneously the buzzword and the zeitgeist of the 1990s.[4] Despite (or because of) its vagueness and lack of precise definition and because of the deepening of the struggle for power everywhere and at all levels, democracy tends to represent the spirit and outlook of the post–Cold War generation. It constitutes a new discourse of hegemonic representation totally associated in the minds of many with the West, free market, and capitalist relations. It allows Western powers to define the political reality of the world in their own terms by defining what constitutes democracy and what is the nature and scope of human rights. For sure, the aspiration for democracy may be viewed as a genuine manifestation of universal and original popular demands for political freedom, representation, participation, and accountability, but the current wave of democratization (i.e., multiparty elections and politics) in developing countries and former centrally planned economies was essentially a by-product of economic restructuring, often imposed from outside as a political model of adjustment to the process of economic liberalization and privatization brought about by SAPs. The correlation between multipartyism and structural adjustment programs is reflected in the discourse of political and economic liberalization: good governance, accountability, and transparency with a new emphasis on human rights, the rule of law, and political participation. An open economic market leads to an open political market. The results are the powerful democratization pressures sweeping the Third World and forcing the autocratic political systems to open up their societies and adapt to the requirements of the global strategy of adjustment. The forms and procedures of this representative democracy include formal equality before the law, open electoral competition, liberties for the articulation and organization of dissenting positions,[5] written constitutions, bills of rights, houses of parliament, guaranteeing the rule of law, and governmental succession by constitutional and electoral procedures.

These trends of democratization are particularly visible in Africa where multipartyism has displaced single-party rule in most countries during the past five years. This dramatic shift in African politics raises critical questions. Why did the *imperative* or *impulse* to democratize African politics become so urgent precisely in the 1990s? Who are the primary agents behind this process? What are the implications of democratization for people's empowerment? In their explanation of the democratic shift in African politics from one-party systems to multipartyism, Michael Bratton and Nicolas van de Walle argued that "external factors serve as precipitating conditions rather than causal ones" and that "African governments introduced political reforms primarily in response to active demands, spontaneous and organized, from a loose, multiclass assemblage of indigenous protest groups."[6] Along the same lines of analysis, Carol Lancaster downplayed the role of foreign governments and international institutions as the agents behind the move toward political pluralism by listing it the last of five causes: economic discontent, reforms in Eastern Europe, diffusion effect from other African countries, educated unemployed, and the role of foreign governments.[7] The underestimation of the common origin and the structural linkages between SAPs and multipartyism in Africa was also echoed by Crawford Young when he said, "In contrast to economic reform, whose agenda has been largely dictated by the policy formulas and neoclassical concepts of the international financial institutions and donor community, political change is primarily defined from within."[8]

The folowing section emphasizes the organic linkages between SAPs and multipartyism and argues that the role of popular protest in bringing about multipartyism to Africa was significant, yet secondary to the role played by Western pressure to liberalize African politics following a decade of endeavor to liberalize African economies through SAPs.

Western Pressure for Democratization in Africa

Although the democratization process was welcomed by opposition groups throughout the continent, most African leaders and governments did not welcome democratization and saw it as imposed upon them by Western lenders/donors as a corollary to SAPs. In their resistance to democratization, most African governments were motivated not only by regime stability but also by a serious concern for the sovereignty of their countries ,as well as by what later became a genuine fear of sociopolitical disintegration.[9] In many countries opposition parties were often led by leftist movements inspired by the Soviet model of single-party rule, which they define as "popular democracy." Therefore they were never enthusiastic about liberal democracy and multipartyism, which they describe as futile bourgeois democracy. It was only when the foundation of single-party rule began to weaken following the adoption of SAPs and the disintegration of the Soviet Union that cohesive opposition movements began to emerge in all African countries and became threatening to governments only in conjunction with external pressure for democratization. As Robert Albert noted,

> In further probing into the economic base of political reform, I argue that, however passionate may be the domestic political impetus for reform, it is nonetheless weak. While Africa is racked with economic disillusion, few mass movements have arisen demanding less government intervention, fewer social programs, less spending, or less regulation. . . . Reformism has strong domestic roots, but it is powerful because it is backed by international agencies and foreign capital. It opposes Africa's governments, but it is often initiated by them.[10]

The democratization process is a facade behind which lies fierce competition between African governments, opposition parties, and Western donors over the politics of control of African economies and societies. In the end, African governments moved to multipartyism to keep the flow of Western loans and grants and to avoid defamatory reports on human rights violations, whereas the industrialized nations pushed for multipartyism to ensure a political environment supportive of market reforms and propitious to the promotion of their industrial exports—a process that requires the opening of the economy and society to Western trade, capital investment, political model, and cultural values. Though African opposition parties seized the moment to undermine their governments, their efforts for democracy and human rights and the overall trajectory of their movements were a priori defined and channeled by Western powers' definition of what constitutes democracy and human rights. Economic and financial policies of privatization may not be sustainable in the long run unless preserved by the appropriate political environment that fragments the internal political forces of the given country and prevents the state and society from organizing any eventual compact bloc in the face of international capital. They equally need an appropriate institutional framework where the rigidities of state regulations are reduced to a minimum. "In short, the economic reform of African states also requires the reform of their domestic politics."[11] In the same way that the one-party system was more congruent with the statist, protectionist economic policies of the 1960s and 1970s, the multiparty system better suits privatization and liberalization policies that have been sweeping the continent since the early 1980s. Until adjustment policies began to take root in Africa in the mid–1980s, military and one-party governments dominated almost all African countries, while multiparty systems were the exception. From 1990 on, dozens of African countries began the process of holding competitive presidential and legislative elections. By 1993, only six countries in Africa adhered to the one-party system,[12] and by 1994 almost the entire continent had converted to the new religion of multipartyism, whether through a civil coup d'etat as in Benin, a violent transition as in Mali, a government/opposition polemic as in Mauritania, a combination of anarchy and civil war as in Somalia, or through violent and still unfolding processes as in Algeria and Egypt.

In all cases, the democratization process was subsequent to the implementation of SAPs (see table 36). By the end of the 1980s most African governments had adopted SAPs, while few of them had begun multiparty political reforms and most democratic reforms in Africa "were initiated by the very governments that were the object of demands for change."[13] The general sequence of change was that IMF/World Bank austerity programs created popular dissent while they reduced the financial ability of the state to fund political clientelism to reward supporters and co-opt/neutralize the opposition. In most cases these austerity programs triggered popular discontent and often violent

Table 36 Sequence of SAPs and Multipartyism in Africa

Country	SAPs Began	Partyism Began	Country	SAPs Began	Partyism Began
Algeria	--/1987	2/1989	Malawi	9/1982	6/1993
Angola	7/1989	7/1990	Mali	10/1988	3/1991
Benin	6/1989	8/1990	Mauritania	4/1985	7/1991
Burkina Faso	3/1991	12/1991	Morocco	10/1983	9/1992
Burundi	--/1986	4/1992	Mozambique	10/1984	11/1990
Cameroon	5/1989	12/1991	Niger	11/1983	4/1991
Central African Republic	6/1981	7/1992	Nigeria	12/1986	10/1992
Chad	10/1989	3/1991	Rwanda	--/1990	6/1991
Congo	7/1986	7/1990	Sierra Leone	9/1977	3/1991
Cote d'Ivoire	5/1984	5/1990	Somalia	3/1985	12/1990
Equatorial Guinea	7/1985	1/1992	South Africa	11/1982	2/1992
Gabon	6/1978	5/1990	Sudan	11/1979	10/1985
Ghana	2/1983	5/1992	Tanzania	9/1986	5/1992
Guinea	4/1986	10/1990	Togo	6/1979	4/1991
Guinea-Bissau	10/1987	4/1990	Tunisia	11/1986	8/1987
Kenya	12/1989	12/1991	Uganda	11/1981	3/1994
Liberia	12/1980	12/1989	Zaire	6/1976	11/1990
Madagascar	4/1981	3/1990	Zambia	5/1983	10/1991

Source: Compiled from: International Monetary Fund, 1994, *Official Financing for Developing Countries*, Washington, D.C.: International Monetary Fund; *The Europa World Year Book 1994*, London: Europa Publications Limited; and *Foreign Broadcast Information Service*.

protest, which were exclusively led by students (SAPs ended the automatic hiring of graduates), civil servants, workers, and professionals, all of whom were the principal victims of SAP austerity measures (including currency devaluation, which sharply reduced the purchasing power of all wage earners). In some cases popular discontent was also expressed by military coups or attempted coups. To a great extent, these discontent movements were initially anti-SAP, protests which opportunist politicians from the opposition shrewdly exploited to undermine the single-party system and establish multipartyism, hoping to win the elections and force the ruling party out of power.

The rapid decline of the model of single-party rule in Eastern Europe and the Soviet Union inspired its critics in Africa in much the same way as its rise inspired most political leadership in Africa throughout the three decades following World War II. Moreover, the international community of lenders and Western media used the retreat of single-party rule in Eastern Europe to encourage Africans to rebel against single-party rule. Dramatized international events such as workers' challenge to one-party rule in Poland in 1981, Mikhail Gorbachev's *glasnost* and *perestroika* reforms following his ascendancy to the position of secretary-general of the Communist Party of the Soviet Union in 1985, the grandiose celebration of the bicentennial of the French Revolution, the fall of the Berlin Wall, and the public execution of Romanian President Nicolae Ceausescu and his wife in 1989 all encouraged Africans to delegitimize the model of one-party rule which was already eroded and weakened by almost a decade of IMF stabilization and World Bank structural adjustment programs. These programs culminated in the denationalization of peripheral states, the globalization of their economies, and the fragmentation of their political systems.

The year 1989 was known as the Year of Revolutions, which shook the foundation of single-party rule in its heartland of Eastern Europe and the Soviet Union and delegitimized it elsewhere. Nigerian President Ibrahim Babangida, noted that "the virtual end of the cold war and the crisis of the state in the previously commandist economies have also dramatised graphically the nature of this African crisis as well as the urgent imperative of pursuing a collective African response to it."[14] But even if the political changes in Eastern Europe and the Soviet Union had inspired the shake-ups in Africa, "the real detonating force was economics," particularly since "the IMF and the World Bank have begun to press African regimes to liberalize their politics as well as their economies."[15] In February 1990, hundreds of representatives from

African governments, grassroots organizations, United Nations agencies, and Northern NGOs, gathering in the Tanzanian city of Arusha, adopted the so-called African Declaration for Popular Participation, which calls for "an opening up of political processes to accommodate freedom of opinion and tolerance of difference."[16] The change from one-party to multiparty political systems was widely described as "the democratic revolution" or the "second independence," particularly since the First Pan-African Conference on Democracy and Control of Transition in Africa was held in Dakar, Senegal, in May 1992. One resolution of the conference reads "the African Political Leaders meeting in Dakar pledged to guide Africa away from the one-party system towards multiparty systems."[17]

However, the above enthusiasm for multiparty politics was less an expression of genuine African popular demands than an official government shift encouraged by the mood created by SAP reforms, which are backed by the international community of lenders and donors who realized how multiparty politics would consolidate adjustment policies by dismantling the rigidities of economic regulations inherent to single-party rule, as the example of democratization in Benin illustrates. The most publicized democratization-related event in Africa was the famous Beninese National Conference of February 1990, which was used as a model for delegitimizing single-party rule in the continent, particularly in the francophone countries. Less publicized, however, was the fact that "the structural adjustment program required by international donors played an important role in Benin's political liberalization despite the program's avowed purely economic and social objectives."[18] Benin's involvement with SAPs began through a dialogue with the World Bank in 1982, the opening of a World Bank mission in Cotonou in 1983, the release of the World Bank country economic memorandum on Benin in 1984, the government adoption of a broad-based adjustment program in 1986–87, and the government commitment to implement the first Beninese structural adjustment program in 1989. The austerity measures decreed by SAPs and the delays and hesitations in the disbursements of World Bank and IMF loans precipitated a financial crisis of the state which triggered violent demonstrations on 16 February and 21 June 1990, thus setting the necessary political context for a national dialogue on SAPs. In this regard, the Beninese National Conference of February 1990 was above all a sort of referendum on SAPs under pressures from the IMF and France amid a fiscal crisis of the Beninese state. The Beninese government stopped paying salaries of its employees for six months, and because of its membership in the Communauté Financière Africaine (better known as the CFA franc zone), it could not cover its fiscal deficit by simply printing money as most financially sovereign governments would do. Despite (or because of) its Marxist-Leninist orientation, the regime was left with the choice of either SAPs or collapse. It is in this context that Beninese President Mathieu Kerekou opened the National Conference by "a pledge to implement the IMF's structural adjustment program," and after ten days of deliberations the conference "adopted plans for multiparty elections and chose Nicephore Soglo, *a former World Bank official*, as interim prime minister" [emphasis added]. How national was the National Conference? Why was it a one-time conference and not an institutionalized democratic forum? There is no doubt that the Beninese people have deep aspirations for democracy, but the real issue for the government was to engineer a consensus for SAPs not for democracy, even though the opposition seized the moment to call for democracy to undermine the government monopoly of power.

A similar sequence of austerity programs, social unrest, and demand for democratization provided the context for further Western pressure for multipartyism in Africa through bilateral, multilateral, and nongovernmental channels. Such Western pressures for multipartyism came particularly from the United States, France, Britain, the IMF, the World Bank, and Amnesty International. This was exemplified by "the unusual vigor"[19] with which the United States pressured the Kenyan government of Daniel arap Moi to adopt multipartyism following its adoption of SAPs in December 1989. British pressure for multipartyism in Kenya was equally conveyed during a visit by British Foreign Secretary Douglas Hurd to Kenya in September 1991. In November 1991, Western donors announced that they would suspend aid to Kenya indefinitely pending the acceleration of both economic and political reforms. In accordance with this policy, the IMF froze a $350 million aid package to Kenya to force economic and political reforms, while the United States and the World Bank continued to press along the same line.[20] Propaganda pressure was also exercised through the Washington-based Human Rights Watch, particularly Africa Watch (now renamed Human Rights Watch/Africa) which published lengthy reports condemning Kenya's human rights records and calling for political pluralism.[21] Following these pressures, Kenyan President Daniel arap Moi warned that "many countries in the African Continent were being forced to adopt political systems that could create chaos in a country" and that "multiparty politics was a luxury in Africa which could disrupt the unified approach to development at this stage."[22] His minister of education, Joseph Kamotho, noted that in 1990 the U.S. Congress had voted $850 million to fund the propagation of democracy and multipartyism in the world and that $30 million of this amount were distributed to the eastern region of Africa, a policy that he described as "international corruption."[23] Western pressures for multipartyism in Kenya continued for two years before the country was finally forced to replace the one-party system by multipartyism in December 1991. The Kenyan opposition was supportive of Western pressure for democratization and led antigovernment riots on many occasions, particularly in February 1990 in the aftermath of the obscure death of Robert Ouko, the minister of foreign affairs and international cooperation. However, the opposition did not play a decisive role in forcing the government to adopt political pluralism, as indicated by its poor performance and defeat in the 1992 general elections and the victory of the ruling party. In the words of Rok Ajulu, the 1992 general elections in Kenya "present an example of an attempt to restructure an authoritarian state through imperialist political conditionality."[24] The real objective of Western powers in Kenya was the liberalization of the economy and the opening of society rather than empowering the average Kenyan citizen as the discourse of democratization suggests. This was further illustrated in late 1994 when Western donors meeting in Paris pledged $800 million in assistance for Kenya, not in response to genuine democratic orientation but rather in response to important economic reforms, such as the liberalization of exchange regulations, the lowering of some tariffs, and the easing of price controls.[25] These reforms were carried out by the same ruling party whose monolithism was vilified prior to its compliance with structural adjustment programs.

In the same context of Western pressure, other long-time single-party states were forced to adopt multipartyism. President Ali Hassan Mwinyi of Tanzania could not disguise the impact of external pressures on his single-party government when he said that because of "political reasons" and "to keep up with the times" in which all countries in Africa are affected by multipartyism, "the national executive committee of the party [the Revolutionary Party of Tanzania] conference had agreed that Tanzania should have a multiparty system even though 80 percent of Tanzanians want only one party."[26] He even told Manuel Marín, vice president of the European Economic Community, that it was not proper for external powers to force political standards on other countries and that the correct approach to democracy was to allow the people of each country to discuss and eventually arrive at their own consensus on what form of government was suitable to them.[27] Under similar circumstances, the ruling Gabonese Democratic Party declared its commitment to implement multipartyism in May 1990 following the adoption of SAPs in July 1989 and the subsequent popular unrest that began in January 1990.[28] Jerry Rawlings, president of Ghana, explained the scramble for Western liberal democracy as a move dictated by the search for external aid because "naturally, countries that adhere only to the democratic patterns of industrialized nations will, without a doubt, benefit from the aid of these countries and international aid agencies."[29] Social and political discontent following Ghana's adoption of SAPs in February 1983 was reflected in a series of attempted coups and widespread student unrest between 1984 and 1987, during which thirty-four people were executed for their alleged involvement in conspiracies to overthrow the government. It was only in response to Western pressure in July 1990 that the government finally announced the establishment of a National Commission for Democracy, which ultimately led in May 1992 to the adoption of legislation ending the ban on the formation of political associations.[30]

The issue of human rights[31] and democracy emerged stronger in the context of Western pressure for the adoption of multipartyism. It was often a convenient two-edged sword for regulation of foreign aid and intervention in other nations' internal affairs. Notwithstanding the incidental climate of tolerance (as well as indifference) concomitant with raising human rights issues, Western powers' concern with the democratization process remains selective, since the real objective behind it is to pressure governments for more liberalization and hence less political sovereignty over their national economies. Western powers support democratization and human rights in sub-Saharan Africa as long as such support will bring to power Westernized and secularized elites eager for further opening of their societies to Western capital investment and cultural values. But the same Western powers view democratization and human rights in North Africa as a different story because in this region the Westernized and secularized elites are increasingly threatened by the Islamists. Here comes the double standard of the *fin de siècle*: support democratization south of the Sahara and suppress it north of it. For example, France strongly supported the suspension of the democratic process in Algeria in January 1992, while the United States turned a blind eye to it.[32] The two Western powers were more interested in the secular outlook of the ruling Front de Liberation Nationale (FLN) and its readiness to implement SAPs than the religious tone of the opposing Front Islamique de Salut (FIS), which is associated with "ideological rigidities" geared to limit the openness required by SAPs.[33]

The end of the Cold War allowed the United States to strongly reaffirm its commitment to use human rights and democracy as the new stick of the New World Order and as one major aid conditionality and a convenient instrument for circumventing the sovereignty of independent nations. U.S. Vice President Dan Quayle zealously addressed the UN Human Rights Commission in Geneva in these terms: "The days when a government charged with human rights abuses could cite 'sovereignty' or 'non-interference in internal affairs' as a defense are gone."[34] "To export democracy, we need only continue doing what we have done since World War II" because "what is good for democracy is good for America."[35] This interventionist foreign policy is exemplified by the U.S. Department of State's *Country Reports on Human Rights Practices*, which monitors (on an annual basis) the respect for human rights in all countries except the United States (up to the summer of 1994). Acquiescence of some African leaders to this new doctrine of intervention contributed to its success. On one occasion, Abdou Diouf, president of Senegal, declared that the principle of nonintervention in internal affairs of sovereign nations "must be attacked vehemently" as far as human rights are concerned.[36] President Diouf's declaration was concomitant to President Bush's announcement that "the U.S. is forgiving $42 million worth of debt which Senegal incurred in the purchase of agricultural commodities."[37]

When African governments began to lose control over their national economies following their adoption of SAPs, external pressure from Western governments, international financial institutions, and NGOs "for pro-democratic change which was once covert has become much more overt and insistent."[38] This political conditionality came to reinforce the overall conditionality of SAPs in that "it is only an *additional* tier of conditionality, a third stage following macroeconomic policy conditionality and sectoral policy conditionality."[39] As the Eastern bloc began to disintegrate, Western lenders/donors intensified their campaign for multipartyism in Africa, where the balance of the Soviet Union was no longer available to African governments in their quarrels with the West. Public statements about a new redeployment of Western aid began to be heard loudly when Herman Cohen, the U.S. secretary of state for African affairs, expressed U.S. determination to link economic aid to progress in the implementation of political pluralism. He made it clear that "for further economic assistance to be forthcoming political reform in a democratic direction would be necessary."[40] Returning from a Chiefs of African Mission meeting in Washington, the U.S. ambassador to Kenya, Smith Hempstone, noted that "there is a strong political tide flowing in our Congress, which controls the purse strings, to concentrate our economic assistance on those of the world's nations that nourish democratic institutions, defend human rights and practice multi-party politics. . . . This may also become a fact of political life in other donor countries tomorrow."[41]

France, believed to be Africa's largest source of bilateral aid,[42] began to link its foreign aid to progress in multiparty politics after the sixteenth Franco-African summit in La Baule, France, in June 1990. Addressing the representatives of thirty-five African nations (twenty-two of them represented by heads of state), French President François Mitterand called on "the African countries to implement multiparty politics and organize elections."[43] Mitterand reminded his African peers that aid and debt relief would be "more tepid for regimes which behave in an authoritarian manner, without accepting the evolution towards democracy." He was reported to have wondered, "Who could then be against democracy?"[44] French pressure for multiparty systems in Africa was described as the African "*Paris*troika." Also in June 1990, British Foreign Secretary Douglas Hurd, speaking paternalistically on behalf of the international community of lenders and donors, stated that "countries tending towards pluralism, public accountability, respect for the rule of law, human rights and market principles should be encouraged." At the same time, he strongly warned and threatened Africans that "governments which persist with repressive policies, corrupt management and wasteful, discredited economic systems should not expect us to support their folly with scarce aid resources which could be better used elsewhere."[45] Hurd also wrote to the European Commission suggesting that aid be cut to developing countries that violate human rights. Japan, too, emphasized that "democratization and economic development must proceed in tandem."[46] In sub-Saharan Africa, Japan pledged $650–$700 million to support democratization and economic liberalization between 1993 and 1995.[47] It is this kind of carrot-and-stick statements and policies that encouraged opposition movements in Africa to put further pressure on incumbent governments, which were finally forced to adopt multiparty politics as a necessary condition for the continuation of the flow of Western loans and grants.

To sum up, even though democratization has a long history in Africa and elsewhere and has a potential of triumph over tyranny, the particular process of democratization that swept across the continent from the late 1980s came after a decade of SAPs to which they are organically linked. The sequence of economic liberalization and political pluralism indicates that the process of democratization is a political restructuring aimed at "constructing political legitimacy for SAP."[48] Political pressure for democratization was channeled by Western powers through the financial and economic pressure of international financial institutions such as the IMF and the World Bank. In the words of David Mulford, U.S. under secretary of the treasury for international affairs, "In the 1990s, the IMF will be called upon to continue to fulfill its responsibilities in the less developed countries and to promote democracy and freedom in Eastern Europe."[49] As the strategy of structural adjustment deepens, democratization became an imperative. It became part of aid conditionality because it can be used as an effective instrument for further opening up societies for business and consolidating financial and economic reforms. Despite complaints and fear that ethnic cleavages could disintegrate many African nations, multiparty politics was almost imposed on many African governments by the international community of lenders and donors to prevent any reversion of SAPs. Recent developments in Africa indicate that Western pressure for democratization slowed down and may no longer be needed because almost all African governments embarked "successfully" on what seems to be irreversible SAPs and also because further pressures could bring to power undesirable social forces, such as the Islamists in Islamic African countries where Western powers did not pressure for genuine multipartyism. Recently, one journalist noted that "all across Africa, dictators, military men and traditional autocrats are showing their resiliency as democratic movements fade, and Western aid donors seem willing to accept economic modernization—without political reform—as sufficient reason to continue the flow of funds."[50]

Western Pressure for Democratization in Mauritania

Pressure for multipartyism in Mauritania came essentially from the outside, from the community of lenders and donors. The contribution of the internal opposition to fostering the process of democratization was secondary to the role played by international pressure for multipartyism. The same opposition is far weaker and more divided three years after the process of democratization began, while the government remained in power after the adoption of multipartyism. The weakness of the internal opposition indicates the important role played by external pressure for democratization, particularly from the United States, human rights organizations, France, and the externally based opposition. The United States used Mauritania's neutral position in the U.S.-led war against Iraq in early 1991 and the country's postcolonial ethnic divide between the Moorish Arab majority and the black African minority as an instrument of pressuring the state. Throughout the Gulf crisis and under overwhelming popular pressure, the Mauritanian government had voiced criticism against both the Iraqi invasion of Kuwait and the U.S.-led invasion of both Kuwait and Iraq. This position was also expressed in a joint communique issued by Mauritania and Sudan at the beginning of the ground war. The communique stated that since the real objective of the ground offensive was to "totally destroy Iraq," Mauritania and Sudan have "condemned the ground war imposed on Iraq by the coalition forces who have ignored all the negotiations undertaken to find a peaceful solution."[51] Even though the Mauritanian government was primarily motivated in this declaration by domestic pressure in favor of Iraq, such a position was not acceptable to the United States, Kuwait, and Saudi Arabia, all of whom immediately suspended aid to Mauritania.

The French did not join the coalition position in this case because they knew the government took such a position under extreme popular pressure, as Mauritanians followed the tragedy of Operation Desert Storm through their transistors with the same passion Americans would watch football or baseball games, and it was suicidal for the regime not to verbally condemn the war. Otherwise, noted President Ould Taya, the regime would have been "swept away."[52] It was in this political context that a series of reports on human rights abuses in Mauritania began to be propagated by the Washington-based Human Rights Watch, particularly its Africa Watch branch. Such reports provided the basis for the publication of the 1991 U.S. congressional reports entitled *Human Rights in the Maghreb and Mauritania*, which have since provided an inexhaustible source of reference for the condemnation and defamation of Mauritania. The externally and ethnically based opposition (Forces de Liberation des Africains de Mauritanie [FLAM])[53] also helped in the conception and propagation of these reports, particularly the congressional one in which the Human Rights Caucus in the U.S. House of Representatives wrote directly to the president of Mauritania in these terms: "As Members of Congress concerned about human rights issues, we are writing to you regarding conditions in Mauritania."[54] A congressional resolution (a "Sense of Congress") on Mauritania "calls upon the U.S. government to take a number of steps, including opposing loans to Mauritania in the multilateral development banks, ending trade privileges under the General System of Preferences, and requesting the appointment of a Special Rapporteur at the United Nations Commission on Human Rights."[55] As a follow-up to this policy, U.S. President Clinton notified the Congress in 1993 of his intent to suspend indefinitely Mauritania as a designated beneficiary developing country under the General System of Preferences because he has "determined that it has not taken and is not taking steps to afford internationally recognized worker rights."[56]

While the practices of racial discrimination described in the 1991 congressional report (*Human Rights in the Maghreb and Mauritania*) do not occur in Mauritania, the report did embarrass the government in its external relations and in international fora. The report claims that the policy of Arabization in Mauritania "discriminates against the black ethnic communities, particularly the Halpulaars" and that "it is fair to say that the Mauritanian government practices undeclared apartheid [without being an apologist for the government, I must say that the phrase "apartheid in Mauritania" is quite misleading and inaccurate] and severely discriminates on the basis of race" and that "what is taking place in southern Mauritania is, in effect, an undeclared war, in which one community [the Arabs] is using the resources and power of the state against another community" [the blacks].[57] The virulence of these allegations may be explained by the active role of two congressmen (Thomas E. Lantos, Democrat from California, and John E. Porter, Republican from Illinois)[58] who distributed and managed to get passed a "Dear Colleague" motion on human rights violations in Mauritania. The motion was exclusively based on FLAM's racist portrait of the government and began with: "In the West African country of Mauritania, the government, which is controlled by persons of Arab/Berber descent (the Beydanes or "white" Moors), continues to perpetrate human rights abuses against non-Arab, black Mauritanians."[59] Shortly after, in August 1991, Amnesty International, USA, published the names of some 339 political prisoners (mainly from the rank and file of the military) who were reported to have been killed between November 1990 and March 1991[60] following an attempted coup in late 1990.

These reports damaged the reputation of the country and forced the government to think about how to handle these serious charges of human rights abuses. In an attempt to put this issue behind and perhaps protect some of those (both in the government and the opposition) accused of human rights abuses, the government issued Law no. 23/93 of 14 June 1993, which states that "a comprehensive and complete pardon is offered to the members of the armed and police forces who, in the period of January 1, 1989 to April 17, 1992, committed criminal acts connected with the incidents which took place among their ranks . . ., and to all Mauritanians who committed crimes, acts of violence and acts of terrorism after the armed operations during the same period."[61] Washington's reading of this amnesty and of the democratic process as a whole is that "while human rights practices in Mauritania improved somewhat in 1992, serious abuses continued and major problems from the unresolved abuses of previous years remained. . . . In 1992 restrictions on certain rights, such as freedom of speech, press, and association, were reduced, although not eliminated" and "the political system still fell far short of a genuine democracy."[62] It should also be noted that during this period of transition to multipartyism in Mauritania, the relations between the two countries were not at all helped by the personality of the U.S. ambassador to Mauritania, Gordon Brown (a former Central Command political advisor[63] for General H. Norman Shwarzkopf), whose tactless comments are widely criticized in Nouakchott.[64]

More than the Americans, the French were flexible and efficient in bringing about multipartyism to the country by relying on quiet diplomacy and without seeking to overthrow the government. France, as the former colonial power, knows Mauritanian politics better than the United States and was less mystified by FLAM's allegations about racial discrimination in Mauritania. On 5 April 1991, French Foreign Minister Roland Dumas met for three hours with Mauritanian President Maaouiya Ould Taya in Nouakchott. At the end of the meeting Dumas declared that democracy goes hand in hand with human rights.[65] Less than two weeks later (on 15 April 1991) came Ould Taya's major speech on democratization in which he declared the intention of the government to hold a constitutional referendum, open up the political system, legalize political parties, and free the press. The July 1991 Constitution[66] was essentially based on the Constitution of the French Fifth Republic of October 1958, which strengthened the executive at the expense of parliament and, within the executive, strengthened the constitutional prerogatives of the presidency. Many critics pointed out that the French Constitution had simply been copied and charged the government with plagiarism in this regard.[67] The preamble of the Constitution began by a solemn adherence to the Universal Declaration of Human Rights (or the Declaration of the Rights of Man of 26 August 1789, which the General Assembly of the United Nations adopted in 1948). Such adherance had direct and immediate positive consequences for the reputation of the government in the West. In a press conference held shortly after the general referendum on the Constitution, Manuel Marín, vice president of the Commission of the European Economic Communities, expressed EEC support for the democratic process in Mauritania and warned the military that "if the EEC found itself confronted with a Coup d'Etat in a country engaged in the democratic process, it is clear that we will take a negative measure. This means immediate suspension of all forms of aid, except naturally, humanitarian aid. Actually we have done this. There are examples."[68]

Once multiparty politics was established, Mauritania became more credible in the eyes of its international partners and the government felt full membership in the international community of lenders and donors. In the words of Minister of Finance Kane Sheikh, "Thanks to democratization we really have the feeling of being better understood by our foreign partners. This brings us a lot of sympathy at the international level."[69] Democratization brought about a great deal of self-confidence for the government in international fora. Leading the Mauritanian delegation to the June 1993 Second UN Conference on Human Rights, Prime Minister Sidi Mohamed Ould Boubacar enthusiastically declared that "Mauritania is a full-fledged democratic state" with not a single political prisoner, and where there are more than fifteen political parties and dozens of press publications and civil associations.[70] The almost complete dependence of the state on the outside world makes the government sensitive and sometimes paranoid of anything that could tarnish its image in the Western community of lenders and donors, particularly after Mauritania paid the price of its verbal sympathy with Iraq.

This hysteria of image-polishing to please the West is illustrated by Mauritania's new fear of showing any sympathy (this time) with Libya—considered by the United States as the West's bête noire because of its support for the liberation of Palestine and its opposition to U.S. and Zionist policies in the Middle East[71]—even though Mauritania and Libya are bound by the Arab Maghreb Union Charter whose Article 15 states that any foreign aggression on any member is an aggression on the entire union. In 1992, rumors circulated worldwide that some Libyan deposits were being transferred from Western banks in Europe to certain Arab countries, including Mauritania, as a response to the U.S.-led international sanctions against Libya. Responding to the question of whether Mauritania received some of these Libyan deposits, the governor of the Mauritanian central bank, Ahmed Ould Zein, responded furiously: "that is false; the BCM did not receive any Libyan deposit. Not one single dollar! This rumor tends to cause harm to our country's image in the West."[72] Hasni Ould Didi, Mauritanian minister of foreign affairs and cooperation, was dismissed while on a visit to Morocco when he declared to a Moroccan newspaper that "the states of the Arab Maghreb Union cannot implement Security Council sanctions against Libya because they are not convinced of their legality." It was reported that, upon hearing the declaration, the speaker of the Mauritanian government went immediately to inform the ambassadors of the United States, Saudi Arabia, and Kuwait in Nouakchott that "Hasni's statement does not reflect the position of the Mauritanian government."[73] The government was determined to adjust to whatever is required by the international community of lenders and donors or face further international isolation, political defamation, and economic sanctions. The current (October 1995) crackdown on the pro-Iraqi Baathist party in Mauritania further illustrates the government's determination to please the United States and its Middle Eastern allies.

The weakening of the state and its submission to the will of the international community of lenders and donors makes Mauritania the first Arab League member to have elected a president of the republic (out of four presidential candidates) by direct universal suffrage. The 1992 elections were so hastily organized that, one month after the elections, the members of the newly elected parliament needed special instructions from the president so that state regional authorities would open their doors to them.[74] The elections did not change much in the structure and relations of power within the state. Indeed, it legitimized and legalized that structure and in this sense continued the political order by means other than the violence of military rule. In the eyes of the opposition party (UFD), the significance of the elections is that "above all, the Colonel [the incumbent President] wanted his Constitution, his Parliament, his State-Party as 'in the days of old' when he had his Charter, his Military Committee and his *Structures d'Education des Masses*."[75] Democratization in Mauritania provided a psychological palliative necessary for a people experiencing the stress of political instability, ethnic tension, and rapid socioeconomic changes brought about by SAPs. As for true democracy, it "goes beyond the formal trappings of democratic political systems (such as multipartyism and elections) to include such elements as accountability and genuine popular participation in the nation's political and economic decision making process."[76]

For many, multipartyism is not democracy. We should not "be dazzled by formal democracy and wait the building of deep democracy."[77] Real democracy should be judged by its outcome (people's empowerment and equality) rather than its process (elections and multiparty politics). In this regard, the rule of the *single party* is certainly monolithic but not less democratic than the rule of the *winning party* within the framework of multipartyism. One can even argue that the inclusive nature (claiming to represent all the people) of the rule of a single party has perhaps more potential for people's empowerment than the exclusive nature (working to implement only the agenda of the winning party) of the ruling party within multipartyism. The concepts of (the respect of) *difference* and the *right to be different* (upon which rest the philosophy of multipartyism) represent the embodiment of social inequality in the distribution of power and wealth. For example, apartheid in South Africa was often justified on the basis of difference and the right to be different. Moreover, the decentralization process accompanying multiparty systems has led to "the retreat of genuine democracy, a victim of the bias of the combined influence of reactionary local forces and depoliticization following the loss of the overall dimension essential to political consciousness."[78] As an ultimate political adjustment to economic privatization and liberalization, decentralization and multipartyism opened the door for, as well as reflected, further social fragmentation.

Fragmentation: Ethnicity, Multipartyism, and Islamism

The denationalization of the state following the adoption of SAPs weakened the public sector and created a sense of social insecurity among people who feel that the state is no longer able and/or willing to protect them. People turned to tribal and clan institutions and identities in search for a minimum of social security. The model of "one-partyism" and "national integration" of the 1960s[79] is giving way to multipartyism, ethnicity, and even trends of national disintegration. This trend is behind much of the various nonnational identities (subnational as well as transnational) mushrooming today in Mauritania and including ethnicity, partyism, Islamism, tribalism, and feminism. Although these identities existed before SAPs, they are being reconstituted anew as part of a process of identity formation that constitutes both a cause and a consequence of the denationalization process. Among these identities, ethnicity, partyism, and Islamism have more impact on the political scene of the country today and will therefore be addressed in this section as an illustration of sociopolitical fragmentation in Mauritania along three distinct paths following the processes of economic liberalization and political democratization.

Ethnicity

The reemergence of tribalism and ethnicity in Mauritania in the 1980s has been observed and thoroughly analyzed.[80] The dissolution of the Mauritanian People's Party in 1978 and the banning of political parties under the military regime were often cited as some of the main causes behind the rise of these nonnational identities and forms of consciousness. These forms of explanation fail, however, to situate the phenomenon within the wider context of social fragmentation arising out of the crisis of the peripheral state and the implementation of structural adjustment policies. The reemergence of ethnicity in Mauritania in recent years "is incontestably linked to the global crisis of the State"[81] and its inability to firmly control the global/local growing connections. Ethnicity in Mauritania is an old internal issue, but its recent resurgence and political significance stem from the ascendence of the international factor over the national one, exemplified by the weakness of the central state and the growing hegemony of the international financial institutions. Ethnicity and ethnic strife represent the most common manifestations of sociopolitical fragmentation taking place amid the process of denationalization of the state and globalization of national economies. In Mauritania, ethnicity is complicated by issues of race and competition between Arab and black nationalism.

The question of Arabism versus Africanism in Mauritania was raised during the first years of political debate about independence. Although it is a question of power struggle and competition between Moorish and black African elites for control of the state, it was expressed in the form of ethnicity, language, and nationalism. Today, this question is exacerbated by the global crisis of the state and the worldwide emergence of nonnational identities arising from SAP denationalization and privatization policies. Given the geopolitics of Mauritania, the ethnic conflicts became the backdrop for Arab and African nationalism, two locally narrow forms of nationalism geared to confrontation more than cooperation. Although Arab and African nationalisms developed generally in response to European colonialism and were strengthened during the period of "national planning" of the 1960s and 1970s, in Mauritania they developed mainly in response to each other and were repressed during the 1960s and 1970s because of their potential for undermining national unity and the process of nation-state building. Originally, "Arab nationalism was a political reaction to Turkish nationalism and European colonialism"[82] in the Arab Mashreq centered around Greater Syria, where later Akram Hourani and Michel Aflaq founded Hizb Al-Baath Al-Arabi Al-Ishtiraqi (the Arab Socialist Baath Party) as a rallying cry for Arab unity and the liberation of Palestine. With Nasser's charisma and the strategic importance of Egypt, Nasser became the father of Arab nationalism, and Nasserism became a populist ideology stressing Arab and Muslim unity and making Arab nationalism the most important political force in the Arab world up to the 1979 Islamic Revolution in Iran, which made Islamism a more militant form of nationalism throughout and beyond the Arab world, even though some critics of both secular and religious nationalism believe that the shift from one to the other is nothing but an "ideological shift from myths to illusions."[83] In Mauritanian, however, the forces of Arab and black nationalism were latent forces throughout the 1960s and 1970s and therefore were not tied to the period of national planning. Ironically, they reemerged stronger with adjustment, when the period of national planning was waning away. This is why they are analyzed here with some detail and as new forms of ethnicity (rather than nationalism proper) arising out of the crisis of the denationalized state and the subsequent social crisis of identity that is contributing both to the constitution of new subnational and transnational identities and affiliations and to new forms of social fragmentation associated with the decline (rather than the rise) of the central power of the state.

From its inception, Arab nationalism in Mauritania had a strong populist element, as its founding leaders did not come from the traditional chieftains or from the modern French-educated elites. They grew outside the state apparatus and the dominant traditional social structures of power. They were able to develop a cultural power focus in between the above two foci, particularly in the education system, which has always been a fierce battle ground in Mauritania between French and Arabic. Up to the mid–1970s Arab nationalists in Mauritania were overshadowed by the leftist Kadihin (inspired by both Soviet

Leninism and Chinese Maoism), but after the mid–1970s Nasserists and Baathists grew rapidly within the education system. With rural-urban migration and the increase of education, the *Arabisants* (as they were labeled by the then-dominant French-educated elite) began to penetrate the administration, particularly since the coming to power of the military in 1978. They saw in the Arabic language and Islamic religion the only instruments capable of thwarting the domination of French language and culture within state institutions. They rejected the idea of Mauritania being depicted as simply "a hyphen" between the Arab world and black Africa. They believe this is an attempt to destroy the Arab and Islamic identity of the country. As the state weakened in the aftermath of SAPs, Arab and African nationalists began to expand beyond the education and cultural spheres to other state institutions and apparatuses, particularly within the military, where the Baathists and the Nasserists (the two offsprings of Arab nationalism in Mauritania) began recruiting adherents and supporters. Generally, the Baathists are more secular in their political outlook and receive direct support from Iraq, while the Nasserists often have more proclivities toward Islam and are more independent, even though they occasionally get support from Libya.

Black nationalism in Mauritania began as an offspring of négritude, a concept developed by French-educated black intellectuals from the West Indies (René Maran, Léon Damas, and Aimé Césaire) and West Africa (Leopold Sédar Senghor, former president of Senegal). They define négritude as the total sum of the qualities possessed by all black men everywhere and the recognition and acceptance of those qualities. They wrote extensively about négritude, black Africa, black character, black civilization, and the black world. Senghor himself (as well as the French existentialist, Jean-Paul Sartre) acknowledged that "there was an element of antiracist racism" in négritude, but he often evoked the idea that "European reason" and "African soul" complement each other, and he is well known for his francophile views and his role among the francophones.[84] In contrast to Arab nationalism, black nationalism in Mauritania was from the outset an elite-based movement that developed essentially among the French-educated black elite, many of whom were influenced at some point by Marxism. The attachment of black intellectuals to *francophonie* (French language and culture) and their susceptibility to Western influence in general often make them a potential scapegoat for anyone who wants to blame them for that attachment and susceptibility.[85] The first violent manifestation of their opposition to the Arabization of the education system began at the Lycée de Nouakchott in 1966 when a government decree made Arabic compulsory in high school. Black African students boycotted classes following this government decision, and the boycott degenerated into ethnic riots in Nouakchott. In 1967 the ruling party adopted bilingualism and established equality between French and Arabic within the education system. Following the massive rural-urban migration of the 1970s and 1980s, the number of *Arabisants* turned out by the education system increased rapidly, while the relative number of *Francisants* declined steadily. The process culminated with the adoption of the 1991 Constitution whose Article 6 stipulates that "the National Languages are Arabic, Poular, Soninke, and Wolof. Arabic is the Official Language," thus dismissing French and ending twenty-five years of official bilingualism. Each reform of the education system increasing Arabization has been vehemently opposed by African nationalists, an attitude that puts them on a collision course with Arab nationalists.

The most radical and most violent form of African nationalism came in the early 1980s as a result of the weakening (denationalization) of the state when a group of about thirty black intellectuals formed the Liberation Forces of Africans in Mauritania or FLAM and issued a thirty-seven–page document entitled Le Manifeste du Négro-Mauritanien Opprimé (the Manifesto of the Oppressed Mauritanian Black) in which they discussed alleged discrimination against black Mauritanians in government appointments and access to education. The authors of the document "included some of the best and most brilliant black Mauritanian intellectuals"[86] who consider the progressive Arabization of society a threat to their well-established privileges within the French-oriented administration and education system. The early declared objective of FLAM was to take over the Mauritanian state after destroying the "Arab/Berber state."[87] At another point, FLAM's objective was to achieve some sort of federalism,[88] while FLAM's most recent demands are concentrating on the "repatriation of the deportees." In 1986, they distributed the manifesto throughout Senegal, where they secured both popular and government sympathy and support. During the same year they also distributed the manifesto as a tract in Addis-Ababa, Ethiopia, during the OAU summit, and in Harare, Zimbabwe, during the summit of the nonaligned countries. The document was written in French and targeted mainly foreign audiences and (arbitrarily) divided the Mauritanian society along racial lines: the Arab-Berbers (the whites) and the black Africans (the blacks), the former exploit the latter.

The authors of the tract were intellectuals and high-ranking civil servants mainly from the Toucouleur ethnic group. They relied on a favorable international context and were encouraged by the domestic situation: the nation-state was going through a financial and legitimacy crisis triggered partly by years of SAP austerity programs. Given their minority status and the unpopularity of their racist views, FLAM elements centered their strategy on race relations and on international public opinion through systematic campaigns of defamation of the Mauritanian government and the Moors as racists who discriminate against blacks. Their message was more effective in the United States (where politics is more sensitive to race relations) than in European countries (where politics is more sensitive to class consciousness). In Senegal, they have the support of the "Halpular lobby" of the river valley and the sympathy of segments from the extreme left. On the African scene, they have support from the Ligue des États négro-africains (financed by Zaire's Mobutu), which finances certain influential Senegalese personalities and circles with "strong anti-Arab and pro-Israeli tonality."[89] These various groups operating in Senegal were known as "the anti Mauritanian lobby," which was centered around the Comité d'Initiative des Ressortissants du Fleuve in Dakar. The Groupe Afrique within the French Socialist Party and the Human Right Caucus within the U.S. Congress all have, for one reason or another, supported FLAM's claim of racial discrimination in Mauritania. The initial racial articulation of the discourse by FLAM elements exacerbated ethnic relations not only within Mauritania but also between Mauritania and Senegal. It culminated in the unprecedented ethnic violence that erupted in both countries in April 1989 and led to the simultaneous repatriation/deportation of Mauritanians and Senegalese. FLAM also sought sympathy and support from the francophone world. The anonymous president of FLAM said once that he was disappointed that the francophone world is abandoning the black Mauritanians, "the only ones who continue to maintain the French language."[90] FLAM rejects Mauritania's Arabness in favor of négritude and the *francophonie*. These issues of cultural identities cannot be separated from the political ramifications of SAPs, which were setting the stage for most changes since the early 1980s.

Even though various conceptualizations of the Senegal-Mauritania conflict had been informed by history, Arab-African identity, ecology, and political economy,[91] one must emphasize the fact that the explosion of ethnicity in Mauritania and Senegal came at the peak of SAP implementation, whose social hardship intensified popular feeling of insecurity and provided the political elites with opportunities to use ethnic divisions as the basis for populist mobilization and political scapegoats. One cannot understand the April 1989 conflict between Mauritania and Senegal unless the political crisis in Senegal at the time is fully understood.[92] Both Mauritania and Senegal were going through deep economic and social crises caused partly and exacerbated by the implementation of SAPs. In Senegal, the crisis was deep, and discontent was expressed by strikes among high school and university students and even policemen. For the first time there were rumors in Dakar about a possible military coup d'etat.[93] Relations with neighboring countries deteriorated and secessionist insurgency in the southern region of Casamance became more and more violent. At the same time, the process of revalorization of the Senegal River valley began to materialize with the completion of the Manantali (upper valley) and Diama (lower valley) dams, whose costs in 1990 (all infrastructure including dam supervision, access roads, population resettlement, and forest clearing) had reached $620 million ($506 million for Manantali, $114 million for Diama).[94] With the completion of the dams and the focus of lender attention on the valley, the dominant classes in both Mauritania and Senegal "believe that quite considerable wealth is to be made in agriculture."[95] This revalorization was achieved by regional cooperation between Mauritania, Mali, and Senegal through the Organisation de la Mise en Valeur du Fleuve Senegal (OMVS). Mauritania played an important role in lobbying Arab countries to assist the OMVS. By 1984 some 54 percent of OMVS's financing was coming from Arab sources.[96] The government of Senegal began to consider the Senegal River valley (a long-neglected region) as the new pole of economic development after the decline of the groundnut producing regions when the price of groundnut plunged from $1,000 to $550/ton between 1985 and 1987 as a result of SAP search for competitiveness in price exports.

In Mauritania too the crisis was deep and was reflected in a great deal of political instability. Discontent was widespread among civil servants whose purchasing power had been deteriorating, particularly following systematic devaluations of the ouguiya. Land reform was being implemented, bringing fundamental changes in the agricultural system on the Mauritanian side of the Senegal River. As the adjustment state began to weaken in the early 1980s, centrifugal forces (ethnic, nationalistic, and so on) began to challenge it. A fierce struggle to take over the state began. In this context, hundreds of Arab nationalists (Baathists and Nasserists) and African nationalists (FLAM members) were arrested, tortured (some of them to death), and imprisoned without trial.

The scramble to take over the state graphically illustrates its unprecedented weakness: in October 1987 as few as fifty FLAM radicals in the army were about to overthrow the government and establish a FLAM-controlled state. As the crisis deepened in both Senegal and Mauritania, these complex problems and relations were articulated by politicians in a way that reduced them to simply ethnic or racial (black and white) conflict, a convenient scapegoat that diverted the attention of the population to an imminent external threat, instead of an assessment of the problems arising out of the interaction between SAP implementation and the internal social relations. This scapegoating helped both governments to stay in power amid deep economic and legitimacy crises of the state. "A temporary national unity sometimes termed the 'Falklands effects' because of the increased support given to a regime when facing an external threat has occurred in both countries" as President Diouf of Senegal benefited from expressions of genuine nationalistic feeling among the Senegalese, while President Ould Taya of Mauritania benefited from a virtual consensus at home.[97] This crisis saved both regimes from collapsing as soon as the energy of their opponents was shrewdly diverted to the confrontation with some outside threats. But the political nature of the conflict cannot be hidden. The so-called racial conflict can be seen as a truly political conflict when one understands "the firm alliance between Senegal and Morocco."[98] Morocco represented Senegal's interest in Mauritania following the break of diplomatic relations in 1989, and it is widely believed that Saudi Arabia somehow supported Senegal while Iraq supported Mauritania in this conflict. Even though the reemergence of Arab as well African nationalism in Mauritania in the 1980s and 1990s is part of the overall emergence of ethnicity following the denationalization of the state, it is also an important power strategy reflecting the interplay between internal social struggles and external intervention.

History repeats itself, at least in power strategies. Today, both the reality and the discourse of the ethnic divide between the Arabic-speaking and the non-Arabic speaking Mauritanians brings to mind the precolonial opposition between warrior and maraboutic tribes among the Moors. Both constitute an internal power struggle that the outside world (France at the turn of the century and the international community of lenders and donors today) has used essentially to strengthen the weak only to weaken the strong. This was the case when the French colonial administration gradually abolished and/or bought all forms of tributes to weaken the warrior tribes, which were a competitor in terms of the use of "legitimate violence." The result was that everyone ended up paying taxes, a new tribute (*Al-Ushr* or *impôt*) to the French colonial administration. Today, the process of weakening the state by taking away its material base (state enterprises), supporting its ethnic-based opposition, and strengthening the private sector and NGOs represents the same power strategy under different circumstances. While democratization did not bring an end to sociopolitical fragmentation along ethnic lines, it overshadowed it by the politics of multipartyism: a legal and nonviolent means of an even deeper sociopolitical fragmentation.

Multipartyism

The political trajectory of postindependence Mauritania has gone from the monolithism of the single-party (the Party du Peuple Mauritanien [PPM] from 1963 to 1978) to the dictatorship of military rule (the Military Committee from 1978 to 1992) to the hegemony of the ideology of multipartyism from 1992 on (Mauritania had some eighteen political parties in 1993 [see table 37]). As the state became denationalized amid the global discourse of democracy, only two of the eighteen political parties have the attribute "Mauritanian" in their names, whereas half of them have the term "democracy" in their names. This transition from a rigid military rule to a seemingly more flexible multiparty rule represents a power strategy already tested at the turn of the century in West Africa as a sophisticated divide-and-rule policy. In fact, the *politique des races* (racial policy) and the *justice indigène* (indigenous justice) that the French colonial administration implemented in West Africa in the late 1900s as a decentralization strategy of control after years of concentration of power in the hands of one administrator[99] bears some resemblance to the coming of multipartyism after years of one-party rule. The political implication of multipartyism resides essentially in the fragmentation and diffusion of national political forces. Once political parties are turned against each other in their selfish and often destructive process of competition for power, they disintegrate and fragment national political forces within the country to the extent that there is no unified and coordinated national policy.

The list of political parties in Mauritania is somehow misleading since it masks a more complex political reality. It is complex because the majority of political parties and groups that were underground prior to

Table 37   Legalized Political Parties in Mauritania in 1993

1. Democratic and Social Republican Party	10. National Avant-Garde Party
2. Union of Democratic Forces, New Era	11. Party of Freedom/Equality/Justice
3. Mauritanian Party for Renewal	12. Party of Labor and National Unity
4. Democratic and Social Popular Union	13. National Party for Unity/Democracy
5. Democratic Justice Party	14. Social and Democratic Union
6. Rally for Democracy and Unity	15. National Rally for Unity and Justice
7. Progressive and Popular Alliance	16. National Charter
8. Mauritanian Democratic Centre Party	17. Union for Democracy and Progress
9. Union for Planning and Reconstruction	18. Union for Democracy/Development

Source: Compiled for the author by Mohamed Ali Ould-Mey, Nouakchott, January 1994.

democratization were not allowed and/or were not willing to register under their real noms de guerre, such as Kadihin, Nasserists, Baathists, FLAM, and Islamists. Instead, they adopt new names or melt into larger coalitions of political parties. This is a clear indication that the democratization process is well regulated and controlled to the extent that certain political activism and certain political emblems are not accepted because of their potential partisanship or divisiveness amid an increasingly fragmented society. This form of administered pluralism (first by Western powers and then by the military government of Ould Taya) is often overshadowed by the euphoria and uproar accompanying the process. It also illustrates that the political agenda of each party is not sufficiently popular and/or democratic to be presented under the true name of the party. Rather than open debates and a transparent decision-making process, interest groups and lobby politics represent the dynamics of multipartyism. This is why after the institutionalization of freedom of speech and association, each political faction continued to keep its nom de guerre away from public rallies and public debates. In addition, each faction is so weak that it must form a coalition with others as a survival strategy. The eighteen political parties are therefore polarized between two major coalitions or political parties that dominate the political scene: the Democratic and Social Republican Party (PRDS) and the Union of Democratic Forces (UFD, later renamed UFD New Era), which were respectively created by the government and the opposition on the eve of the January 1992 presidential elections.

The PRDS represents virtually an elephant's belly,[100] bringing together high-ranking state officials, tribal leaders, businessmen, the leading wings of the Baathists, the Nasserists, and the Islamists, some former leaders of the leftist Kadihin Party, and other leaders from the El-

Hor movement (a sociopolitical movement for the total emancipation of the Haratins from the residues of slavery). Relying on his incumbency and on the state's administrative channels and institutions, Ould Taya was able to build a sort of consensus between these various elements, sometimes by brandishing the specter of FLAM and the phenomenon of national disintegration and civil wars taking place in other African countries. Ultimately, this strategy worked well despite the wide spectrum of real and potential divisions among the various components of the PRDS coalition. The election campaign was for the most part based on demagoguery and propaganda. Though the campaign was open and democratic (as many European observers witnessed), it deliberately avoided political/economic discourse and focused on the Arab/Islamic cultural identity of the country and the necessity of preserving it in the face of an ever-expanding Western culture through various real or imaginary local "fifth columns." It praised the incumbent government for succeeding in the prevention of civil war that had destroyed other countries such as South Yemen, Somalia, Yugoslavia, and Liberia. The political discourse became more realistic once the election was over. In his inaugural address, the newly elected president shifted his campaign's major theme of "returning to ourselves, to our culture and history"[101] to a new discourse of adjustment: "our society must adapt to the contemporary realities of modernism. Technology is the only way for the salvation of our people."[102]

The second party (UFD) was dominated mainly by elements from the former PPM and its former opposition. These include many dignitaries and former ministers (such as Mohamedhen Ould Babbah and Hamdi Ould Mouknass) from the Ould Daddah government (1958–78), the leftist Democratic National Movement (MND)—including the so-called Kadihin Mariem, who joined the PPM after 1974—an important wing of El-Hor, and elements of the FLAM. At some point it was reported that Hizb Al-Umma (a nonlegalized Islamist party) joined the UFD coalition. As a whole the UFD was even less homogeneous than the PRDS, and it had a hard time finding a political leader. After an intense debate and dialogue, the leaders of the UFD finally agreed on Ahmed Ould Daddah as a symbol of the premilitary era and someone with "a big name" since he is half-brother and former minister of finance of former President Mokhtar Ould Daddah. He also worked for the Kuwaitis and the World Bank, two important lenders/donors for Mauritania. But these outstanding qualities were canceled by three others: (1) his de facto alliance with FLAM, (2) his detachment from the national political reality and dynamics since he had been away from the country for years, and (3) his underestimation of the power of the military and the appeal of Arab nationalism. No wonder then that the UDF lost the 1992 presidential elections[103] (with only one-third of the total vote), boycotted the April 1992 legislative ones, suffered membership losses in 1993 following the creation of the Union pour la Démocratie et le Progrès (UDP), and finally accepted the terms of "the Ould Taya's democracy." Yet Ahmed Ould Daddah, the leader of the UFD, maintained that election fraud was widespread and that he got more votes than his adversary, Ould Taya. In the latest municipal elections of January 1994, the ruling party (PRDS) won in 160 out of 208 communes, the main opposition party (UFD) won only in 32 communes, and the remaining communes were shared among independent candidates.[104] Although presidential and municipal elections are different, the UDF's share (only 15 percent of the communes) reflects further decline of its position as a major political party, a trend that may not change in the foreseeable future, despite the party's confidence in the forthcoming legislative and presidential elections of 1997 and 1998.

From the beginning, the UFD rejected the outcome of the presidential and parliamentary elections in the following declaration of 17 April 1992: "The UDF which rejected the results of the presidential elections and boycotted the parliamentary elections proclaims its total rejection of institutions born out of those elections which it considers illegal."[105] This also was the position of FLAM, whose leadership (based in Senegal and France) issued a communique in late January 1992 rejecting the outcome of the presidential elections and the democratic process, which "did not meet all the conditions of openness required for a healthy, legal, and unbiased competition."[106] But less than two years after its creation, the opposition party began to disintegrate and suffered large membership losses following the creation of the UDP, believed to be pro-Moroccan. In fact, in 1993 Hamdi Ould Mouknas, former Mauritanian foreign minister and leader of the UDP was briefly arrested by the authorities and questioned about the meeting he organized in Morocco between King Hassan II and former Mauritanian President Mokhtar Ould Daddah. After his release, he praised Mokhtar Ould Daddah and described King Hassan II of Morocco as "the greatest and most qualified world leader today."[107]

This schism within the opposition and perhaps the disillusionment of some of its leaders finally forced the UFD to reconsider its position vis-à-vis the government and to decide to abide by the rules of the political game and to "struggle within the limits of possibilities offered by the constitution" and to declare its readiness to open a "responsible, constructive and serene" dialogue with the president and other political parties.[108] The UFD and its leaders were discredited politically mainly because of their de facto alliance with FLAM. In this regard, Ahmed Ould Sidi Baba, a former influential member of the PPM and a strong behind-the-scenes element of the Ould Taya government, had the following comment on the leader of the UFD: "Ahmed Ould Daddah is and will continue to be a friend, but he gave a written commitment to one party whose elements constitute a danger for our country."[109] But Ahmed Ould Daddah insists that his party (UDF) "represents all the communities in Mauritania. There is the Arab community, that is to say with all its components, including the Haratins, and the black community."[110] FLAM, which portrays Mauritania as an "intrinsically racist, tribalist, and slavist white system,"[111] was and is still considered by many (including the government) as a racist, francophone-backed, chauvinist movement opposed to Islam and Arabism, that was created by Senegal to destabilize Mauritania through a civil war, a necessary prelude to a Senegalese takeover of the entire Senegal River once the OMVS dams were completed. Moreover, FLAM is still bitterly remembered as the agent behind the April 1989 events during which the millennial fraternal relations between the two Muslim peoples of Senegal and Mauritania were destroyed in one week and where hundreds of thousands of Mauritanians lost their properties in Senegal, probably forever.

> From May 1986 "The Mauritany Question" becomes for Senegal an essential element of home policy and a favorite theme for election campaigns. The hostile operations against Mauritania, particularly against the Moors as an ethny [*sic*] went far beyond outbursts of temper. They took on the form of a systematic campaign first indirectly and then directly financed by the Senegalese power . . . responsible for the creation of the FLAM. . . . After the proclamation of this movement [FLAM] in Dakar, the Senegalese authorities will consider as political refugees all its well known militants, most of them being Senegalese, and will help them to get a registration certificate from the [UN] "High Commission Office for Refugees." Moreover the private and official Senegalese press will offer them a large tribune by popularizing their racist proclamations and their unambiguous threats against peace and interethnic cohabitation in Mauritania.[112]

But whatever credit this or that party may have in the domestic arena, international connections, particularly with the West, are always crucial for success. It is widely believed that France is behind the PRDS, the United States and the Arab Gulf states are behind the UDF, and Morocco is behind the UDP. Of all these countries, France is by far the most important for any political party aspiring to rule Mauritania. France remains the favorite mecca for both government and opposition leaders. They know very well that its position is determinant for the rise as well as for the demise of most political regimes in Mauritania. In 1993 President Maaouiya Ould Taya and his two major opponents (Ahmed Ould Daddah and Hamdi Ould Mouknas) visited France in search of support and sympathy.[113] But the difference between these political parties is formal and has more to do with competition between their leaders than with real antagonism of their political or economic agendas. The UFD's proposed economic policy was carefully articulated as liberal economy, free competition, and restoration of macroeconomic equilibrium of public finances and balance of payments.[114] These were essentially the policies of adjustment advocated by the World Bank and adopted by the military government and ultimately by the PRDS. The economic policy of the government and the opposition was the same. Their difference stemmed less from their programs than from differences in style and, more important, differences in the interpretation of past management of the state.[115] As long as they do not question SAPs or multipartyism, the government/opposition struggle is essentially about who governs rather than how to govern. In the eyes of many, they are embarking on a vicious circle that is inherent to the fragmented and egoistic politics of multipartyism, where each party must defeat its rival by destroying its achievements and plans, since the failure of the ruling party is necessary for the success of the opposition.

Fragmentation of the political system is also reflected in the fragmentation of opinion, despite striking similarities in the political agendas of all parties. Between January 1991 and October 1992, the Ministry of Interior issued some ninety-three permits for free publication of independent newspapers (weekly, monthly, and so on), of which fifty-three were to be published in Arabic, twenty-two in both Arabic and French, and fifteen in French.[116] Such great diversity of opinion could be described as part of strong democratic practices, and it certainly reflects a growing printing business. It also represents a fragmentation of national politics, with so many factions competing openly with each other and engaging in intense, yet partly empty, political and cultural debates. Empty debates because major national socioeconomic policies are conceived and designed by international financial institutions and not by these factions, even if some of them benefit from those policies. Before this fission of opinion, there was only one daily (*Al-Shaab* in both

Arabic and French) and a couple of periodicals. The same trend of fragmentation is taking place among workers' unions, where the Union of Mauritanian Workers (UTM) is in the process of splitting apart, into the General Confederation of Mauritanian Workers (CGTM)[117] and the Confederation of the Free Syndicates of Mauritania (CSLM). Some trade unions leaders are concerned that the increased competition among unions for members could fragment and weaken labor's bargaining strength[118] as it already did for political parties. While the discourse of ethnicity and partyism are still dominant, militant Islamism may soon enter the official political scene of Mauritania as a real and potential third path of sociopolitical fragmentation.

Islamism

The constant resort to Islamic discourse in legitimizing power[119] has been an important ideological factor in both pre- and postcolonial Mauritanian society. This historical legacy continues to force both government and opposition to include Islamic discourse in their political agendas and propaganda efforts to win support from large segments of the public that may not be reached or influenced otherwise. The flexibility of Islam in coexisting with and even legitimizing a variety of political systems illustrates Muslims' capacity to interpret religion in accordance with sociopolitical interests. The first great schism in Islam, which gave birth to the first Sunna/Shia divide during the formative century of Islam, was initially a power struggle framed in religious discourse to legitimize the claim of each side in a *superior court*. This historical experience made Islamic discourse an important weapon in the dynamics of social struggle, particularly in the process of legitimizing or delegitimizing social power, as was the case with the Al-Murabitun movement in the eleventh century and the Zouaya and Toroodo revolts in the seventeenth century. Even French colonial penetration in Mauritania was legitimized and delegitimized on the basis of Islam, as was reflected in the *Fatawi* (singular *Fatwa*, religious decree or legal opinion) and letters of the great shaykhs of the time: Shaykh Sidya Baba and Shaykh Ma Al-Ainin. The flexibility and instrumentality of Islamic discourse in legitimizing power continues today, as illustrated by the use of such discourse in Iran and Saudi Arabia to legitimize two diametrically opposed political agendas.[120] Such duality exists today within all Muslim states, where traditional Muslim leaders (Salafi Ulemas and Sufi Sheikhs) are increasingly criticized by a new generation of militant Islamists (Muslims whose main political goal is to establish an Islamic state based on Islamic law), who are inspired partly by the success of Khomeinism in Iran in moving beyond Islamic discourse of the Ulema to a political economy of Islamic power in government practice. In the words of Abdessalam Yassine, an Islamist from Morocco,

> It is very interesting, what a few ulema are doing, but it is not enough. They are (no doubt) in the opposition, (but it is) an opposition based on principle, which is eternal. They only point with their finger at the things which they consider immoral. This is not sufficient. It is necessary to move to the next step, which is to have a program. . . . With a few rare exceptions, they never speak about economic problems, and rarely about politics, when what is essential is to realize that there exists a close relationship between immorality and the economic and political system. . . . We demand power. . . . that is permitted by democracy, that is what we want.[121]

Despite their awareness that "today, the Islamic World is experiencing a clear religious *Sahwa*" (awakening),[122] most Mauritanian Ulemas never seriously challenged the political system, and on many occasions they have openly supported it—in contrast to more recent Islamist militant groups, who are moving away from the tradition of acquiescence to the established power and want nothing short of a comprehensive and full implementation of the *Sharia* (Islamic Law) in every facet of life, even though the appeal of their program is still overshadowed by the politics of ethnicity and secular nationalism. These Islamists have encouraged opposition to the government, particularly since the 1991 Constitution excluded them by banning religious parties. Article 99 states that amendment of the Constitution is not possible if it seeks to change the republican formula of the political order or the pluralist nature of Mauritanian democracy. Though Article 5 of the 1991 Constitution stipulates that "Islam is the religion of the people and the state," the ordinance on political parties carefully excluded the possibility of legalizing religious parties, i.e., Islamist parties, and consequently the Islamist Hizb Al-Umma party was not legalized. Hence the paradox of an Islamic republic outlawing any Islamic or Islamist party. From the government viewpoint, Islamist parties were outlawed precisely because Mauritania was an Islamic republic. This irony represents a stark illustration of the importance of Islamic discourse in legitimizing power.

In banning Islamist parties, the government argues that no party should monopolize Islam's powerful appeal in a 100 percent Muslim society.

This decision was welcomed by the leaders of most political parties, who realized their inability to compete with adversaries using Islamist discourse in their appeal to the population. The potential of increased Islamism in Mauritania cannot be disregarded if the movement continues to rise in the other Maghreb states and Egypt. While many leaders of the Islamists supported the PRDS during the 1992 elections, they were not allowed to form an Islamist party, even under a secular name. This is perhaps an indication of the weakness of the ideological foundations of the peripheral nation-state and the limits to the kind of democratization that was carefully tailored to serve SAP needs only. The banning of Islamist parties remains a latent political issue that will undoubtedly continue to undermine the ideological foundation of multipartyism and the overall credibility of the democratic process. Following an attack in 1993 on two French Roman Catholic priests, who were stabbed in the gardens of the Catholic mission in Nouakchott, the Mauritanian government expelled five Algerian students who were allegedly preaching a militant form of Islam. They were part of some 100 students mainly from Algeria, Tunisia, Pakistan, and Afghanistan who study at Koranic colleges in Mauritania.[123] President Ould Taya warned these and other Islamists that "Al-Shanaguita do not receive any lesson of Islam or Arabism from anyone."[124] In November 1993, an armed man opened fire (while shouting "Allah Akbar!" [God is great]) and injured two policemen in a party attended by some government ministers in Nouakchott.[125] This act was described as an "isolated incident," its perpetrator as "mentally disturbed," and the Islamists denied any responsibility in the incident.[126] However, the banning of Hizb Al-Umma in Mauritania and the resurgence of Islamist movements throughout the Arab world cannot be excluded as important factors that may have inspired the "mentally disturbed" perpetrator.

In October 1994, confrontation between the Islamists and the government escalated when the authorities arrested some sixty Islamist leaders, including a former minister, ten imams, and six foreigners for belonging to "secret foreign organizations."[127] The current Iranian and Sudanese political systems are perceived by many Islamists as political models, since they were the first in this century to translate the power of Islamist discourse into government practice. It is worth noting that in the aftermath of the 1991 Gulf War, the first Arab-Islamic Popular Congress was held in Khartoum, Sudan, in April 1991, and the second one was also held in Sudan in December 1993. Both gatherings included not just the Islamists but also some Marxists and secular nationalists. In October

1994, 100 top Islamists and Arab nationalists (including at least one Christian priest) met in Beirut, Lebanon, to discuss ways of ending decades of ideological rivalries between them. The 1994 joint declaration by the heads of state of the Arab Maghreb Union in Tunis condemning Islamist terrorism indicates this growing phenomenon in the Arab world. In February 1995, the Paris-based *Jeune Afrique* reported under the heading *Confidentiel* that Mali, Mauritania, and Senegal are collaborating closely in the fight against the Islamists. Along the same lines, the North Atlantic Treaty Organization (NATO) declared a Mediterranean Initiative (February 1995) that calls for direct dialogue between NATO and the non-NATO countries of Egypt, Morocco, Tunisia, Israel, and Mauritania aimed at establishing security arrangements and strategies designed to contain the rise of the Islamists in the Middle East and North Africa. It was reported in June 1995 that this bizarre dialogue was being conducted at the ambassadorial level in Brussels. In his study of the Islamic movement in North Africa, François Burgat came to the conclusion that "nearly everywhere in the Arab world today, it is the forces emanating from the vast movement of political Islam that appear to be the leading candidates to replace the regimes linked to the national movements."[128] While this scenario cannot be excluded, it needs to be articulated within the process of denationalization of Middle Eastern states following their adoption of SAPs. It has been argued that Islamic radicalism represents "a postmodern reaction to dependent modernization" and that its emergence "can best be understood in the global context of the crisis of statism in general and of inwardly-oriented industrialization in the Third World in particular."[129]

Three factors seem to have played an important role in inspiring and/or encouraging the increasing militancy of the Islamists. The first one is the existence of an important historical and political Islamic model or blueprint that includes: an Islamic state (*Al-Khilafa Al-Islamiya*), a Muslim community (*Al-Umma Al-Islamiya*), and an Islamic constitution (*Al-Sharia Al-Islamiya*). The Islamists believe that the restoration of a new political system based on this model is both feasible and desirable in the light of the failure of secular nationalism, Western capitalism, and Soviet Marxism to bring about radical solutions to the many problems facing Muslim societies today. In this regard, their re-Islamization movement could be viewed as a response to the strong de-Islamization policy inaugurated by Moustapha Kamal (Ataturk) in the 1920s. The second factor that ironically inspires and encourages Islamic fundamentalism is the success and power accumulated by Jewish fundamentalism in the Middle East since the end of World War II. Israel is the only religious state in the region whose legitimacy is exclusively based on religious stories and tales. It is founded on Jewish fundamentalism of restoring an alleged Old Testament order, and its success and regional hegemony (thanks to Western support) will continue to inspire fundamentalism in general and Islamism in particular. The third and perhaps the most important factor behind the rise of the Islamists is the extreme weakness of Middle Eastern states in the aftermath of their denationalization following over a decade of intensive structural adjustment programs. This failure is illustrated not only by their capitulation to Western imperialism and Zionism following the disintegration of the Soviet Union and the Iraqi defeat in the 1991 Gulf War but also by the increasing reliance of many states on foreign intervention. For example, the political systems in the six states of the Gulf Cooperation Council can no longer continue without direct U.S. military protection. By the same token, the Algerian and Egyptian governments cannot contain their opposition without strong economic and diplomatic support from France and the United States, respectively. Such weakness and dependence of peripheral states and their inability to mediate some of the interactions and transactions brought about by the process of globalization gave rise to subnational as well as transnational forces and identities that, while resisting globalization, are nevertheless accelerating it by their circumvention of the power of central states. They are expressed in various types of sociopolitical fragmentation (such as ethnicity, multipartyism, and Islamism) and forms of consciousness reflected partly in the growing mosaic of postmodern geographies of fragmentation, ephemerality, and instantaneity.[130]

To sum up, the collapse of the central power of the peripheral state following its denationalization and the emergence of more powerful international financial institutions are giving rise to decentralization trends at the national level while increasing centralization at the global level. This process is unleashing trends of globalization that contributed to the revival of centrifugal forces and to the potential interaction between the global and the local, and more generally awakened the old academic debate between "the universal" and "the particular." Today, Western liberal democracy, civilization, and way of life are increasingly portrayed as universal, while other alternatives are dismissed as particularist and nationalist. Because "European imperialist expansion had to be presented in terms of a universal civilizing function of modernization, . . . the resistances of other cultures were presented not as struggles between particular identities and cultures, but as part of an all-embracing, epochal struggle between universality and particularisms—the notion of peoples without history expressing precisely their incapacity to represent the universal."[131] One example of this dichotomy may be found in the increasing confrontation between the Islamists and the unidimensional Western model of liberal democracy and free market, which continues to present itself as pluralist, diverse, and tolerant while rejecting any other alternative of socioeconomic organization. "Too often analysis and policymaking have been shaped by a liberal secularism that fails to recognize it too represents a world view, not the paradigm for modern society, and can easily degenerate into a 'secularist fundamentalism' that treats alternative views as irrational, extremist, and deviant."[132] In the same way communist states in Eastern Europe and the Soviet Union defined themselves as popular democracies during the Cold War era, many Islamic movements portray themselves as democratic movements and define democracy as the *Shura* (consultation) principle in the Quran. While various interpretations of democracy by liberals, communists, and Islamists are an indication of its centrality to contemporary power struggles and theories, they are also an indication that neither of these three models represents genuine democracy, where power and wealth are in the hands of the people and where individuals have sovereignty over their mind and their labor. Such a genuine democratic model (often portrayed as utopian) exposes the limits to the current process of democratization, which is tailored on SAPs.

9

Democratization or Democracy?

It is the central thesis of this work that the global strategy of adjustment of the 1980s and 1990s has reconstituted and reinvigorated the political, economic, and military power of the West and accelerated the recompradorization of the peripheral states of the world economy by reversing their nationalist policies. In contrast to the Cold War era, where peripheral states had at least the option of alignment with one of two superpowers and hence had a greater latitude within which to frame independent policies, the New World Order era allows only one option: Western capitalism and multipartyism. Any political economic system outside this straitjacket model of socioeconomic organization is considered an international pariah at best and crushed by military force at worse. However, this unidimensional philosophy of development is defined and presented by the dominant discourse of liberalism as the embodiment of pluralism, diversity, and difference, even though it does not tolerate any political or economic alternative. Under such unequal power relationships, the peripheral states are literally deprived of their national sovereignty, while the transfer of resources from South to North increases amid a hegemonic discourse of economic aid, technical assistance, and humanitarian relief. The systematic devaluation of national currencies in developing countries, far from providing benefits from international aid, is redirecting the flow of resources from South to North. In terms of resource transfer, devaluation seems to be as effective as the earlier forms of "primitive accumulation" achieved through war and violence during the first centuries of European expansion. The denationalization of the peripheral state is the key to the success of the processe of globalization. Indeed the new national security threats of fragmentation along the lines of ethnicity, religion, and partyism are actually providing an opportunity for the forces of globalization to further pressure states and obtain more concessions on sovereignty matters. The process of denationalization prevents the state and the multiparty society from forming any cohesive coalition or bloc to enable steadfastness in the face of international capital strategies of resource transfer. This process of denationalization of the state and the globalization and devaluation of the economy is creating an unmelting global pot and unleashing mass poverty and sociopolitical fragmentation. It is also exacerbating a crisis of identity where individuals are swinging between the identity of the economic man (world citizen) and other subglobal, transnational, and nationalist forms of cultural identities embodied for the most part in ethnicity and religion, partly because political and economic identities (other than market economy and multipartyism) are no longer tolerated. The current resonance and revival of Islam and Muslim identity (Islamism) in Islamic states represents the most visible antagonism between the global and the local and illustrates the failure of the dependent and peripheral nation-state to provide a minimum of national honor and/or economic success despite its constant adjustment to the imperatives of the Western-led global economy at the expense of nationalist policies. Antagonism and interaction between the global and the local is better reflected in, and exacerbated by, the profound transformation of the peripheral state from a nation-state to a multilateral state, as the case of Mauritania demonstrates.

After a decade of systematic adjustment to the above global strategy, the Mauritanian state is being transformed from a national to a multilateral state, that is, a denationalized state overwhelmed by the process of globalization and haunted by the specter of national disintegration. It is losing control over its money and credit system. Its sovereignty over lawmaking and budget allocation is eroding. Even its monopoly over internal politics and the use of violence are sometimes challenged. Its capacity to conceive, design, fund, implement, monitor, and evaluate original development programs is almost vanishing. Regional, ethnic, tribal, religious, linguistic, and cultural adherence and loyalties are accelerating sociopolitical fragmentation and seriously undermining national cohesiveness and, indeed, the whole project of nation/state building. Global state-like institutions such as the IMF, the World Bank, the Paris Club, the Consultative Group, and dozens of NGOs are increasingly bypassing, circumventing, and penetrating the

Mauritanian state at all levels. The nerve center of real decision making is actually shifting away from the state bureaucracy to these collective instruments of financial and economic policy. A new rearticulation of political space and a new geography of power relations are emerging within the Nouakchott-Washington-Paris triangle, and a variety of national interest groups are being systematically connected to a variety of international interests.

However, the process of denationalization does not eliminate the state. Other developments seem to empower the state. For example, the creation of municipalities in 1986–88 constituted an enlargement of the spatial and institutional scope and capacity of the state; the general referendum on a new constitution in 1991 and the subsequent parliamentary and presidential elections in 1992 contributed to sharpening state legitimacy; and the current slogan, "the state of law," may be seen as an indication of an increasing encroachment by the state in modeling and regulating the social life of people in a slow but steady process of separation of politics and work. SAPs could not have succeeded without the state, which remains an important source of power and access to resources. It is the major institution within which internal conflicts are settled and the sole one through which international agreements are negotiated and implemented. Viewed pragmatically, however, the apparent empowerment of the state is nothing but a reinforcement of its capacity to maintain internal order as a sine qua non condition for implementing unpopular economic policies advocated from outside and containing their internal social and political ramifications. The apparent empowerment of the state at a time when the nerve center of real decision making in economic and financial matters is shifting away from state apparatuses to international financial institutions is only paralleled by the apparent democratization of society at a time when the great majority of the people has little control over the conception and design of SAPs, which affect their lives in many ways. Since neither the state nor civil society have full sovereignty over SAPs, it is justifiably right to question the most praised aspect of SAPs: the process of democratization. This process needs to be further studied and above all demystified, since democratic relations at the domestic level will remain superficial amid undemocratic relations at the international level, where SAPs are conceived and designed.

My main critique of democratization under SAPs arises from an understanding of democracy as above all an act of sovereignty and self-determination, whether assessed at the international, state, or individual level. If a country does not have control over its economic policy, its democratization or militarization do not matter because, without sovereignty, the state will be more responsive to international pressure than to internal demand. The current democratization did not achieve a significant redistribution of political power among the people since much of the power taken away from the central government was essentially recuperated by multilateral institutions or NGOs that are dominated by the G–7 states. The process of economic liberalization and political democratization provides counterweights that limit the power of the central state, but many of those counterweights are not placed in the hands of the ordinary citizen since "some of them will be in the hands of multinational corporations which can take decisions that have far-reaching effects on the indigenous population."[1] Within the framework of SAPs, the crucial economic decisions of budget allocation, investment, credit, and so on, are excluded from the sphere of democracy and left to the bureaucracy of international financial institutions and their partners in government committees, who are neither elected by, nor accountable to, the people. In other words, democratization did not bring about people's sovereignty over SAPs, and the process of weakening the state does not seem to empower the people. Democratic relations at the domestic level will remain superficial amid undemocratic relations at the international level (the veto power within the UN Security Council, the voting power within the IMF and the World Bank, and so on). Even a grassroots participation in the process of decision making at the local level will not make much difference as long as the above global structures of monopoly of power and resources remain unchallenged. "For how long shall the world wait for the democratization of the United Nations?" exclaimed Cuba's Fidel Castro during the commemoration of the fiftieth anniversary (1995) of the United Nations. Some critics of SAPs point out that democracy is incompatible with such monopoly of power where SAPs are developed and imposed in an undemocratic manner.[2] Oxfam, a United Kingdom and Ireland NGO, has extensive experience in Africa, where in 1992 it managed and administered grants worth 23 million pounds, funding 1,200 projects in twenty-five countries across the continent. As a Northern NGO, Oxfam had an unusually candid assessment of adjustment that raised fundamental questions about the implications of SAPs for African democracy:

> Is genuine democracy compatible with the *de facto* transfer of economic policy sovereignty to Washington-based institutions, which are manifestly not accountable

to the communities which their policies affect? Similarly, is a democratic contract between state and civil society possible where externally-imposed stabilisation programmes undermine the ability of governments to meet minimum welfare needs, forcing them instead to rely on donor-funded and designed safety nets?[3]

Even supporters of SAPs realize the dimensions of the crisis of legitimacy facing African governments that are caught in between the devil of international forces and the deep sea of internal social pressures. "[African] governments must, in fact, constantly adapt to the economic logic of structural adjustment programmes and the political logic of democratization processes and reconcile the demands of their constituencies at home (the voters) with the demands of their constituencies abroad (the funders)."[4] Since African governments have more control over the voters than the funders, it is always the demands of the latter that matter. There is little balance between the pressures of international financial institutions and domestic popular demands. The ultimate goal of the current democratization is multiparty politics, which opens up and fragments society and therefore benefits global capitalism by weakening the power of the peripheral nation-state, curbing resistance to workplace rules, and diffusing collective work action. Such sociopolitical fragmentation is a necessary prelude to the success of market mechanisms.

Some critics of SAPs go farther to remind advocates of the liberalization and democratization processes that "many of the contemporary efforts to 'develop' and 'democratize' the Third World are really nothing more than replays of the 'White Man's Burden' of a bygone era" where similar efforts to "civilize" and "modernize" had led to enslaving peoples.[5] Within the context of SAPs, democratization is not a goal in itself. Like the Social Dimension of Adjustment, which attempts to cushion SAP economic austerity, democratization is an instrument that guarantees a lasting economic privatization and a political environment suitable for conducting business. Its emphasis is on openness, governance, and accountability rather than popular empowerment and equality. While strong states with integrated "civil societies" can handle multipartyism without fatal disintegration, in many weak and impoverished peripheral states the combination of SAP austerity programs and multipartyism could lead to fragmented and tension-plagued societies where ethnicity, tribalism, individualism, and other forms of national dislocation place society on the brink of civil war by pitting all against all amid uncertainty and confusion. For example, the 1994 Rwandan tragedy is not simply the result of the century-old ethnic divide between the Hutus and the Tutsis. The economic hardship created by the 1990 structural adjustment program (which included a 66 percent devaluation of the Rwandan franc) contributed to a sharp decline of the standard of living of urban Rwandans and exacerbated social tension, which ultimately exploded following the tragic death of the Rwandan president in the Summer of 1994.[6] So far the "transition to democracy" has been bloody and violent in the former Soviet Union, former Yugoslavia, Liberia, Somalia, Algeria, Egypt, and, more recently, Chechnya. In societies where the democratization process was completed without state disintegration or civil war, the transition was formal and did not undermine the fundamental social and spatial inequalities in the distribution of wealth and power. Change was more noticeable, however, in the world of representation and perception, i.e., the change was not in the power structure but in the way people perceive and judge that structure, particularly its legitimacy. As noted earlier, the structure of power in Mauritania survived (almost intact) the transition from a military regime to a civilian regime based on multipartyism, free elections, and free press. To caricature it, the colonel took off his military fatigues and wore a business suit as a cosmetic constitutional reform designed more for appeasing Western pressure and disarming the internal opposition than genuinely empowering the people, the ultimate objective of *direct* democracy as opposed to *representative* democracy.

The central tenets of the contemporary representative democracy go back to the political reforms and revolutions of the seventeenth and eighteenth centuries in Britain (trial and execution of King Charles I in 1649), the United States (American Revolution against British rule in 1776), and France (French Revolution against the Old Regime in 1789), which brought the European Renaissance to a new peak: the European Enlightenment. I say "European" because in the rest of the world, the seeds of long-term decline were already sown, thus announcing the beginning of a new Dark Age during which the Atlantic slave trade devastated the African continent, settlement of the Americas almost exterminated the American Indians, the Ottoman, Mughal, and Chinese empires were experiencing severe setbacks and retreats from the eighteenth century on, thus leaving Europe the sole master of the world. As far as power and democracy in Europe are concerned, the Enlightenment was essentially about the replacement of the monarchy by the republic and the abolition of the divine right of kings, which held that rulers had an inherent right to exercise power and that the subjects had a responsibility to obey. It was the demystification of this power dogma that opened the door to various facets (cultural, political, economic, and so on) of the Enlightenment or modernity. The change allowed people to select or elect their representatives or rulers rather than represent or rule themselves directly. The political fetish of the divine right of kings was replaced by new ones: parliaments and governments as the *true* representatives of the people. As perhaps the most important democratic theorist of the Enlightenment, Jean-Jacques Rousseau described the transition from the monarchy to the republic as a shift from an *hereditary aristocracy* to an *elective aristocracy*. Though Rousseau acknowledged the supremacy of direct democracy, he thought it could not be implemented since "it is impossible to imagine that the people should remain in perpetual assembly to attend public affairs."[7] This is when the divine right of kings dogma was replaced by the often unquestioned principle of *representation*, which continues to maintain power in the hands of the few on behalf of the many.

More than two centuries after Rousseau, the debate about democracy is far from being settled, despite the current *supremacist* thesis that Western liberal democracy and capitalism represent "the end of history." This supremacist idea is gaining ground not only among the political right but also among the political left, as Richard Rorty asserts that "it is going to take a long period of readjustment for us Western leftist intellectuals to comprehend that the word 'socialism' has been drained of force as have been all other words that drew their force from the idea that an alternative to capitalism was available."[8] By the same token, liberal intellectuals believe that there is no alternative to representative democracy. But a careful examination of liberal democracy reveals that it is formal, procedural, and, above all, representative, not direct. Its current hegemony is not the result of its moral superiority or of its veracity and rightness, rather it is the result of military power that maintains and imposes representative democracy by crushing any alternative. Moreover, the values proclaimed in the French Revolution—liberty, equality, fraternity—"have not yet gone beyond bourgeois democracy to democracy in politics and economics, beyond equality of rights to social equality, beyond polarization to the confraternity of the world's peoples."[9] Abraham Lincoln's definition of democracy as the government of the people, by the people, and for the people "remains a grand aim, not an achievement"[10] since "barely half of the [U.S.] electorate votes, often much less than half," while the rate of reelection is around 90 percent, a phenomenon that marginalizes the masses, makes political leaders a quasi-separate caste relying heavily on "the increasingly insidious media hegemony" over electoral processes.[11]

Unfortunately, dominant social theories have put more emphasis on how power makes history rather than on how to put power in the hands of the people. Power struggle was and still is the most important force in the making of human history. It is at the center of Ibn Khaldun's model of *asabya* struggle, which is behind the eternal movement of elites and the rise and fall of dynasties. It is also at the heart of Marx's class struggle and the rise and fall of modes of production. Power determines and shapes human history, as well as our representation of that history. The connection between truth and power is important since power is above all the ability to define reality in one's own terms and impose that definition on others. On the global scale of representation and production of knowledge and culture, Edward Said pinpointed and emphasized the intricate relationship between power and knowledge and between power and culture,[12] while on a micro/local scale, Michel Foucault revealed and analyzed "the mutual unwrapping, interaction and interdependence of power and knowledge."[13] Power is also intricately linked to the principle of representation, since one aspect of power is to "represent others," "speak on behalf of others," "define others," "claim to be others," and so on. Therefore, any serious critique of power and democracy must begin by a serious critique of the very principle of *representation*, which continues to distort true democracy, where "there can be no representation in lieu of the people, for representation is fraud" and democracy is the expression of freedom rather than the freedom of expression.[14]

Notes

Chapter 1: Concrete and Theoretical Contexts

1. Pickles, J., and Watts, M. 1992. Paradigms for Inquiry. In *Geography's Inner World: Pervasive Themes in Contemporary American Geography*, eds. Ronald F. Abler, Melvin G. Marcus, and Judy M. Olson. New Brunswick, New Jersey: Rutgers University Press, 301-26.

2. Pickles, J., and Woods, J. 1992. South Africa's Homelands in the Age of Reform: The Case of QwaQwa, *Annals of the Association of American Geographers* 82(4):649.

3. Bok, D. quoted in Boyer, B. 1990. *Scholarship Reconsidered*. Princeton, New Jersey: The Carnegie Foundation for the Advancement of Teaching, 76.

4. Guitàn, M. 1992. *Rules and Discretion in International Economic Policy*. Washington, D.C.: International Monetary Fund, 3.

5. Lovering, J. 1989. The Restructuring Debate. In *New Models in Geography: The Political-Economy Perspective*, Volume 1, eds. Richard Peet, and Nigel Thrift. London: Unwin Hyman, 218.

6. Lerner, D. 1958. *The Passing of Traditional Society*. Glencoe, Illinois: Free Press.

7. Peet, R., and Thrift, N. 1989. Political Economy and Human Geography. In *New Models in Geography: The Political-Economy Perspective*, Volume 2, eds. Richard Peet and Nigel Thrift. London: Unwin Hyman, 1.

8. Emmanuel, A. 1972. *Uneven Exchange: A Study of the Imperialism of Trade*. New York: Monthly Review Press; and Amin, S. 1977. *Imperialism and Unequal Development*. New York: Monthly Review Press.

9. Harvey, D. 1982. *The Limits of Capital*. Oxford: Basil Blackwell; Smith, N. 1984. *Uneven Development: Nature, Capital and the Production of Space*. New York: Blackwell; and Harvey, D. 1985. *The Urbanization of Capital*. Baltimore, Maryland: John Hopkins University Press.

10. Smith, N. 1989. Uneven Development and Location Theory: Towards a Synthesis. In *New Models in Geography: The Political-Economy Perspective*, Volume 1, eds. Richard Peet and Nigel Thrift. London: Unwin Hyman, 151.

11. Lipietz, A. 1977. *Le Capital et son espace*. Paris: Maspero; and Aglietta, M. 1979. *A Theory of Capitalist Regulation: The U.S. Experience*. London: New Left Books.

12. United Nations Conference on Trade and Development, Programme on Transnational Corporations, *World Investment Report 1993: Transnational Corporations and Integrated International Production*, New York: United Nations, 1993, Table I.1, 14.

13. Harvey, D. 1988. The Geographical and Geopolitical Consequences of the Transition from Fordist to Flexible Accumulation. In *America's New Market Geography: Nation, Region and Metropolis*, eds. George Stenlieb and James W. Hughes. New Bruwnswick, New Jersey: Rutgers Press, 101. After a long career in the apartheid state, F. W. de Klerk noted the formal nature of the change brought about by restructuring by stating that the value of color in South Africa today is no longer as important as the value of free enterprise. See CNN live coverage of the debate between Nelson Mandela and Frederik W. de Klerk, 14 April 1994.

14. Bowles, S., and Gintis, H. 1987. *Democracy and Capitalism: Property, Community, and the Contradictions of Modern Social Thought*. New York: Basic Books, 95.

15. Corbridge, S. 1989. Marxism, Post-Marxism, and the Geography of Development. In *New Models in Geography: The Political-Economy Perspective*, Volume 1, eds. Richard Peet and Nigel Thrift. London: Unwin Hyman, 247.

16. Qaddafi, M. 1980. *The Green Book*. Tripoli, Libya: The Green Book Center for Research and Study, 5.

17. Taylor, P. 1993. Full Circle, or New Meaning for the Global. In *The Challenge for Geography: A Changing World, A Changing Discipline*, ed. R. J. Johnston. Oxford, UK: Blackwell, 191.

18. These are Canada, France, Germany, Italy, Japan, the United Kingdom, and the United States. Originally, it was a group of five nations that later admitted Italy and Canada not only because of the importance of their economies but also because of their particular significance for the U.S. global military strategy during the Cold War.

19. Clark, G. 1989. The Geography of Law. In *New Models in Geography: The Political-Economy Perspective*, Volume 1, eds. Richard Peet and Nigel Thrift. London: Unwin Hyman, 310, 314.

20. The term Third World here refers to all countries of the world except the United States, Canada, European countries, the former Soviet Union, Japan, Australia, and New Zealand. Other concepts, such as the South, the periphery, and developing countries will be used as synonymous to the Third World, even though I realize the different specific connotations related to each one of them and the recent questioning of the relevance of the concept of the Third World after the end of the Cold War.

21. Two months after the G-7 summit of June 1982, Mexico declared that it could not continue to service its debt as originally contracted.

22. Mahjoub, A. 1990. Structural Adjustment or Delinking: The Question Posed. In *Adjustment or Delinking? The African Experience*, ed. Azzam Mahjoub. London: Zed Books, 157-169.

23. El-Naggar, S., ed. 1987. *Adjustment Policies and Development Strategies in the Arab World*. Washington, D.C.: The International Monetary Fund.

24. Until 1984, the *Direction de la Statistique et de la Comptabilité Nationale* within the Mauritanian Ministry of Planning used to compute regularly two price indexes for consumption, one for low-income Mauritanians and the other for high-income (European-like) households. With the beginning of adjustment, the IMF requested that this system

be abolished and replaced by a single price index for middle-income Mauritanians only. The undeclared objective is to hide the growing disparity between the rich and the poor and make the evaluation of disparity from the available statistics almost impossible since there is no price index for either the poor or the rich. More details on this manipulation of statistics can be found in Fonds monetaire international, Bureau des statistiques, Rapport de Mission en Mauritanie, etabli par Le Marois, M., 20 mars 1986. See also Nelson, J., ed. 1989. *Fragile Coalitions: The Politics of Economic Adjustment.* Oxford: Transaction Books. Providing advice to international financial institutions, Nelson argues (111) that "analysis and data collection by external agencies, or such efforts by governments with support from external agencies, should not focus narrowly on the bottom third. From both welfare and *political perspectives*, it is important to keep track of trends and conditions among the middle decile as well" [italics added].

25. McCloskey, D. 1985. *The Rhetoric of Economics.* Madison: University of Wisconsin Press, 31.

26. During my field work in Mauritania, I found that state officials were willing to release information related to how much foreign aid (loans and grants) entered the country, but they were reluctant to provide precise information (if they knew at all) related to how much money (profit remittance and debt servicing) left the country.

27. Banque mondiale. 1991. *Rapport Annuel 1991.* Washington, D.C.: World Bank, 3.

28. Fauntroy, W. 1990. Opening Statement. In United States Congress, *Role of the International Monetary Fund: hearing before the Subcommittee on International Development, Finance, Trade, and Monetary Policy of the committee on Banking, Finance, and Urban Affairs, House of Representatives, One Hundred First Congress, second session, March 1, 1990.* Washington, D.C.: U.S. Government Printing Office, 55–60.

29. Nelson, J., ed. 1990. *Economic Crisis and Policy Choice: The Politics of Adjustment in the Third World.* Princeton, New Jersey: Princeton University Press, 8.

30. Laishley, R. 1993. Renewed Calls for Less Debt, More Aid. *Africa Recovery* 6(4):4.

31. In 1992, Italy (with a population of 57 million) had a GDP of $965 billion. The same year, the entire Middle East and North Africa (the twenty-one Arab League members, Iran, Turkey, and Israel), with a population of 360 million, had a combined GDP of only $767 billion. See Central Intelligence Agency, (Vital Statistics) *World Factbook 1993.* In 1992 consumer price inflation fell to 3.75 percent in industrial countries, while in developing countries it averaged near 40 percent (see the 1993 IMF Annual Report cited in *IMF Survey,* 20 September 1993, 284). Moreover, external debts of developing countries reached $1,662 billion in 1992 (See *Asharq Al-Awsat,* 17 December 1993).

32. United Nations. 1991. *World Economic Survey 1991/2: A Reader.* New York: United Nations, 8.

33. Computed from table 7.2, United Nations. 1993. *World Economic Survey 1993/94,* Student Edition. New York: United Nations, 155.

34. Papic, A. 1991. Net Transfer of Financial Resources from the South, *South Letter,* no. 11, September 1991, Published by the South Centre – the Follow-Up Office of the South Commission, 10. See also Turok, Ben, 1991, Introduction, 1–13; and Campbell, H. Restructuring the World Economy, 17–39. In *Alternative Strategies for Africa: Debt*

and Democracy, Volume 3, ed. Ben Turok. London: Institute for African Alternatives.

35. Kirdar, U. 1992. Antalya Statement. In *Change: Threat or Opportunity for Human Progress?*, Volume 1: Political Change, ed. Uner Kirdar. New York: United Nations, 20.

36. Rojas-Suàrez, L. 1991. Risk and Capital Flight in Developing Countries. In *Determinants and Systematic Consequences of International Capital Flows*, Washington, D.C.: The Research Department of the International Monetary Fund, Occasional Paper no. 77, March, 83–84.

37. Riddel, J. B. 1992. Things Fall Apart Again: Structural Adjustment Programmes in Sub-Saharan Africa, *Journal of Modern African Studies* 30(1):66.

38. World Bank. 1993. *World Development Report 1993*. Washington, D.C.: World Bank, 239.

39. Philip, G. 1993. The New Economic Liberalism and Democracy in Latin America: Friends or Enemies? *Third World Quarterly* 14(3):555–571.

40. Bortot, F. 1990. ECA-OAU and World Bank Analyses and Strategies on African Development: The Converging Alternatives, *African Review of Money, Finance and Banking* 1:115.

41. Roth, M. 1991. Structural Adjustment in Perspective: Challenges for Africa in the 1990s. In *Democratization and Structural Adjustment in Africa in the 1990s*, eds. Lual Deng, Markus Kostner, and Crawford Young. African Studies Program, University of Wisconsin-Madison, 31.

42. Latouche, S. 1992. Preface. In *Rituels et Développement ou Le Jardin du Soufi*, eds. Philippe Lassale and Jean-Bernard Sugier. Paris: Éditions L'Harmattan, 13.

43. UN Economic Commission for Africa. 1989. *African Alternative Framework to Structural Adjustment Programmes for Socio-economic Recovery and Transformation (AAF-SAP)*. New York and Addis Ababa, 16.

44. George, S. 1992. *The Debt Broomrang: How Third World Debt Harms Us All.* Boulder, Colorado: Westview Press. Mosley, P. and Weeks, J. 1993. Has Recovery Begun? "Africa's Adjustment in the 1980s" Revisited. *World Development* 21(10):1583–1606. Adedeji, A. 1985. Intra-African Economic Cooperation in Light of the Final Act of Lagos. In *Economic Crisis in Africa: African Perpectives on Development Problems and Potentials*, eds, Adabayo Adedeji and Timothy M. Shaw. Boulder, Colorado: L. Rienner Publishers, 77. Sandbrook, R. 1993. *The Politics of Africa's Economic Recovery.* Cambridge: Cambridge University Press, 103, 139. Ravenhill, J. 1993. A Second Decade of Adjustment: Greater Complexity, Greater Uncertainty; and Callaghy, T. and Ravenhill, J. How Hemmed In? Lessons and Prospects to Africa's Responses to Decline. In *Hemmed In: Responses to Africa's Economic Decline*, eds. Thomas Callaghy and John Ravenhill, 41, 560.

45. U.S. Congress. 1989. *Structural Adjustment in Africa: Insights from the Experiences of Ghana and Senegal.* Report of a Staff Study Mission to Great Britain, Ghana, Senegal, Cote d'Ivoire, and France, 29 November – 20 December 1988, submitted to the Committee on Foreign Affairs, U.S. House of Representatives, Washington, D.C.: U.S. Government Printing Office, 2.

46. Adams, P. 1992. The World Bank and the IMF in sub-Saharan Africa: Undermining Development and Environmental Sustainability, *Journal of International Affairs* 46(1):117.

47. World Bank. 1990. Islamic Republic of Mauritania, Structural Adjustment Program. Completion Report, January 12, Washington, D.C., para. 71.

48. The Nigerian president (Babangida, I.) has prepared a detailed reparations proposal. See Noble, K. 1990. Nigeria's Leader to Seek Slavery Reparations, *New York Times*, December 24, A, 4:3. Mazrui, A. 1993. The Building Debate over Reparations: Who Should Pay for Slavery? *World Press Review* (August):22–3. The issue of reparations is also increasingly raised by many African-American leaders (for example, Leonard Jeffries, chairman of the African Studies Department at City College of New York), particularly since the opening of the United States Holocaust Memorial Museum in April 1993 and the coming out of the Schindler's List film in 1994. African-Americans feel strongly that the Atlantic slave trade is worse than the Nazi Holocaust and deserves reparations, memorials, museums, and immortalizing films. Notwithstanding the class dimension of the recent racial tension between Jews and blacks (the former at the top and the latter at the bottom of American society) in the United States, the issue of material and moral reparations for some rather than for all is at the heart of that racial tension which may even intensify.

49. Michaels, M. 1992. Retreat From Africa, *Foreign Affairs* 72(1):93–108.

50. Ong'Wen, O. 1993. Another "Lost Decade" for Africa, *World Press Review*, May, 41.

51. Jaycox, E., vice president, Africa Region, World Bank (interviewed by Margaret A. Novicki in 1987), *Africa Report* 32(6):32.

Chapter 2: Globalization and Peripheral States

1. Substantial parts of this chapter are reprinted as originally published or with changes from: Ould-Mey, M. 1994. Global Adjustment: Implications for Peripheral States, *Third World Quarterly* 15(2):319–36. Reprinted with permission.

2. Lipietz, A. 1982. Towards Global Fordism, *New Left Review*, no. 132, March–April, 34.

3. Cornia, G. et al. eds. 1988. *Adjustment with a Human Face, Volume 1: Protecting the Vulnerable and Promoting Growth*. Oxford: Clarendon Press, 13.

4. Lipietz, A. 1984. How Monetarism Has Choked the Third World Industrialization, *New Left Review*, no. 145, 64.

5. Kirdar, U. 1992. Antalya Statement. In *Change: Threat or Opportunity for Human Progress?* Volume 1: Political Change, ed. Uner Kirdar. New York: United Nations, 20.

6. Banque mondiale, Memorandum economique, Republique Islamique de Mauritanie, 10 juillet 1985, Table 2.2, 101.

7. Banque mondiale, *Rapport Annuel 1991*, 118.

8. Ohmae, K. 1990. *The Borderless World: Power and Strategy in the Interlinked Economy*. New York: Harper Business.

9. UN Document A/AC. 166L.48: Proposal Titled: Programme of Action on the Establishment of a New International Economic Order, 30 April 1974.

10. UN Document A/RES/3200 (S-VI) – 3202 (S-VI): Resolutions adopted by the General Assembly during its sixth special session, 16 May 1974.

11. For example, "it costs from $250 to $300 per ton to dispose of waste under current U.S. environmental regulations while developing countries will accept waste for as little as $40 a ton." See Chepesiuk, R. 1991. From Ash to Cash: The International Trade in Toxic Waste. In *Annual Editions: Third World 92/93*, Fourth Edition. Guilford, Connecticut: The Dushkin Publishing Group, 224–28. For labor comparative advantage in developing countries, see also Samatar, A. 1993. Structural Adjustment as Development Strategy? Bananas, Booms, and Poverty in Somalia, *Economic Geography* 69(1):25–43. Samatar analyzes how child labor was the foundation of the banana plantation industry in Somalia.

12. Bluestone, B., and Harrison, B. 1982. *The Deindustrialization of America: Plant Closing, Community Abandonment, and the Dismantling of Basic Industry*. New York: Basic Books Inc., 42.

13. See Lipietz, A. 1992. *Towards a New Economic Order: Postfordism, Ecology and Democracy*. New York: Oxford University Press, 19. He attributes the crisis to a fall in profits and a drop in demand.

14. The Union of Banana Exporting Countries (UPEB), the Association of Natural Rubber Producing Countries (ANRPC), the Intergovernmental Council of Copper Producing Countries (CIPEC), the International Bauxite Association (IBA), and Café Mondiale were all established between 1967 and 1974.

15. Agnew, J., presentation at the University of Kentucky, 2 April 1993, entitled What is the Third World After the Cold War? He suggested that the geopolitical concept of Third World is no longer appropriate in the post–Cold War era. See also Ahmad, A. 1992. *In Theory: Classes, Nations, Literatures*. London: Verso, 309. He argues that "the collapse of the Second World" has, of course, made shambles of the "Three Worlds Theory." However, the gap between the North and the South continues to grow.

16. Neff, D. 1993. Lessons to be Learned from 66 U.N. Resolutions Israel Ignores. *The Washington Report on Middle East Affairs* 11(8):42.

17. Haggard, S., and Kaufman, R. eds. 1992. *The Politics of Economic Adjustment*. Princeton, New Jersey: Princeton University Press, 12.

18. Southall, A. 1991. Democracy and Development: Tangled Meanings. In *Democratization and Structural Adjustment in Africa in the 1990s*, eds. Lual Deng, Markus Kostner, and Crawford Young. Madison, Wisconsin: African Studies Program, University of Wisconsin-Madison, 116.

19. Langley, W. 1990. What Happened to the New International Economic Order, *Socialist Review* 20(3):45–62.

20. U.S. Department of State, *Dispatch*, vol. 2, no. 37, 16 September 1991, 694.

21. Berger, S. U.S. State Department, Briefing on President's Trip to G–7 Summit, Halifax, Bureau of Public Affairs, 6 June 1995. Commenting on the communique issued by the 1995 G-7 economic summit, Michel Camdessus, the managing director of the IMF has this to say: "I welcome, in particular, the G–7's conclusion that the role of the IMF, in an environment of increased globalization, calls for a strengthening of its surveillance. I also consider important the G–7's call to ensure that the IMF has sufficient resources to meet its responsibilities and appropriate financing mechanisms to operate on a scale and with the timeliness required to manage shocks effectively." See IMF *News Briefs*, 6 June 1995.

22. U.S. Department of State, *Bulletin*, no. 1902 (8 December 1975), 805–807.

23. U.S. General Services Administration, *Weekly Compilation of Presidential Documents*, vol. 13, no. 11, 1977, 322.

24. Hajnal, P. ed. 1989. *The Seven-Power Summit: Documents from the Summits of Industrialized Countries 1975-1989*. New York: Kraus International Publications, xxv.

25. See the London Declaration of the G-7, in U.S. Department of State, *Bulletin*, no. 1980, 6 June 1977, 583-86.

26. World Bank. 1979. *World Development Report, 1979*. Washington, D.C.: World Bank, August, 3.

27. World Bank. 1980. *World Development Report, 1980*. Washington, D.C.: World Bank, August, 13.

28. World Bank. 1990. *World Development Report, 1990*. Washington, D.C.: World Bank, 24.

29. U.S. Department of State, *Bulletin*, no. 2041, August 1980, 11.

30. Ainley, M. 1984. *The General Arrangements to Borrow*. Pamphlet Series no. 41, Washington, D.C.:IMF, 41.

31. Harvey, D. 1989. *The Condition of Postmodernity*. Cambridge: Basil Blackwell, 170.

32. Boughton, J. 1994. IMF Since 1979: Revolutions in the World Economy. *IMF Survey* 23(14):221.

33. Campbell, B., and Loxley, J. eds. 1989. *Structural Adjustment in Africa*. New York: St. Martin's Press, 1.

34. Mingst, K. 1990. *Politics and the African Development Bank*. Lexington: University Press of Kentucky, 6.

35. George, S., and Sabelli, F. 1994. *Faith and Credit: The World Bank's Secular Empire*. San Francisco: Westview Press, 249.

36. U.S. Congress, *Foreign Assistance and Related Programs Appropriations for 1984: Hearing before a Subcommittee on Appropriations, House of Representatives, Ninety-Eight Congress, First Session, 1983*. Washington, D.C.: U.S. Government Printing Office.

37. Boughton, J. 1994. IMF Since 1979: Revolutions in the World Economy. *IMF Survey* 23(14): 221.

38. See the 1993 Annual Report of the IMF cited in The Whole-Earth IMF and A World Economy in Transition, *IMF Survey*, (20 September 1993):285.

39. *Quota Increase of the International Monetary Fund*, hearing before the Subcommittee on International Development, Finance, Trade and Monetary Policy of the Committee on Banking, Finance and Urban Affairs, House of Representatives, One Hundred Second Congress, First Session, 10 July 1991, Washington, D.C.: U.S. Government Printing Office, 67 and 99.

40. Polak, J. 1991. *The Changing Nature of IMF Conditionality*. Princeton, New Jersey: International Finance Section, Department of Economics, Princeton University, 1.

41. U.S. Department of State, *Dispatch*, vol. 2, no. 29, 22 July 1991, 529.

42. U.S. General Accounting Office, National Security and International Affairs Division. 1994. *Multilateral Development: Status of World Bank Reforms*. Briefing Report to Congressional Requester. Washington, D.C.: USGAO, 11 and 15.

43. Jackson, R. H. 1990. *Quasi-States: Sovereignty, International Relations, and the Third World*. Cambridge: Cambridge University Press, 191.

44. U.S. Department of State, *Bulletin*, no. 2137, August 1988, 49–52.

45. Today the World Bank has archives so voluminous that they can no longer all be housed in its Headquarters in Washington, and consequently some 65,000 cubic meters of them are kept in cheaper storage space in Pennsylvania. See George, S., and Sabelli, F. 1994. *Faith and Credit: The World Bank's Secular Empire*. Boulder, Colorado: Westview Press, 2.

46. Brown, R. 1988. Evaluating the World Bank Major Reports: A Review Essay, *Issue: A Journal of Opinion* 16(2):5–10.

47. Clapham, C. 1993. Democratization in Africa: Obstacles and Prospects, *Third World Quarterly* 14(3):431.

48. Callaghy, T. 1988. Debt and Structural Adjustment in Africa: Realities and Possibilities, *Issue: A Journal of Opinion* 16(2):11–18.

49. Green, R., and Allison, C. 1986. The World Bank's Agenda for Accelerated Development: Dialectics, Doubts and Dialogues. In *Africa in Economic Crisis*, ed. John Ravenhill. New York: Columbia University Press, 80.

50. World Bank. 1981. *Accelerated Development in Sub-Saharan Africa: An Agenda for Action*. Washington, D.C.: World Bank, 4, 132, 133.

51. Berg, E. 1986. The World Bank's Strategy. In *Africa in Economic Crisis*, ed. John Ravenhill. New York: Columbia University Press, 58.

52. World Bank. 1981. *Accelerated Development in Sub-Saharan Africa: An Agenda for Action*. Washington, D.C.: World Bank, v.

53. Loxley, J. 1987. The IMF, the World Bank, and sub-Saharan Africa: Policies and Politics. In *The IMF and the World Bank in Africa*, ed. Kjell Havnevik. Uppsala: Scandinavian Institute of African Studies, 48.

54. World Bank. 1989. *Sub-Saharan Africa: From Crisis to Sustainable Growth*. Washington, D.C.: World Bank, 14.

55. World Bank. 1994. *Adjustment in Africa: Reforms, Results, and the Road Ahead*. Washington, D.C.: World Bank, 219.

56. World Bank. 1991. *World Development Report 1991*. Washington, D.C.: World Bank, 9.

57. World Bank. 1987. *World Development Report 1987*. Washington, D.C.: World Bank, 58 and 60.

58. U.S. General Accounting Office, National Security and International Affairs Division. 1994. *Multilateral Development: Status of World Bank Reforms*. Briefing Report to Congressional Requesters. Washington, D.C.: USGAO, Appendix II, note d.

59. Payer, C. 1987. The IMF and India. In *The IMF and the World Bank in Africa*, ed. Kjell Havnevik. Upsala: Scandinavian Institute of African Studies, 67.

60. Banque mondiale, RIM, Memorandum economique, 10 July 1985, 8, 74–85.

61. Amin, S. 1982. A Critique of the World Bank Report Entitled "Accelerated Development in sub-Saharan Africa," *Africa Development* 7(1/2):29.

62. Bangura, Y. 1987. IMF/World Bank Conditionality and Nigeria's Structural Adjustment Programme. In *The IMF and the World Bank in Africa*, ed. Kjell Havnevik. Upsala: Scandinavian Institute of African Studies, 104.

63. *The Economist*, 24-30 April 1993, 43.

64. Oxfam. 1993. *Africa, Make or Break: Action for Recovery*. Oxford: Oxfam Print Services, 22.

65. Laishley, R. Africa's Debt Burden Continues to Grow, *Africa Recovery*, December 1993–March 1994, 12–14.

66. Heginbotham, S. J. 1994. Rethinking International Scholarship. *Items: Social Science Research Council* 48(2-3):36. In 1992, 20 percent of all foreign students (419,590) in the United States were majoring in business and management, the largest field of study for international students in the United States (see Zikopoulos, M. ed. 1993. *Profiles 1991/1992: Detailed Analyses of the Foreign Student Population*. New York: Institute of International Education, table 4.6, 46).

67. El-Naggar, S. 1987. Summary of the Seminar. In *Adjustment Policies and Development Strategies in the Arab World*, ed. Said El-Naggar. Washington D.C.: International Monetary Fund, 4.

68. El-Naggar, S. ed. 1989. *Privatization and Structural Adjustment in the Arab Countries*. Papers presented at a seminar held in Abu Dhabi, United Arab Emirates, 5-7 December 1988. Washington D.C.: International Monetary Fund.

69. El-Naggar, S. 1989. Privatization and Structural Adjustment: The Basic Issues. In *Privatization and Structural Adjustment in the Arab Countries*, ed. Said El-Naggar. Papers presented at a seminar held in Abu Dhabi, United Arab Emirates, 5-7 December 1988. Washington, D.C.: IMF, 4.

70. Walters, A. 1989. Liberalization and Privatization: An Overview. In *Privatization and Structural Adjustment in the Arab Countries*, ed. Said El-Naggar. Papers presented at a seminar held in Abu Dhabi, United Arab Emirates, 5-7 December 1988. Washington, D.C.: IMF, 18.

71. Gill, D. 1989. Privatization: Opportunities for Financial Market Development. In *Privatization and Structural Adjustment in the Arab Countries*, ed. Said El-Naggar. Papers presented at a seminar held in Abu Dhabi, United Arab Emirates, 5-7 December 1988. Washington, D.C.: IMF, 120.

72. Abdel-Rahman, H., and Abu Ali, M. S. 1989. Role of the Public and Private Sectors with Special References to Privatization: The Case of Egypt. In *Privatization and Structural Adjustment in the Arab Countries*, ed. Said El-Naggar. Papers presented at a seminar held in Abu Dhabi, United Arab Emirates, 5-7 December 1988. Washington, D.C.: IMF, 143.

73. Camdessus, M. 1989. Forward. In *Privatization and Structural Adjustment in the Arab Countries*, ed. Said El-Naggar. Papers presented at a seminar held in Abu Dhabi, United Arab Emirates, 5-7 December 1988, vii. Washington, D.C.: IMF.

74. Pfeifer, K. 1992. Economic Liberalization in the 1980s: Algeria in Comparative Perspective. In *State and Society in Algeria*, eds. John Entelis and Philip Naylor. Oxford: Westview Press, 98.

75. Rijnierse, E. 1993. Democratisation in Sub-Saharan Africa: Literature Review, *Third World Quarterly* 14(3):656.

76. Murphy, G., and Angelli, E. 1993. International Institutions, Decolonization, and Development, *International Political Science Review* 14(1):81.

77. Drysdale, A., and Blake, G. 1985. *The Middle East and North Africa*. Oxford: Oxford University Press, 328.

78. *The Washington Post National Weekly Edition*, 20-26 December 1993, 15.

79. Ramsay, W. 1993. Oil in the 1990s: The Gulf Dominant. In *Riding the Tiger: The Middle East Challenge After the Cold War*, eds. Phebe Marr and William Lewis. Boulder, Colorado: Westview Press, 51.

80. See also Blum, W. 1995. *Killing Hope: U.S. Military and CIA Interventions Since World War II.* Monroe, Maine: Common Courage Press.

81. Zunes, S. 1993. The U.S.-GCC Relationship: Its Rise and Potential Fall, *Middle East Policy* 2(1):104.

82. Cockburn, A., and Cockburn, L. 1991. *Dangerous Liaison: The Inside Story of the U.S.-Israeli Relationship.* New York: Harper Collins Publishers, 321 and 322.

83. During the four decades following World War II (1947–1988), the United Nations had organized some twelve peacekeeping operations in the Third World, while in the last five years (1988–1993) it organized some twenty peacekeeping operations, including one in Europe (UN Protection Force in Yugoslavia). See also Glassner, M. 1993. *Political Geography.* New York: John Wiley & Sons, 408–9.

84. Not withstanding China, considered in the West as the last empire to be opened as it once was following the Opium Wars of the nineteenth century.

85. In the 1980s, the United States suspended its participation in UNESCO and later stopped paying much of its assessment to the UN, thus plunging the organization into a financial crisis that made it comply willy nilly with U.S. policy. The marginalization of the UN General Assembly was also observed by Taylor, P. 1993. Geopolitical World Orders. In *Political Geography of the Twentieth Century: A Global Analysis*, ed. Peter Taylor. London: Belhaven Press, 59.

86. Falk, R. 1993. In Search of a New World Model, *Current History* 92(573):146.

87. Neff, D. 1993. Lessons to be Learned from 66 U.N. Resolutions Israel Ignores. *The Washington Report on Middle East Affairs* 11(8):40–42.

88. Martin, L. 1993. Peacekeeping as a Growth Industry, *The National Interest*, Summer, 5.

89. Anderson, J. 1990. Bankruptcy America. In *Economic Adjustment After the Cold War*, hearings before the Joint Economic Committee, Congress of the United States, One Hundred First Congress, first and second sessions, 12 and 19 December 1989 and, 20 March 1990. Washington, D.C.: U.S. Government Printing Office, 283 and 288.

90. Speech by Richard Nixon on American-Japanese relations broadcast by C-SPAN on 25 April 1993.

91. Murphy, C. 1990. Freezing the North-South Bloc(k) after the East-West Thaw, *Socialist Review* 20(3):41.

92. According to Noam Chomsky (Chomsky, N. 1992. *Deterring Democracy*. New York: Hill and Wang,409–10) the Gulf war was misnamed because it did not involve two sides in combat. The first stage involved Iraqi troops invading Kuwait with almost no military resistance since Kuwait's ruler and most of his government fled to Saudi Arabia. The next phase began with the U.S.-led attack of 16 January 1991. The first component of the attack (massive air carpet bombing) targeted the civilian infrastructure, including power, sewage, and water systems in Iraq, and the second component (the ground war) was simply the slaughter of Iraqi soldiers in the desert while they were retreating from Kuwait.

93. Berman, L., and Jentleson, B. 1989. Bush and the Post-Cold-War World: New Challenges for American Leadership. In *The Bush Presidency First Appraisal*, eds. Colin Campbell and Bert Rockman. Chatham, New Jersey: Chatham House Publishers, 98. Teddy Roosevelt's imperialist world view and vicious diplomacy have been famous since 1901 when he declared: "Speak softly and carry a big stick; you will go far."

94. *Newsweek*, 11 March 1991, 30.

95. Lipietz, A. 1992. *Towards a New Economic Order: Postfordism, Ecology and Democracy*. New York: Oxford University Press, 172 and 178.

96. The early Pentagon estimates were 100,000 Iraqi soldiers killed and 300,000 wounded. See also *New Internationalist*, October 1992, 18–19. In 1993 (two years after the war), John Heidenrich attempted to "civilize" the war by asserting that "military effectiveness is not synonymous with human slaughter" and that the early Pentagon estimates were exaggerated. See Heidenrich, J. 1993. The Gulf War: How Many Iraqis Died? *Foreign Policy* 90:108–125.

97. Ibrahim, Y. M. 1992. Gulf War's Cost to Arabs Estimated at $620 Billion, *The New York Times*, 8 September, A8.

98. Brynen, R., and Noble, P. 1991. The Gulf Conflict and the Arab State System: A New Regional Order? *Arab Studies Quarterly* 13(1-2):117–40.

99. *Asharq Al-Awsat*, 17 December 1993.

100. Lippman, T. W. 1994. The Saudi Economy: Over a Barrel, *The Washington Post National Weekly Edition*, 20-26 December, 15; and Lancaster, J., and Mintz, J. 1994. They'll Gladly Pay Tomorrow for Weapons Today: The Saudis are a little short of cash and U.S. arms-makers are a little worried, *The Washington Post National Weekly Edition*, 17-23 January, 21.

101. Todd Gitlin, quoted in Lifton, R. 1993. *The Protean Self: Human Resilience in an Age of Fragmentation*. New York: Basic Books, 223.

102. In 1993, Voice of America (VOA) had a budget of $355 million and 3,068 full-time permanent positions. VOA Charter states that "VOA will present the policies of the United States clearly and effectively." VOA broadcasts these policies on shortwave from a central station in Washington, D.C., three transmitters located in California, North Carolina, and Ohio; and from ten other relay stations in Belize, Botswana, Germany, Greece, Kuwait, Morocco, Philippines, Sao Tome, Sri Lanka, and Thailand, in the following forty-seven languages: Albanian, Amharic, Arabic, Armenian, Azerbaijani, Bengali, Bulgarian, Burmese, Cantonese, Creole, Croatian, Czech, Dari, English, Estonian, Farsi, French, Georgian, Greek, Hausa, Hindi, Hungarian, Indonesian, Khmer, Korean, Kurdish, Lao, Latvian, Lithuanian, Mandarin, Pashto, Polish, Portuguese, Romanian, Russian, Serbian, Slovak, Slovene, Spanish, Swahili, Thai, Tibetan, Turkish, Ukranian, Urdu, Uzbek, and Vietnamese. In the summer of 1994, VOA moved to the so-called information superhighway by offering digital audio newscasts on the Internet.

103. Marash, D. in *TV Guide*, April 1979, 17.

104. Quoted in Kaplan, R. 1993. *The Arabists: The Romance of an American Elite*. New York: Free Press, 4.

105. Ott, M. 1993. Shaking Up the CIA, *Foreign Policy* 93:147.

106. Fukuyama, F. 1989. The End of History, *The National Interest*, Summer, 3–18.

107. President Reagan once said: "We knew that the USSR was in reality frailer than it looks. So I reproduced in my artistic imagination the star-wars of the cinema and hurried the preparation of the Strategic Defense Initiative (SDI). This meant challenging the already overstretched technological and financial capabilities of the USSR, to limits when even the marshals, generals, strategists and financiers of the formidable military-industrial complex had to cry, most appropriately in both senses: PAX!" See Ionescu, G. 1993. The Painful Return to Normality. In *Democracy and Democratization*, eds. Geraint Parry and Michael Moran. London: Routledge, 110.

108. Agnew, J. 1993. The United States and American Hegemony. In *Political Geography of the Twentieth Century: A Global Analysis*, ed. Peter Taylor. London: Belhaven Press, 233.

109. Clinton, B. 1992. A Democrat Lays Out His Plan, *Harvard International Review*, Summer, 63.

110. *Financial Times*, 18 July 1991.

111. *The Wall Street Journal*, 16 April 1993.

112. U.S. President Clinton speaking from Moscow on ABC's "Nightline" on 13 January 1994. However, the World Bank estimate is that approximately 7,000 state-owned enterprises in more than 70 countries have been privatized since the early 1980s. See World Bank. 1992. World Bank Cites Increase in Privatization, *Business America* 113(11):19–20.

113. Cited by John Lindgren on Local News, *ABC Network*, Lexington, Kentucky, 14 March 1994.

114. Reich, R. 1993. U.S. secretary of labor, speaking to National Press Club on 12 October 1993.

115. United Nations. 1993. *Report on the World Social Situation 1993*. New York: United Nations, 179.

116. Greenwald, J. 1994. The Economy: Picking Up Speed, *Time*, 10 January, 18.

117. Kortunov, A., quoted in Lambeth, B. 1992. *Desert Storm and Its Meaning: The View from Moscow*. A Project AIR FORCE Report prepared for the United States Air Force, Santa Monica, California: RAND, 38.

118. Gorostiaga, X. 1990. Resisting "Low-Intensity Democracy," *Socialist Review* 20(3), 21.

119. Boutros-Ghali, B. 1992. *An Agenda for Peace*. New York: United Nations, 5.

120. Stein, D., executive director, Federation for American Immigration Reform (FAIR), Statement, in *Administration's Proposed Refugee Admission Program for Fiscal Year 1993*, hearing before the Subcommittee of International Law, Immigration and Refugees of the Committee on Judiciary, House of Representatives, One Hundred Second Congress, Second Session, 30 July 1991. Washington, D.C.: U.S. Government Printing Office, 181.

121. United Nations. 1993. *Report on the World Social Situation 1993*. New York: United Nations, 16.

122. See *Alternatives: Social Transformation and Humane Governance* 19(2), 1994. Special Issue: Against Global Apartheid: Contemporary Perspectives on World Order and World Order Series. See particularly Mazrui, A. Global Apartheid: Structural and Overt, 185–87.

123. Bello, W., with Shea Cunningham and Bill Rau. 1994. *Dark Victory: The United States, Structural Adjustment, and Global Poverty*. London: Pluto Press, 107.

124. King, R., and Oberg, S. 1993. Introduction: Europe and the Future of Mass migration. In *Mass Migrations in Europe: The Legacy and the Future*, ed. Russell King. London: Belhaven Press, 3.

125. Montary, A., and Cortese, A. 1993. South to North Migration in a Mediterranean Perspective. In *Mass Migrations in Europe: The Legacy and the Future*, ed. Russell King. London: Belhaven Press, 229.

126. Chomsky, N. 1992. *Deterring Democracy*. New York: Hill and Wang, 107.

127. *Time*, 25 October 1993, 18.

128. Layne, C., and Schwarz, B. 1993. American Hegemony—Without Enemy, *Foreign Policy* 92:6.

129. Quoted in Volman, D. 1993. Africa and the New World Order, *The Journal of Modern African Studies* 31(1):1,2.

130. Clinton, B. 1992. A Democrat Lays Out His Plan: A New Covenant for American Security, *Harvard International Review*, Summer, 26-27.

131. Quoted in Simons, G. 1993. *Libya: The Struggle for Survival*. New York: St. Martin's Press, 329. In September 1994, President Clinton warned the United Nations General Assembly that U.S. military intervention in Haiti is a prime example in what he called "the struggle between democracy and tyranny and between openness and isolation."

132. Broadcast on C-SPAN and quoted in Falk, R. 1993. In Search of a New World Model, *Current History* 92(573):145.

133. Falk, R. 1993. In Search of a New World Model, *Current History* 92(573):146.

134. Maynes, C. 1992. America's Third World Hang-Ups. In *Change: Threat or Opportunity for Human Progress?*, Volume 2: Economic Change, ed. Uner Kirdar. New York: United Nations, 211.

135. Kinzer, S. 1992. German Unrest Expected to Bring Tightening of Law on Immigration, *New York Times*, 2 September, A1, A8.

136. See Huntington, S. 1993. The Clash of Civilizations? *Foreign Affairs* 72(3):22–49. He identifies what he calls "a Confucian-Islamic connection" which challenges Western interests, values, and power. He also believes that the Islamic threat is perhaps more serious than the Chinese one because of what he calls the "bloody borders of Islam."

137. Isenberg, D. 1993. Desert Storm Redux?, *Middle East Journal* 47(3), 436.

138. Lesieur, J. 1993. Quand la CIA armait les Islamistes, *L'Express*, 2 December, 18–23.

139. Nixon, R. 1992. *Seize the Moment: America's Challenge in a One-Superpower World*. New York: Simon and Schuster, 195.

140. Khalidi, R. 1995. Is There a Future for Middle East Studies?, *Middle East Studies Association Bulletin* 29(1):1–6.

141. Youssef Choueiri argued that "whereas culture and politics resonate with Islamic overtones, the economy lurches in an open-ended void. By considering socioeconomic and political affairs as mere administrative technicalities, both Sunni and Shiite radicalism divest society of its human agencies." See Choueiri, Y. 1990. *Islamic Fundamentalism*. Boston: Twayne Publishers, 160. Even without a clear economic model, the Islamist discourse today may represent the only political and cultural challenge (not threat) to the triumphing Western values of liberal democracy and market economy.

142. Mohaddessin, M. 1993. *Islamic Fundamentalism: The New Global Threat*. Washington, D.C.: Seven Locks Press, v.

143. Grossette, B. 1992. U.S. Official Calls Muslim Militants a Threat to Africa, *The New York Times*, 1 January, 3.

144. Pelletreau, R., Jr., Pipes, D., and Esposito, J. 1994. Symposium: Resurgent Islam in the Middle East, *Middle East Policy* 3(2):1–21, 3.

145. Collin, F. 1993. Israel's Untouchable Entitlement Programs, *The Washington Report on Middle East Affairs*, March, 15. According to *Africa Recovery*, December 1993–March 1994, 13, Clinton's budget proposals for fiscal year 1995 would "eliminate specific, country-by-country funding—except for Israel, Egypt and Russia—in favor of flexible promotion of broad policy objectives such as democracy, free trade, anti-terrorism and environment." If one realizes that U.S. aid to Egypt is actually part of the overall U.S. aid to Israel and that aid to Russia is tied to market reforms, it became clear that Israel is the only country receiving unconditional American aid even after the end of the Cold War and Gulf War.

146. Yoram Ettinger (an Israeli diplomat) noted that "President Bill Clinton has held U.S. Jewish activists in high political esteem, appointing an unprecedentedly large number of Jews to executive positions. He is aware of their centrality in the domestic political scene, their unique role in his 1992 victory [there are 118 pro-Israel Political Action Committees in the United States] and their potential impact on the future of critical legislation." See Ettinger, Y. 1994. American Jewry's Clout, *The Jerusalem Post International Edition*, 26 February, 7. Clinton's very partial attitude towards Israel was also observed by David Steiner, president of the American Israel Public Affairs Committee, when he referred to Clinton by saying: "He's got something in his heart for the Jews, he has Jewish friends. Bush has no Jewish friends. . . Clinton is the best guy for us. . . Gore [who received $133,640 from pro-Israel PACs between 1984 and 1990] is very committed to us. . . We'll have access. . . We're talking now." See (Steiner, D.) AIPAC President Steiner's Phone Conversation with Harry Katz: The Complete Unexpurgated AIPAC Tape, *The Washington Report on Middle East Affairs*, December 1992/January 1993, 13–16. See also Curtiss, R. 1991. *Stealth PACs*. Washington, D.C.: American Educational Trust, 202. According to Avinoam Bar-Yosef (an Israeli journalist), in the U.S. National Security Council, seven out of eleven top staffers are Jews: Sandy Berger is the deputy chairman of the council; Martin Indyk, the intended ambassador to Israel, is a senior director in charge of the Middle East and South Asia; Dan Shifter, the senior director and advisor to the president, is in charge of Western Europe; Don Steinberg, the senior director and advisor to the president is in charge of Africa; Richard Feinberg, the senior director and advisor to the president, in charge of Latin America; Stanley Ross, the senior director and advisor to the president, is in charge of Asia. See Bar-Yosef, A. 1994. The Jews Who Run Clinton's Court, *Maariv*, 2 September. Note also President Clinton's nomination of James D. Wolfensohn as the ninth president of the World Bank Group.

147. Levau, R. 1993. *Le Sabre et le Turban: l'Avenir du Maghreb*. Paris: Éditions François Bourin, 260.

148. Israeli, R. 1993. *Fundamentalist Islam and Israel: Essays in Interpretation*. Jerusalem: The Jerusalem Center for Public Affairs, 201.

149. Mazrui, A. 1990. Satanic verses or a satanic novel? Moral dilemmas of the Rushdie affair, *Third World Quarterly* 12(1):124, 137.

150. Esposito, J. 1993. *The Islamic Threat: Myth or Reality?* Oxford: Oxford University Press.

151. Arnold, G. 1993. *The End of the Cold War*. London: St. Martin's Press.

152. Chomsky, N. 1993. *Year 501: The Conquest Continues*. Boston: South End Press, 33. According to American Public Radio (2 March 1994) the United States exported over 100,000 tons of toxic wastes outside North America in 1992. Also *World Watch*

magazine reported that Western companies had dumped more than 24 million tons of hazardous waste in Africa alone during 1988. See Kumar, P. 1994. Stop Dumping On the South: The Lure of Loose Laws. In *Annual Editions: Third World 94/95*. Guilfort, Connecticut: The Dushkin Publishing Group, 204–5.

153. World Bank. 1988. *Adjustment Lending: An Evaluation of Ten Years of Experience*. Washington, D.C.: World Bank.

154. Morrisson, C. ed. 1992. *Adjustment and Equity in Developing Countries: A New Approach*. Paris: OECD Development Centre Studies.

155. Aglietta, M. 1982. World Capitalism in the Eighties, *New Left Review* 136:5.

156. Abdoun, R. 1990. Algeria: The Problem of Nation-building. In *Adjustment or Delinking*, ed. Azzam Mahjoub. London: Zed Books, 43.

157. Koo, H. 1987. The Interplay of State, Social Class, and World System in East Asian Development: The Cases of South Korea and Taiwan. In *The Political Economy of the New Asian Industrialism*, ed. Frederic Deyo. London: Cornell University Press, 178.

158. Jackson, R. H. 1990. *Quasi-States: Sovereignty, International Relations and the Third World*. Cambridge: Cambridge University Press.

159. Cox, R. W. 1992. Towards a Post-Hegemonic Conceptualization of World Order: Reflections on the Relevancy of Ibn Khaldun. In *Governance without Government: Order and Change in World Politics*, eds. James Rosenau and Ernst-Otto Czempiel. Cambridge: Cambridge University Press, 143–44.

160. Amin, S. 1990. *Delinking: Towards a Polycentric World*. London: Zed Books.

161. Ibn Khaldun (1332–1406) stated in the Muqaddima that "differences of condition among people are the result of the different ways in which they make their living" and he was probably the first thinker to discern the relationship between politico/military history and social/economical evolution. Marx's historical materialism seems congruent with these two aspects of Ibn Khaldun's thought. Both Ibn Khaldun and Marx set forth a conception of historical change based on dialectical conflict. See Lacoste, Y. 1984. *Ibn Khaldun: The Birth of History and the Past of the Third World*. London: Verso, 153. Based on an extensive analysis of the Muqaddima, Lacoste portrayed Ibn Khaldun as a precursor of historical materialism. See also Baali, F. 1988. *Society, State, and Urbanism: Ibn Khaldun's Sociological Thought*. Albany, New York: State University of New York Press, 142. Baali noted that H. Simon stated in (*Ibn Khalduns Wissenschaft on der Menschlichen Kultur*, Leipzig, 1959) that the French translation of Ibn Khaldun's work, in the 1860s, could very well have reached Engels and Marx, who were very much interested in new objective and systematic publications.

162. Chase-Dunn, C. 1990. World-State Formation: Historical Process and Emergent Necessity, *Political Geography Quarterly* 9(2):120.

163. Waker, R. B. J. 1988. *State Sovereignty, Global Civilization, and the Rearticulation of Space*. World Order Studies Program, Occasional Paper no. 18, Center of International Studies, Princeton University, 42. See also Smith, A. 1993. *National Identity*. Reno, Nevada: University of Nevada Press, 175.

164. Helman, G., and Ratner, S. 1992. Saving Failed States, *Foreign Policy* 89:3-20. I would like to thank John Agnew for bringing this article to my attention.

165. Miyoshi, M. 1993. A Borderless World? From Colonialism to Transnationalism and the Decline of the Nation-State, *Critical Inquiry* 19:726-51.

166. See Lenin, V. 1969. *Imperialism: The Highest Stage of Capitalism*. New York: International Publishers; and Addo, H. 1986. *Imperialism: The Permanent Stage of Capitalism*. Tokyo: The United Nations University.

167. Quoted in Roussanne, A. 1991. *L'homme suiveur de nuages: Camille Douls, Saharien (1864–1889)*. Rodez, France: Editions du Rouergue, 33.

168. Ould-Mey, M. 1989. Cash Crops versus Food Crops in Africa: A conflict between Dependency and Autonomy, *Annales de la Faculté des Lettres et Sciences Humaines*, University of Nouakchott, no. 1, 21.

169. Quoted in Hammond, R. 1994. Structural Adjustment Policies in Africa Have Failed, *Third World Network Features*, Internet, 15 March.

170. *IMF Survey*, 21 February 1994, 59.

Chapter 3: The Mauritanian Context

1. While in the southwestern and coastal regions, the term Al-Gibla means south; in the central and eastern parts of the country, the term Al-Gibla means west. It derives from the Arabic term Al-Qibla, which refers to the direction of the Kaaba shrine in Mecca toward which all Muslims turn in ritual prayer. This is perhaps an indication that the Arab tribes who migrated to North Africa came from both eastern (where Al-Qibla is to the west) and northern (where Al-Qibla is to the south) Arabia.

2. According to Ibn Khaldun, the term Sanhaja is an Arabized form of the term Zenaga, which designates the Berber ethnic group to which belong the original tribes of Lemtuna, Messufa, and Gudala which dominated the Sahara before and during the Almoravid period. However, Ibn Khaldun, Ibn Al-Kalby, and other historians think that among the Berbers of the Maghreb, the Sanhaja and the Kutama were originally Yemenite tribes brought by Ifriqish (from which the name Africa came), the leader of the Hymyarite Al-Tababi'a who ruled Yemen centuries before Islam. See Ibn Khaldun. 1959. *Tarikh Al-Allamah Ibn Khaldun*, vol. 6. Beirut: Dar Al-Kitab Al-Lubnani, 26, 177, 425.

3. Traoré, A. Quoted in Marchesin, P. 1992. *Tribus, ethnies et pouvoir en Mauritanie*. Paris: Karthala, 48.

4. Ould Bah, M. 1971. Introduction à la poésie mauritanienne, *Arabica* 18(1):7.

5. See Ibn Khaldun. 1959. *Tarikh Al-Allamah Ibn Khaldun*, vol. 6. Beirut: Dar Al-Kitab Al-Lubnani 118–121. Ibn Khaldun noted that originally the Maqil formed a small group (less than 200) within the Banu Hilal, but their numbers increased substantially as they gradually absorbed other tribes from the Banu Hilal, the Banu Sulaym, and possibly the Zenata of Morocco with whom they had a long alliance. He believes that, genealogically, the Maqil are neither from the Banu Hilal as some Hilalians claim nor from the Banu Hashim, Prophet Mohammed's clan among the Quraysh of Mecca, as the Maqil themselves claim. He thinks they are Yemeni Arab tribes (probably the Kahlan) since tribes bearing the name Maqil exist in Yemen and some of them supported the Qaramita takeover in Bahrain before they were deported with the Banu Hilal and Banu Sulaym to Egypt. He also believes that Banu Hashim were all city dwellers and did not include Bedouins like the Maqil. *If* Ibn Khaldun is correct, one may add that the Banu Hashim/Maqil connection was perhaps related to Maqil's support for the Qaramita Shiia who consider Ali (from Banu Hashim) their first Imam. Today the name Ali continues

to be more common among many Maqil tribes than the names of the other Rashidun Khalifs: Abu Bakr, Omar, and Uthman.

6. Ibn Khaldun. 1959. *Tarikh Al-Allamah Ibn Khaldun*, vol. 6. Beirut: Dar Al-Kitab Al-Lubnani, 28.

7. Ibn Khaldun. 1959. *Tarikh Al-Allamah Ibn Khaldun*, vol. 6. Beirut: Dar Al-Kitab Al-Lubnani, 408.

8. Ould Cheikh, A. W. 1988. *Eléments d'histoire de la Mauritanie*. Institut Mauritanien de Recherche Scientifique et Centre Culturel Français Antoine St-Exupéry, Nouakchott, 49, 55.

9. Norris, H. T. 1977. An Introduction to the Desert Moors and their Arabic Literature. In *The Pilgrimage of Ahmad, Son of the the Little Bird of Paradise: An Account of a 19th Century Pilgrimage from Mauritania to Mecca*, ed. Harry Thirlwall Norris. Warminster, England: Aris & Phillips, viii.

10. For useful comments on this and other nomenclatures of what will be Mauritania, see Ould El Hassene, A. G. 1989. L'expression de la conscience "maure" à travers la litérature classique pré-coloniale. In *Mauritanie entre arabité et africanité*, Revue du Monde Musulman et de la Mediterranée 54:83–88.

11. See Massignon, L. 1909. Une bibliothèque saharienne: la bibliothèque du Cheikh Sidia au Sahara, *Revue du monde musulman* 8:409–18. See also Stewart, C. C. 1988. Haroun Ould Cheikh Sidia Library Microfilm Project, *Islam et sociétés au sud du Sahara* 2:189–91.

12. Soudan, F. 1993. La pluie, les "Afghans" et la santé du président, *Jeune Afrique* 1707:37.

13. The white/black categories are not always based on color so much as class since social status in the traditional society was for the most part symbolized by blood and ancestry, i.e., real or constructed Arab genealogies following the male line and regardless of both the female line and the color of the skin. To be (or to claim to be) a Sharif (a descendent of Prophet Mohammed) is the ideal in this system of values. Even in other West African countries, it is not unusual to come across black Muslim families who claim to be Sharif (plural Shurafa or Ashraf). Along the same lines of ideological construction, historians of the Ottoman Empire made up genealogies for Turkish sultans tracing their Arab origin back to the Prophet Muhammed. More recently, Slavic, German, Khazar, and other European Jews claim to be descendent of the Biblical Israelis and even of Abraham.

14. Smith, A. 1993. *National Identity*. Reno, Nevada: University of Nevada Press, 82.

15. *Human Rights Quarterly*, vol. 11, no. 3, August 1989, cited in United Nations *Report on the World Social Situation 1993*, New York: United Nations, 1993, table XII.2, 150.

16. Shaykh Sidya Baba (d. 1924). A History of the Western Sanhaja. Norris' translation in Norris, N. 1972. *Saharan Myth*. Oxford: Oxford University Press, 168.

17. Stewart, C. 1972. Political Authority and Social Stratification in Mauritania. In *Arabs and Berbers: From Tribe to Nation in North Africa*, eds. Ernest Gellner and Charles Micaud. Lexington, Massachusetts: Lexington Books, 392.

18. Dubie, P. 1953. La vie matérielle des Maures. In *Mélanges Ethnologiques*, Mémoire de l'Institut Français d'Afrique Noire (IFAN), no. 23, Dakar, 115.

19. Soudan, F. 1992. *Le Marabout et le Colonel: La Mauritanie de Ould Daddah à Ould Taya*. Paris: Jalivres, 17.

20. See De Chassey, F. 1977. *L'Étrier, la Houe et le Livre*. Paris: Anthropos; and Levau, R. 1993. *Le Sabre et le Turban: l'Avenir du Maghreb*. Paris: Éditions François Bourin.

21. Ould As-Saad, M. 1989. Émirats et espace émiral maure: Trarza aux XVIIIe–XIXe siècle. In *Mauritanie, entre arabité et africanité*, Revue du Monde Musulman et de la Mediterranée 54:56.

22. Ngaido, T. 1993. Land Tenure and Social Structure of the Halaybé. In *Risk and Tenure in Arid Land: The Political Ecology of Development in the Senegal River Basin*, ed. Thomas K. Park. Tucson, Arizona: University of Arizona Press, 146.

23. Ould Cheikh, A. W. 1982. *Problèmes et avenir du pastoralisme sahelien: le cas de la Mauritanie*. Nouakchott: Institut Mauritanien de Recherche Scientifique, 42.

24. Marchesin, P. 1992. *Tribus, ethnies et pouvoir en Mauritanie*. Paris: Karthala, 62.

25. See Park, T., Baro, M., and Ngaido, T. 1993. Les Conflits Fonciers et la Crise du Nationalism en Mauritanie. Paper prepared for the USAID and the Land Tenure Center at the University of Wisconsin-Madison, LTC paper 142–F, 4. See also Barry, B. 1972. *Le Royaume du Waalo*. Paris: Maspero.

26. These include the Al-Horma or Al-Gharama (individual tribute), Abbakh (on agricultural land under cultivation), Al-Ghafr (paid by passing caravans or tribes), Al-Mudarat (occasional levy paid to avoid potential raid or to get back something lost in a previous one), Kubul Al-Melh (salt tax), Amkubul (dues paid by French trade companies in the colony of Senegal to the emirs of Trarza, Brakna, and Tagant to provide for free trade on the river ports). For more details see Dubie, P. 1953. La vie matérielle des Maures. In *Mélanges Ethnologiques*, Mémoire de l'Institut Français de l'Afrique Noire (IFAN), no. 23, Dakar, 111–252; Stewart, C. C. 1972. Political Authority and Social Stratification in Mauritania. In *Arabs and Berbers: From Tribe to Nation in North Africa*, eds. Ernest Gellner and Charles Micaud. Lexington, Massachusetts: Lexington Books, 375–393; and Ould As-Saad, M. 1989. Émirats et espace émirale maure: Trarza aux XVIIIe–XIXe siècle. In *Mauritanie, entre arabité and africanité*, Revue du Monde Musulman et de la Mediterranée 54:53–82.

27. The term *goum* refers to a unit of native soldiers under French officers in North Africa. It is derived from the Hassania Arabic dialect term *gawm*, which is a variation of the classic Arabic term *qawm* (a band or group of people).

28. Dubie, P. 1953. La vie matérielle de Maures. In *Mélanges Ethnologiques*, Mémoire de l'Institut Français de l'Afrique Noire (IFAN), no. 23, Dakar, 174, 182, 183.

29. Stewart, C. C. 1972. Political Authority and Social Stratification in Mauritania. In *Arabs and Berbers: From Tribe to Nation in North Africa*, eds. Ernest Gellner and Charles Micaud. Lexington, Massachusetts: Lexington Books, 385.

30. Ould Cheikh, A. 1990. Mauritania: Nomadism and Peripheral Capital. In *African Agriculture, The Critical Choices*, eds. Hamid Ait Amara and Bernard Founou-Tchuigoua. London: Zed Books, 82.

31. Marchesin, P. 1992. *Tribus, ethnies et pouvoir en Mauritanie*. Paris: Karthala, 45.

32. Delcourt, A. 1952. *La France et les etablissements français au Sénégal entre 1713 and 1763*. Mémoire de l'IFAN, no. 17, Dakar, Senegal. Hamès, C. 1979. L'évolution des émirats maures sous l'effet du capitalisme marchand européen. In *Pastoral Production and Society: Proceedings of the International Meeting on Nomadic Pastoralism*, Edited by L'Équipe écologie et anthropologie des sociétés pastorales. New York: Cambridge University Press, 375–98.

33. Le Chevalier Boufflers, quoted in Audibert, J. 1991. *Miferma: une aventure humaine et industrielle en Mauritanie*. Paris: Edition L'Harmattan, 15.

34. Stewart, C. C. 1972. Political Authority and Social Stratification in Mauritania. In *Arabs and Berbers: From Tribe to Nation in North Africa*, eds. Ernest Gellner and Charles Micaud. Lexington, Massachusetts: Lexington Book, 385.

35. Lapidus, I. 1988. *A History of Islamic Societies*. Cambridge: Cambridge University Press, 833.

36. The famous ones were René Caillié, who stayed for a period of time among the Brakna of Mauritania, and Camile Douls, who spent five months among Oulad Dlim of the Western Sahara. See Caillié, R. 1830. *Journal d'un voyage à Tombouctou et à Djenné dans l'Afrique Central*. Paris: Imprimerie Royale; and Douls, C. 1888. Cinq mois chez les Maures nomades du Sahara occidental, *Le Tour du Monde* 55:177–224.

37. International Court of Justice. 1975. *Western Sahara: Information and Documents Supplied by the Spanish Government to the Court in Accord with Paragraph 2 of Resolution 3292 (XXIX) of the United Nations General Assembly*. Africana L964.8 S131X, vol. 1–6, Book V, Appendix 3 to Annex 21. La Hague: International Court of Justice.

38. Gillier, Commandant breveté. 1926. *La pénétration coloniale en Mauritanie*. Paris: P. Geuthner.

39. Marty, P. 1915–16. *L'Islam en Mauritanie et au Senegal*, Revue du Monde Musulman 31:59.

40. Balans, J. 1975. La Mauritanie entre deux mondes, *Revue Française d'Études Politique Africaines* 113:54–64.

41. Jean-Michel Pérille, Delegate of the Commission of the European Community in Nouakchott and Hamdi Ould Mouknas, former Mauritanian foreign minister, quoted respectively in *The Courier* 137(1 January 1993):39, 35.

42. Baduel, P. R. 1989. Editorial: Un pays-frontière, la Mauritanie. In *Mauritanie, entre arabité et africanité*, Revue du Monde Musulman et de la Mediterranée 54:6.

43. See respectively, Ould Cheikh Abdallahi, S. 1990. Long-Term Perspectives for Sub-Saharan Africa: The Situation in Mauritania. In *Long-Term Perspectives Study of Sub-Saharan Africa: Background Papers*, volume 1: Country Perspectives. Washington, D.C.: World Bank, 9; and Stewart, C. C. 1989. Une interprétation du conflit Sénégalo-mauritanien. In *Mauritanie, entre arabité et africanité*, Revue du monde Musulman et de la Mediterranée 54: 163.

44. Marchesin, P. 1992. *Tribus, ethnies et pouvoir en Mauritanie*. Paris: Karthala, 72, n. 2.

45. Baduel, P. R. ed. 1989. *Mauritanie, entre arabité et africanité*, Revue du Monde Musulman et de la Mediterrannée 54.

46. A similar political movement was created in Dakar in the 1980s by the name of Union Amicale des Ressortissants de la Vallée du Fleuve: UARF (Friendly Union of Nationals from the River Valley). One of its objectives was to overthrow the Moor-dominated Mauritanian government.

47. *Le Monde*, 29–30 June 1958.

48. Baduel, P. R. 1989. Mauritanie 1945–1990 ou l'État face à la Nation. In *Mauritanie, entre arabité et africanité*, Revue du Monde Musulman et de la Mediterranée 54: 21.

49. Zouheiry, Q. 1991. *Muthakkirat Diblumacy An Al-Alalqat Al-Maghribya Al-Muritanya*. Rabat, Morocco: Arabian Al Hilal, 91–92.

50. Quoted in RIM, Deuxième Plan de Développement Économic et Social 1970–1973, 47.

51. Fahem, A. 1993. Les phenomenes migratoires et l'urbanisation comme objet d'enseignement: la Mauritanie, *International Review of Education* 39(1–2):82.

52. Annuaire statistique de l'Office National de la Statistique 1991.

53. Nielsen, C. 1993. Stopping the Sand, *One World* (March):8–10.

54. Audibert, J. 1991. *Miferma: une aventure humaine et industrielle en Mauritanie*. Paris: Editions L'Harmattan, 192.

55. Ministère de l'Economie et des Finances, Synthèse du Projet RAMS, S 1, août 1981, 84.

56. Banque Mondiale, RIM, Memorandum Economique, 10 July 1985, 5.

57. POLISARIO represents the Spanish generic terms for the Popular Front for the Liberation of the Saguia Al-Hamra and the Rio d'Oro (the Western Sahara). In seeking the independence of the Western Sahara, the POLISARIO launched an armed struggle against Spanish occupation in 1973, founded the Arab Sahrawi Democratic Republic in 1976, fought against Mauritania between 1975 and 1978, and against Morocco between 1975 and September 1991, when a cease-fire agreement was reached between the POLISARIO and Morocco. As of March 1995, the cease-fire continues to hold and the parties agreed in principle on a UN proposed referendum to determine the fate of the territory, i.e., independence or integration with Morocco. The major problem that continues to delay the referendum is the disagreement between Morocco and the POLISARIO over the eligibility of Moroccan settlers in the Western Sahara for vote in the proposed referendum. In early 1984, Mauritania recognized the Arab Sahrawi Democratic Republic declared by the POLISARIO Front in February 1976 and maintained a neutral position vis-à-vis the conflict since December 1984.

58. Government Policy Letter to the World Bank detailing the restructuring of the public enterprise sector, 25 May 1990, para. 2.

59. It was the heyday of Dependency Theory in Latin America and Africa. In Mauritania, opposition to the ruling party (Hizb Al-Shaab) was led by the underground Hizb Al-Kadihin, whose main leaders were strongly inspired by Marxist-Leninist ideology, particularly its Maoist offspring.

60. Banque mondiale, RIM, Memorandum Economique, 10 July 1985, tables 7.1 and 7.4.

61. Some nine coups, attempted coups, or plots took place within the Mauritanian state between July 1978 and December 1984. The failed coup of March 1981 (which was backed by Morocco) led to the death of eight people and the trial and execution of three army officers. This political instability reflects partially the period of transition from a national to a multilateral state.

62. In 1981, the Socialist-led government in France engineered the term *restructuration* (restructuring) as a euphemism for privatization (of ownership and/or management) of certain French state enterprises.

63. Negotiations between the Ould Haidalla government and the Bank and the IMF broke off in early 1984.

64. The idea of PFP was endorsed and developed by the executive directors of the Bank and the Fund following U.S. Secretary of State James Baker's initiative in 1985.

65. IMF, Treasurer's Department 1991 *Financial Organization and Operations of the IMF*, Pamphlet Series No. 45, Second Edition, Washington, D.C., 79.

66. Sideri, S. 1993. Restructuring the Post-Cold War World Economy: Perspectives and Prognosis, *Development and Change* 24:19.

67. Drawing upon examples of cocoa, coffee, and cotton in Africa, Campbell and Loxley found that "the widespread adoption of Fund/Bank programs has led to an expansion of world supply and a corresponding decline in world prices." See Campbell, B., and Loxley, J. eds. 1989. *Structural Adjustment in Africa*. New York: St. Martin's Press, 6.

68. Dadzie, K. 1992. The Outlook for Development in the 1990s. In *Change: Threat or Opportunity for Human Progress?* volume 2: Economic Change, ed. Uner Kirdar. New York: United Nations, 71.

69. UN Development Program, Co-operation au Development, Mauritanie, Rapport 1990, Novembre 1990, 23.

70. Central Intelligence Agency, Vital Statistics, Mauritania, *World Factbook 1993*.

71. Ould Ahmed Hadi, S. Quoting Ahmed Ould Daddah in *Al Bayan*, no. 36, 12–18 October 1992, 3.

72. Banque mondiale, Etude: Gestion de l'Aide et de la Dette Exterieure en Afrique Subsaharienne, version preliminaire. This document was disseminated by the World Bank among state bureaucrats in Mauritania and probably other sub-Saharan countries to influence their perception of the debt problem.

Chapter 4: Denationalization: From National to Multilateral State

1. Harvey, D. 1989. *The Condition of Postmodernity*. Cambridge: Basil Blackwell.

2. Haggard, S., and Kaufman, R. 1992. eds. *The Politics of Economic Adjustment*. Princeton, New Jersey: Princeton University Press, 25.

3. Morris, D. 1994. Globalism, *Utne Reader* 62:73.

4. Hollow, J. 1994. Global Capital and the National State, *Capital and Class* 52:33.

5. Amin, S. 1990. *Maldevelopment: Anatomy of a Global Failure*. London: Zed Books, 176.

6. George, S. 1992. Uses and Abuses of African Debt: The International Squeeze on Poor Countries, *Dissent* 39(3):341–42.

7. I have not come across any study of adjustment policies based primarily on the analysis of primary adjustment documents such as the texts of World Bank loan agreements, policy framework papers, IMF standby arrangements, Paris Club accords, and minutes of proceedings of meetings between a government and the multilateral institutions.

8. Deuxième Plan de Développement Economique et Social, 1970–1973, 9.

9. Synthèse du Projet RAMS, S1, août 1981, 23.

10. U.S. Department of State, U.S. Agency for International Development (USAID), Country Development Strategy Statement, FY 1981, Mauritania, January 1979, unabridged version, 23.

11. Many diagnostic studies of the Mauritanian economy were carried out by consultants from Louis Berger International, Inc., 100 Halsted Street, East Orange, New Jersey 07019, USA, particularly since the latter signed an agreement (Convention no. 533/5 of 16 December 1986) with the Mauritanian government. For more details on how the Bank supervises international consultants, see World Bank Guidelines for International Consultants, August 1981.

12. United States Congress, House, Committee on Foreign Affairs, Subcommittee on Africa, *Africa, the World Bank, and the IMF: An Appraisal.* Hearing before the Subcommittee on Africa of the Committee on Foreign Affairs, House of Representatives, Ninety-Eighth Congress, second session, 23 February 1984, Washington, D.C.: U.S. Government Printing Office, 1.

13. United States Congress. 1989. *Structural Adjustment in Africa: Insights from the Experiences of Ghana and Senegal.* Report of a Staff Study Mission to Great Britain, Ghana, Senegal, Cote d'Ivoire, and France, 29 November – 20 December 1988, submitted to the Committee on Foreign Affairs, U.S. House of Representatives. Washington D.C.: U.S. Government Printing Office, 5.

14. Emmerij, L. 1987. The Future of Development Research in the OECD Development Center: Reflections on the Conclusions of the Seminar. In *Development Policies and the Crisis of the 1980s,* ed. Louis Emmerij. Paris: OECD Development Centre, 14. See also Stephan Haggard and Robert R. Kaufman. 1992. eds. *The Politics of Economic Adjustment.* Princeton, New Jersey: Princeton University Press, 18.

15. Callaghy, T. 1988. Debt and Structural Adjustment in Africa: Realities and Possibilities, *Issue: A Journal of Opinion* 16(2):18.

16. Projet DIAR, Rapport sur l'état d'avancement du projet de développement institutionnel et administrative et de la réforme au 31/12/1990.

17. World Bank, Mauritanie—Projet de Développement Institutionnel, Rapport aux autorités mauritaniennes, 9 décembre 1985.

18. PDIAR financing amounted to about UM 637 million spent on the following: civil engineering (12 million); consultants (268 million); equipment (226 million); management (107 million); civil servant training (24 million). See Rapport sur l'etat d'avancement du PDIAR, 31 December 1990. Note the amount spent on consultants.

19. PDIAR, Rapport sur l'état d'avancement du projet de développement institutionnel et administrative et de la réforme au 31/12/1990. See also PDIAR, Evaluation du Volet Formation, Turkia Daddah, Mission de Juillet 1991.

20. Synthèse du Projet RAMS, S1, août 1981, 19.

21. Troisième Plan de Développement Economique et Social 1976–80, 11.

22. Conrow, J. 1987. Statement. In United States Congress, House, Selected Committee on Hunger, *The World Bank in Africa: hearing before the Select Committee on Hunger, House of Representative, One Hundredth Congress, first session, July 23, 1987,* Washington, D.C.: U.S. Government Printing Office, 59–61.

23. Document-cadre de politique economique pour la periode 1987–90.

24. Bilan d'execution du PREF (1985–88), preparé pour le 2e Groupe Consultatif pour la Mauritanie, Paris, les 25, 26, 27 juillet 1989.

25. Document-cadre de politique économique, 1989–91.

26. Procès verbal des discussions entre le gouvernement de la RIM et la Banque mondiale sur les conditions de deboursement de la 2eme tranche du crédit d'ajustement structurel, le programme d'investissement 1989–91, et le cadre macroeconomique, signé

le 22 février 1989 à Washington D.C.

27. Projet de Document-cadre de politique economique pour 1990–93.

28. Lettre du Fonds Monetaire International au gouverneur de la Banque Centrale de Mauritanie, le 27 juillet 1990.

29. United States Congress, House, Committee on Foreign Affairs, One Hundredth Congress, First Session, *Human Rights in the Maghreb and Mauritania: hearing, June 19, 1991, before the Subcommittee on Human Rights and International Organizations and on Africa*, Washington, D.C.: U.S. Government Printing Office, 21.

30. Following the signing of the fourth PFP, I talked over the phone with three Mauritanian nationals (Tiam Samba, Sidi Mohamed Ould Boubacar, and Sarr Bassirou) holding advisory positions at the headquarters of the IMF and the World Bank in Washington, D.C., to get more information about the fourth PFP or even a copy of the document. Thinking the document was top secret, they were not able and/or willing to even confirm or deny that it was finally signed. They seemingly fear serious consequences if any substantial information about the PFP leaks through their offices. I thank Miguel Saponara (country officer and economist at the World Bank) who sent me a copy of the fourth PFP one year later, in November 1993, following the August 1993 new policy on disclosure of some World Bank operational information.

31. Amin, S. 1980. *Class and Nation: Historically and in the Current Crisis.* New York: Monthly Review Press, 24.

32. Harvey, D. 1982. *The Limits to Capital.* Chicago: University of Chicago Press, 281.

33. Camdessus, M. 1992. Conference de Presse, *Horizons*, no. 294, 16–17 July; and *Le Temps*, no. 48, 19–26 July.

34. *IMF Survey*, 20 September 1993, 283.

35. Mauritanie: Demande d'accord de confirmation. Document du Fonds Monetaire International, ESB/87/73, le 7 avril 1987.

36. The mission is composed of E. Sacerdoti (head of the mission, Africa Department), Y. Fassassi (Africa Department), P. Marciniak (Africa Department), T. Ramtoolah (Institute), and A. M. Réolon (secretary, Bureau of Linguistic Services). It was assisted by M. R. Vaurs (from the World Bank) who was in Nouakchott at the time.

37. See The Whole-Earth IMF and A World Economy in Transition, *IMF Survey*, 20 September 1993, 285.

38. Cherif, M. 1991. Mauritanie: Projet de Soutien à la Reflexion Endogène. An EC-funded report.

39. To some extent, Mauritanian society was polarized along ethnolinguistic and cultural lines during the 1992 presidential elections. Most of the Arabic-speaking Moor majority espoused the political discourse of Arab nationalism and Islamic traditions, which was perceived as anti-West, while most non-Arabic-speaking black minorities espoused the cosmopolitan discourse prevailing in francophone West Africa and considered as pro-West.

40. On the secretive character of the IMF, Michel Camdessus (IMF managing director) is candidly clear: "Each time we take a decision we share all the elements of this decision with 178 countries in the world, through our Executive Board. Of course, we do not share that with the academic community or with all of you ladies and gentlemen. The interested countries just do not want it." See *IMF Survey*, 7 February 1994, 43.

41. Letter of the Director of Credit at the Central Bank, no. 0032/DC/SMS/92, 23 February 1992.

42. Banque mondiale, RIM, Memorandum Economique, no. 5535-MAU, 10 July 1985, para. 2.15. For the above debt statistics, see Declaration du Gouvernement Mauritanien Presentée par le Ministre du Plan et de l'Emploi, Reunion Gouvernment Mauritanien - Donateurs, Paris Mercredi 26 et Jeudi 27 Juillet 1989. See also U.S. Central Intelligence Agency, Vital Statistics, Mauritania, *Factbook 1993*; and various issues of IMF's *International Financial Statistics*.

43. Procès verbal agrée relatif à la consolidation de la dette de la RIM, Paris, 26–27 avril 1985.

44. *Foreign Broadcast Information Service*, (NES) 2 February 1993, 14.

45. U.S. Department of State, 1990, *Dispatch* 1(9):223.

46. U.S. Department of State, 1990, *Dispatch* 2(37):529.

47. Réunion des Bailleurs de Fonds pour la Mauritanie, Résumé des Débats, le 12 août 1989.

48. Bilateral lenders: the United States, France, Italy, Japan, Morocco, Brazil, and the Netherlands. Multilateral lenders: African Development Bank, Islamic Development Bank, Commission of European Communities, Arab Fund for Economic and Social Development, International Fund for Agricultural Development, Kuwait Fund for Arab Economic Development, Arab Monetary Fund, International Monetary Fund, Saudi Development Fund, and United Nations Development Program.

49. Declaration du Gouvernement Mauritanien, presentée par le Ministre du Plan et de l'Emploi, Réunion Gouvernement Mauritanien - Donateurs, Paris, Mercredi 26 et Jeudi 27 Juillet 1989.

50. Biktash, S. 1992. *Al-Niza' Al-Singhali Al-Muritany*. Al-Qahira: Dar Al-Mustaqbal Al-Arabi, 244.

51. Even though those deported from Senegal outnumber ten times those deported from Mauritania, the Senegalese government and part of the Mauritanian opposition organized refugee camps south of the Senegal River for many of those who either fled or were deported from Mauritania and channeled to them international assistance through the UN High Commission for Refugees, while Mauritania dismantled in few months its refugees camps and did not register them with the UN High Commission for Refugees. This policy covered the crimes and abuses committed against the Moors in Senegal, while it exposed crimes and abuses committed against the blacks in Mauritania. It obscured the fact that many of the Moors deported from Senegal and many of the blacks deported from Mauritania were actually Senegalese citizens.

52. Agricultural projects financed by the lenders on the Mauritanian side of the Senegal River were endangered in 1989 following disputes over the borders between Mauritania and Senegal and the subsequent massive deportations of nationals from both countries due to bloody ethnic clashes.

53. The distribution of investment per sector in 1989 was as follows: rural development (34 percent), industrial development (13.2 percent), zoning (25.1 percent), human resources (10.1 percent), public and parapublic (3.1 percent), and SNIM (14.2 percent).

54. Ould Abdel Jelil, Y. 1989. A Brief Presentation of the Mauritanian Experience in Public Investment during the Period of SAPs. Paper presented at the Arab Planning Institute, Kuwait, 2–20 December, Ministry of Planning and Employment, Nouakchott.

Chapter 5: Denationalization: Lenders and NGOs within the State

1. Cited by Smith, P. Aid Conditionality is "Swamping" Africa, *Africa Recovery*, December 1993–March 1994, 15.

2. Martin, M. 1991. *The Crumbling Façade of African Debt Negotiations: No Winners*. London: McMillan.

3. Through interviews with state officials and reviews of dozens of World Bank missions' *aide-mémoires* (memos or reports), as well as minutes of proceedings of meetings between international lender missions and government committees.

4. Report and Recommendation of the President of the International Development Association to the Executive Directors for a Proposed Development Credit of SDR 11.7 million and a Proposed Special African Facility Credit of SDR 21.4 million to the Islamic Republic of Mauritania for a Structural Adjustment Program, 11 May 1987.

5. World Bank, Country Operations Division, Sahelian Department, Africa Region, Islamic Republic of Mauritania, Structural Adjustment Program, Program Completion Report, 12 January 1990, para. 5.

6. World Bank, Country Operations Division, Sahelian Department, Africa Region, Islamic Republic of Mauritania, Structural Adjustment Program, Program Completion Report, 12 January 1990, para. 24.

7. World Bank, Country Operations Division, Sahelian Department, Africa Region, Islamic Republic of Mauritania, Structural Adjustment Program, Program Completion Report, 12 January 1990, para. 25.

8. World Bank, Country Operations Division, Sahelian Department, Africa Region, Islamic Republic of Mauritania, Structural Adjustment Program, Program Completion Report, 12 January 1990, para. 25.

9. World Bank, Country Operations Division, Sahelian Department, Africa Region, Islamic Republic of Mauritania, Structural Adjustment Program, Program Completion Report, 12 January 1990, para. 26.

10. World Bank, Country Operations Division, Sahelian Department, Africa Region, Islamic Republic of Mauritania, Structural Adjustment Program, Program Completion Report, 12 January 1990, para. 81.

11. A study of the agricultural private sector in Mauritania (by Miller, a consultant for the World Bank in 1988) argues that in three years of reforms the private sector irrigated more lands than did the public sector in fifteen years.

12. The preparation of the project began with a World Bank mission led by Salah Darghouth (with consultants from the government and other lenders) who stayed in Mauritania between 19 May and 16 June 1988. The project is part of the sectoral priorities defined by the first structural adjustment loan. The mission had discussions in Nouakchott with officials from the government, the private sector, and the community of foreign lenders. Then it went to the regions of Trarza, Brakna, Gorgol, and Al-Assaba for field visits and discussion with regional authorities, technical staff, and peasants. The conclusions and recommendations of the mission were presented to the government during a meeting led by the general secretary of the Ministry of Rural Development held on 13 June 1988.

13.   *Actions*   *Deadlines*
-Preparation of mission reports   June/July 1988
-Sending mission reports   July 1988
-Complementary government reports   June/September 1988
-Sending government reports to the Bank   15 September 1988
-Mission for final preparation and evaluation   September/October 1988
-Negotiation   December 1989
-Presentation to the Bank's executive board   March 1989

14. The prenegotiation mission, composed of Salah Darghouth and Doublet from the World Bank, stayed in Mauritania 11–16 March 1989. They worked in close collaboration with the newly created Technical Support Committee of the project and had discussions with government authorities, the private sector and the community of foreign lenders in Nouakchott. They went also to Rosso, Boghé, and Kaedi for field visits and discussions with the regional authorities, the technical staff of the national agency for rural development (SONADER), and the peasants. The mission also held meetings with the ministers of rural development, economy and finance, and the general secretary of the Ministry of Interior to inform them and record their suggestions on the different steps of the mission.

15. Aide-Mémoire, mission de pre-négociation du PASA, du 11 au 16 mars 1989.

16. *Actions*   *Deadlines*
-Approval of the project document (President's Report)
  by the Bureau of Senior Vice President, Bank Operations   25 March 1989
-Signing Letter of Development Policy for the agricultural sector   3 April 1989
-Negotiation of the project in Washington, D.C.   3–7 April 1989
-Presentation of the project to the Bank executive board   13 May 1989
-Release of the first tranche of the adjustment loan   September 1989
-Release of the second tranche of the adjustment loan   September 1990

17. This supervision mission took place between 27 June and 10 July 1991. It was composed of Anne Marie Frenehard (from the French Ministry of Cooperation), Gerard Ancey and Yves Ficatier (from the Caisse Centrale de Cooperation Economique), and David Jones and Jacques Gastaldi (from the World Bank). Simultaneously, Gerard Vacca (also from the World Bank) was conducting another supervision mission focusing on investment aspects of the project that are managed by SONADER, and he issued a separate report. The conjoint mission began its official work by a meeting with officials held on 29 June. Then a series of meetings was held (30 June–4 July) with the different subgroups of the project headed by Baro from the planning cell in the Ministry of Rural Development. On the other hand, the mission visited the region of Rosso on 6–7 July. This field visit allowed the mission to discuss the project with the Wali (governor) of Trarza and the members of the local administration, as well as with the different technical partners of the project, particularly: (1) Federation of Farmers and Grazers of Mauritania, (2) Association of Group Studies for Agricultural Techniques, (3) Land Bureau, (4) Branch of the Union des Banques de Developpement in Rosso, (5) owners and managers of ricemills, and (6) regional management of SONADER. In Nouakchott, the members of the mission met with the ministers of interior and rural development and the governor of the central bank to keep them informed on the progress of their mission. The conclusions and recommendations of the mission were presented to the government during a meeting (held on 8 July 1991) headed by the director of planning.

18. Telex de la Banque mondiale, Washington D.C., 13 août 1991, aux ministères du Développement Rural, du Plan, de l'Interieur, et des Postes et Télécommunications concernant le PASA, Mission de supervision du 27 juin au 10 juillet 1991.

19. Letter of Sarbib, J., deputy director, Sahel Department, Africa Region, World Bank dated 9 December 1991. The letter was officially sent to the minister of planning and the governor of the central bank and copies were transmitted to ten other ministers.

20. Peace Corps (U.S.). 1991. Mauritania. Washington, D.C., 17.

21. *Le Temps*, no. 11, 22–28 September 1991.

22. Union of International Associations. ed. 1992. *Yearbook of International Organizations, Volume 1, 1992/93*. New York: K. G. Saur Munchen, entry no. 08287, 1206.

23. See James D. Wolfensohn: Dilettante or Visionary?, *West Africa* 26 June-2 July 1995, 993-96.

24. See Hamzata, D. 1992. Une ONG: Caritas Mauritanie, *Le Temps*, no. 45, 21–27 June.

25. Mbutu, P. 1988. *Status of Christianity Profile: Mauritania*. Nairobi: Research Department, Daystar University College, 29, 26. The above report also mentioned that the failure to convert any native Mauritanian to Christianity is encouraging some missionaries to plan strategies "to reach . . . the hundreds of Mauritanian students who are studying in various Universities, especially in France."

26. Clark, J. 1990. *Democratizing Development: The Role of Voluntary Organizations*. Kumarian Press, West Hartford, Connecticut, 43.

27. Conversation with Bella Ould Cheibani, advisor to the Secrétaire Permanent du CMSN, fall 1991.

28. Africa 70, Association Française des Volontaires du Progres, Caritas Mauritanie, Communaute Doulos, Federation Lutherienne Mondiale, Oxfam, Terre des Hommes, World Vision International, Lumiere Vie Amour, and Pharmaciens sans Frontières.

29. Rapport Final du 1er Seminaire National sur les Communes Rurales, ONG et Développement à la Base Organisé par la Cellule d'Appui aux Petits Projets du 15, 16 et 17 octobre 1989.

30. Giddens, A. 1985. *The Nation-State and Violence, Volume Two of A Contemporary Critique of Historical Materialism*. Los Angeles: California: University of California Press, 282.

Chapter 6: Globalization and Devaluation of the Economy

1. Inasmuch as the government has little input in the formulation of development policy (which is essentially based on World Bank economic diagnoses) and the articulation of development strategies (which are based on the PFP), an IMF/World Bank document described by the IMF as "a forward-looking document, updated annually on a three-year rolling basis, that identifies the country's macroeconomic and structural policy objectives, the strategy of the authorities to achieve these objectives, and the associated financing requirements." See IMF, Treasurer's Department, 1991, *Financing Organization and Operations of the IMF*, Pamphlet Series no. 45, Second edition, Washington, D.C., 79.

2. United States Senate, *The Internationalization of Capital Markets*. Hearing before the Committee on Banking, Housing, and Urban Affairs, Ninety-Ninth Congress, second session, 26–27 February 1986. Washington, D.C.: U.S. Government Printing Office, 18.

3. United Nations. 1993. *World Economic Survey 1993/94*. Student Edition, New York: UN, 196.

4. Economic sanctions and the blocking or freezing of foreign assets in U.S. domestic banks and some of their owned branches abroad were used by the U.S. government against countries such as Cuba, former East Germany, Vietnam, Iran, Libya, Iraq, and, more recently, Haiti.

5. Kim, S. 1984. *The Quest for a Just World Order*. Boston: Westview Press, 191.

6. World Bank. 1993. *World Development Report 1993*. Washington D.C.: Oxford University Press, 238–9.

7. Brett, E. 1985. *The World Economy since the War: The Politics of Uneven Development*. New York: Praeger, 17.

8. Brecher, J. 1993. Global Village or Global Pillage? *The Nation*, 6 December, 685.

9. O'Brien, R. 1992. *Global Financial Integration: The End of Geography*. New York: Royal Institute for International Affairs, 70.

10. Brunn, S., and Leinbach, T. eds. 1991. *Collapsing Space and Time: Geographic Aspects of Communication and Information*. London: Harper Collins Academic.

11. Radice, H. 1984. The National Economy: A Keynesian Myth?, *Capital and Class* 22:111–40. Dicken, P. 1993. The Changing Organization of the Global Economy. In *The Challenge for Geography*, ed. R. J. Johnston. Oxford, UK: Blackwell, 47.

12. Ohmae, K. 1990. *The Borderless World: Power and Strategy in the Interlinked Economy*. New York: Harper Business, 172.

13. Gumbel, P., and Davis, B. 1994. G–7 Countries Show Limits of their Power, *The Wall Street Journal* (July 11):A3, A7.

14. Cited in *Africa Recovery*, December 1993–March 1994, 9.

15. In the 1990s, the SDR valuation basket consists of the currencies of the five members (the United States, Germany, Japan, France, and Britain) having the largest export of goods and services during the period 1985–89. The weights for their currencies is: U.S. dollar, 40 percent; Deutsche Mark, 21 percent; Japanese yen, 17 percent; and French franc, and pound sterling, 11 percent each. In 1993, one SDR is equivalent to 1.3 to 1.4 dollars.

16. As a reward for the government's successive agreements with the IMF, the Paris Club agreed to reschedule Mauritania's debt five times: in April 1985 ($68 million), in May 1986 ($27 million), in June 1987 ($90 million), in June 1989 ($52 million), and in January 1993 ($218 million). See IMF. 1994. *Official Financing for Developing Countries*. Washington, D.C.: IMF, 62.

17. In recent years, fish exports have tended to become more important than those of iron ore.

18. Document of the World Bank, "Report and Recommendation of the President of the International Development Association to the Executive Directors for a Proposed Development Credit of SDR 11.7 million and a Proposed Special African Facility Credit of SDR 21.4 million to the Islamic Republic of Mauritania for a Structural Adjustment Program," Washington, D.C., 11 May 1987, para. 99.

19. Sidi Mohamed Ould Boubacar (interviewed by David, D.). Country Report, Mauritania, *The Courier* 137 (1 January 1993):31.

20. World Bank. RIM, Memorandum Economique, 10 July 1985, para. 1.11 and 3.28.

21. Economic and Financial Recovery Program 1985–88, para. 19.

22. *Business America* 8(7), 1 April 1985, 26–27.

23. Pressler, L. 1993. Opening Markets for U.S. Wheat. *Congressional Record* (Daily ed., 29 April):S5100.

24. Economic and Financial Recovery Program 1985–88, para. 13–15.

25. IDA President's Report no. P–4550–MAU, 11 May 1987, para 12. Compared to others, the Mauritanian government's performance in its compliance with the conditions of SAPs is impressive indeed. In a World Bank study of fifty-one SAPs and SALs in fifteen developing countries (including five from Africa) between 1980 and 1987, only 60 percent of adjustment conditionality was implemented. See Bangura, Y., and Gibbon, P. 1992. Adjustment, Authoritarianism and Democracy: An Introduction to Some Conceptual and Empirical Issues. In *Authoritarianism, Democracy, and Adjustment: The Politics of Economic Reform in Africa*, eds. P. Gibbon, Y. Bangura, and A. Ofstad. Uppsala: Nordiska Afrikainstitutet, 11–12.

26. IDA President's Report no. P–4550–MAU, 11 May 1987, para. 78.

27. World Bank (internal document), Mauritania, Structural Adjustment Program, Completion Report, 12 January 1990, para. 17, World Bank Country Operations Division, Sahelian Department, Africa Region, Washington, D.C.

28. World Bank, Mauritania's Structural Adjustment Program, Completion Report, 12 January 1990, para. 7.

29. Bilan d'exécution du PREF 1985–88, juillet 1989, 12–15.

30. Troisième Plan de Développement Economique et Social 1976–80, tableau 3, 11.

31. Bilan d'exécution du PREF 1985–88, juillet 1989, 2.

32. UN Development Program, Governing Council, *Program Planning, Country and Intercountry Programs and Projects, Fourth Program for Mauritania*, 14 December 1992, 2.

33. Document diagnostic [*sic*] de la Banque Mondiale intitulé: Projet de Développement Institutionnel, Rapport aux Autorités Mauritaniennes, 5 avril 1987, para. 46.

34. IDA President's Report no. P–5293–MAU, 30 May 1990, para. 22.

35. Sectoral Policy Letter, Public Enterprise Sector, 25 May 1990, para. 2.

36. Computed from Bulletin Trimesteriel de Statistique, Direction des Etudes, BCM, juin 1991.

37. Banque mondiale, RIM, Memorandum Economique, 10 July 1985, para. 3.29.

38. Organisation des Nations Unies pour le Développement Industriel (UNIDO/10/R.166), Séminaire sur la Stratégie du Développement Industriel de la République Islamique de Mauritanie, organisé dans le cadre de la décennie du développement industriel de l'afrique, Nouakchott, Mauritanie, 28 juin 1985.

39. The companies from which the state withdrew on the eve of adjustment are: Banque Mauritanienne Arabe Africaine (BMAA), 1985; Centre National des Energies Alternatives (CNEA), 1984; Mauritanienne de Frigorifique et de Conservation (MAFCO), 1984; Office National du Cinema (ONC), 1984; Office du Tapis Mauritanien (OTM), 1984; Société Nationale de Confection (SNC), 1985; Office du Complexe Olympique (OCO), 1984; Société Mauritanienne d'Industrie de Raffinage (SOMIR), 1985; Société Mauritanienne de Tourisme et d'Hotelerie (SMTA), 1984; and Société Mauritanienne de Connaissement d'Acconage et de Transit (SOMACAT), 1985. Source:

Cellule de Rehabilitation des Entreprises Publiques, Ministère de la Planification et des Finances, Informations non publiées concernant the secteur public, 1986.

40. Document of the World Bank, Report and Recommendation of the President of the International Development Association (Report no. P–5293–MAU) to the Executive Directors on a Proposed Development Credit of SDR 30.7 million the Islamic Republic of Mauritania for a Public Enterprise Sector Adjustment Program, 30 May 1990, Annex VII. World Bank, Washington, D.C.

41. IDA President's Report no. P–5293–MAU, para. 62.

42. Communication du Ministre du Plan en Conseil des Ministres (sans date), 1990.

43. In late 1990, negotiations for financing the M'Haoudat Project indicate a cofinancing distributed as follows: Caisse Central de Cooperation (FF 350 million), European Investment Bank (ECUS 30 million), and African Development (UCB 46.81 million). See Rapport SNIM, Realisation 1990, Direction de la Dette Exterieure, Ministère des Finances.

44. Ould Heyine, S. (interviewed by David, D.). Country Report, Mauritania, *The Courier* 137(1 January 1993):23.

45. IDA President's Report no. P–4550–MAU, 11 May 1987, para. 53.

46. IDA President's Report no. P–4550–MAU, 11 May 1987, para. 54 and 55.

47. See Convention de Financement no. 98 26 00 91 030 entre la RIM et la CCCE, le 10 février 1992.

48. *L'Indépendant*, no. 003, 9 October 1991; and *Le Temps*, no. 13, 6–12 October, 1991.

49. *Jeune Afrique*, no. 1735, 7–13 April 1994, 7.

50. The Economist Intelligence Unit. 1991. *Guinea, Mali, Mauritania, A Country Profile 1991–92*. London: EIU, 73.

51. World Bank, Agricultural Sector Adjustment, the Private Sector in Mauritania, June 1988.

52. Economic and Financial Recovery Program 1985–88, Mauritania, prepared for the Consultative Group for Mauritania, 26–7 November 1985, para. 10.

53. IDA President's Report no. P–4550–MAU, 11 May 1987, para. 24.

54. Computed from Bulletin Trimesteriel de Statistique, Direction des Etudes, BCM, juin 1991.

55. Martin, F. 1985. Mauritania: Cereal Policy Reform in the Sahel, A Report Prepared for the OECD/Club du Sahel/CILSS, Elliot Berg Associates, para. 152–3.

56. Oxfam, UK and Ireland. 1993. *Africa, Make or Break: Action for Recovery*. Oxford: Oxford Print Services, 28.

57. Ould Didi, H. 1990. Liberalisation de la filière riz en Mauritanie. Paris: Institut de Recherche et d'Application des Méthodes de Développement, 15.

58. The mission was composed of Birger Fredriksen (chief of the mission, economist and specialist in education planning), Bernard Abeille (specialist in architecture), Steve Berkman (specialist in technical and professional training), Diana Risen (operation assistant), Alain Mingat (consultant/economist), and Jorn Mygind (scientific education consultant).

59. Etude du Projet de Restructuration du Secteur de l'Education en Mauritanie, par Burger Fredriksen, Bernard Abeille, Steve Berkman, Diana Risen, Alain Mingat, et Jorn Mygind, Projet Education III, Ministère du Plan, Nouakchott, 1988.

60. Governor of the central bank, instructions no. 4, 5, 6, 7, and 8, 14 June 1988.

61. World Bank document, Mauritania: Policy Framework Paper (October 1992–September 1995), Washington, D.C., 13 November 1992, para. 14.

62. These are: Ciment de Mauritanie (3.4 percent), Abdou Ould Maham (3 percent), Abdallahi Ould Noueigedh (2 percent), Mohamed Abdallahi Ould Abdallahi (2 percent), Ould Marcou family (Mohamed, Hassanna, and Sidi Mohamed) (1.6 percent), and Ahmed Ould Sidi Baba (1.2 percent).

63. These are: Sidi Mohamed Ould Abbass (36.76 percent), Moulaye El Hacen Ould Mokhtar El Hacen (22 percent), Limam Ould Ouleida (22 percent), Abdallahi Ould Noueiguedh (4 percent), and Mohamed Abdallahi Ould Abdallahi (4 percent).

64. Ghai, D., and Alcantara, C. H. 1990. The Crisis of the 1980s in Sub-Saharan Africa, Latin America and the Caribbean: Economic Impact, Social Change and Political Implications, *Development and Change* 21:406.

65. World Bank. 1989. *World Development Report 1989*. Washington, D.C.: World Bank, 132.

66. *Jeune Afrique*, 13–20 January 1994.

67. Bentsi-Enchill, N. K. Devaluation Hits the African Franc Zone, *Africa Recovery*, December 1993–March 1994, 3, 42.

68. Moffett, M., and Friedland, J. 1995. Queasy Capital: Mexico Peso Collapse Presents Stark Choices to Latin Economies, *Wall Street Journal* (January 6):A, 1:6.

69. IDA President's Report no. P–5293–MAU, 30 May 1990, para. 12.

70. IDA President's Report no. P–5293–MAU, 30 May 1990, Annex 8, para. 18, note 8.

71. *Shaab*, 26 December 1993, 3.

72. Moustapha Ould Abeiderrahmane (interviewed by Dominique, D.). Country Report, Mauritania, *The Courier* 137(1 January 1993):27.

73. Banque mondiale, RIM, Memorandum Economique, 10 July 1985, para. 2.16.

74. Banque mondiale, RIM, Memorandum Economique, 10 July 1985, para. 6.20.

75. UN Development Program, Cooperation au Développement, Mauritanie, Rapport 1990, novembre 1990.

76. Banque mondiale, RIM, Memorandum Economique, 10 July 1985, Tableau 4.2.

77. *Shaab*, 26 December 1993.

78. United Nations Conference on Trade and Development, Programme on Transnational Corporations. 1993. *World Investment Report 1993: Transnational Corporations and Integrated International Production*. New York: United Nations, Box I.2, 19.

79. United Nations Conference on Trade and Development, Programme on Transnational Corporations *World Investment Report 1993: Transnational Corporations and Integrated International Production*, New York: United Nations, 1993, Box I.2, p. 29.

80. See conditions of World Bank credit (1943–MAU, August 1988) for restructuring the education sector.

81. See the preamble of the loan agreement between IBRD and SNIM and the Guarantee Agreement between IBRD and RIM dated January 1986. See also the July 1980 agreement between Mauritania and SNIM's lenders.

82. Mauritanie: Evolution de la situation économique et financière, *Moniteur du Commerce International*, no. 1013, 24 February 1992, 10.

83. Banque mondiale. 1991. *Rapport sur le Développement 991*. Washington, D.C.: World Bank, 118.

84. UN Development Programme Governing Council. 1992. *Programme Planning, Country and Intercountry Programs and Projects: Fourth Country Programme for Mauritania.* 14 December, 2.

85. The Economist Intelligence Unit. 1991. *Guinea, Mali, Mauritania, Country Profile 1991-92*. London: EIU, 65.

86. Ould Michel, M., quoted by Jean-Baptiste Placca, Démocratie en construction, *Jeune Afrique economie*, April 1993, 124.

87. Ould Mahfudh, H. In *Al-Bayane*, no. 22, 13-19 May 1992.

88. Ould Dey, S., quoted in *Al-Qafila*, no. 004, 25 December 1991.

89. Ould Daddah, A. (interviewed by David, D.). Country Report, Mauritania, *The Courier* 137(1 January 1993):33.

90. Doumou, A. 1987. The State and Popular Alliances: Theoretical Preliminaries in the Light of the Moroccan Case. In *Popular Struggles for Democracy in Africa*, ed. Peter Anyang' Nyong'o. London: United Nations University, 48-77.

Chapter 7: Social Dimension of SAPs

1. Jolly, R. 1985. *Adjustment with a Human Face*. New York: UNICEF.

2. Cornia, G., Jolly, R., and Stewart, F. eds. 1988. *Adjustment with a Human Face, volume 1: Protecting the Vulnerable and Promoting Growth.* Oxford: Clarendon Press for UNICEF, 288.

3. Cornia, G., Jolly, R., and Stewart, F. eds. 1988. *Adjustment with a Human Face, volume 2: Country Case Studies.* Oxford: Clarendon Press for UNICEF, 1.

4. World Health Organization, Repercussions of the World Economic Situation, Provisional Report by the Director-general, 39th World Health Assembly, A39/4, 16 May 1986.

5. UN Development Program. 1987. Assessment of Social Dimensions of Structural Adjustment in Sub-Saharan Africa' Project Document, UNDP Fourth cycle, RAF/86/037/A/01/42.

6. United Nations Economic Commission for Africa (UNECA), African Alternative Framework to Structural Adjustment Programmes for Socio-economic Recovery and Transformation, Addis Ababa: ECA, 1991.

7. Petit, B. 1993. Democracy and Structural Adjustment in Africa, *The Courier* 138(March):74-5.

8. Ghai, D. 1992. *Structural Adjustment, Global Integration and Social Democracy.* Geneva: United Nations Research Institute for Social Development, Discussion Paper no. 37, October, 11.

9. Serageldin, I. and Noel, M. 1990. Tackling the Social Dimensions of Adjustment in Africa, *Finance and Development* (September):18.

10. Coetzee, S. and Jahed, M. 1993. Structural Adjustment: A Review of the State of the Art, *Africa Insight* 23(2):84.

11. World Bank. The Social Dimensions of Adjustment in Africa: A Policy Agenda. SDA Document, Washington, D.C.: World Bank, March, 1990, 8, 6, 10, 23, respectively.

12. World Bank. 1990. *World Development Report 1990*. Washington, D.C.: World Bank, iii.

13. Sawyerr, A. Les politiques d'ajustement: problèmes politiques, Report on Conference Internationale sur le Facteur Humain dans le Redressement Economique et le Developpement de l'Afrique, Khartoum, Soudan, 5–8 mars 1988, Economic Commission of Africa, ECA/ICHD/88/29.

14. World Bank. 1990. *World Development Report 1990*. Washington, D.C.: World Bank, 26.

15. United Nations Development Program, Evaluations of the Social Dimensions of Adjustment, national technical cooperation assessments and programmes, and UNDP assistance to intergovernmental organizations in Africa, Report of the Administrator, UN Document DP/1991/17, 30 April 1991, para. 6, 7, 8.

16. Smith, S. 1992. The Social Dimensions of Structural Adjustment: A Change of Direction or a Figleaf? In *Structural Adjustment and the Crisis in Africa: Economic and Political Perspectives*, ed. D. Kennet and T. Lumumba-Kasongo. New York: The Edwin Mellen Press, 134.

17. Morrisson, C. 1992. ed. *Adjustment and Equity in Developing Countries: A New Approach*. Paris: OECD, 89.

18. Economic and Financial Recovery Program 1985–88, para. 79; Economic Consolidation and Growth Program 1989–91, page 14–15; policy framework paper 1989–91, para. 37; and policy framework paper 1992–95, para. 30.

19. During the academic year of 1990–91, I was a lecturer at the University of Nouakchott. I requested and was given permission to be on leave (with pay) for a couple of months to complete my Ph.D. course work in the United States. At my return I found that the University's accountant (Maheed Ould El Mokhtar, who perhaps assumed that I would not return to the University of Nouakchott) had counterfeited my signature and withdrawn my monthly salary (about the equivalent of $500) for four consecutive months before he was dismissed from the University for other reasons and returned to his previous position as an employee in the Ministry of Finance. Hoping to reverse the decision of his dismissal, Maheed did not return the university official keys and records. Instead, he went to the town of Atar, where he is believed to have solicited support from an influential religious sheikh (Ely Sheikh Ould Memma) whose moral influence on certain top state officials and army officers could be used to reverse the university's decision. When I pressured the president of the university (Mohamed El Hacen Ould Lebbat) to get the money back and sue the delinquent accountant, I was immediately paid from the university budget and was (indirectly) told that the rest is not my business. Three months later I came across the name of Maheed Ould El Mokhtar running for senator in the April 1992 parliamentary elections.

20. Chenonceau, T. Etude de Politique de Gestion des Agents de l'Etat, Dossier Technique, Effectifs, Societé Française de Conseil en Développement, SEDES-CEGOS, juin 1990, tableau 2.

21. The Economist Intelligence Unit. 1991. *Guinea, Mali, Mauritania, A Country Profile 1991–92*. London: EIU, 68. See also World Bank. 1994. Five Decades of Development: 100 Examples of the World Bank in Action. World Bank documents distributed during the World Bank celebrations of its fiftieth anniversary.

22. President Ould Taya declared that 10,000 Moors died in ethnic clashes in Senegal while only 35 Senegalese died in Mauritania. See *Foreign Broadcast Information Service*, (NES), 26 March 1991, 10.

23. RIM, *Book of Facts: Conflict with Senegal*, Nouakchott, 31 August 1989, 69.

24. Dubie, P. 1953. La vie matérielle des Maures. In *Mélanges Ethnologiques*, Institut Français de l'Afrique Noire (IFAN), 235–6.

25. *Mauritanie Nouvelles*, no. 16, 10–17 May 1992.

26. World Bank document, IDA President's Report no. P–5293–MAU, 30 May 1990, para. 62.

27. Rapport d'activité du Commissariat à la Securité Alimentaire, Novembre 1989.

28. Cohen, A. 1994. The Help That Hurts, *The Progressive* 58(1):27–30.

29. Government Letter of Development Policy for the first structural adjustment loan, 1987, para. 77, 91, 92, 95.

30. RIM, Economic Consolidation and Growth Program 1989–91, 14.

31. Mauritanie: Document-cadre de politique économique, 1989–91, 25 avril 1989, para. 37.

32. Economic Consolidation and Growth Program 1989–91, 15.

33. Other estimates run as low as one pound of grain per person per day. According to Prime Minister Sidi Mohamed Ould Boubacar, during the first six months of 1993, some sixty-eight community development projects were implemented. They created temporary jobs estimated at 295,000 working days for which the government paid 135 tons of food, or about one pound of cereal per working day. See *Shaab*, 26 December 1993.

34. RIM, Economic Consolidation and Growth Program 1989–91, 15.

35. *Shaab*, 26 December 1993, 3.

36. Policy framework paper 1992–95, para. 31.

37. U.S. Congress, House, Committee on Foreign affairs, 1989, *Structural Adjustment in Africa: Insights from the Experiences of Ghana and Senegal*, Report of a Staff Study Mission to Great Britain, Ghana, Senegal, Cote d'Ivoire, and France, 29 November-20 December 1988. Washington, DC: U.S. Government Printing Office, 18.

38. Synthèse du Rapport d'Evaluation du Programme d'Actions Prioritaires, 1989?, Ministère du Plan.

39. Document of the World Bank, Report and Recommendation of the President of the International Development Association (Report no. P–4550–MAU) to the Executive Directors for a Proposed Development Credit of SDR 11.7 million and a Proposed Special African Facility Credit of SDR 21.4 million to the Islamic Republic of Mauritania for a Structural Adjustment Program, 11 May 1987. Washington, D.C.: World Bank, para. 99.

40. *Le Temps*, no. 48, 19–26 July 1992.

41. Walton, J., and Seddon, D. 1994. *Free Markets and Food Riots: The Politics of Global Adjustment*. Oxford: Blackwell.

42. Mauritanie: Document-cadre de politique économique, 1989–91, para. 37.

43. Ghai, D. *Structural Adjustment, Global Integration and Social Democracy*, Geneva: United Nations Research Institute for Social Development, Discussion Paper no. 37, October 1992, 18. See also Ghai, D., and de Alcantara, C. H. 1990. The Crisis of the 1980s in Sub-Saharan Africa, Latin America and the Caribbean: Economic Impact, Social Change and Political Implications, *Development and Change* 21:389–426.

44. *Al-Bayan*, no. 83, 27 December 1993, 4.

45. Ould Cheikh Bounenna, M. Le Speaker dans l'avion juste avant l'atterrissage à Nouakchott, *Le Temps*, no. 48, 19–26 July 1992.

Chapter 8: Political Implications of SAPs

1. Substantial parts of this chapter are reprinted as originally published or with changes from: Ould-Mey, M., (forthcoming). Democratization in Africa: The Political Face of SAPs, *Journal of Third World Studies*, Fall 1995.

2. Frank, A. G., and Fuentes, M. 190. Civil Democracy: Social Movements in Recent World History. In *Transforming the Revolution: Social Movements and the World System*, eds. Samir Amin, Giovanni Arrighi, Andre Gunder Frank, and Immanuel Wallerstein. New York: Monthly Review Press, 178.

3. See respectively Fukuyama, F. 1989. The End of History, *The National Interest* (Summer):3–18; and Laclau, E. 1990. *New Reflections on the Revolution of Our Time*. New York: Verso, 82.

4. Qadir, S., et al. 1993. Sustainable Democracy: Formalism vs Substance, *Third World Quarterly* 14(3):415; and Lancaster, C. 1993. Democratization in Sub-Saharan Africa, *Survival* 35(3):49.

5. Roberts, K. 1985. Democracy and the Dependent Capitalist State in Latin America, *Monthly Review* (October):14.

6. Bratton, M., and Nicolas van de Walle. 1992. Popular Protest and Political Reform in Africa, *Comparative Politics* 24(4):420.

7. Lancaster, C. 1993. Democratization in Sub-Saharan Africa, *Survival* 35(3):38–50.

8. Young, C. 1994. Democratization in Africa: The Contradictions of a Political Imperative. In *Economic Change and Political Liberalization in Sub-Saharan Africa*, ed. Jennifer A. Widner. Baltimore, Maryland: Johns Hopkins University Press, 247.

9. Burundi Domestic Service. 1990. President Buyoya Speaks Against Multiparty System, *Foreign Broadcast Information Service*, Sub-Saharan Africa, March 15, 2. See also Nairobi KNA in English. 1990. Mwinyi Criticizes Pressure on Political system, *Foreign Broadcast Information Service*, Sub-Saharan Africa, June 11, 4.

10. Bates, R. 1994. The Impulse to Reform in Africa. In *Economic Change and Political Liberalization in Sub-Saharan Africa*, ed. Jennifer A. Widner. Baltimore, Maryland: Johns Hopkins University Press, 25-26.

11. Clapham, C. 1993. Democratization in Africa: Obstacles andpects, *Third World Quarterly* 14(3):432.

12. Dowden, R. 1993. A Continent Sleeping into Darkness, *World Press Review* (January):16–17.

13. Widner, J. 1994. Introduction. In *Economic Change and Political Liberalization in Sub-Saharan Africa*, ed. Jennifer A. Widner. Baltimore, Maryland: Johns Hopkins University Press, 3.

14. Babangida, I. 1992. Address by the President. In *First Pan-Africa Conference on Democracy and Control of Transition in Africa*, Dakar, Senegal, 25–28 May.

15. Beyer, L. 1990. Continental Shift, *Time* 135(21):43–36.

16. Lone, S. 1990. Africans Adopt Bold Charter for Democratization, *Africa Recovery* 4(1):1,14.

17. Dakar Declaration of African Political Leaders. In *First Pan-African Conference on Democracy and Control of Transition in Africa*. Dakar, Senegal, 25–28 May.

18. Westebbe, R. 1994. Structural Adjustment, Rent Seeking, and Liberalization in Benin. In *Economic Change and Political Liberalization in Sub-Saharan Africa*, ed. Jennifer A. Widner. Baltimore, Maryland: Johns Hopkins University Press, 87.

19. Bonner, R. 1990. A Reporter at Large: African Democracy, *New Yorker* 66(29):93–105.

20. *West Africa* 3936:347, 1993. See also *Africa News* 37(2):6, 1992.

21. Africa Watch Committee. 1991. *Kenya: Taking Liberties*. New York: Africa Watch.

22. Nairobi Kenya Broadcasting Corporation Network. 1991. Moi Cited on Introduction of Multipartyism Soon, *Foreign Broadcast Information Service*, Sub-Saharan Africa, 2 December, 6.

23. Nairobi KTN Television. 1991. Minister: U.S. Pursuing, Financing Multipartyism, *Foreign Broadcast Information Service*, Sub-Saharan Africa, 21 November, 4.

24. Ajulu, R. 1993. The 1992 Kenya General Elections: A Preliminary Assessment, *Review of African Political Economy* 56:98–102, 98.

25. Richburg, K. 1995. A Line of "Big Men" Has Thrown Democracy for a Loss, *The Washington Post National Weekly Edition* 12(10):18.

26. Dar es Salam Radio Tanzania. 1992. President Mwinyi on Introduction of Multipartyism, *Foreign Broadcast Information Service*, Sub-Saharan Africa, 25 February, 11.

27. Nairobi KNA in English. 1990. Mwinyi Criticizes Pressure on Political system, *Foreign Broadcast Information Service*, Sub-Saharan Africa, 11 June, 4.

28. Libreville Africa No. 1. 1992. Democratic Party Affirms Respect for Multipartyism, *Foreign Broadcast Information Service*, Sub-Saharan Africa, 17 March, 2.

29. Abidjan Fraternité Matin. 1992. Rawlings Comments on Impact of Multipartyism, *Foreign Broadcast Information Service*, Sub-Saharan Africa, 15 June, 38.

30. *The Europa World Year Book 1994*, London: Europa Publications Limited.

31. The Washington based Human Rights Watch comprises Africa Watch, [Latin] America Watch, Asia Watch, Helsinki Watch, Middle East Watch, and the Fund for Free Expression. Human rights and democratization also constitute the major theme of all programming of Voice of America, Radio Free Europe, Radio Free Asia, and Radio and TV Martí.

32. Paul-Marie de la Gorce revealed a secret visit to Washington in October 1993 by Algerian Defense Minister General Khaled Nizzar. See de La Gorce, P. 1993. Algerie: Les Américains s'en Mêlent, *Jeune Afrique* 1719:26–28.

33. The United States and France have recently agreed to support the Paris Club rescheduling of over $5 billion in Algerian official debt. See Rodman, P. 1995. A Time Bomb Is Ticking in Algeria, *The Washington Post National Weekly Edition* 12(10):24.

34. Quayle, D. 1992. Human Rights: An International Responsibility. Address before the UN Human Rights Commission, Geneva, Switzerland, 10 February. *U.S. Department of State Dispatch* 3(7):103-4.

35. Muravchik, J. 1991. *Exporting Democracy: Fulfilling America's Destiny*. Washington, D.C.: The AEI Press, 221–222.

36. Diouf, A. speaking to Radio France International, 8 September, 1991.

37. U.S. Department of State. 1991. U.S.-Senegal: A Special Relationship. *U.S. Department of State Dispatch* 2(37):691.

38. Riley, S. 1992. The Democratic Transition in Africa: An End to One-Party State? *Conflict Studies* 245:7.

39. Gibbon, P. 1992. Structural Adjustment and Pressures toward Multipartyism in Sub-Saharan Africa. In *Authoritarianism, Democracy, and Adjustment: The Politics of Economic Reform in Africa*, eds. Peter Gibbon, Yusuf Bangura, and Arve Ofstad. Uppsala: Nordiska Afrikainstitutet, 143–4.

40. Riley, S. 1992. The Democratic Transition in Africa: An End to One-Party State? *Conflict Studies* 245:1–37, 12.

41. Lone, S. 1990. Africans Adopt Bold Charter for Democratization, *Africa Recovery* 4(1):1,14.

42. Wilson, E. III. 1993. French Support for Structural Adjustment Programs in Africa, *World Development* 21(3):332.

43. Agence France Press. 1990. Franco-African Summit Opens in La Baule, *Foreign Broadcast Information Service*, West Europe, 21 June, 1.

44. Casteran, C., and Hugo Sada. 1990. Sommet de La Baule: L'Avertissement, *Jeune Afrique* 1539:14–16.

45. Oxfam UK and Ireland. 1993. *Africa Make or Break: Action for Recovery*. Oxford: Oxfam Print Services, 38. See also Riley, S. 1992. The Democratic Transition in Africa: An End to One-Party State? *Conflict Studies* 245:10.

46. Tokyo Kyodo. 1993. Central American Aid Linked to Democratization, *Foreign Broadcast Information Service*, East Asia, 15 March, 5.

47. Laishley, R. 1993/4. Africa's Debt Burden Continues to Grow, *Africa Recovery* (December–March):32.

48. Beckman, B. 1992. Empowerment or Repression?: The World Bank and the Politics of African Adjustment. In *Authoritarianism, Democracy, and Adjustment: The Politics of Economic Reform in Africa*, eds. Peter Gibbon, Yusuf Bangura, and Arve Ofstad. Uppsala: Nordiska Afrikainstitutet, 86.

49. Mulford, D. 1990. Statement. In *Role of the International Monetary Fund: Hearing before the Subcommittee on International Development, Finance, Trade, and Monetary Policy of the committee on Banking, Finance, and Urban Affairs, House of Representatives, One Hundred First Congress, second session, 1 March 1990*. Washington, D.C.: U.S. Government Printing Office, 61–72.

50. Richburg, K. 1995. A Line of 'Big Men' Has Thrown Democracy for a Loss, *The Washington Post National Weekly Edition* 12(10):18.

51. Agence France Press. 1991. Taya, Sudan's Al-Bashir Condemn Ground Offensive, *Foreign Broadcast Information Service*, Near East and South Asia, 27 February, 11.

52. Soudan, F. 1992. *Le Marabout et le Colonel: La Mauritanie de Ould Daddah à Ould Taya*. Paris: Jalivres, 109.

53. FLAM is an umbrella organization bringing together a number of small factions of black African nationalists which include: Union Democratique Mauritanienne (UDM), Movement Populaire des Africains de Mauritanie (MPAM), Organization pour la Defense des Interets des Négro-Africains de Mauritanie (ODINAM), and Front Walfougui for the self-determination of Walo, Fouta, and Guidimaka. The Mauritanian government maintains that many FLAM leaders are actually Senegalese, not Mauritanian citizens.

54. United States Congress, House, Committee on Foreign Affairs, *Human Rights in the Maghreb and Mauritania*, Hearing before the Subcommittee on Human Rights and International Organizations and on Africa, 19 June 1991. Washington, D.C.: U.S. Government Printing Office, 111.

55. Burkhalter, H. (Washington Director of Human Rights Watch), Human Rights in Mauritania, Tunisisa, and Morocco: Testimony. In United States Congress, House, Committee on Foreign Affairs, *Human Rights in the Maghreb and Mauritania*, Hearing before the Subcommittee on Human Rights and International Organizations and on Africa, June 19, 1991, Washington,D.C.: U.S. Government Printing Office, 25.

56. Clinton, B. 1993. *Communication from the President of the United States Transmitting Notification of His Intent to Suspend Indefinitely Mauritania from Their Status as GSP Beneficiaries, Pursuant to 19 U.S.C. 2462(a)*. Washington, D.C.: U.S. Government Printing Office.

57. Burkhalter, H. Human Rights in Mauritania, Tunisisa, and Morocco: Testimony, 30; and Amnesty International, Mauritania: Human Rights Violations in the Senegal River Valley, 109. In United States Congress, House, Committee on Foreign Affairs, *Human Rights in the Maghreb and Mauritania*, Hearing before the Subcommittee on Human Rights and International Organizations and on Africa, 19 June 1991. Washington, D.C.: U.S. Government Printing Office.

58. The two congressmen were co-chairmen of the Congressional Human Rights Caucus and had received donations of $76,450 from pro-Israel Political Action Committees between 1980 and 1990. See Curtiss, R. 1990. *Stealth PACs: Lobbying Congress for Control of U.S. Middle East Policy*. Washington, D.C.: American Educational Trust, 192, 195.

59. Lantos, T., and Porter, J. Human Rights Violations in Mauritania. In United States Congress, House, Committee on Foreign Affairs, *Human Rights in the Maghreb and Mauritania*, Hearing before the Subcommittee on Human Rights and International Organizations and on Africa, 19 June 1991. Washington,D.C.: U.S. Government Printing Office, 110.

60. Amnesty International, USA, Mauritania, Personal Details on 339 Political Prisoners Reported to Have Been Killed Between November 1990 and March 1991, August 1991.

61. *Foreign Broadcast Information Service*, (NES) 15 June 1993, 19.

62. See respectively *Human Rights in Africa*, U.S. Congressional Record, Daily ed., 29 April 1993, S55084; and U.S. Department of State, *Country Reports on Human Rights Practices for 1993*, Report to the House Committee on Foreign Affairs and the Senate Committee on Foreign Relations, February 1994. Washington, D.C.: U.S. Government Printing Office, 177.

63. Schwarzkopf, H. N. 1992. *It Doesn't Take A Hero: General H. Norman Scharzkopf, the Autobiography (written with Peter Petre)*. New York: Bantam Books, 355.

64. Many Mauritanians believe that Ambassador Gordon Brown provided support for the ethnic based opposition (FLAM) and does not want to improve U.S.-Mauritanian relations as long as President Ould Taya (believed to be "a friend of Iraq") is in power. His style and attitude were also widely criticized. For example, he is believed to have said that it is the Mauritanian president who should visit the U.S. ambassador, not the other way round. This may explain his replacement by Ambassador Dorothy Myers

Sampas in September 1994.

65. *Foreign Broadcast Service*, Near East, 9 April 1991, 19.

66. The draft Constitution was submitted to a national referendum on 12 July 1991 and obtained 97.9 percent (a figure reported by the government and contested by the opposition) of those who voted (85.3 percent of the registered electorate). The new Constitution accorded extensive powers to the president of the Republic who is to be elected, by universal suffrage, for a period of six years (no limitations regarding the renewal of the presidential mandate were stipulated). Provision also was made for a bicameral parliament comprising a national assembly (to be elected every five years) and a senate (with a six-year mandate). By April 1992, the above institutions were established amid the cacophony of government/opposition polemic.

67. Ould Amar, I., quoted in *Mauritanie Nouvelles*, no. 16, 10–17 May 1992; Diagana, M., quoted in *Al-Mouchahid*, no. 4, 7 June 1992; and Ould Bedredine, M., quoted in *Mauritanie Demain*, no. 23, August 1991.

68. Marín, M., quoted in *L'Indépendant*, no. 003, 9 October 1991.

69. Kane, S., quoted in Placca, J. Démocratie en construction, *Jeune Afrique economie*, April 1993, 119.

70. *Foreign Broadcast Information Service*, (NES) 18 June 1993, 14.

71. Ould-Mey, M. Al-Jamahirya Wal Nitham Al-Dawly Al-Jadid, Lecture Series, Student Solidarity Committee, University of Nouakchott, Mauritania, April 1992.

72. Ould Zein, A., quoted in *Mauritanie Nouvelles*, no. 16, du 10 au 17 mai 1992.

73. *Al-Bayan*, no. 6, 11–18 March 1992.

74. President's special instructions to regional authorities during Cabinet Council Meeting of 27 May 1992.

75. *Livre Blanc sur la Fraude ou Chronique d'un Putsch Electoral Programmé*, Direction de la Campagne du Candidat Ahmed Ould Daddah aux Elections Presidentielles du 24 Janvier 1992 en Mauritanie.

76. Martin, G. 1993. Preface: Democratic Transition in Africa, *Issue: A Journal of Opinion* 21(1–2):6–7.

77. Qadir, S., et al. Sustainable Democracy: Formalism vs Substance, *Third World Quarterly* 14(3):422.

78. Amin, S. 1990. *Delinking: Towards a Polycentric World*. London: Zed Books, 27.

79. See Moore, C. 1965. One Partyism in Mauritania, *The Journal of Modern African Studies* 3(3):409–20; and Coleman, J., and Rosberg, Carl G., Jr., eds. 1964. *Political Parties and National Integration in Tropical Africa*. Berkeley: University of California Press.

80. Marchesin, P. 1992. *Tribus, ethnies et pouvoir en Mauritanie*. Paris: Karthala.

81. Baduel, P. R. Mauritanie 1945–1990 ou l'État face à la Nation. In *Mauritanie, entre arabité et africanité*, Revue du Monde Musulman et de la Mediterranée, no. 54, 1989/4, 44.

82. Haddad, M. 1994. The Rise of Arab Nationalism Reconsidered, *International Journal of Middle East Studies* 26(2):217.

83. Tibi, B. 1990. *Arab Nationalism: A Critical Inquiry*. New York: St. Martin's Press, 26.

84. See Vaillant, J. 1990. *Black, French, and African: A Life of Léopold Sédar Senghor*. Harvard University Press, Cambridge, Massachusetts, 244, 251, 258.

85. Ould El Yassa, A. In *Al-Bayan*, no. 22, du 13 au 19 mai 1992.

86. Parker, T., Baro, M., and Ngaido, T. Conflicts over Land and the Crisis of Nationalism in Mauritania, LTC Paper no. 142, prepared for USAID and The Land Tenure Center, University of Wisconsin-Madison, February 1991, 6.

87. *Al-Bushra*, no. 15, 20 March–5 April1993, 4.

88. *Foreign Broadcast Information Service*, NES, 26 March 1991, 10.

89. Soudan, F. 1992. *Le Marabout et le Colonel: La Mauritanie de Ould Daddah à Ould Taya*. Paris: Jalivres, 99.

90. *Foreign Broadcast Information Service*, (NES), 26 March 1991, 10.

91. Magistro, J. 1993. Crossing Over: Ethnicity and Transboundary Conflict in the Senegal River Valley, *Cahiers d'Études africaines* 130 (XXXIII–2):226.

92. Biktash, S. 1992. *Al-Niza' Al-Singhaly Al-Muritany*. Al-Qahira: Dar Al-Mustaqbal al-Arabi, 109.

93. Stewart, C. Une interpretation du conflit sénégalo-mauritanien. In *Mauritanie, entre arabité et africanité*, Revue du Monde Musulman et de la Mediterranée, no. 54, 1989/4, 161–71.

94. Fall, E. 1989. Sénégal-Mauritanie: Le dossier du conflit, 1. Les enjeux de l'après-barrages, *Jeune Afrique* 1491:40.

95. Horowitz, M. 1989. Victims of Development, *Development Anthropology Network* 7(2):5.

96. Biktash, S. 1992. *Al-Niza' Al-Singhaly Al-Muritany.*, Al-Qahira: Dar Al-Mustaqbal Al-Arabi, 88.

97. Parker, R. 1991. The Senegal-Mauritania Conflict of 1989: A Fragile Equilibrium, *The Journal of Modern African Studies* 29(1):165–6.

98. Sklar, R., and Strege, M. Finding Peace Through Democracy in Sahelian Africa, *Current History*, May 1993, 227.

99. Marty, P. *L'Islam en Mauritanie et au Senegal*, Revue du Monde Musulman, vol. XXXI, 1915–6.

100. See Cheikhou, Partis-Pouvoir: Frenesie Politique, *Mauritanie Demain*, no. 23, August 1991. (This issue was censored by the authorities).

101. Presidential candidate Ould Taya's address to the people, 9 January 1992.

102. President Ould Taya's inaugural address, 18 April 1992.

103. Ould Taya was elected by 62.7 percent of those who voted (the rate of participation was 51.7 percent of the registered electorate), Ould Daddah obtained 32.8 percent, and the remaining 4.5 percent was shared by the two other presidential candidates: El-Mustapha Ould Mohamed Salek (a retired army colonel and a former president) and Mohamed Mahmoud Ould Mah (a university professor and former mayor of the city of Nouakchott).

104. *West Africa*, 7–13 February 1994, 224.

105. Leaflet distributed by the UDF in Nouakchott.

106. *Foreign Broadcast Information Service*, NES, 29 January 1992, 26.

107. Ould Mouknas, H., quoted by Ahmed Al-Wely in *Al-Sayyad*, no. 9, 11 July 1993, 7. In his first public declaration (*Le Calame*, no. 70, 24–31 January 1995) since his overthrow in 1978, Mokhtar Ould Daddah expressed his support for the opposition and his intention to return to public life when he noted that the decomposition of state institutions, the aggravation of ethnic conflicts, the seriousness of the social situation, and the extreme tension on all Mauritanian borders make him fear the worst. His declaration further widens the gap between those who view Mauritania as an Arab country and those

who view it as a *trait d'union* between the Arab world and sub-Saharan Africa. This political cleavage is essentially cultural and political (not racial, as it may superficially appear) where the *trait d'union* idea is more popular among the elites of the region of Al-Gibla (Trarza, Brakna, Gorgol, and Guidimaka) mainly because French education and cultural influence are stronger here than in the rest of the country.

108. The Economist Intelligence Unit. *Country Report: Senegal, The Gambia, Mauritania,* fourth Quarter 1993. London: EIU, 28–29.

109. Ahmed Ould Sidi Baba, leader of the Rassemblement pour la Democratie et l'Unité (RDU), in a press conference aired on Radio Mauritanie on 9 January 1992.

110. Ould Daddah, A. (interviewed by David, D.) *The Courier* 137(1 January 1993):32.

111. *Foreign Broadcast Information Service,* AFR, 28 June 1990, 42.

112. Islamic Republic of Mauritania. 1989. *Book of Facts.* Nouakchott, 31 August, 19.

113. *Al-Bayan,* no. 81, 13 December 1993, 8.

114. *Horizons,* no. 142, 15 January 1992.

115. Cheikhou. Parti-Pouvoir: Frenesie Politique, *Mauritanie Demain,* no. 23, August 1991.

116. *Al-Tanmya,* no. 10, 26 November 1992.

117. CGTM was legalized in January 1994. See *Foreign Broadcast Information Service,* NES, 7 January 1994, 15.

118. U.S. Department of State, *Country Reports on Human Rights Practices for 1993,* Report to the House Committee on Foreign Affairs and the Senate Committee on Foreign Relations, February 1994. Washington, D.C.: U.S. Government Printing Office, 184.

119. Ould Cheikh, A. W. Nomadisme, Islam et Pouvoir Politique dans la Societé Maure Precoloniale (X ème siècle – XIX ème siècle): Essai sur quelques aspects du tribalisme, Thèse de doctorat en sociologie, Paris V Rene Descartes, 1985, 1000.

120. Anti-Islamist Middle Eastern governments are themselves increasingly forced to rely on Islamic ideology and Islamic discourse as a strategy of containing the Islamists and competing with them. King Fahd of Saudi Arabia has added a new emblematic title: The Guardian of the Two Holy Shrines (in Mecca and Medina). King Hussein of Jordan has claimed to have historic custody over the third holiest shrine in Islam, Al-Masjid Al-Aqsa in Jerusalem (despite strong Palestinian opposition) even though his family is neither from Jordan nor from Palestine. It originally belongs to Mecca from which it was taken by the British and given the crowns in Iraq and Jordan after World War I. King Hassan II of Morocco has built the second-largest mosque in the world in Casablanca to prove that he is a good Muslim who cares about Islam. In 1991, Iraq added the phrase *Allah Akbar* (God is Great) to its national flag, and in 1994 Iraqi engineers completed plans for Saddam Grand Mosque, the largest mosque in the world, to be built in central Baghdad.

121. Quoted in Burgat, B. 1993. *The Islamic Movement in North Africa.* Austin: Center for Middle Eastern Studies, University of Texas at Austin, (Translated from French by William Dowell), 21.

122. Ould Abdallahi, B., quoted in *Al-Umma Al-Wasat,* no. 1, 7 May 1992.

123. The Economist Intelligence Unit. *Country Report: Senegal, The Gambia, and Mauritania,* fourth Quarter 1993, London: EIU, 30.

124. *Jeune Afrique,* no. 1707, du 23 au 29 Septembre 1993, 37.

125. Ould Mohamdi, A. *Asharq Al-Awsat,* 29 November 1993, 1.

126. *Akhbar Al-Usbu*, no. 23, 5 December 1993.

127. Dateline, Mauritania: Islamic Leaders Arrested. 1994. *West Africa* 4019:1759.

128. Burgat, F. 1993. *The Islamic Movement in North Africa*. Austin: Center for Middle Eastern Studies, University of Texas at Austin, (Translated from French by William Dowell), 309.

129. Gulalp, H. 1992. A Postmodern Reaction to Dependent Modernization: The Social Roots of Islamic Radicalism, *New Perspective on Turkey* 8:22.

130. Massey, D. 1992. A Place Called Home? *New Formations* 17:7; and Harvey, D. 1990. *The Condition of Postmodernity: An Inquiry into the Origins of Cultural Change*. Cambridge, Massachusetts: Blackwell, 117.

131. Laclau, E. 1992. Universalism, Particularism, and the Question of Identity, *October* 61:86.

132. Esposito, J. 1994. Political Islam: Beyond the Green Menace, *Current History* 93(579):24.

Chapter 9: Democratization or Democracy?

1. Pinkney, R. 1994. *Democracy in the Third World*. Boulder, Colorado: Lynne Rienner Publishers, 172.

2. Danaher, K., ed. 1994. *50 Years Is Enough: The Case Against the World Bank and the International Monetary Fund*. Boston, Massachusetts: South End Press.

3. Oxfam, UK and Ireland. 1993. *Africa, Make or Break: Action for Recovery*. Oxford: Oxfam Print Services, 25.

4. Petit, B. 1993. Democracy and Structural Adjustment in Africa, *The Courier* 138:74–75.

5. Bauzon, K. E. 1992. Introduction: Democratization in the Third World—Myths or Reality? In *Development and Democratization in the Third World: Myths, Hopes, and Realities*, ed. Kenneth E. Bauzon. Washington, D.C.: Taylor & Francis, 7.

6. See also Michel Chossudovsky, IMF-World Bank Policies and the Rwandan Holocaust, *Third World Network Features*, Internet, 26 January 1995.

7. Rousseau, J. (1712–1778). 1901. The Social Contract. In *Ideal Empires and Republics*, ed. Oliver H. G. Leigh. Washington, D.C.: M. Walter Dunne, 59.

8. Rorty, R. 1992. For a More Banal Politics, *Harper's* 284:16.

9. Amin, S. 1993. Historical and Ethical Materialism, *Monthly Review* 45(2):56.

10. Southall, A. 1991. Democracy and Development: Tangled Meanings. In *Democratization and Structural Adjustment in Africa in the 1990s*, eds. Lual Deng, Markus Kostner, and Crawford Young. African studies Program, University of Wisconsin-Madison, 118. See also Rijnierse, E. 1993. Democratization in Sub-Saharan Africa? Literature Review, *Third World Quarterly* 14(3):651.

11. Southall, A. 1991. Democracy and Development: Tangled Meanings. In *Democratization and Structural Adjustment in Africa in the 1990s*, eds. Lual Deng, Markus Kostner, and Crawford Young. African Studies Program, University of Wisconsin-Madison, 115.

12. Said, E. 1979. *Orientalism*. New York: Vintage Books; and 1993. *Culture and Imperialism*. London: Chatto and Windus.

13. Foucault, M. 1980. *Power/Knowledge: Selected Interviews and Other Writings 1972–1977*. New York: Pantheon Books.

14. Qaddafi, M. 1980. *The Green Book*. Tripoli, Libya: The Green Book World Center for Research and Study, 5.

Index

308   *Global Restructuring and Peripheral States*

SDI 48
Star Wars 47, 48
Strategic Defense Initiative 48
U.S. Central Command 53
veto power 2, 28, 34, 45, 254
voting power 108, 254
Warsaw Pact 24, 44, 48
Puerto Rico 30
Qadir, S. 213, 231
Qatar 187
Radice, H. 148
Ramsay, W. 43
Ratner, S. 60
Ravenhill, J. 19
Reich, R. 50
Richburg, K. 221, 225
Riddel, J. 17
Rijnierse, E. 42, 257
Riley, S. 223, 224
Roberts, K. 214
Rodman, P. 223
Rojas-Suarez, L. 17
Rorty, R. 257
Roth, M. 18
Roussanne, A. 61
Rousseau, J. 257
Russia 45, 49, 55, 56, 149
  Chechnya 49, 56, 256
Rwanda 92, 217
Sahara 36, 65, 66, 68-71, 74-78, 82, 84, 85, 86, 210, 222
Sahel 65, 66, 78, 82, 120, 136-139, 152, 175
Said, E. 258
Samatar, A. 27
Sandbrook, R. 19
SAPs 2-6, 8, 11, 14, 15, 18-21, 23, 26, 29, 33, 38, 41, 54, 56, 57, 61, 62, 63, 65, 87, 93, 112, 124, 126, 140, 141, 148, 149, 158, 159, 167, 174, 179, 182, 191, 193, 195-204, 206-211, 213-220, 222, 223, 225, 231, 232, 234, 236, 237, 244, 248, 250, 253-255
  adjustment 1-12, 14-21, 23-25, 27, 28, 29-45, 47, 50-52, 57-62, 87-100, 103, 104, 106-109, 111,

112, 114-116, 119-129, 131-133, 136, 138, 140-143, 147, 148, 149-154, 156-159, 163, 165, 167, 168, 173, 174, 176, 178-181, 185, 186, 190-192, 195, 196, 197-210, 214, 216, 218-221, 223-225, 231-233, 237, 241, 244, 249, 251, 252, 254-258
  administrative reform 99-103, 105, 151, 152, 160
  agricultural sector 38, 113, 122, 123, 124, 129, 131, 132, 152, 163, 174, 175, 191
  banking sector 105, 158, 159, 162, 177, 178, 179
  education sector 152, 163, 174, 176, 190, 191
  health and population 151, 152, 177, 191
  political implications 6, 180, 210, 213
  privatization 7, 40-42, 49, 58, 87, 95, 160, 162-167, 175, 178, 179, 188, 214, 216, 231, 232, 255
  public enterprises 7, 41, 58, 86, 95, 105, 110, 113, 128, 151, 155, 156, 159, 163-169, 201, 203, 208, 209
  rural sector 96, 162, 174
  SDA 197-201, 206
  sectoral adjustment 5, 126, 129, 132, 133, 149-151, 153, 154, 163, 165, 167, 173, 176
  social differentiation 5, 6, 195, 207, 209-211
  social dimension 5, 122, 195-198, 201, 206, 255
  social policy 5, 195-197, 199-201, 203, 204, 206
  stabilization programs 57, 156, 158, 163, 191, 200
  structural adjustment 5, 7, 9, 15, 16, 17-20, 25, 27, 29, 31-33, 36, 39, 40-42, 51, 57, 62, 88, 91, 98, 99, 104, 109, 112, 121, 126-129, 131, 147, 149-154, 156, 158, 159, 163, 165, 191, 196, 197, 200,

About the Author

Mohameden Ould-Mey is an Assistant Professor in the Department of Political Science and Geography at Francis Marion University. He has taught at the University of Nouakchott and the University of Kentucky and published in *Third World Quarterly* and *Journal of Third World Studies*. His research and teaching interests include development policy and theory, the Middle East and Africa, and the development of geographic thought.